HARVARD HISTORICAL STUDIES

PUBLISHED UNDER THE DIRECTION OF
THE DEPARTMENT OF HISTORY

VOLUME XXXII

HARVARD HISTORICAL STUDIES

HARVARD UNIVERSITY PRESS

CAMBRIDGE, MASS., U. S. A.

THE SCHLESWIG-HOLSTEIN QUESTION

BY

LAWRENCE D. STEEFEL

ASSISTANT PROFESSOR OF HISTORY IN THE
UNIVERSITY OF MINNESOTA

CAMBRIDGE
HARVARD UNIVERSITY PRESS
LONDON: HUMPHREY MILFORD
OXFORD UNIVERSITY PRESS
1932

PRINTED AT THE MESSENGER PRESS
ST. ALBANS, VERMONT, U. S. A.

TO

THE MEMORY OF MY FATHER

SIMON L. STEEFEL

1859 - 1931

PREFACE

THIS monograph has grown out of a thesis presented in 1923 in partial fulfilment of the requirements for the degree of Doctor of Philosophy at Harvard University. The Schleswig-Holstein question is treated here with special emphasis on the years 1863 and 1864 when it played its most important rôle in international politics. After sketching the development of the question and the wearisome and futile attempts to settle it, I have described in more detail the crisis that brought on the German-Danish war of 1864 and have followed the policies of the Great Powers until June 1864, when, at the close of the London Conference, all but Austria and Prussia practically renounced their interest in the issue.

There is already a vast literature on the Schleswig-Holstein question. Practically all of the existing books and articles, however, deal with special problems or with the question as an episode in the career of Bismarck or in the history of Denmark or of Germany. The present monograph attempts to amalgamate the results of previous studies with new materials made available by the recent opening of the most important European archives.

The best treatment of the subject has been that of the Danish historian and politician, N. Neergaard in his *Under Junigrundloven*. But as is natural in a history of Denmark, it contains a more detailed account of Danish politics than is necessary for the presentation of the question as a problem in international relations. The standard German works remain von Sybel's *Die Begründung des deutschen Reiches* and Jansen and Samwer's *Schleswig-Holsteins Befreiung*, the former representing the Bismarckian, the latter, the Augustenburg point of view. There is no detailed German work which deals with the whole subject in the light of the material that has been published during the last thirty years. The best treatment in English is that of the late Sir Adolphus Ward in his *Germany, 1815-1890*, published in the

Cambridge Historical Series. Sir Adolphus has made a thorough use of the available printed materials in German, French, and English, but like most writers on the problem outside of the Scandinavian countries, has neglected the Danish works.

A great stimulus to the study of the international aspects of the Schleswig-Holstein question was given by the publication by the French government in 1910 of the first volumes of *Les Origines diplomatiques de la guerre de 1870-1871.* The publications based on them, both in France and in Germany dealt mainly with the policy of Napoleon III and suffered from lack of materials from the other European archives, for which the British *Blue Books* and the works of von Sybel, Neergaard, and Koht were an inadequate substitute. Shortly before the war of 1914, Professor Erich Brandenburg was allowed to use a few but only a few of the dispatches in the Prussian archives concerning Franco-Prussian relations in 1864. Even then, however, much remained to be learned.

The thesis on which this monograph is based was the first study to supplement the published materials by the unpublished resources of the archives of London, Copenhagen, Paris, Vienna, and Berlin. The British archives offered a surprisingly rich field for research. The voluminous *Blue Books* published in 1863 and 1864 omitted practically all of the confidential conversations with foreign statesmen and sovereigns. Very little of this has since been used for the section on the Schleswig-Holstein question in the *Cambridge History of British Foreign Policy.* Of the material in the Danish archives, that for the period up to December 1863 had been used by Thorsøe and that for the whole period by Neergaard. But, as their work was done with Danish interests in the foreground, something of value from the international point of view remained to be gleaned. The publication of *Les Origines diplomatiques de la guerre de 1870-1871,* which covers most of the period of this study, made the use of the French archives almost unnecessary but the unpublished documents for the first eleven and a half months of 1863 offered much of interest and value. Some of the Austrian documents, up to February 1864, had been published by Hengelmüller in his articles on *Graf*

Alois Karolyi in the *Deutsche Revue*. Except for that, the Austrian archives were virgin soil. The Prussian archives (with the exception of the protocols of the Crown Councils of 1864, which I was one of the first students of history to utilize) had been used by von Sybel and by the authors of the General Staff history of the German-Danish War. Hitherto, however, these works had not been subject to control and, in addition, the evidence needed to be studied from an up-to-date and neutral point of view.

Since the presentation of the first results of my study in 1923, more of the unpublished documents, especially from the Prussian archives, have appeared in print and a number of the problems have been worked on by other writers. The more important papers written or dictated by Bismarck have now been published in the definitive edition of his collected works. Some of the important reports from the Prussian ambassador in Paris may be found in H. Oncken's book on *Die Rheinpolitik Kaiser Napoleon III*, the materials on the question of the division of Schleswig in Platzhoff's *Bismarck und die Nordschleswigsche Frage* and in Hähnsen's *Ursprung und Geschichte des Artikels V des Prager Friedens*, and the protocols of the Prussian Crown Councils of January and February 1864 in Stern's *Geschichte Europas*. These and other recent publications make it only the more desirable to synthesize what has already appeared with the unpublished materials.

One of the greatest difficulties in studying the diplomacy of this period is the fact that for many important discussions, only one source exists. This is true particularly of the confidential conversations of Bismarck and of Napoleon III. It is, of course, impossible to be sure that they have been reported accurately in detail or that the summaries available represent the impression intended to be conveyed. The cumulative impression gained from studying many documents from many sources offers some basis for judgment but is something which cannot be defined in footnotes. I have quoted freely from the documents as it seemed that in many cases, where there was only one source, a further summary might depart farther from what had actually been said. In many cases, too, it is less important to know what was said than what was reported. Statesmen make many decisions in the light of information at hand and that information is contained sometimes in a single document.

In the preparation of this work, I have received advice and assistance from many people. I wish to acknowledge first of all the generous support given by the officials in the various archives in which it was my privilege to work. To the assistance of the Hon. John W. Davis, formerly Ambassador at London, and the courtesy of the British Foreign Office, I owe the permission to study the British archives for a period then not normally open to students. Other American representatives abroad, especially in Copenhagen and Berlin, were of great service in aiding me to secure access to materials I needed. I owe much to the opportunity of discussing the problems of the Schleswig-Holstein question with European scholars, especially the late Sir Adolphus Ward, himself a source, Professors Friis and Fabricius of Copenhagen, Meinecke of Berlin, and Stern of Zürich. To Dr. Robert H. Lord, formerly of Harvard University, I am indebted for the suggestion to undertake this study. His advice and keen criticism have been of the utmost value. Professors C. H. Haskins, C. K. Webster, and the late A. C. Coolidge have all given me encouragement and valuable criticism. Finally, Mr. F. B. Tiffany of St. Paul and Dean Guy Stanton Ford of the University of Minnesota have read the manuscript and given me the benefit of their knowledge and experience. In the preparation of the manuscript, I have received valuable assistance from Elizabeth Slator Dunn, and, above all, from my wife, Genevieve Fallon Steefel, whose work in collating and correcting has removed many errors of copying and of style.

Lawrence D. Steefel.

Minneapolis, Minn.
September 1930.

CONTENTS

APPENDICES

CHAPTER I

INTRODUCTION: THE SCHLESWIG-HOLSTEIN QUESTION TO 1863

I

The Schleswig-Holstein question is the name commonly given to a complex of problems which concerned the relations of the duchies of Schleswig and Holstein to each other, to the kingdom of Denmark, and to the German Confederation.[1] In it were involved dynastic and constitutional controversies which had their roots in the Middle Ages and had often been causes of disputes and wars. Yet the old controversies might have continued on the same lines for centuries more and have acquired no greater place in history than belongs to so many dead and gone dynastic and territorial squabbles, had they not been given new life by the rise of the spirit of nationalism. Early in the nineteenth century, the Schleswig-Holstein question became a vital factor in the national development of Denmark and Germany. Finally, in 1863, Bismarck took up the question and turned it to his own advantage. By winning in it his first great diplomatic victory he consolidated his power in Prussia. He then used the problem of Schleswig-Holstein as his main instrument in bringing about the solution of the German question.

The earlier centuries may be left to antiquarians, legists, and specialists in local history. The first decades of the nineteenth

---

[1] In contemporary documents and discussions, it is often referred to as the Danish question, the question of the duchies of the Elbe, or even as the Schleswig question. Its complexity is notorious. "La questione danese, o per meglio dire dello Schleswig-Holstein era talmente complicata e oscura, che Lord Palmerston non essendo riuscito diplomaticamente a impedire quella guerra, soleva spiritosamente raccontare, che tre soli individui conoscevano a fondo quella imbrogliata controversia. Uno era il principe Alberto, che disgraziamente era morto; il secondo un uomo di Stato danese, che era impazzito; il terzo, lui Lord Palmerston, che l'aveva dimenticata." A. la Marmora, *Un po' più di luce sugli eventi politici e militari dell' anno 1866*, pp. 30 f.

century furnish an adequate approach to the modern phase of the question.

After the close of the Napoleonic wars, the European dominions of the King of Denmark consisted of the Kingdom of Denmark (Jutland and the Danish islands) and the Duchies of Schleswig, Holstein, and Lauenburg. These territories which were linked in a loosely organized monarchy, differed greatly in size and importance. Lauenburg, which had been acquired as a compensation for the much more valuable Norway, was a tiny rural duchy of some four hundred square miles with a population of about fifty thousand.[2] Schleswig and Holstein were more substantial, each nearly three thousand five hundred square miles in area and with four hundred thousand and five hundred thousand inhabitants respectively. The kingdom proper had an area of nearly fifteen thousand square miles and a population of one million, five hundred thousand.[3]

The population of the kingdom was exclusively Danish; that of Holstein and Lauenburg, German. Schleswig, with the probable exception of the extreme southern portion, was Danish at the beginning of its history,[4] but early in the Middle Ages, German settlers began to penetrate it. In the later Middle Ages, the rulers and the great landowners were German. With the Reformation, the process of Germanization was accelerated by the introduction of the German language in the church services as far north as the present boundary between Denmark and Germany. The advance of the German language and culture continued into the third decade of the nineteenth century when the people of Angeln, the region south of Flensburg Fiord, gave up the use of Danish for "Platt-deutsch."[5] In the nineteenth

[2] Mention of Lauenburg, which played a very minor part in the following developments, can generally be omitted.

[3] Statistics from Gosch, *Denmark and Germany since 1815*, pp. 1 f., but reduced to round numbers. Population statistics based on Danish census of 1860.

[4] Cf. F. de Jessen, *Manuel historique de la question du Slesvig*, parts I, II, part III, pp. 89-93. J. B. Høyer, "En Rejse gennem Overgangsegnene fra Dansk til Tysk", in Dahl and Linvald, *Sønderjylland*, I, pp. 96 f.

[5] Dahl and Linvald, *Sønderjylland*, I, pp. 96 f; 120-136; 185-194. Adler, "Die Volkssprache in dem Herzogthum Schleswig seit 1864," in *Z. f. s-h. G.*, XXI (1891), especially pp. 49 ff.

century, the population of the rural areas of northern Schleswig was almost exclusively Danish, that of central Schleswig and of the towns to the north, mixed German and Danish, that of southern Schleswig almost exclusively German.[6]

The differences in size and in nationality of the parts of the Danish Monarchy were complicated by differences in international position. Holstein and Lauenburg, which had been parts of the Holy Roman Empire, were included after 1815 in the German Confederation; Schleswig, in spite of the fact that it contained a considerable German population, was not.

The kings of Denmark, who were absolute monarchs in law in the kingdom and in fact in the duchies, were interested primarily in the maintenance of the monarchy and in the consolidation and centralization of their power over its parts. But they were slow and cautious, hesitant to stir up opposition to innovations, and almost before they realized it, the rising liberalism and nationalism of the early nineteenth century brought them face to face with problems which they were unable to solve and which led to the destruction of their monarchy.

The growth of liberalism and of nationalism was closely connected both in the duchies and in the kingdom. For a time, the liberal elements among Germans and Danes coöperated. But in the 1830's, the national antagonisms began to gain the upper hand, and by 1848, the two peoples stood in irreconcileable opposition.[7] The national, or Schleswig-Holstein party in the duchies looked forward to the establishment of a more closely united German national state which should include not only Lauenburg and Holstein, which were already members of the German Confederation, but also Schleswig. The nationalist party in the kingdom, with which may be included the Danish nationalists of Schleswig, cared little what became of Lauenburg

---

[6] Cf. maps, I and II. Especially in the mixed districts and in such towns as Flensburg, language was not always an accurate guide to national sympathy. Cf. Mackeprang, *Nordslesvig*, 1864-1909, pp. 8 f.

[7] Cf. especially Brock, *Vorgeschichte der schleswig-holsteinischen Erhebung*; Ottosen, *P. H. Lorentzen*; Lauridsen, *Da Sønderjylland vaagnede*; Gebauer, *Christian August von Schleswig-Holstein-Augustenburg*. Also Springer, *Dahlmann*; Jansen, *U. J. Lornsen*; Droysen, *J. G. Droysen*. The literature on this subject is extensive.

and Holstein, but aimed at a close connection of Schleswig with Denmark. Some of them looked even beyond this to the formation of a great pan-Scandinavian state. From the river which marked the boundary between Schleswig and Holstein, they became known as "Eider-Danes" and the object of their ambitions as "Eider-Denmark."

These two conflicting parties based their theories on their interpretation of the long history of the relations of the duchies to the crown of Denmark and each believed sincerely and passionately in the accuracy and justice of its point of view. The German or Schleswig-Holstein claims may be summed up in three main points: that Schleswig and Holstein were independent, sovereign states, connected with Denmark only in personal union; that Schleswig and Holstein were inseparably united in a real union with each other, whence the name of Schleswig-Holstein; and that the succession in the duchies followed the Salic law. The Eider-Danes, on the other hand, maintained that Schleswig was rightfully a province of the kingdom, having been incorporated with it in 1721; that the inseparable union of the two duchies was justified neither by law nor by history; and that in Schleswig, the succession was the same as in the kingdom, where the *Lex Regia* of 1665 permitted it to pass through females.

As a member of the German Confederation, Holstein was a sovereign state.[8] The legal status of Schleswig involves difficult problems of political theory but it is, at least, clear that the Danes were mistaken in believing that the duchy had been incorporated with the kingdom.[9] On the second point, the real union of the duchies, the Danes were justified in denying the applicability of the medieval charters on which the claim was based— the fact that the duchies had been fiefs of different suzerains seems conclusive against it—but a *de facto* union had developed that had long been recognized in practice. With regard to the third point, the most authoritative opinion now is that the *Lex*

---

[8] Federal Act organizing the German Confederation annexed to the Treaty of Vienna (1815), Art. I; Final Act of Vienna, May 15, 1820, Arts. I and II.

[9] Erslev, *Frederik IV og Slesvig.*

Regia had never formally been established in Schleswig and that the old law of male succession still applied.[10]

According to this, on the impending extinction of the direct male line of the royal house,[11] the kingdom and the duchies would go each its own way. The kingdom would pass to the nearest heir of the last king, which meant through the female line, while the duchies would pass to the nearest male line, that of the dukes of Augustenburg.[12]

Alarmed at this prospect, the Eider-Danes attempted to force the government's hand. In 1846, in answer to a question from the Estates of the Danish islands, a royal proclamation, the famous "Open Letter," declared that the succession in Schleswig was the same as that in the kingdom. Only with reference to some parts of Holstein was any doubt admitted and this the government was exerting itself to clear.[13] This categorical denial of the Schleswig-Holstein claim was answered by protests from the agnates and by an outburst of indignation in the duchies and in Germany. The Estates of Holstein appealed to the German Confederation but before the Diet at Frankfurt had secured a satisfactory solution, the Revolution of 1848 burst upon Europe.

In March 1848, the Eider-Danes gained the upper hand in Copenhagen. A liberal constitution was established in the Kingdom of Denmark and one was planned for the whole monarchy which would link Schleswig more closely to the kingdom than to Holstein. The duchies rose in revolt and were at first aided by Prussia acting as the mandatory of the Frankfurt Parliament. But under pressure from Russia[14] and Great Britain, the Prussians withdrew from the duchies, making separate peace

[10] Erslev, *Augustenborgernes Arvekrav.*

[11] The Crown Prince, later King Frederick VII, had no children and little prospect of any. The only other male in the direct royal line was his uncle, Prince Ferdinand, who lived until July 1863, but was also childless.

[12] See genealogical table in Appendix, below, based on Gebauer, *Christian August, Herzog von Schleswig-Holstein,* Appendix.

[13] Falck, *Sammlung der Wichtigsten Urkunden, welche auf das Staatsrecht der Herzogthümer Schleswig und Holstein Bezug haben,* No. CVI.

[14] Schiemann, *Russland unter Nikolaus I,* IV, pp. 164 f, believes that the Russian threats were pure bluff. Nevertheless, they had the desired effect.

with Denmark, and the hostilities ended with the Schleswig-Holsteiners in control of Holstein and the Danes, of Schleswig.

II.

The Schleswig-Holstein question, after the Revolution of 1848, turned less on the theories that have just been outlined than on a new legal basis, established under the auspices of the Great Powers. Because of its location at the entrance to the Baltic Sea, the Danish Monarchy has been an object of international interest. Considerations like those that have made the Great Powers unwilling to see one of their number predominant at Constantinople,[15] influenced their attitude toward Denmark and made the independence and integrity of the Danish Monarchy an axiom of European politics.[16]

After the suppression of the revolt in the duchies, the Powers took counsel as to how Denmark could best be secured against a recurrence of the danger that had threatened her. Ignoring the significance of the national antagonism of Germans and Danes in the monarchy, they acted as though the root of the difficulty lay in the uncertainty of the succession to the crown.[17] To remedy this, it was arranged that Prince Christian of the Glücksburg branch of the Danish royal house should succeed in case of the extinction of the direct line. The other claimants to the succession, except the Duke of Augustenburg, renounced their rights in favor of Prince Christian. The Danish government steadfastly refused to admit the rights of the Duke of Augustenburg, who had taken a leading part in the revolt, and declined

[15] Cf. Bloomfield to Palmerston, No. 66, St. Petersburg, March 4, 1850, (Record Office, London); Sir A. Malet, *The Overthrow of the Germanic Confederation*, pp. 22 f.

[16] E. g.: Palmerston to Sir Henry Wynn, (draft), Private, Sept. 18, 1846. ''In reply to your letter of the 10th Instant I have to inform you that Her M. Govt. have not yet had time thoroughly to examine the Question of the succession to the throne of Denmark so as to enable them to form an opinion upon it, but that on general principles the British Government would regret any thing which might tend to diminish the extent and impair the resources of the Danish Monarchy.'' (Record Office, London.)

[17] Cf. Sir A. W. Ward in *Cambridge History of British Foreign Policy*, II, pp. 530 f.

to ask him for a direct renunciation but for various reasons, most important of which was the insistence of the King of Prussia, a compromise was reached. The Duke ceded his estates, which had been sequestered, to the Danish government for a large sum of money and signed an agreement to live outside of the Danish Monarchy and to do nothing that might disturb its peace or the established order of succession.[18] Finally, at London, on May 8, 1852, the Great Powers (Austria, France, Great Britain, Prussia, Russia) and Sweden-Norway made a treaty with Denmark in which they recognized the principle of the integrity of the Danish Monarchy as a permanent element of the European balance of power and agreed to recognize the succession of Prince Christian of Glücksburg to "all the States at present united under the sceptre of His Majesty the King of Denmark."[19]

In the meantime, negotiations which were to prove of greater importance had been carried on between Austria, Prussia, and Denmark. The treaty ending hostilities between Prussia and Denmark had provided that the King of Denmark might appeal to the German Confederation to restore his legitimate authority in Holstein. It was understood that he should not attempt to reconquer it himself.[21] In accordance with this agreement, at the end of 1850, Austrian and Prussian troops occupied Holstein.[22] But before restoring the duchy to its sovereign, and before they

[18] The negotiations with the Duke were conducted by Bismarck at Frankfurt. Cf. Gebauer, *Christian August, Herzog von Schleswig-Holstein*, pp. 316-332, and a few additional documents in Bismarck, *Die gesammelten Werke*, I.

[19] Cf. Appendix, II, pp. 265 ff. It should be noted that this treaty does not "guarantee" the succession or the independence and integrity of the Danish Monarchy. In Germany, it is generally known as the "London Protocol" although that term is more correctly applied to the Protocol of August 2, 1850. Cf. *Cambridge History of British Foreign Policy*, II, pp. 530 ff.; Thorsøe, *Kong Frederik den Syvendes Regering*, II, parts 1 and 3; Neergaard, *Under Junigrundloven*, I, pp. 696-745; and some additional documents in Hoetzsch, *Peter von Meyendorff*, II. There is an extensive controversial literature on the treaty of London. Most of the other European states, including some members of the German Confederation, adhered to the treaty but, as Austria and Prussia were parties, it was not thought necessary to secure the adhesion of the Confederation.

[21] Treaty of Berlin, July 2, 1850. *Nouveau Recueil Général de Traités*, XV, pp. 340-346.

[22] Cf. Thorsøe, *Kong Frederik den Syvendes Regering*, II, pp. 99 ff.; Neergaard, *Under Junigrundloven*, I, pp. 501 ff.; Stern, *Geschichte Europas*, VII, p. 471.

would agree to the new order of succession for the Danish Monarchy the two Powers demanded to know what the future organization of the re-united monarchy was to be.

On the German side, the lead in these negotiations was taken by the Austrian Minister President, Prince Schwarzenberg, then at the height of his power. The reaction in Germany and in Europe was in full swing and Austria, with Prussia in her wake, was preparing to crush out the liberal constitutions which 1848 had left in the German Confederation.[23] Denmark was not, it is true, part of the Confederation and her institutions and those of Schleswig were not subject to revision by the Diet of Frankfurt; but if it was in the interest of the ''Balance of Power'' to maintain the integrity of the Danish Monarchy by the suppression of Schleswig-Holsteinism, it was in the interest of the ''Conservative Principle'' to keep the liberal Danish constitution of June 1849 within as narrow limits as possible by the suppression of Eider-Danism.[24]

The first proposals of the Danish government for the reorganization of the monarchy maintained an intimate constitutional connection of Schleswig with the kingdom and were rejected as unsatisfactory by the two German Powers. In September 1851, the Austrian and Prussian Ministers President argued that the restoration of the system of local Estates for Holstein alone would result in a temporary conclusion of the events of the past few years but not in a permanent solution of the problem. They demanded the restoration of the Assembly of Estates in Schleswig as well as in Holstein and the submission to both bodies of the plan for the reorganization of the monarchy. ''Can a real solution of the difficulties be expected,'' wrote Schwarzenberg, ''when the promise to follow constitutional methods is limited to Holstein? Are not the Estates of Holstein linked to those of

[23] H. Friedjung, *Oesterreich von 1848 bis 1860*, II, pp. 149 f.

[24] ''Baron Manteuffel further stated that he should entertain strong objections to the establishment of a Democratic constitution in Sleswig which would have effects injurious to the tranquillity of the North.'' Howard to Palmerston, Berlin, November 16, 1851, No. 104, (Record Office, London). Cf. Gooch, *Later Correspondence of Lord John Russell*, II, p. 44; Thorsøe, *Kong Frederik den Syvendes Regering*, II, pp. 153 ff.; Neergaard, *Under Junigrundloven*, I, pp. 510 ff.

Schleswig by the *nexus socialis* of the Ritterschaft?[25] Will not their first actions consist of objections to the plan of reorganization laid before the late assembly of notables, of reclamations for their ancient rights, and of complaints to the German Confederation?'"[26] In a second dispatch of the same date, he wrote

The re-establishment of the Provincial Estates of Holstein, ... is looked upon by the Imperial Cabinet. . . as an important and favorable change in the Danish question. But the Danish Ministers will hardly be able, at the moment when the future of their country is to be founded anew, to cast their eyes on the position of Denmark and of Europe without being obliged to confess to themselves that that salutary resolution is but a first step made towards the re-establishment of the vital conditions of the Danish Monarchy. *The idea of separating Holstein still more from the other Provinces of the Monarchy, in order more closely to unite Schleswig with the Kingdom of Denmark, is repugnant to the principle of the integrity of the Monarchy.* . . . . That idea. . . arises from a tendency which manifests itself more or less in every country and which aspires to the formation of a new map of Europe according to nationalities. *The steps taken in order to realize that idea. . . and the. . . object of which is the incorporation of Schleswig with Denmark, are the results of the innovations of the year 1848, which it would be quite time definitely to restrict.* . . . The Duchy of Schleswig has always been an intermediate link between Denmark and Holstein.

The attempts which had been made to alienate the institutions of Schleswig from those of Holstein, ''in order to unite them with the institutions of a democratic Denmark,'' were stated to be infringements of the permanent interests of the monarchy as well as of existing rights.[27] Baron von Manteuffel, the Prussian

---

[25] Cf. Appendix I.

[26] Thorsøe, *Kong Frederik den Syvendes Regering*, II, p. 158; *British and Foreign State Papers*, XLI, pp. 1014 f.

[27] Schwarzenberg to Vrintz, Vienna, September 9, 1851, No. 2, (Vienna Archives). English translation in *Correspondence between Austria, Prussia and Denmark, 1851-52*. The italics are mine. Two other dispatches of September 9, 1851, to Freiherr von Vrintz at Copenhagen are important for an understanding of Austrian policy in the Schleswig-Holstein question. In No. 4, Schwarzenberg recommended a unitary customs system for the Danish Monarchy, ''mit Vorbehalt des eventuellen Anschlusses Holsteins an eine allgemeine deutsche Zoll- und Handelseinigung,'' and he emphasized the importance of establishing the customs frontier at the Elbe. The consequence would be, of course, to prevent the inclusion of Holstein in the Prussian ''Zollverein'' or in any tariff union from which Austria was excluded. The influence of the rivalry of Austria and Prussia appears even more clearly in No. 5. ''Ich füge meinen heutigen Erlassen einige Worte vertraulich bei über unser und Preussens Verhältniss zu der dänischen Angelegenheit. In

minister, emphasized the loyal and conservative character of the
Estates of the duchies and he too pointed to the position of
Schleswig as an intermediate link between Holstein and Den-
mark. ''By the summoning of these Estates, not only for
Holstein but also for Schleswig,'' he wrote,

the Danish government will provide itself with the proper means of again
establishing the influence of the sound, conservative elements of these lands
and will secure to them the position that becomes them in the Danish
Monarchy. Schleswig will thus again become the intermediate link between
Holstein and the other parts of the Monarchy, in which latter, those tendencies which cannot in the long run be reconciled with the development of
the monarchical form of government will lose their preponderance. There
will, at the same time, thereby be established a durable and satisfactory
basis for relations with Germany and for the protection of the constitutional
rights of the German Confederation.[28]

Schwarzenberg summed up his suggestions for the reorganization of the Danish Monarchy as: ''community for every part of
the Monarchy of the order of succession and of the political
institutions essential to the unity of the Monarchy; no incorporation, either expressed or *de facto*, of Schleswig with the
Kingdom; provincial Estates in the Duchy of Schleswig as well
as in the Duchy of Holstein; and a settlement of the position of
Holstein in its relations to the German Confederation. ... ''[29]

unserem Vortheile liegt eine in ihrer Integrität wahrhaft gesicherte dänische
Monarchie. Preussen ist in dem entgegengesetzten Falle und fügt sich nur einer
Notwendigkeit wenn es zu ihrer Herstellung mitwirkt. Der Kaiser müsste Sich
aber, ungeachtet des Londoner Protokolles, aus der ganzen Sache zurückziehen,
könnte Er Seine Mitwirkung nicht mit Seiner deutschen Stellung vereinigen.
Welche Folgen daraus bei der schwankenden Politik Preussens, und der Möglichkeit
eines neuen Systemwechsels in Berlin, für Dänemark entstehen könnten habe ich
wohl nicht nöthig vorauszusagen. Unterlassen Sie also Nichts um dem Könige und
Seinen Minister klar zu machen, dass wenn es ihnen um die Gesamt-monarchie zu
thun ist, und nicht der Lohn aller ihren Anstrengungen völlig ungewiss bleiben soll,
die gegenwärtge Conjunctur benützt werden müsse um eine Lösung im Sinne unserer Rathschläge herbeizuführen.'' Drafts Nos. 4 and 5, Sept. 9, 1851, (Vienna
Archives). Cf. Krieger, *Dagbøger*, I, p. 133. Fear that Prussia would gain advantage in Germany by a more ''national'' policy in the Schleswig-Holstein question
was an important factor in Austrian policy until the end of the war of 1864.

[28] Thorsøe, *Kong Frederik den Syvendes Regering*, II, p. 159. The date is mis-
printed *December*.

[29] Schwarzenberg to Vrintz, Vienna, September 9, 1851, No. 2, (Vienna
Archives).

Acceptance of these demands would mean the abandonment of the Eider policy but there was nothing else for Denmark to do. Great Britain and Russia had intervened when her integrity was at stake but they would not support her in questions of constitutional detail.[30] The Danish ministry resigned, a new one on a more conservative basis was formed, and in December of 1851 the negotiations were completed. The Danes promised that they would not incorporate Schleswig with the Kingdom nor take any steps directed to that end; the two German Powers gave up the claims of the Schleswig-Holstein party. But the clause which was to cause the most difficulty and which finally wrecked the whole settlement was that in which the King of Denmark declared his intention of establishing a constitution for the affairs of the monarchy as a whole, to bring about "an organic and homogeneous union of all parts of the Monarchy in a legal and constitutional manner; that is, by means of the deliberative Provincial Estates of each of the said Duchies separately, and so far as regards the Kingdom, by means of resolutions of the Rigsraad; as well as, in reference to Lauenburg, with the coöperation of the Knights and Representatives of the country."[31]

In the years that followed, "Schleswig-Holstein" and "Eider-Danish" theories continued to influence public opinion and so to put pressure on the governments but the international aspects of the question depended upon the complex and ambiguous agreements of 1851-52.

III.

For a few years after 1852, while the liberal and national forces were recuperating from the shock of defeat, the Danish government was left practically undisturbed to deal with the

---

[30] Thorsøe, *Kong Frederik den Syvendes Regering*, II, pp. 166 ff.; Neergaard *Under Junigrundloven*, I, pp. 542 f.

[31] Cf. Appendix II, pp. 267-273. English translations of the document may be found in *Correspondence between Austria, Prussia and Denmark, 1851-52* and in Gosch, *Denmark and Germany since 1815*, pp. 380-400. The main points were summed up in a Danish royal proclamation of January 28, 1852. *Nouveau Recueil général des Traités*, XV, pp. 407-412; Gosch, *op. cit.*, pp. 395-398.

problem of the duchies.   During the Crimean War, Napoleon
III suggested to the Prussian government that Holstein and
southern Schleswig might be its reward for entering the war
against Russia.[32] Otherwise none of the Powers took an active
interest in the Schleswig-Holstein question until 1856.

In the duchies, the attitude of Austria and Prussia as expressed
in the agreements of 1851-52 made the realization of the national
aims of the Schleswig-Holstein party seem hopeless.   In Schleswig, which was now rigorously separated from Holstein, the mass
of the German population stubbornly resisted the anti-German
measures of the administration.   But most of the political leaders
were in exile or despondent and inactive.   In Holstein, on the
other hand, where German nationality was not exposed to
pressure, the middle classes and the peasantry were generally
apathetic.   The leadership there, of the opposition to the Danish
government, passed from the liberals to the conservative aris-
tocrats, the right wing of the *Ritterschaft*.[33]   Most influential
among this group were Count Adolf Blome and Baron Carl von
Scheel-Plessen.[34] Their goal was not the separation of the duchies
from the Danish Monarchy but the establishment of a conservative 'Whole State,' in which the German and Danish nationalities should be on an equal footing.   Even the old-fashioned
royal absolutism seemed to them preferable to a state in which
the 'democracy' of Copenhagen could rule the aristocracy of
Holstein.[35] Their emphasis on the 'historic rights' of the duchies
was not inconsistent with the prevailing currents of reaction,
and their ultra-conservative and aristocratic policy gained them
the sympathy of conservative Europe.[36]

In the kingdom, all parties, with the exception of a small group
of the National Liberals, recognized the necessity of yielding to
the pressure of the Great Powers and of abandoning the Eider

[32] Neergaard, *Under Junigrundloven*, I, pp. 936 f.

[33] Cf. Appendix I.

[34] Hagenah, "1863.   Die nationale Bewegung in Schleswig-Holstein." in
Z. *f. s-h. G.*, LVI, pp. 283 ff.

[35] Hagenah, *op. cit.*, pp. 285 f. Neergaard, *Under Junigrundloven*, II, pp. 71 f.
Bismarck, *Die gesammelten Werke*, VII, p. 34.

[36] Cf. Poschinger, *Preussens auswärtige Politik, 1850 bis 1858.* pp. 220 f.

policy. The working out of the new organization of the monarchy fell to the Conservatives, the so-called *Helstat*[37] party, who aimed at the preservation of the monarchy as a whole and who regarded with equal disfavor the disruptive forces, both Schleswig-Holstein and Eider-Dane. For a time, the *Helstat* party was supported by the *Bondevenner*, or Peasants Party, and by the tacit acquiescence of some of the National Liberals, in its general policy and especially in the passing of the new law of succession called for by the Treaty of London.

But before the program could be completed by the establishment of the projected common constitution,[38] it had become more difficult for the government to deal with the *Rigsdag*[39] of the kingdom.

The ministry was becoming increasingly reactionary and by a royal proclamation of July 26, 1854, without the coöperation of the *Rigsdag* or of the Estates of the duchies, it established a constitution for the affairs common to the monarchy as a whole.[40] This vested the legislative power in a *Rigsraad* of fifty members, thirty to be elected by the representative bodies of the kingdom and of the three duchies,[41] twenty to be appointed by the King.

In 1854, however, the European reaction had reached its height and the defeats of the Russians in the Crimea gave new hope to the liberal and national elements in Europe, not least to those of Denmark.[42] In December 1854, a less reactionary ministry came

[37] 'Whole State.'

[38] This seems to be the most satisfactory term to use for the constitution of the monarchy as a whole. It is usually called *Fællesforfatning*, in Danish, *Gesamtverfassung*, in German. The term 'Federal' will be used for the constitution of the German Confederation.

[39] *Rigsdag* is the term usually applied to the legislature of the kingdom, *Rigsraad* to that of the monarchy as a whole. The *Rigsdag* had legislative (*besluttende, beschliessende*) powers, the Estates of the duchies merely deliberative (*raadgivende, berathende*).

[40] According to the royal proclamation of January 28, 1852, these were to be foreign affairs, army, navy, and common finance; according to section 5 of the Constitution of 1854, common affairs were all those not specifically reserved as local for the individual parts of the monarchy. Cf. Neergaard, *Under Junigrundloven*, I, pp. 571 f., 893.

[41] 18 for Denmark, 6 for Holstein, 5 for Schleswig, and 1 for Lauenburg.

[42] Cf. Karl Ploug's stirring poem "Sebastopols Fald." *Digte*, I, pp. 264-267.

into office in Copenhagen and preparations were made to revise the constitution in accordance with the wishes of the representatives of the kingdom.[43]

The second common constitution was signed by the King on October 2, 1855 and was accepted, though informally, by the *Rigsdag*, but was not submitted in any way to the influence of the representatives of the duchies. Its main feature was a unicameral *Rigsraad* of eighty members, twenty appointed by the King, thirty elected by the members of the four local assemblies, and thirty chosen by direct election of voters who met a certain property qualification. By the apportionment of representation to the various parts of the monarchy and by the method of election, a Danish majority was assured.[44]

The Constitution of 1855 proved as unsatisfactory to the German leaders as the preceding one to the Danes. Under the leadership of Baron von Scheel-Plessen, eleven of the German members of the first *Rigsraad* introduced a resolution petitioning the King to lay the constitution and the electoral law before the Estates of Schleswig, Holstein, and Lauenburg; and to present to the *Rigsraad* a draft taking account of their advice. When this was defeated by the Danish majority in the assembly, the 'eleven' protested against the constitution as contrary to the royal proclamation of January 28, 1852, and to the agreements with Austria and Prussia.[45]

The failure of the Danish government to give the Estates of the duchies an opportunity to deliberate on the provisions regulating their position in the common constitution of the monarchy

---

[43] The change in ministry was due in part to the Danish opposition, in part to Court intrigues. Cf. Neergaard, *Under Junigrundloven*, I, pp. 896-905, 942-968.

[44] Of the appointed members, 12 were to be residents of the kingdom, 3 of Schleswig, 4 of Holstein, 1 of Lauenburg; of the indirectly elected, 18 were from the kingdom, 5 from Schleswig, 6 from Holstein and 1 from Lauenburg; of the directly elected, 17 were from the kingdom, 5 from Schleswig and 8 from Holstein. 47 members were thus allotted to the kingdom and although the composition of the assembly of the Estates of Schleswig favored the Germans, some Danish representatives were sure to be elected directly in Schleswig. Cf. Neergaard, *Under Junigrundloven*, II, pp., 23-33; and P. Andrae, *Andrae og Fællesforfatningen af 5 October 1855.*

[45] *Rigsraadstidende*, 1856, Columns 1135-1409, 1665-1880.

was a serious mistake, whose effects were intensified by the way in which the Constitution of 1855 was established. It is true that, formally, the constitution was created by the King after consultation with the *appointed* members of the existing *Rigsraad*. But practically, the Danish *Rigsdag* had had an opportunity to accept or reject it,[46] while the representatives of the duchies had been completely disregarded. Even if the Estates of both duchies had maintained the Schleswig-Holstein point of view and opposed the policy of the government, their right was merely to discuss and to advise, not to accept or reject. The government would have been as free to disregard their advice concerning the common constitution as it was to decline it with reference to the constitutions for local affairs. Its refusal even to hear the opinion of the Estates gave a legitimate basis for the complaints of the Schleswig-Holsteiners and of the German Powers.

IV.

The conflicts that developed in the *Rigsraad* led to the diplomatic intervention of Prussia and Austria. The immediate occasion was a law passed by the *Rigsraad* authorizing the government to dispose of certain domain lands in Holstein. The royal proclamation of January 28, 1852, had included the income from domain lands with the common finances of the monarchy but had left their administration and control under the head of local affairs. This division had been retained in the local constitutions of the duchies but article 50 of the Common Constitution of 1855 gave the *Rigsraad* control of the alienation and acquisition of the domains of the monarchy. The local constitution of Schleswig was modified in this sense by royal ordinance but the Estates of Holstein refused to accept a parallel amendment.[47] The point of view of the government was that, as, in the past, the King alone had exercised the unquestioned right of selling the domains in the duchies, he now had the right to limit his power

[46] Neergaard, *Under Junigrundloven*, II, pp. 23-34, 36-52.
[47] *Ibid.*, p. 109.

by giving the *Rigsraad* a share of it. But with the legal situation in a transitional stage, it was politically unwise for the government to raise the question. The Schleswig-Holstein opposition protested against the transference of the control of the domains from the local to the common legislature and broadcast the charge that the Danish government had broken its agreements on a second point. The opinion widely held in Germany that the wealth of the duchies was being used to lighten the financial burdens of the kingdom thus gained new emphasis and apparent confirmation.

In a note dated June 1, 1856, Manteuffel instructed the Prussian minister at Copenhagen to call the attention of the Danish government to the grievances of the duchies. ''We have followed the deliberations of the Holstein Estates and of the Danish *Rigsraad* with the liveliest interest. We have observed with regret that the situation of the duchies has again reached a state of tension that gives cause to fear more serious developments.'' In an attached memorandum, he specified the objections of the Prussian government to the action of the Danish government with regard to the domain lands and to the way in which the Constitution of 1855 had been established.[48] This note of the Prussian government was followed on June 23 by a similar one from Buol in Vienna to the Austrian minister at Copenhagen.[49]

Neither Manteuffel nor Buol had objected to the more reactionary constitution of 1854, which had been promulgated with equal disregard for the procedure prescribed by the agreements of 1851-52. They had even replied with expressions of cordial approval when notified by the Danish government of the establishment of that of 1855.[50] After the Crimean War, however, German public opinion had begun to follow the situation in the duchies and in Denmark with renewed interest. Pamphlets and books on the 'Danish oppression' of the 'German duchies' appeared in increasing numbers. The cause of the duchies was one

---

[48] *Urkundenbuch zur Geschichte der Holstein-Lauenburgischen Angelegenheit, 1851-1858*, No. 12.

[49] *Ibid.*, No. 13.

[50] Neergaard, *Under Junigrundloven*, II, p. 124.

in which liberals and conservatives could unite on the basis of a common hostility to Denmark. The former were in close touch with the exiled leaders of the Schleswig-Holstein revolt, the latter sympathized with the *Ritterschaft* in its conflict with the more liberal tendencies of Copenhagen. "I cannot look on in silence at what has come to pass over there," King Frederick William IV of Prussia told a Danish envoy.

At Copenhagen, they have quite forgotten that the Confederation exists and has rights and, too, that it is a land of forty-five millions of people. They carry on as though Germany were not a power and not deserving of respect. That I cannot accept. ....I cannot and will not hear without protest that a part of Germany, a German land is to be only a foreign province, that Holstein is to be a Danish province. ....Certainly the King has the best of intentions, but I want to tell you this, to express my opinion frankly: ... There was Revolution in Denmark and it still shares in the government. There are some respectable men in the Ministry, that I gladly admit, but you are flirting with Revolution, with the revolutionary rabble. It has been my duty everywhere to stand against injustice and against the Revolution. ...[51]

Because of the influence of public opinion on the governments of the minor states, it was feared that a complaint by the Holstein or Lauenburg Estates to the Diet of the Confederation would result in awkward discussions. The Prussian government decided, therefore, to make what political capital it could by taking the initiative in a popular cause and to forestall the action of the minor states at Frankfurt. The Austrian government dared not risk its influence in Germany by falling too far behind Prussia.[52]

Scheele, the Danish minister for foreign affairs, took the situation very lightly and by his dilatory and intransigeant handling of the negotiations envenomed the controversy. His replies to the notes of Austria and Prussia offered a few slight concessions in the matter of the domain lands but passed over the more important issue, the Constitution of 1855. Manteuffel and Buol renewed their complaints in sharper notes in October 1856 and

[51] Bülow to Scheele, September 18, 1856, Neergaard, *Under Junigrundloven*, II, p. 134.
[52] Neergaard, *Under Junigrundloven*, II, pp. 124 ff; Sybel, *Begründung des deutschen Reiches*, III, pp. 92 ff.; Bismarck to Manteuffel, May 27, 1856, in Poschinger, *Preussen im Bundestag*, III, pp. 1-4. Cf. note 27, pp. 11 f. above.

threatened that if Denmark did not regulate the position of Holstein and Lauenburg by constitutional methods, they would refer the question to the Diet of the German Confederation.[53]

Scheele's reply, in February 1857, [54]argued that the Common Constitutions of 1854 and 1855 had been promulgated in all due form because the constitution of Holstein had previously been amended in such a way as to withdraw from the competence of the Estates of the duchy, all matters which were ''common affairs'' of the monarchy.[55]

The negotiations were obviously leading to no results and Austria and Prussia prepared to bring the question before the Diet. Scheele insisted that any further yielding on Denmark's part was ''a constitutional impossibility'' and was prepared to regard any attempt at Federal Execution by the Frankfurt Diet as the beginning of war.[56] He fell from power in April 1857, and his ministry was succeeded by one under the leadership of the abler and more conciliatory Carl Christian Hall.[57] The first act of the Hall ministry was to inform Austria and Prussia that Denmark agreed to do what Scheele had merely suggested: to submit the local constitution for Holstein to the Estates by August 1857.[58]

It was becoming too late for even this temporary solution. The meeting of the Estates brought the conflict no nearer to an end. The government's proposals offered Holstein more exten-

---

[53] Neergaard, *Under Junigrundloven*, II, pp. 127 ff.; *Urkundenbuch zur Geschichte der Holstein-Lauenburgischen Angelegenheit, 1851-1858*, pp. 76-89.

[54] The delay was due in part to Scheele's wish to see what would happen in the Neufchâtel question, which monopolized the attention of the Prussian government in the autumn and winter of 1856, in part to his attempt to have the controversy brought before a European conference. Neergaard, *Under Junigrundloven*, II, p. 136.

[55] *Urkundenbuch zur Geschichte der Holstein-Lauenburgischen Angelegenheit, 1851-1858*, pp. 90-98.

[56] Scheele to Bülow, March 16, 1857. Neergaard, *Under Junigrundloven*, II, p. 141, footnote 2.

[57] On Hall, cf. especially C. St. Bille, ''Carl Christian Hall'' in Bricka, *Dansk Biografisk Lexikon*, VI, pp. 493-508, and N. N[eergaard], ''Hall, Carl Christian'' in *Salmonsens Konversationslexikon*, X, (1920), pp. 684-687.

[58] *Urkundenbuch zur Geschichte der Holstein-Lauenburgischen Angelegenheit, 1851-1858*, p. 104.

sive constitutional rights, but as before, all references to the position of Holstein in the common constitution were omitted. At the end of October, then, Austria and Prussia referred the question to the Diet at Frankfurt which took formal cognizance of the state of the negotiations and prepared for action.[59]

On February 11, 1858, the Diet adopted a resolution that it could not regard the Constitution of 1855 as valid in Holstein and Lauenburg. Denmark was called upon to inform the Diet of the way in which it intended to secure the constitutional position of those duchies in the monarchy in accordance with the principles of the constitution of the German Confederation and the promises of 1851-1852.[60] On February 25, the Diet expressed the expectation that the Danish government would refrain from any measures in Holstein and Lauenburg which were not in accordance with the above mentioned resolution of February 11.[61] Attempts of the Danish government to compromise were rejected and finally, under pressure from the Diet, in November 1858 the application of the Constitution of 1855 to Holstein and Lauenburg was suspended and the Holstein Estates called for January 3, 1859 to deliberate on the position of that Duchy in the Monarchy.[62]

The net result of the negotiations from 1856 to 1858 was the *de facto* establishment of the Eider-Denmark. Since 1856, its partisans had been increasing in number and in influence on public opinion and on the government. They found cogent arguments in the obvious difficulty of establishing a constitution that would be acceptable to Holstein and to Germany and in the danger to the development of liberal institutions in the rest of the monarchy from the intervention of the German Confederation in Holstein. The government was not yet ready to break completely with its opponents by boldly adopting the Eider program. Nevertheless, the decision not to offer armed

---

[59] At the same time a formal complaint was received from Lauenburg. *Ibid.*, pp. 117-125.

[60] *Ibid.*, pp. 132-138.

[61] *Ibid.*, p. 140.

[62] *Urkundenbuch zur deutsch-dänischen Angelegenheit vom 29 October 1857 bis 26 December 1861*, pp. 48-54.

resistance but to suspend the operation of the constitution in the Federal lands of the monarchy was really the parting of the ways. Hall, the President of the Council, emphasized as the great advantage in fulfilling the demand of the Diet, the fact that this would be in accordance with the wishes of the Great Powers and would therefore temporarily free Denmark from pressure and give time to look about for another way out of the difficulty. Yielding would not prejudice the future, but would leave the way open for an approach to the Eider policy or a return to the 'Whole State' organization as circumstances demanded.[63] As the future showed, the Holstein Estates and their German supporters would accept no common constitution that was not based either on absolute monarchy or on equal representation of all four parts of the Monarchy, regardless of the population. The people of Denmark, however, had advanced too far constitutionally to accept a return to absolutism. The alternative, equal representation regardless of population, would have given fifty thousand Lauenburgers equal power with one and one half million Danes and would have given the German minority full control of the legislature. It was out of the question for Denmark to submit to such an arrangement. The return to the 'Whole State' organization was impossible.

V.

During this phase of the controversy, from 1856 to 1858, the Danish government received no support for its policy except from Sweden-Norway. There the renewal of the Danish-German conflict had caused a revival of interest in the idea of a Scandinavian union. In the latter part of the eighteenth century, the idea had begun to spread in learned and literary circles in the three Scandinavian countries that Danes, Swedes, and Norwegians were at bottom one people and, in spite of unpleasant memories from the days of the Kalmar union of the fourteenth century, their relationship should be closer than that of other nations. The policy of Sweden during the last years of the

[63] Neergaard, *Under Junigrundloven*, II. pp. 183-186.

Napoleonic wars checked the movement for a time but, influenced by the romanticism of the first generation of the nineteenth century, it revived with increased strength. Poets turned back to the early days when there was little to distinguish the three peoples, and celebrated the glories common to them all. In the 1840's, came a series of meetings of the university youth of the three countries, who were soon joined by the Liberals of the cities in their support of the Scandinavian ideal.

As the conflict of nationalities in Schleswig became acute, the Scandinavian movement became more political and the Eider-Danes, especially, dreamt of a union of the three peoples to defend "the northland's frontier" against the Germans. "Not Schleswig, not Denmark," proclaimed Carl Ploug in 1844 to the Danish Schleswigers, "but the whole northland, great and beautiful, is your fatherland. Good courage, Schleswigers, for you are Scandinavians! .... There are not thirty-three millions of Germans who are going to overwhelm a hundred and fifty thousand poor peasants; there are thirty thousand, yea, only three thousand, or, strictly speaking, perhaps only thirty fool-hardy Schleswig-Holsteiners who have thrown down the gauntlet to six million Scandinavians."[64] In 1848, Swedish and Norwegian volunteers had flocked to the Danish army and a Swedish-Norwegian auxiliary corps was landed on the island of Fyn (Fünen). There was talk of solving the Danish succession question by the adoption of the King of Sweden-Norway as the heir of Frederick VII.[65] Whether or not such a plan was seriously considered in official circles, the Treaty of London ended it as a possible solution and it was not discussed again until 1856.

In June of that year, a group of students from the Universities of Copenhagen, Christiania, and Lund gathered at Uppsala, where Carl Ploug, editor of the influential National Liberal *Fædrelandet* and the recognized leader of the Danish 'Scandinavians' eloquently advocated the dynastic union of the three kingdoms. On their return, King Oscar entertained the students at his palace of Drottningholm near Stockholm, listened to the

---

[64] Neergaard, *Under Junigrundloven*, I, pp. 23 f.
[65] *Sveriges Historia*, XII, p. 104.

enthusiastic speeches, and in reply proclaimed the future brother-hood-in-arms of the northern peoples: "Our swords" he pro-claimed, "are ready for the common defense."[66] Crown Prince Charles (soon to be King Charles XV) as Viceroy of Norway, addressed the Norwegian students on their return to Christiania, and King Frederick VII of Denmark gave a banquet to the Danish delegation.

Naturally the Eider-Danes, who disliked the 'Whole State' system, would seek to overturn the order of succession upon which it was based.[67] Their aim was to associate Sweden and Norway with the policy of excluding Holstein and to enlist their aid in the defense of the historic and 'national' Eider frontier. In political circles in Sweden, the point of view was somewhat different. To the royal house, a third crown was of itself some-what tempting. In addition, it was felt that the union of the three Scandinavian kingdoms would form a respectable counter-weight against Russia, which had been angered by the hostile attitude of Sweden during the Crimean War[68] and by the treaty made with England and France in November 1855.[69]

In September 1856, when Prince Jerome Napoleon visited Christiania and Stockholm, Prince Charles and King Oscar gained the impression that England and France were seriously interested in modifying the Danish succession and bringing about the Scandinavian union. From the 16th to the 22nd of September, Prince Charles visited Copenhagen where he was received with enthusiasm. His conversations with leading 'Scandinavians' and particularly with Carl Ploug, led to the appointment of a more sympathetic Swedish minister to Denmark and to a negotiation between the Kings of Sweden and Denmark. Early in December, Ploug sent a memorandum to King Oscar, in which he pointed out that there were three forms of alliance possible for their states: a purely defensive alliance, excluding the "purely German" territories of Denmark; an offensive and

---

[66] H. Koht, *Die Stellung Norwegens und Schwedens*, p. 34; *Sveriges Historia,* XII, p. 106; Neergaard, *Under Junigrundloven*, II, p. 120.

[67] Cf. Krieger, *Dagbøger*, I, p. 177. (January 5, 1856).

[68] *Sveriges Historia*, XII, p. 105.

[69] *Ibid.*, pp. 129 f.

defensive confederation, limited in territorial extent like the first, but with common army, navy, and representation, with gradual extension of the constitution; and a complete dynastic union. The last must be their ultimate aim. It, like the second, was contrary to existing treaties and would be opposed by Russia and Germany, but it could be attained if Sweden-Norway would begin by offering a defensive alliance on the basis of the Eider policy. As the Danish people would never consent to the German demands for the duchies, a severe conflict was almost sure to arise. Then, if Sweden-Norway gave armed aid to Denmark and the German duchies were actually separated from the monarchy, the way to the dynastic union would be prepared. King Oscar accepted the idea. On February 25, 1857, he wrote to Frederick VII, suggesting the conclusion of an alliance and in March, explained his plan in greater detail. Whereas in 1848, the Swedish government had limited its aid to the defense of the kingdom proper, it was now prepared to help defend the Eider.[70]

Under the influence of his minister for foreign affairs, who was opposed to the Scandinavian movement and who frequently acted with scant regard for the views of his colleagues in the ministry, the Danish King rejected an alliance that did not include the defense of his whole monarchy. When a dispatch of von Scheele's of February 20 became generally known, in which he spoke of the Scandinavian movement as "a poetic idea" and rather brusquely rebuffed the Swedish government, the negotiations lost all prospect of immediate success.[71]

For a short time, however, political Scandinavianism became what it had hardly been before, a European question, and was discussed in pamphlets and newspapers.[72] An article in the Paris *Presse*[73] signed Charles Edmond, aroused especial attention. The author, a Polish émigré,[74] had accompanied Prince Jerome Napoleon on his journey in northern waters and was supposed to

[70] H. Koht, *Die Stellung Norwegens und Schwedens*, pp. 36 f., 42 ff. *Sveriges Historia*, XII, p. 110.

[71] H. Koht, *op. cit.*, pp. 39 ff., *Sveriges Historia*, XII, pp. 110-113.

[72] H. Koht, *op. cit.*, pp. 37 f.

[73] Dec. 20, 1856.

[74] His real name was Choiecki.

reflect his views.   In his article, which was later expanded into
a chapter of a book, *Voyage dans les Mers du Nord*[75] Edmond
proposed that Lauenburg, Holstein, and South Schleswig be
joined in a state for Prince Christian of Glucksburg, and that
the rest of Schleswig and Denmark be united with Sweden-
Norway under the Bernadotte dynasty.[76]

These discussions led to no practical results.   Napoleon III
was the only one of the great monarchs in sympathy with the
pan-Scandinavian movement.   He generally included the formation of a united Scandinavia in his many editions of the new map
of Europe but, although he discussed the matter with various
European statesmen, he subordinated his interest to the more
immediate object of an *entente* with Alexander II.   For several
years, therefore, the official policy of France in the Schleswig-
Holstein question followed that of Russia.[77]

Russia had taken the lead in supporting the action of Prussia
and Austria.   In February 1856, Nesselrode, then in charge of
Russian foreign affairs, had spoken to the Prussian minister at
Petersburg of his fear that the controversy between the Danish
government and the Estates of Holstein might lead to serious
consequences.   His most intimate friend for forty years, he said,
had been the late Danish minister to Russia, Count Blome.
That friendship had now been transferred to his nephew, Baron
Blome, the leader of the Holstein opposition.[78]

In July 1856, Nesselrode's successor, Gorchakov told the
Danish minister at Petersburg that, in spite of his sympathy for
Denmark, the Emperor was sincerely and seriously alarmed at
conditions there.[79]   Somewhat later he remarked that he could no
longer perform for Denmark the same services that he had as

[75] Paris, 1857.

[76] H. Koht, *op. cit.*, p. 38.

[77] Bismarck, *Die gesammelten Werke*, II, p. 212; T. Martin, *The Life of His
Royal Highness the Prince Consort*, IV., p. 111; F. Charles-Roux, *Alexandre II,
Gortchakoff et Napoléon III*, pp. 207-210.   Cf. Appendix V.

[78] Werther to Manteuffel, February 26, 1856.   In Poschinger, *Preussens auswärtige Politik, 1850 bis 1858*, III, pp. 220 f.

[79]   Otto Plessen's report from St. Petersburg, July 30, 1856; Neergaard, *Under
Junigrundloven*, II, 138.

Russian representative at Frankfurt in 1850, and added, "I owe it to you to say that perhaps I don't even want to!"[80] In Otto Plessen's words, "from the moral standpoint, the government of St. Petersburg sees the Holstein opposition as a conservative element in contrast with the government; and from the political standpoint, it is anxious lest our conflicts should lead to complications which would expose the whole constitutional organization so toilsomely completed, to serious danger."[81] Even Baron Brunnow, the Russian ambassador at London, long the strongest supporter of the Danish cause, pointed out to a Danish diplomat that the situation was quite different from that of 1848-50. "Russia is now favorably disposed to Prussia, unfavorably to Denmark. You know that we regard the Holstein question as one of German domestic politics. England will support you with notes but nothing more; France will risk nothing for your sake. You will come to be entirely isolated. Follow our example! Although a Great Power we have yielded and made concessions that were humiliating to our self-esteem in order to attain peace and avert worse evils. Win over the Holsteiners, cajole them, when they are in Copenhagen lay the constitution before them! You are no longer dealing with revolutionary forces but with conservative ones, both in Holstein and in Germany."[82]

The Russian government persisted in regarding the conflict over the position of Holstein as within the jurisdiction of the German Confederation. "It has grown out of measures taken by your government," Gorchakov told the Danish minister at St. Petersburg, "and it is your affair to come to an understanding with the German cabinets."[83]

Great Britain made some efforts to persuade Austria and Prussia not to lay the matter before the Diet at Frankfurt, but failed to convince those two powers or Russia. At the same time, the British cabinet urged the Danish government to save itself from conflict with Germany by redressing the "legitimate grievances"

[80] Otto Plessen's report, September 5, 1856. *Ibid.*
[81] Report of November 14, 1856. *Ibid.*
[82] *Ibid.*, p. 139.
[83] *Ibid.*, II, p. 138, pp. 158 f; and K. v. Schlözer, *Petersburger Briefe*, pp. 38, 47.

of its German subjects.[84] British sympathy for Denmark was stimulated by the attitude of Denmark's opponents, Austria and Prussia, during the Crimean war and by the Austrian policy in Italy which irritated English friends of the *Risorgimento*. Suspicion of Germany's—or Prussia's—aspirations for naval supremacy in the Baltic disturbed some English minds and added to the growing assumption that Great Britain was bound in honor to protect 'little Denmark.' But in the Foreign Office, this sentiment was counteracted by knowledge of the grievances of the Duchies, especially as represented in a confidential report of Mr. John Ward, the British representative at Hamburg, who made a detailed study on the ground and who was sympathetic to the German liberal aspirations. Lord Clarendon, the foreign secretary, maintained a watchful but non-aggressive policy.[85] ''It is the earnest desire of Her Majesty's Government,'' he wrote to the British chargé at Copenhagen,

> that this question of the duchies should be settled in a manner honorable to the King of Denmark; and no advice will ever be offered by them which it would be contrary to His Majesty's honor to adopt; but it is to be remembered that the national good faith of Denmark would suffer, and the Powers which are ill-disposed to her would obtain a great advantage, if existing engagements were not scrupulously observed.
>
> I enclose herewith a memorandum which has been drawn up at this office in regard to the union between Schleswig and Holstein and which contains the assurances to be found in public documents. These, together with the usage of 400 years, constitute the title of the Duchies to union among themselves and separate existence from Denmark under the common Sovereign.[86]

VI.

The assembly of the Estates of Holstein met in January 1859. The royal commissioner laid before it the Common Constitution of October 2, 1855, the electoral law, and the draft of a new constitution for the local affairs of Holstein; the two former for

---

[84] Neergaard, *Under Junigrundloven*, II, 139-140. Clarendon to Buchanan, March 11, 1857; Clarendon to Seymour, March 25, 1857 and March 31, 1857; Clarendon to Orme, July 1, 1857; (Record Office, London).

[85] *Cambridge History of British Foreign Policy*, II, 542-543.

[86] Clarendon to Orme, draft, July 1, 1857, (Record Office, London).

deliberation, the latter for decision. Encouraged by the knowledge that they were backed by German public opinion, the Estates refused to compromise. They declared that they would continue to accept the King's proclamation of January 28, 1852, as the basis for the organization of the monarchy, but that if they had been left a free choice, they would have preferred the *status quo* of 1848, "the legislative and administrative union of the duchies...with such modification as the times demanded." They had never accepted the abolition of that union and they took this opportunity formally to protest against it. They were opposed to the Constitution of 1855, to the electoral law and indeed to any common representative body. If population formed the basis for representation, the German parts of the monarchy would be subordinated to the Danish, contrary to the agreements of 1851-52. Even if the parts of the monarchy were represented equally, their autonomy [Selvstændighed] would not be adequately safeguarded. The lack of knowledge of the Danish language on the part of the Germans and the difficulties involved in meeting in a distant and Danish speaking capital were additional objections to a common legislature. The only arrangement that would be satisfactory would be to maintain the existing spheres of common and local administration and legislation, with the exception that the control of the domains should be local, and to vest the legislative power, not in the ministry and the *Rigsraad* but in the ministry and the assemblies of the individual parts of the monarchy. Laws affecting the common affairs should become valid only when passed unchanged by the Danish *Rigsdag*, the Estates of Schleswig and of Holstein and the Diet of Lauenburg.[87]

Not only did the Estates reject the belated concessions of the government but they opened an attack on the administration of Schleswig. It was a subject with which they were legally incompetent to deal but it, and not the position of Holstein in the monarchy, was the real object of conflict. Although almost ten years had passed since the reconquest of Schleswig, it was governed with little more civic freedom than it had been immediately

---

[87] Neergaard, *Under Junigrundloven*, II, pp. 305-317.

after the suppression of the revolt.[88] Shortly after the peace
treaty between Denmark and Prussia in July 1850, F. F. Tillisch
had been appointed royal commissioner in Schleswig. His
policy, like that of the Danish government since 1848, was to
work for the closest possible union of Denmark and Schleswig
and to maintain the separation of Schleswig and Holstein. The
dismissal of pastors and officials who had taken part in the revolt,
the interference by the officials and the police with the life of
the Germans in middle and south Schleswig, and in general the
Eider-Danish tendencies of Tillisch's administration called forth
such protests from the German Powers and pressure from Russia
and even England, that in July 1851, he resigned.[89]

From the beginning of 1852, when the Danish government
returned to the 'Whole State' basis, until December 1854,
Schleswig was administered by Karl Moltke, an absolutist
German, and the repression weighed equally on Eider-Danes
and Schleswig-Holsteiners. But from then on, the administration
concentrated its attention on the latter. For over a decade after
the suppression of the revolt, Schleswig was governed on much
the same lines as under Tillisch. Freedom of the press, of
assembly and association did not exist. Meetings could not take
place without the preliminary permission of the authorities, any
association could be dissolved by administrative action, and the
press was restricted as it had been in the days of the absolute
monarchy. The opposition press was abolished and only two
political journals, both pro-government, were allowed to appear.
Foreign newspapers and books were carefully watched but after
1854, the restrictions were limited to literature from the south.

In December 1858, just before the meeting of the Holstein
Estates, the minister for Schleswig suppressed a number of asso-
ciations common to the two duchies on the ground that their
activities masked political aims,[90] and the formation of associa-

[88] Neergaard, *Under Junigrundloven*, II, p. 387.

[89] *Ibid.*, I, pp. 523-543, 545, 553. Schwarzenberg admitted that "Certes ce
n'est pas nous qui avons le droit de vous interroger sur les mesures de rigueur."
Quoted in Wynn to Palmerston, Copenhagen, May 15, 1851. No. 55, (Record
Office, London).

[90] The most important of these were the *Schleswig-Holstein-Lauenburg Gesell-*

tions whose objects were to unite the inhabitants of the duchies for any common purpose, was prohibited.

The most important objects of German complaint, however, were the language regulations, initiated by Tillisch and his secretary, T. A. J. Regensburg, put into force by Karl Moltke, and retained by subsequent administrators.[91] Their chief point was the establishment of the so-called 'mixed' district, which included some districts where the ordinary language of the people was entirely Danish, some where, at least among the younger generation 'Plattdeutsch' was almost exclusively used.[92]

In the 'mixed' district, Danish was made the language of instruction in the schools, with four hours per week instruction in German. Church services were to be alternately in German and Danish and ceremonies in the language chosen by those concerned. In accordance with the promise of equal protection to Danish and German made in the proclamation of January 28, 1852, Tillisch's successors gave the right of using either language in communication with the authorities and decreed that the one chosen should be used in the reply. In civil cases, each party could use his own language. The court would use the plaintiff's language for its first decree and thereafter the defendant's. In criminal and police cases, the language of the accused was to be employed. Contracts and other legal documents were to be drawn in both languages if the parties could not agree on one.

These regulations seem sufficiently liberal. But even apart from the fact that over-zealous pastors and officials used undue influence to promote the use of Danish, the population of the 'mixed' districts was generally opposed to the introduction of the additional Danish. German was regarded as more genteel and, from its use in church services, had become sanctified as

schaft für vaterlandische Geschichte, the S.-H.-L. Gesellschaft fur Sammlung u. Erhaltung vaterländischer Alterthümer, Kunstverein im Kiel, Verein zur Verbreitung wissenschaftlicher Kenntnisse, and the Gartenbau Verein der Herzogthümer S., H., und L. Thorsøe, Kong Frederik des Syvendes Regering, II, 660, n. 1.

[91] Cf. the detailed study of H. Hjelholt, Den danske Sprogordning og det danske Sprogstyre i Slesvig mellem Krigene (1850-1864).

[92] Cf. maps I and II.

the language of prayers and of Holy Writ.[93] Mr. (later Sir)
Augustus Paget, the British minister to Denmark, reported in
February 1861 that an investigation conducted by the British
Vice-Consul appeared to establish the following points: "that
there is almost universal dissatisfaction in the 'Mixed districts'
at the existing regulations respecting the languages; that the
compulsory education in Danish produces hostility and bad
feeling towards the Danish government instead of creating Danish
sympathies; that the effect of the regulations respecting Divine
worship is to demoralize the population; that the complaints
respecting the proceedings of the government employees in the
south of Schleswig and 'Mixed districts' are in many instances
well founded; and, that the Danish government cannot do
greater injury to their own interests, or better serve the cause of
their opponents, than by allowing the grievances which are well
founded to remain unredressed.[94]

VII.

The action of the Estates of Holstein in 1859 and especially
the way in which they emphasized the national conflict, merely
made reconciliation more difficult.   In a circular dispatch to the
Danish representatives abroad, Hall expressed his government's
opinions on the proposals of the Estates and declared that submission of propositions to the consent of four local legislatures
would mean that no definite organization of the monarchy could
be established.[95]

The outbreak of the Italian war in April 1859 distracted the
attention of Germany from the north and the period of the war
had little immediate effect on the Schleswig-Holstein question.
A few bold spirits wished Prussia to take advantage of the
opportunity to adopt a vigorous policy and, at least, to free

---

[93] H. Hjelholt, "Mellem Krigene," p. 274, in Dahl and Linvald, Sønderjylland,
I, pp. 267-288.

[94] Paget to Russell, Copenhagen, Feb. 22, 1861, enclosing report of Vice-
Consul Rainals of Feb. 15, 1861; Reports. . .respecting the Duchies of Schleswig and
Holstein, presented to the House of Lords, 1864.

[95] Thorsøe, Kong Frederik den Syvendes Regering, II, pp. 675 f.

Holstein and Schleswig from Denmark,[96] but the idea was premature. The mobilization of the Federal army brought home to the Danes the inconvenience of their relationship to Holstein by raising the problem of Danish neutrality in a war of the Confederation against France. On the other side, the quickening of German national feeling resulted in a more intense propaganda in favor of the duchies and an increased desire to protect the nationality of the Germans in Schleswig.

The Estates of Schleswig began a session on January 20, 1860, which was almost as stormy and attracted as much attention as that in Holstein in the preceding year. The Schleswig-Holstein majority in the assembly attacked the administration of the Duchy and protested against the continuance of the *Rigsraad* for Denmark and Schleswig alone. The patent of November 1858, suspending the operation of the common constitution for Holstein and Lauenburg, was declared to be an indirect incorporation of Schleswig with the kingdom. Schleswig had never accepted the removal of the old link with Holstein and desired its restoration as essential to the welfare of the duchies. An attempt of the government, supported by the Danish minority in the assembly, to split the German party by an attack on the privileges of the aristocracy, failed completely and led to a bitter discussion between members of the opposing national groups.

The proceedings of the Estates attracted much attention in Denmark and Germany. Meetings in many Danish towns voted addresses of thanks to the minority and in Germany the recently established *Nationalverein* organized meetings in support of the majority. In the Prussian House of Representatives, petitions for the protection of the rights of Schleswig were received and after a two days debate, the House voted unanimously to present the petitions to the government ''in the expectation that it, in coöperation with the allied German states, will neglect nothing to help the duchies of Schleswig and Holstein to the full enjoyment of their severely violated rights.'' The speech of the Prussian minister for foreign affairs, Herr von Schleinitz expressed

---

[96] H. Oncken, *Rudolf von Bennigsen*, I, p. 319; cf. also Ringhoffer, *Im Kampfe für Preussens Ehre*, p. 405, R. Haym, *Ausgewählter Briefwechsel*, p. 173

the sympathy of the government for the action of the house. Hall's protests against the discussion of the domestic affairs of a non-German state by a foreign parliament and his attempt to maintain that the agreements of 1851-52 were not binding international agreements were sharply controverted by Schleinitz.[97]

The exchange of views led to no immediate results but Schleswig had at last been brought into the negotiations. Hall tried to convince the Powers that Prussia and Germany were attempting to meddle unjustifiably in the affairs of the non-federal parts of the monarchy but his arguments were coolly received.

The question now came again before the Diet at Frankfurt. In July, 1860, the Oldenburg representative proposed Federal Execution in Holstein on the ground that, at the beginning of the month, the Danish government had published the Holstein budget for the fiscal year 1860-61 without reference to the Estates. This was declared to be a violation of the Federal decree of March 8, 1860 which had stated that no law for common affairs would be recognized as valid in Holstein and Lauenburg unless accepted by the Estates. The reply of the Danish government that the publication was not of a law but merely a statistical summary of provisions legally established prior to the decree of the Diet, was rejected and on February 7, 1861, the Diet declared that the budget and a Danish proclamation of September 25, which made certain temporary regulations for the constitutional position of Holstein, were invalid. Under threat of Federal Execution, Denmark was called on to give within six weeks a declaration that she would submit to the decree of March 8,1860, by laying the budget for the fiscal year beginning April 1, 1860, before the Estates of the two German duchies. The threat of Execution received additional force from the speech of the new King of Prussia at the opening of the Prussian *Landtag* on January 14, 1861, in which he had declared it to be a national

[97] Extracts of proceedings of the Prussian House of Representatives, May 3 and 4, 1860; Danish circular dispatch of May 25, 1860; Schleinitz to the Prussian minister in Copenhagen, June 29, 1860; in *Urkundenbuch zur deutsch-dänischen Angelegenheit vom 29, October 1857 bis 26, December 1861*, pp. 236-260. Also cf. *Das Staatsarchiv*, II, Nos. 244-247.

duty of Prussia to bring about, in coöperation with her allies, a satisfactory solution of the problem of the duchies.[98]

There was much sentiment in Denmark for letting matters come to a head, but the Great Powers were strongly opposed to a violent settlement. On March 1, 1861, the Ministers of France, Russia, Great Britain and Sweden-Norway made a collective *démarche*, urging the Danish government to accept the Diet's decree of March 8, 1860, which concerned only Holstein and was a domestic question of the German Confederation in which the Powers could not intervene.

The meeting of the Estates of Holstein from March 6 to April 11, 1861, was as futile as those that had preceded it. The assembly rejected the government propositions and reiterated its complaints about the treatment of Schleswig and its demand for the union of Schleswig and Holstein. During the session, the Danish government decided to yield to the pressure from the Powers and to submit the budget to the Estates, but although this decision was communicated to the foreign Powers, the royal commissioner at Itzehoe, who happened also to be minister for Holstein, was not kept informed of the course of negotiations. His statements to the Estates were for some time inconsistent with those of the minister for foreign affairs to the diplomats. This gave the impression of ambiguity and even bad faith on the part of Denmark.

The negotiations with the Estates had failed again. The time limit of the resolution for Federal Execution of February 7 had expired late in March. During April, there were many national demonstrations in Denmark and military and naval preparations were made. On April 27, 1861 the Diet at Frankfurt was officially informed of the results of the meeting of the Holstein Estates and referred the report to the usual committee. Then months passed and nothing happened.

It was quite obvious that for the time being, the German Powers were unwilling to bring on a crisis. The harmony of the 'new era' in Prussia was disturbed by the first stages of the 'constitutional conflict' while Austria was busied with the reor-

[98] H. Kohl, *Dreissig Jahre preussisch-deutscher Geschichte*, p. 22.

ganization of the empire. The embarrassments of its opponents
made the Danish government more anxious to attempt a solution
in its own way. But the foreign Powers, although they too
wanted to see the long conflict ended, disapproved of the Danish
attitude and did not regard the issues at stake of sufficient
importance to justify the risk of a war that might easily involve
all of Europe.

During the rest of 1861 and 1862, therefore, the diplomats
developed a more active interest and a series of schemes were
brought forward in an attempt to reconcile Denmark and
Germany. The initiative in the new attempts to settle the
Schleswig-Holstein question by negotiations under the auspices
of the neutral Powers was taken by the Swedish government.
Charles XV, who became Prince Regent in September 1857, and
succeeded his father as King in July 1859, had begun his administration by reversing Oscar I's policy toward Denmark. He
dropped the project of an alliance with Frederick VII.[99] He
recalled Admiral Virgin, the Swedish minister to Denmark since
the end of 1856, lest the envoy's zealous activity in favor of the
Scandinavian union compromise his government, and replaced
him by Count Wachtmeister, who was reputed to be unsympathetic towards it. All this was probably due, however, to the
Regent's desire to follow a policy of his own rather than one
marked out by his father and not to any real opposition in
principle. Charles had often manifested his sympathy for the
pan-Scandinavian movement and, after an exchange of visits
with Frederick VII in the summer of 1860, he abandoned his
reserve and stood forth ostentatiously as the friend of Denmark
and the apostle of the Scandinavian ideal.[100]

Ludvig Manderström, who in 1858 had become minister for
foreign affairs, was less enthusiastic for the Scandinavian union
than was his royal master. He was a trained diplomat and a
skilful drafter of notes but not a strong-willed, independent

[99] Cf. p. 25 above.

[100] On the character and policy of Charles XV, cf. C. Hallendorff, *Illusioner
och Verklighet*, pp. 23-32; *Sveriges Historia* XII, pp. 219-232, 305-345; H. Koht,
Die Stellung Norwegens und Schwedens im deutsch-dänischen Konflikt, passim.

statesman. His foreign policy represents a compromise between his own views of what was practicable and the King's temperamental and sometimes fantastic intentions. Charles XV, like Napoleon III, was in the habit of discussing political questions with foreign sovereigns and diplomats and of employing private individuals to conduct negotiations behind the back of his responsible minister. The formal diplomacy of the state was left to Manderström but he was not always informed of what the King had said or done and was constantly embarrassed by the monarch's gasconades and hampered by his intrigues.[101]

In a dispatch of March 29, 1861, to the Swedish-Norwegian ministers at London, Paris, and St. Petersburg, Manderström made a proposal for the settlement of the German-Danish controversy. He recommended the complete administrative separation from the rest of the monarchy of the duchy of Holstein, to which would be left, besides its local affairs, its own army. The affairs common to the whole monarchy should thus be restricted to the civil list, foreign relations, the navy, the posts and telegraphs. Then after the King of Denmark had fulfilled his promises concerning the organization of Schleswig, the Powers which had signed the Treaty of London should issue a declaration recognizing what had been done and assuring, for the future, the cessation of all interference by Germany in the affairs of that duchy. Finally, to assure the efficacy of the other conditions, Holstein should be neutralized and placed under the guarantee of the powers signatory to the Treaty of London.[102]

These proposals met with scant attention from the Powers. Russia and France were not favorable to the neutralization of Holstein[103] and Lord John Russell replied that as the chance of obtaining the consent of Germany seemed infinitely small, there was no need of discussing the policy involved in the Swedish proposition.[104]

---

[101] Cf. *Sveriges Historia*, XII, pp. 312-314.

[102] "Aktstykker vedkommende den dansk-tydske Strid" in *Historisk Tidsskrift* (Copenhagen), 3 R. III, pp. 693-704.

[103] H. Koht, *Die Stellung Norwegens und Schwedens im deutsch-dänischen Konflikt*, p. 72.

[104] Russell to Jerningham, London, April 19, 1861, *Das Staatsarchiv*, V, No. 733.

At the same time, however, Russell suggested to the governments of Sweden, France, and Russia, a somewhat similar scheme. The essential points were:

1.   That the quota of the common budget of the Monarchy which affects the Duchies of Holstein and Lauenburg should be submitted to the States of Holstein and Lauenburg respectively for their assent, amendment, or rejection.

2.   That the laws which are to affect the Duchies of Holstein and Lauenburg shall be submitted to the Diets of Holstein and Lauenburg respectively for their assent, amendment, or rejection.

3.   That the Duchy of Schleswig shall send representatives to the Parliament of Denmark, to vote in that Parliament the common expenses of the Monarchy, and to vote on all laws affecting the Monarchy.

4.   That the separate Diet of Schleswig shall continue to be elected and to meet according to the present law. The functions of that Diet to consist in voting such sums as may be necessary for the maintenance of churches and schools and other local expenses, and in providing by equal laws for the welfare of the Danish, German, and other inhabitants of Schleswig.

5.   When these terms are assented to, and solemnly proclaimed by the King of Denmark, the four Powers, viz. France, Great Britain, Russia, and Sweden, to guarantee to the Crown of Denmark the possession of the Duchy of Schleswig.

6.   That Commissioners be appointed...to define the boundary of the Duchy of Schleswig.

7.   That the Treaty and Engagements of 1852, so far as they are not altered by these articles, should be inviolably maintained.[105]

In a second dispatch of May 8, Lord Russell gave a more detailed explanation of his rather superficial plan[106] in an attempt to anticipate criticism by the other cabinets. He summed up the solution as separating Holstein from the Danish provinces as completely as Luxemburg is separated from Holland, uniting Schleswig with Denmark for purposes common to the Monarchy, but retaining in Schleswig, a local representative body as a guarantee ''for those rights and interests of the German inhabitants of Schleswig the neglect of which has given rise to so much complaint.''[107]

The scheme differed little from the *status quo*. It failed to win the support of the other Powers[108] and at the end of May, Lord

---

[105]   Russell to Cowley *et al.*, London, April 19, 1861, *Das Staatsarchiv*, V, No. 732.
[106]   Cf. Neergaard, *Under Junigrundloven*, II, pp. 480 f.
[107]   Russell to Cowley *et al.*, London, May 8, 1861, *Das Staatsarchiv*, V, No. 739.
[108]   *Ibid.*, Nos. 742, 746, 748.

Russell abandoned it. He informed the Danish minister at London that the Danish government should lose no time in making such arrangements as they thought advisable and that he entirely approved the idea of giving a separate constitutional position to Holstein.[109]

For the Danish government, the significance of these negotiations lay in the fact that two of the Powers which were parties to the Treaty of London of May 1852, Sweden and Great Britain, were now advocating a solution on lines corresponding to the wishes of the Eider-Danes, the further separation of Holstein from the parts of the monarchy that were not members of the German Confederation. It decided, therefore, to give up its attempts to reach an agreement with the Estates of Holstein and to try to secure a settlement by diplomatic action.[110] In a dispatch of May 11, to the Danish minister at London, Hall, the Danish Minister President, declared that the only course to follow would be to grant to Holstein an independent position which would permit the King of Denmark, without infringing on the rights of the other parts of the monarchy, to fulfil the demands made upon him as Duke of Holstein ''which he seems, by the existing political situation, called upon to fulfil, although they are not justified by German constitutional law.''[111]

This plan, too, was not favorably received. Russia was opposed to the separation of Holstein as, among other reasons, it was feared that this would facilitate the development of German seapower in the Baltic with its base at Kiel. France, in the Schleswig-Holstein question was following the lead of Russia. The one plan that might have solved the problem, the division of Schleswig in accordance with nationality, proposed by Herr von Schleinitz, the Prussian minister for foreign affairs, was rejected by the Danish minister at Berlin without reference to the cabinet at Copenhagen, which completely approved his action. A British suggestion for an international conference was rejected by Austria and Prussia and the negotiations reached

---

[109] Paget to Russell, Copenhagen, May 30, 1861, *Das Staatsarchiv*, V, No. 749.
[110] Neergaard, *Under Junigrundloven*, II, pp. 482 f.
[111] Hall to Bille, Copenhagen, May 1, 1861, *Das Staatsarchiv*, V, No. 744.

another deadlock. But in spite of the failure of the negotiations, Austria and Prussia were not unwilling to avoid complications and the attitude of the other Great Powers was against violent action. Another Danish concession to give the Diet a passable excuse for postponing the Execution, was called for.[112]

On July 29, 1861, Hall, in dispatches to the Danish ministers at Berlin and Vienna, stated that he had been informed by the British minister at Copenhagen that the Prussian minister for foreign affairs had indicated to the British government that there was still a way, if the Danish government chose to follow it, of averting the threatened Execution in Holstein, and at the same time, of initiating fresh negotiations of an international character between Denmark and Germany, which might bring about a quicker and easier solution of the question of the Holstein Constitution. In accordance with this suggestion, on the advice of the English and other friendly governments and with the understanding that it was a purely provisional arrangement, the Danish government declared that for the current fiscal year it would limit the quota of Holstein to the general expenses of the monarchy, to the sums laid down in the 'normal budget' of February 28, 1856.[113] On August 12, the Execution procedure was again suspended.[114] Sentiment in political circles in Denmark was unfavorable to the concession. To neutralize this opposition, Orla Lehmann was taken into the cabinet on September 15. Lehmann was unquestionably the most popular leader of the National Liberals. He had been one of the earliest advocates of the Eider-Danish views and, now, in contrast to the opportunism of the cabinet, he stood for the frank abandonment of the 'Whole State' policy. His entrance into the government would smooth its path at home but it was likely to create an unfavorable impression abroad, especially in Russia and Ger-

[112] Neergaard, *Under Junigrundloven*, II, pp. 481, 486-487.

[113] *Das Staatsarchiv*, I, No. 60. In his dispatch to the Prussian minister at Copenhagen, Berlin, August 12, 1861, Herr von Schleinitz denied the initiative of the Prussian government in this compromise and stated that it was due to the desire of the British government to avert the Execution by any possible means. *Ibid.*, No. 62.

[114] *Ibid.*, No. 63.

many, where Lehmann was known as a violent radical, as ultra-Scandinavian, and as the author of the phrase: "We will write upon their [the Schleswigers'] backs with bloody swords that they are Danes." At home and abroad, the appointment was taken as a signal that Denmark had again adopted the aim of "Denmark to the Eider."[115]

Attempts of the Danish government in the late summer of 1861 to begin conversations were put off by the two German Powers on the pretext that the members of the Federal Diet were taking their vacations.[116]

Negotiations were resumed in October 1861, after Count Bernstorff had replaced Schleinitz as Prussian minister for foreign affairs. In a dispatch to the Danish minister at Berlin on October 26, 1861, Hall proposed a provisional regulation of the position of Holstein, reserving a detailed and final development for a more quiet future.[117] To attain this purpose Holstein should receive a more independent position in the monarchy, on the lines of the proposals made to the estates in March.[118] At the beginning of December, Count Bernstorff, after consultation with the cabinet of Vienna, replied by rejecting the Danish plan. He expressed surprise at the idea of merely temporary arrangements and at the fact that Hall's only proposition was one that had already been rejected by the Estates of Holstein. This hardly offered a basis for negotiation and the exchange of views would be of little value unless the cabinet of Copenhagen gave some information as to the way in which it expected to carry out its obligations derived from the agreements of 1851-52, with reference to Schleswig.[119] In his reply of December 26, Hall rebutted the attempt to bring Schleswig into the negotiations and the exchange of notes dragged on into March of 1862 without

[115] Cf. Neergaard, *Under Junigrundloven*, II, pp. 492 ff.

[116] Thorsøe, *Kong Frederik den Syvendes Regering*, II, p. 800; Neergaard, *Under Junigrundloven*, II, p. 486.

[117] The Danish Minister at Berlin had reported that Bernstorff seemed convinced that at the moment, a final settlement was impossible. Neergaard, *Under Junigrundloven*, II, p. 501.

[118] Hall to Quaade, Copenhagen, October 26, 1861. *Das Staatsarchiv*, II, No. 236.

[119] Bernstorff to Balan, Berlin, December 5, 1861. *Ibid.*, No. 237.

bringing the parties any closer to an understanding. Hall insisted that the negotiations he had in mind concerned merely the position of the two German duchies and that the situation in Schleswig was a domestic question of the Danish Monarchy in which Germany had no right of interference.[120]

It was not until late in August that the cabinets of Berlin and Vienna replied to Hall's note of March 12, 1862. They justified their claim to discuss the question of Schleswig and insisted that Denmark had not lived up to her obligations with respect to that duchy. They demanded that the Constitution of 1855 be suspended for Schleswig as it had been for Holstein because it had been established illegally, without reference to the Estates of the duchies. Proposals for a new common constitution should then be submitted to the representative bodies of the separate parts of the monarchy as stipulated by the agreements of 1851-52 and these proposals must be of a nature to safeguard the duchies against a permanent Danish majority.[121] The Prussian government demanded that, until the new common constitution was accepted, equal influence on legislation for common affairs and on the ministry should be exercised by all the local representative bodies of the Danish Monarchy. For Schleswig, both Prussia and Austria asked for the restoration of the *status quo ante 1848* of the language regulations and the definite settlement of this problem by a law passed with the advice and consent of the Estates of Schleswig.[122]

The main points in the Austrian and Prussian notes, the insistence on discussing the situation in Schleswig and the illegality of the Common Constitution of 1855 for that duchy,

[120] Hall to the Danish Ministers at Vienna and Berlin, March 12, 1862. *Das Staatsarchiv*, II, No. 242.

[121] The Prussian note stated definitely, "worin das unbedingte Princip der Repräsentation nach Volkzahl aufgegeben sein muss."

[122] *Das Staatsarchiv*, III, Nos. 799, 800. The Austrian memorandum emphasized the importance of removing the constitutional arrangement from the too great influence of the Danish nationalists and suggested that, since the succession to all parts of the monarchy had been made uniform by the Treaty of London, it would be safe for the Danish government to restore the time-honored connection of Schleswig with Holstein.

were supported by the British Foreign Secretary. Earl Russell[123] had accompanied the Queen to the continent in the summer of 1862 and, in the strongly anti-Danish environment of the Court of Saxe-Coburg-Gotha, on September 24, issued to the British representatives at Berlin, Vienna, and Copenhagen, another suggestion for the settlement of the Schleswig-Holstein question.

It appears, [he wrote] that the correspondence between Austria, Prussia, and Denmark, which, it was asserted, would lead to a settlement of the dispute so long subsisting between Germany and Denmark in regard to the obligations of Denmark in the affairs of Holstein, Lauenburg, Schleswig and the Common Constitution of the Danish Monarchy, has grown more and more bitter. The longer the lapse of time, and the further the negotiation is carried, the wider is the space that separates the two parties, and the stronger the language they use towards each other.

Upon considering, with pain and regret, this unsatisfactory aspect of the affair, and contemplating the unfavorable results which may be expected from further direct communications between Powers so adverse in their opinions, Her Majesty has directed that you should be furnished with instructions which may, it is hoped, tend to the long desired settlement.

In framing these instructions it is advisable to throw out of the calculation, in the first place, those matters upon which controversy may be said to be exhausted.

The first of these matters relates to the question whether any taxes can be imposed, or any laws enacted, in Holstein or Lauenburg without the express consent of the representatives of those Duchies.

This question has been resolved in the negative by the German Confederation, of which the Duchies of Holstein and Lauenburg are members.

Another question which need not be further discussed is the Constitution of 1855.

It is clear that whether a representation according to numbers of the Kingdom, as well as the Duchies, be a good or a bad Constitution, yet, not having been accepted by the Duchies, the Constitution of 1855 has no force in Holstein, Lauenburg, or Schleswig.

Neither is it necessary to discuss the rights of Denmark in reference to her Rigsraad. It is quite clear that Denmark can legislate for herself, and impose taxes to be levied upon her own people, without the consent of Holstein, Lauenburg, or Schleswig.

Two questions of great importance remain. The first regards the Duchy of Schleswig; the second, the common Constitution of the Monarchy.

For the solution of the former, Earl Russell recommended the grant of complete autonomy to Schleswig, to allow the Diet of Schleswig fairly to treat and independently to decide upon

[123] He was raised to the Peerage in July 1861, but was generally known as, Lord John Russell for years after.

questions affecting their university, their churches and schools,
the language to be used where the Danish population prevails,
where the Germans preponderate, and where the races are mixed.

He came then to the question of the Constitution,

the most entangled and the most embarrassing question of all those in
discussion.

Treaties, protocols, and despatches afford us little light upon this subject,
and the glimmering rays which they do afford tend rather to lead us astray
than to guide us right.

For what could be more destructive of all union, all efficiency, all strength,
and indeed, of all independence, than to lay down as an absolute rule that
no law should be passed, and no Budget sanctioned unless the four states of
the Monarchy all concurred...?

The remedy, he found in a proposal for a normal Budget, to be
laid before the *Rigsraad*, and before the Diets of Holstein,
Lauenburg, and Schleswig for their consent.

It is obvious that the Government of an independent kingdom like Denmark must, for the maintenance of that independence, require a certain
amount of expenditure for the Civil List of the Sovereign, for the Diplomatic
Service, for the Army and Navy of the State. ....

Obtain that sum from the four Representative Bodies. Confide its distribution to a Council of State formed, two-thirds of Danes and one-third of
Germans. Let the votes of this Council be taken in public, and accounts of
the expenditure published yearly.

The normal Budget to be voted in gross for ten years. The distribution
or expenditure to be voted yearly.

Extraordinary expenses beyond the normal budget to be voted freely by
the Kingdom and the three Duchies separately.

The suggestions I have made may be summed up in a few words:—

1.   Holstein and Lauenburg to have all that the German Confederation
ask for them.

2.   Schleswig to have the power of self-government, and not to be represented in the Rigsraad.

3.   A normal Budget to be agreed upon by Denmark, Holstein, Lauenburg, and Schleswig.

4.   Any extraordinary expenses to be submitted to the Rigsraad, and to
the separate Diets of Holstein, Lauenburg, and Schleswig.[124]

These proposals, which resemble the demand of the Estates
of Holstein for a quadripartite organization of the Danish
Monarchy, mark a great change in Russell's attitude. In the

---

[124] *Das Staatsarchiv*, III, No. 801.

preceding spring he had recommended a separate constitutional position for Holstein in what was little more than personal union with Denmark-Schleswig.[125] To Bismarck, who visited London at the beginning of July 1862, Russell seemed Eider-Danish and disposed to argue that the limit of Danish concession ought to be the autonomy of Holstein on the analogy of Luxemburg.[126] Since the beginning of the year, however, Russell had been impressed by the fact that the questions of Schleswig and Holstein were closely connected and that the failure to settle the former might result in war. The German interpretation of the agreements of 1852 and the reality of the German grievances in Schleswig were presented to him in the dispatches of Lord Loftus, the British minister at Berlin, of Mr. John Ward, the British representative at Hamburg, and, especially, in the private letters of Robert Morier, who was becoming his confidential adviser on German questions.[127]

Morier, who acted as Russell's private secretary during the visit to Gotha, claimed to be the 'moral author' of the dispatch. "In suggesting Lord John Russell's mediation," he wrote many years later, "which I never expected would be accepted, I wished to give Her Majesty's Government the means of withdrawing on legitimate grounds from the obligations of the Treaty of London. ... My wish had...been that Lord John Russell, in the event of one party agreeing to the proposal and the other not, should declare, that having failed to obtain the constitutional basis presupposed by the Treaty of London, Great Britain withdrew from obligations which would involve the violation of constitutional rights that the other parties of the Treaty had refused to call into existence." Lord Russell, may, as Morier says, have seen this,[128] but the 'Gotha despatch,' the main points of which

---

[125] Cf. p. 38 above.

[126] Bismarck, *Die gesammelten Werke*, III, pp. 386, 392 f.

[127] Cf. Loftus, *Diplomatic Reminiscences*, A. W. Ward in the *Cambridge History of British Foreign Policy* II, pp. 552 f.; John Ward, *Experiences of a Diplomatist*, passim; Wemyss, *Memoirs and Letters of Sir Robert Morier*, I, ch. XV.

[128] Wemyss, *Memoirs and Letters of Sir Robert Morier*, I, pp. 388 ff. Lord Loftus, too, claimed the paternity. Järta to H. Hamilton, Berlin, November 10, 1862. Carlquist, *Ur H. Hamiltons Brefsamling*, II, p. 82.

were established before Russell arrived at Gotha,[129] represents in the main, a sincere, if somewhat naïve, attempt to secure a settlement by pressing upon Denmark an arrangement that would be acceptable to Germany.[130] Although the plan was accepted in principle by Austria and Prussia and urged on the Danish cabinet by the ministers of Russia, France, and England, it was refused firmly by Denmark and soon abandoned by Russell.[131]

Public opinion in England rejected the 'Gotha dispatch' more emphatically than did the Danish government. The announcement on September 9, 1862, of the betrothal of Princess Alexandra, eldest daughter of Prince Christian of Denmark, to the Prince of Wales called forth renewed enthusiasm in England for the cause of Denmark, and renewed hope in Denmark of English support. The English press regarded it as most offensive that the first action of the British government after the engagement should have been of a character so unfriendly to Denmark.[132] Even Russell's colleagues in the cabinet seem to have disapproved of the dispatch and when Parliament opened at the beginning of February, 1863, Russell was attacked from all sides. The arrival of the Princess Alexandra in England early in March called forth renewed demonstrations in favor of Denmark. Her charm and increasing popularity became one of the most valuable assets of the Danish cause in England; but a source of false hopes and confidence in Denmark. In view of the clearly expressed disapproval of press and parliament, the admonition of the British

[129] Russell outlined them for Paget during their visit to Brussells early in September. In a private letter of August 6, the original suggestions were communicated to Berlin. The Record Office, London, contains the memorandum of "Count Bernstorff's observations on proposals contained in Earl Russell's private letter of August 6, 1862 for the arrangement of the Danish Duchies Question."

[130] Cf. p. 147 below.

[131] This statement is substantially true although the acceptances, the recommendations and the refusal were hedged in with diplomatic verbiage. Cf. *Das Staatsarchiv*, V, Nos. 802 ff; A. W. Ward, in *Cambridge History of British Foreign Policy*, II, 554-557; and Neergaard, *Under Junigrundloven*, II, pp. 550 ff.

[132] Queen Victoria noted on September 9, 1862: "Saw Lord Russell and talked of Bertie's marriage, of France, Germany, and the Schleswig-Holstein Question. We discussed the importance of Bertie's marriage being in *no* sense considered a *political* one....."*Letters of Queen Victoria*, 2nd series, I, p. 44.

minister at Copenhagen and Earl Russell's advice to the Danish minister at London naturally made little impression.

In the meantime, at the end of January 1862, the *Rigsraad* met at Copenhagen. Since the end of 1858, Holstein and Lauenburg had no longer been represented in it, and during the following years some of the German members from Schleswig had refused to attend. To meet the situation, a number of amendments to the constitution were introduced by the government. One, a bill changing the quorum from 41 to 31 members was passed, but the more far-reaching revisions were buried in committee. This was a tacit acceptance of the protests of Austria and Prussia.[133]

During the course of the negotiations, in March, Austria and Prussia had reported the negative results to the Diet which approved their policy in general and especially their protests against the constitutional amendments. The Danish protest against this action was rejected by the Diet, and Hall again called the attention of the neutral powers to the way in which the Diet was meddling in the affairs of a state which was not part of the Confederation.

All in all, the negotiations had been of little value to Denmark. The meeting of the *Rigsraad* had not strengthened the government's position at home, and the neutral Powers, with the exception of Sweden-Norway had shown themselves more and more unfavorable to the Danish point of view. In Germany, the isolation of Denmark was noticed and there was a rapidly growing belief that the internal tension of the Confederation could be eased by forcing the question of Schleswig to a head.[134]

Count Bernstorff[135] had wished to follow an active course in the Schleswig-Holstein question. He believed that if Prussia was to win the confidence of German national opinion for her political leadership, it would be necessary to secure a solution that would wrest Holstein and at least the German parts of Schleswig from Denmark. During his year in office, he showed a sound under-

[133] Cf. Neergaard, *Under Junigrundloven*, II, p. 516.
[134] E. g. *Aus dem Leben Theodor von Bernhardis*, IV, pp. 331, 334.
[135] K. Ringhoffer, *Im Kampfe für Preussens Ehre*, pp. 424, 426-435.

standing of the elements of the international situation. He succeeded in bringing the question of Schleswig into the foreground
and in winning the support of British diplomacy. But so long as
the constitutional conflict lasted in Prussia, he felt that his
foreign policy would be paralyzed.[136] Just as his efforts bore fruit
in Earl Russell's 'Gotha dispatch', he yielded his offices to Bismarck and returned to the embassy at London.

VIII.

From the beginning of his career as a diplomat, Bismarck had
been in intimate contact with the Schleswig-Holstein question.
One of his first tasks after his arrival at Frankfurt in 1851 had
been to carry on the delicate negotiations with Duke Christian
August of Augustenburg. A few years later, he was called upon
to advise his government at nearly every important step in the
controversy. As Prussian envoy at Frankfurt, he had become
familiar with the Federal aspects of the question and with the
involved procedure of the committees and plenum of the Diet.
He had listened to Napoleon III's views at Paris in 1857 and
1862, he had discussed the problem with Gorchakov at St.
Petersburg, with Palmerston and Russell at London in 1862.
On a visit with Blixen Finecke to Denmark and Sweden in 1857,
he had met Frederick VII, Hall, and other Scandinavian leaders.
Rechberg, in Vienna, he knew from their service together at
Frankfurt. At Frankfurt, at the other capitals at which he
served, or on his vacation journeys, he had become personally
acquainted with nearly every monarch, diplomat, and politician,
who was playing or was destined to play an important rôle in the
affair.

Bismarck had never yielded to the general enthusiasm for the
cause of Schleswig-Holstein. In a speech in the Prussian House
of Representatives in December, 1850, he had welcomed the end
of "the unhappy war in Schleswig-Holstein in which the rash
and frivolous policy of the year 1848" had involved the state.[137]

---

[136] K. Ringhoffer, *Im Kampfe für Preussens Ehre*, ch. XVI.

[137] Speech of December 3, 1850. H. Kohl, *Die politischen Reden des Fürsten
Bismarck*, I, p. 268.

At Frankfurt, he rapidly developed from Junker to a European
statesman but his confidential writings and utterances show that
he continued to look at the problem of the duchies from the point
of view of a conservative Prussian.[138] When, in May 1856, it
appeared likely that a formal complaint against the Danish
government would be laid before the Diet at Frankfurt, Bismarck
advised Manteuffel that he saw no reason "in the interest of
Prussian policy" to head off such an action and suggested that
the situation might offer the Prussian government the opportunity to strike an attitude before the eyes of Germany which
would be politically advantageous. He did not, however, believe
that the cause of the duchies would be helped materially by even
the most satisfactory resolutions of the Diet. The action of
Denmark, he pointed out, would be determined by the extent to
which the Cabinet of Copenhagen believed that it could count
upon the protection of the Great Powers.[139] The international
situation would determine how much could be done for the
duchies.

How much should be done for them was, in Bismarck's opinion,
a question of Prussian interests. "...It is hard to see how any
harm would be done," he wrote in 1857, "if we let the affair
become a few months older, and personally I do not see what *we*
will gain if the conflict is settled quickly and to the complete
satisfaction of both parties. It is, to be sure, a good idea to
manage our action so that people will not get the impression
that we are evading the clear and definite demands of our mission
to stand up for Germany abroad; but as soon as the Holsteiners
are living very happily under their Duke, they will have no more
interest in Prussia. That interest, however, if not at the present
moment, may still possibly be useful for us. In my opinion, then,
the whole affair should be kept going at all times with emphasis
on its German aspects but with dilatory caution, enduring a bit
of outcry rather than undertaking expense and trouble without

[138] Cf. A. O. Meyer, "Die Zielsetzung in Bismarcks schleswig-holsteinischer
Politik von 1855 bis 1864" in *Z. f. s.-h. G.*, LIII pp. 103-134.
[139] May 27, 1856. Bismarck, *Die gesammelten Werke*, II, No. 158.

any prospect of practical profits.''[140] If as we may well assume, Bismarck meant by ''practical profit,'' the acquisition of one or more of the duchies by Prussia, it was much too early to recommend this in plain words.[141] In his discussions of the subject, he confined himself to pointing out both to friends and opponents that the continued existence of the Danish Monarchy was more advantageous to Prussia than anything that was likely to take its place. He said that he was ''no friend of the sentimental or national policy,'' the Danish Minister reported from Frankfurt, ''and too much of a Prussian to make any distinction between Spaniards, Bavarians, or Danes. The only question for him was whether Prussia had any interest in quarrelling with Denmark or in the disruption of the Danish Monarchy. That was, for the time being, not the case. The existing Danish Monarchy was much more advantageous for Prussia than to have a new Grand Duchy on the Elbe to coquette with Austria and to have one or all of the pretty islands by the Sound come under English or Russian domination. The other Great Powers would permit neither a Scandinavian union or the union of Holstein with Prussia. The *status quo*, then, was best for Prussia.''[142]

It was, in Bismarck's opinion, undesirable to let the controversy between Germany and Denmark reach a stage where decisive action would be necessary, until the international situation became such as to offer Prussia a chance for positive profit. This situation did not exist in 1858 when the Diet was dealing with the position of Holstein and Lauenburg under the Common Constitution of 1855. Bismarck followed the instructions of his government to help initiate the cumbersome course of procedure preliminary to Federal Execution. At the same time, however, he used all his contacts with foreign statesmen to have enough international pressure put on Denmark to ensure acceptance of

---

[140] To Manteuffel, July 2, 1857. Bismarck, *Die gesammelten Werke*, II, No. 258.
[141] A. O. Meyer, *loc. cit.*, p. 120.
[142] B. v. Bülow's report, November 5, 1856, cited in Neergaard, *Under Juni-grundloven*, II, pp. 126 f. Cf. Bismarck to Leopold v. Gerlach, March 12, 1857, Bismarck's report of his words to Napoleon III, *Die gesammelten Werke*, II, No. 237; and Cowley to Clarendon, April 10, 1857, Appendix III (4), pp. 277-280.

the demands of the Diet.[143] He feared that Prussia, in case of Federal Execution, would be pushed forward into a position where Prussian honor would be involved and in which the risks and burdens of the conflict would fall mainly on Prussia. He realized clearly, moreover, that Federal Execution would not solve the Schleswig-Holstein question. It would not satisfy the complaints of Holstein for the cost would, in the long run, merely increase the financial burden of that duchy. It would not satisfy German national sentiment because of the legal limitations of Federal action. "The Diet passes judgment on Holstein, Europe on Schleswig."[144]

With Austria and Prussia sincerely united, Germany might have defied Europe. Bismarck's own activity at Frankfurt, however, had contributed much to the growing suspicion and hostility of Berlin and Vienna. The Schleswig-Holstein question became one of the fields of their rivalry.[145]

When Bismarck, in October, 1862, took the management of Prussian foreign policy into his own hands, he continued to deal with the Schleswig-Holstein question on the lines he had recommended while minister at Frankfurt.

In his first discussion of the subject with the new British ambassador on October 16, he assured Sir Andrew Buchanan that he was no fanatic on this question and that he had been much gratified by Earl Russell's dispatch of September 24, which he considered an acceptable basis for an arrangement. He could give no decided opinion on the subject, he said, until he had submitted the dispatch to the King and taken His Majesty's orders. He observed, however, that public opinion, both in Prussia and in Germany was very much excited on this question, viewing it as one of nationality, and that Prussia must take that into account in any arrangement proposed. He, personally, would gladly seize any fair and honorable means of bringing the question to an amicable adjustment.[146]

[143] A. O. Meyer, *loc. cit.*, pp. 117 ff.
[144] Bismarck, *Die gesammelten Werke*, II, Nos. 336, 414.
[145] Cf. A. O. Meyer, *Bismarcks Kampf mit Oesterreich 1851-1859*, pp. 324-366.
[146] Buchanan to Russell, No. 564, confidential, October 18, 1862, (Record Office, London).

After the unsatisfactory replies of the Danish government to the Austrian and Prussian notes of the preceding August, Bismarck arranged with Rechberg that the two powers would inform the Diet of the state of the negotiations. They did not, however, intend to press matters and would not recommend Federal Execution unless faced by some action of the Danish government that could not be disregarded.[147] If Federal Execution could not be avoided in the face of Danish disregard for the decrees of the Diet, it should take its course. The Prussian representative at Frankfurt was urged, however, to act *pari passu* with the Austrian minister, to avoid any specifically Prussian initiative, and to place the federal side of the question in the foreground. The situation was not ripe for an active policy.[148] As Bismarck wrote in a well-known letter on December 22, 1862:

> ... I regard it...as most expedient to hold fast to the basis of the English proposals[149] and to the favorable attitude of Russia and France towards them and to recommend Lord Russell's program both to the Diet and to the Estates of Holstein as the basis for action.
>
> I am certain of this, that the whole Danish business can be settled in a way desirable for us only by war. The occasion for such a war can be found at any moment that we find favorable for waging it. Until then, much more depends on the attitude of the non-German Great Powers towards the affair than on the intrigues of the Würzburg coalition governments and their influence on German sentiment. The disadvantage of having signed the London Protocol [sic], we share with Austria and cannot free ourselves from the consequences of that signature without war. If war comes, however, the future territorial status of Denmark will depend upon its results.
>
> It cannot be foreseen what development of German Federal relations is destined for the future; as long, however, as they remain about the same as in the past, I cannot regard it as in the interest of Prussia to wage a war in order, as the most favorable result, to install in Schleswig-Holstein a new Grand Duke, who in fear of Prussian lust for annexation, will vote against us in the Diet and whose government, in spite of the gratitude due to Prussia for its installation, will be a ready object of Austrian machination.....[150]

Late in November, 1862, Bismarck had warned the military authorities of the possibility of an eventual military solution

---

[147] Bismarck, *Die gesammelten Werke*, IV, Nos. 13, 15, 16.
[148] Bismarck to Usedom, December 16, 1862. *Ibid.*, No. 16.
[149] Cf. pp. 43 f. above.
[150] Bismarck, *Die gesammelten Werke*, IV, No. 17.

of the German-Danish conflict and von Moltke prepared a memorandum on the subject.[151] For the time being, however, the dominant interest of Bismarck was the relationship with Austria and the impending vote in the Diet on the Austrian proposals for the reform of the Confederation. Bismarck insisted that Prussia would not yield to a majority vote in this question and would rather declare the Federal Act as broken and the Federal obligations at an end. Then, just as the decisive vote at Frankfurt resulted in the defeat of the Austrian motion, news arrived at Berlin on January 24, 1863, that a revolt had broken out in Russian Poland.

IX

When the Estates of Holstein met at Itzehoe on January 24, 1863, the political atmosphere was not one in which a reasonable compromise would be probable. The preceding year had been marked by demonstrations of national feeling on both sides. In June 1862, some 750 Swedish and Norwegian students visited Copenhagen and in July, King Charles XV was enthusiastically received there. Equally enthusiastic demonstrations accompanied the unveiling in Flensburg churchyard of a monument to the Danish soldiers killed in 1850 at the victory of Idsted. As the relations with Germany became more strained, the Pan-Scandinavian sentiment in Denmark became the more ardent. The Swedish government continued to support the Eider policy and was the only one to uphold Denmark's objections to Lord Russell's 'Gotha dispatch.'[152] The Danish and Scandinavian celebrations called forth counter-demonstrations among the Schleswig-Holsteiners. In July, a great festival of the gymnastic

[151] Cf. Bismarck's memorandum of February 3, 1863. *Die gesammelten Werke*, IV, No. 32; also, Nos. 36 and 54.

[152] In the eyes of the Danish conservatives and of some European statesmen, the attitude of the Swedish government in favor of the separate organization of Holstein was regarded as a Machiavellian attempt to create a situation which would bring about the Scandinavian union under Swedish domination. To the ultra-Scandinavians in Denmark, that would not have been unwelcome, and to all but the 'Whole State' party, Sweden seemed to be the one friend in time of need.

societies at Rendsburg answered the students' meeting at Copenhagen and an assembly of choral societies at Husum replied to the unveiling of the Idsted monument. Attempts to hold other meetings in Schleswig were forbidden by the police but there could be little doubt as to the sentiments of the Germans in the duchies. In the rest of Germany, the press was too much occupied with other things to devote much space to the Schleswig-Holstein Question except when one side or the other took a step that seemed to bring the break nearer.[153] Nevertheless, the sad fate of the Germans in the duchies and especially in Schleswig called forth frequent expressions of indignation and such books as Gustav Raasch's *Vom verlassenen Bruderstamm*, which represented the Danish administration of Schleswig as little better than Radetzky's in Lombardy and King 'Bomba's' in Naples, were widely read.[154]

The Danish government maintained its theoretical opposition to the decree of the German Diet of March 8, 1860, which claimed for Holstein full legislative power in all 'common' legislation, including the budget. It made the practical concession, however, of laying before the Estates all of the propositions with which the *Rigsraad* had dealt during the preceding year. The Estates continued recalcitrant. They felt secure of the support of German public opinion and believed that the apparent change in British policy had weakened the position of their Danish opponents. Attack after attack was directed against the government and the session ended on March 21 with an open declaration of hostilities: an appeal to the Diet of the German Confederation to protect the rights and interests of Holstein.[155]

[153] Nirrnheim, *Das erste Jahr des Ministeriums Bismarck und die öffentliche Meinung*, pp. 389, 396.

[154] Neergaard, *Under Junigrundloven*, II, pp. 574 ff.

[155] *Ibid.*, pp. 589 ff.

CHAPTER II

THE APPROACH OF THE CRISIS

I

On March 30, 1863, a royal ordinance, the so-called March Patent, was issued to regularize the position of Holstein and Lauenburg in the monarchy. By this act, the Danish government took the step that was destined to lead to the final settlement of the long quarrel with Germany. The German Confederation had demanded the establishment of a constitution for the common affairs of the Danish Monarchy on conditions which the Danes regarded as unacceptable. At the same time, the resolutions of the Diet at Frankfurt, which required that no law for the common affairs of the monarchy should be promulgated without the consent of the Estates of Holstein and Lauenburg, made it practically impossible to secure any common legislative action. To make it possible for the development of the rest of the monarchy to go on regardless of the veto of Holstein, the Hall ministry in Denmark, in issuing the March Patent, carried out a plan that had long been under consideration.[1]

Motivated by the constant interference of the German Confederation in the affairs of the Danish Monarchy and by the impossibility of reaching an agreement with the Holstein Estates, the Patent established a constitution for the affairs of Holstein, and provided that, while no law could go into force in that duchy without the consent of its Estates, their opposition could not prevent a law, passed by the *Rigsraad* of Denmark and Schleswig from going into effect in those parts of the monarchy.[2] Thus, the attempt to establish a constitution and a legislature for the Danish Monarchy as a whole, was abandoned.

---

[1] Thorsøe, *Kong Frederik den Syvendes Regering*, II, p. 886; Neergaard, *Under Junigrundloven*, II, p. 613.

[2] Neergaard, *Under Junigrundloven*, II, pp. 613-616.

To make this scheme more attractive to Holstein, the intention was expressed of developing its institutions on a more liberal basis. Indeed, in his circular to the Danish representatives at the Courts of the Great Powers, Hall declared that the Patent was a concession to Holstein and Lauenburg which was well adapted to simplify and improve Denmark's relations to Germany,[3] but it could hardly have been expected that this would be taken at face value. Even so sympathetic an observer as the British minister at Copenhagen found it impossible to deny that, as a definitive arrangement, the March Patent was contrary to the stipulations entered into by the Danish government with Austria and Prussia in 1851-52[4]

As a matter of fact, the Hall ministry had been tending since 1858 toward the policy of the Eider-Danes. Yielding step by step to the demands of the German Diet in regard to Holstein and resolutely rejecting any attempt to negotiate on the position of Schleswig, they had succeeded in averting the threatened Federal Execution, and had attained the situation which had been foreseen—the de facto establishment of an Eider-Denmark, brought about by this very yielding.[5] That the March Patent was intended to pave the way for the incorporation of Schleswig seemed the more obvious from the fact that two days before the publication of the Patent, a meeting at the Casino theater in Copenhagen, like the one which had ushered in the crisis of 1848, had demanded the suppression of all but the dynastic union with Holstein and the maintenance and consolidation of the union between the Kingdom and Schleswig.[6]

The March Patent was followed by an outburst of indignation in Germany, but for some months public opinion did not maintain the constant interest that might have been anticipated in such a popular question. Other problems seemed, at the moment, of even greater importance. Only the broader phases of the negotiations were published and only when one side or another

---

[3] April 1, 1863, *Denmark and Germany, No. 2, 1864*, No. 24.
[4] Paget to Russell, April 29, 1863, *Denmark and Germany, No. 2, 1864*, p. 60.
[5] Cf. Neergaard, *Under Junigrundloven*, II, pp. 181, 617 f.
[6] *Ibid.*, pp. 610-613

took a definite step was there much debate in the press. All parties, with the possible exception of the Prussian conservatives, were agreed that something in favor of the duchies should be done and that the honor of Germany was at stake. The Liberals, and especially the *Nationalverein*, saw no hope of a proper solution of the question so long as Bismarck's ministry was in control of Prussian policy.[7] As one of their leaders expressed it in a discussion in the Prussian House of Representatives:

The Danes would hardly have ventured at this moment to risk such a flagrant violation of their treaty obligations...if they did not believe that Prussia was now in no position to vindicate its own rights derived from the negotiations of the years 1851 and 1852 and the rights of the duchies.... They know that in the present circumstances, a Prussian government, which is sharply at variance with its own land, whose following in the body that represents its own people hardly deserved the name of party, which in consequence of conditions at home is entirely without influence in Germany and has no possibility of vigorously seizing the initiative, that a government which, in addition, has brought Prussia to complete isolation, whose policy in the Polish question has produced a state of extreme tension with the western Powers, that such a government is absolutely not in a position to wage a war against Denmark; and if, under existing conditions, the Prussian government should show any inclination to do so, we should have in my opinion, to take a decided stand against it, because we cannot regard the present conditions as those in which even a successful outcome of the war would allow us to expect a satisfactory solution of the question. Perhaps the Danes think that the party which at present carries on the government would really have no inclination to take measures against Denmark:.... The Minister President spoke in 1849 of the war against Denmark as a most unjust, frivolous and pernicious undertaking in support of an entirely motiveless rebellion.

Bismarck's reply, that "if we find it necessary to wage war, we will do so with or without your sanction," was received with indignation by his opponents.[8]

Neither Austria nor Prussia desired to bring the matter to a crisis at this time when the Polish question demanded all their attention.[9] So, in brief identic notes, they reserved their rights

[7] Nirrnheim, *Das erste Jahr des Ministeriums Bismarck und die öffentliche Meinung*, pp. 389-414.

[8] H. Kohl, *Die politischen Reden des Fürsten Bismarck*, II, pp. 168 f. Nirrnheim, *Das erste Jahr des Ministeriums Bismarck und die öffentliche Meinung*, pp. 392, 399, 404.

[9] Copy of extract of private letter from Werther to Bismarck, Vienna, April 12, 1863: " ......Graf Rechberg (eben so wie unser Deputirter Twesten) scheint

and those of the Confederation and, in separate dispatches, sharply criticised the Danish policy.[10]   Further action was turned over to the slow procedure of the Diet at Frankfurt.

The March Patent was laid before the Diet by the Danish Minister at the session of April 16 and was referred to the committee for the affairs of Holstein and Lauenburg.   Two months later, on June 18, the committee presented its report and, on July 9, this was accepted by the majority vote of the Diet.   It declared that Denmark had failed to carry out the previous decrees of the Diet in a satisfactory manner, that the March Patent showed that she had no intention of doing so, and that the Patent was a violation of the Danish promises of 1851-52 as to the position of Holstein in the monarchy and a step towards the incorporation of Schleswig with the kingdom.   Denmark was to be called upon to revoke the March Patent and to announce that she was prepared to carry out the agreements of 1851-52. In case Denmark did not give a satisfactory answer within six weeks, the committee on the affairs of Holstein and that on Federal Execution were to recommend measures to compel compliance.

The Danish reply,[11] presented to the Diet on August 27, was a flat refusal to revoke the Patent.   Hall claimed that the March Patent had established the arrangement called for by the Federal decrees and accused the Diet of overstepping the limits of its powers in considering the position of Schleswig except through

eine gewisse Ungeduld zu haben um zu erfahren, wie wir die neueste dänische Regierungs-Akte betrachten und was wir zu thun gedenken in Schleswig-Holsteinische Angelegenheit. Ausser der Auffassung, dass Dänemark die Verabredungen von 1851-52 gebrochen, hat Graf Rechberg selber keine Ansicht ausgesprochen, obgleich ich ihn dazu aufgefordert habe. Bundes-Execution in Holstein hilft nichts fur Schleswig und drückt Holstein. Abbruch der diplomatischen Relationen mit Copenhagen, meint Graf Rechberg, wird nichts bewirken und in der Lage der Sache nichts verändern.   Ein deutscher Krieg für Schleswig-Holstein scheint durch die sonstige Lage Europas für uns nicht indicirt.'' (Berlin Archives). Cf. also, Talleyrand to Drouyn de Lhuys, Berlin, February 28 and April 18, 1863. (Paris Archives).

    [10] Brenner to Hall, Balan to Hall, April 17, 1863, *Das Staatsarchiv*, V, No. 839. Rechberg to Brenner, April 13, Bismarck to Balan, April 15, *Ibid.*, Nos. 836, 837. Cf. Bismarck, *Die gesammelten Werke*, IV, Nos. 67, 69, 70; and *Anhang zu den Gedanken und Erinnerungen*, I, Nos. 56, 57.

    [11] Text in *Das Staatsarchiv*, V, No. 905.

the organs of international negotiation. The rejection of the German demands was intended to be complete and, so far as it referred to the threatened Execution, to let "the right and will of the Royal Government to regard such a step as a *casus belli* appear in definite and unambiguous form."[12] Only in the expression of willingness for further negotiations about the position of Holstein in the monarchy on the basis of the March Patent was there to be an opening for the retreat of the Diet.[13]

II.

The Danish Government hoped that this truculent attitude on its part would make the German Diet hesitate. At the least a firm stand would make the non-German Great Powers realize the gravity of the situation and move them to put pressure on Germany to avert serious complications.[14]

Certainly when the Danish reply was drawn up, the situation in Europe and in Germany seemed no less favorable for a bold policy than when the March Patent had been published five months before. In April, the first intervention of France, England, and Austria in favor of Poland had taken place and had been politely rejected by Russia. The next months were filled with rumors of war and, in June, the three Powers again addressed themselves to Petersburg and again their suggestions were rebuffed. In the middle of August, a third series of notes reached the Russian capital and their almost identic conclusions sounded like a threat of war.[15]

With Austria and Prussia occupied elsewhere, Denmark had little to fear from Germany. Even leaving out of account the preoccupation of the two former powers, with the Polish crisis, vigorous action in the Schleswig-Holstein question seemed impossible. In Prussia, the conflict between the ministry and the Liberal majority in the House of Representatives had

[12] Neergaard, *Under Junigrundloven*, II, pp. 653 f.

[13] *Ibid.*

[14] *Ibid.*, p. 655; Hall to Danish representatives abroad, Sept. 3, 1863, *Das Staatsarchiv*, V, No. 906.

[15] A. Stern, *Geschichte Europas*, IX, pp. 176 f.

reached a new high level of bitterness. The session of the House had been closed at the end of May and at the beginning of June, the ministry had strained the constitution by a series of ordinances which muzzled the opposition press and called forth a public expression of disapproval from the heir to the throne.[16]

Austro-Prussian relations had been notoriously strained since the publication of Bismarck's famous conversations with Count Karolyi, the Austrian minister, in the preceding December, when the former had practically served notice on Austria to give up its influence in Germany. In January Bismarck had instructed the Prussian representative to withdraw from the Diet if the Austrian proposal for the reform of the Confederation were carried against the vote of Prussia. The two Powers had taken opposite sides in the Polish question and Bismarck was bitterly angry at the Austrian action in summoning the 'Congress of Princes' at Frankfurt in August 1863 without a preliminary understanding with Prussia.[17]

In spite of the fact that both France and Great Britain, because of their desire to keep Austria and Prussia apart during the Polish crisis, had pressed upon the Danish government the expediency of acting with the greatest prudence and caution in the Holstein question, it was believed at Copenhagen that in an emergency their support could be counted upon. Drouyn de Lhuys, the French minister for foreign affairs, told the Danish minister at Paris that he regretted the March Patent as it might unite Austria and Prussia, whom the Polish question was tending to separate. But he added that, in spite of this, the attitude of France would be more favorable to Denmark than in the past and that the Imperial cabinet would do all in its power to hinder a conflict between Denmark and Germany.[18] When M. Dotézac, the French minister to Denmark imparted the substance of his instructions to Count Hamilton, the Swedish Minister at Copenhagen, the latter was struck by the persistency with which he

[16] A. Stern, *Geschichte Europas*, IX, pp. 301-307.

[17] *Ibid.*, pp. 293 ff., 307 ff.

[18] Moltke-Hvitfeldt to Hall, April 26, 1863; Neergaard, *Under Junigrundloven*, II, pp. 646 f.

spoke of the advantage to Denmark if an actual rupture with the German Powers could be delayed only three or four months.[19]

In England Earl Russell's 'Gotha dispatch' of the previous September had been bitterly attacked in both houses of Parliament and the marriage of Princess Alexandra with the Prince of Wales in March 1863 had called forth enthusiastic demonstrations of sympathy for Denmark. Danish participation in the representations to Russia in favor of Poland, and the acceptance of the throne of Greece by Prince William of Denmark were regarded as having added to the Danish credit account with the two 'Western Powers.'[20]

Even more striking was the fact that in answer to a question in the House of Commons, Lord Palmerston gave weight to Earl Russell's notes of warning to Germany by expressing, amidst the applause of the House, his opinion that if the Germans made any violent attempt to overthrow the rights and to interfere with the integrity of Denmark, they would find that it would not be Denmark alone with which they had to deal.[21]

This was merely bombast. ''Denmark needs to be encouraged a bit and strengthened in her resistance,'' was Palmerston's reply to the criticisms of the Prussian ambassador, ''for she is weak and being bullied by Germany.''[22] In diplomatic circles, Earl Russell made little effort to conceal his disapproval of his colleague's

[19] Paget to Russell, No. 105, Confidential, April 30, 1863; (Record Office, London); Krieger, *Dagbøger*, II, p. 303.

[20] Neergaard, *Under Junigrundloven*, II, pp. 552-556, 661-673.

[21] Reply to Mr. Seymour Fitzgerald, July 23, 1863, Hansard, 3rd series, clxxii, p. 1250.

In explaining this speech of Palmerston, the following memorandum in his handwriting is not without significance. "This is highly probable and indeed more than probable and the gentlemen in Frankfort and the crazy minister at Berlin should have this impressed upon them. Any aggressive measure of Germany against Denmark would most likely lead to an aggressive move of France against Germany, and specially against Prussia the main instigator of that aggression. The Prussian Provinces would at once be occupied by France and in the present state of the Prussian army . . . the first serious encounter between it and the French would be little less disastrous to Prussia than the Battle of Jena. P 27/6—63." (The Layard Papers, Correspondence, general, 1863, British Museum, Add. Ms. 38,989.)

[22] Bernstorff to Bismarck, No. 294, London, July 29, 1863, (Berlin Archives). Summarized in H. von Sybel, *Die Begründung des deutschen Reiches*, III, p. 127.

words.[23] The threat seems to have aroused little comment in England or Germany[24] but it was taken more seriously in Scandinavia. Hall spoke to the British minister at Copenhagen of Lord Palmerston's speech in terms of the most lively satisfaction and said that he was convinced that it would have the most salutary effect in checking the aggressive policy of the Confederation. He refused, however to adopt Sir Augustus Paget's suggestion of taking advantage of the great moral support which the Danish Government had now received, to come forward with some conciliatory propositions.[25] Manderström, the Swedish minister for foreign affairs wrote to Count Hamilton, the Swedish minister, at Copenhagen, that "we are the more justified in taking note of the words of the noble lord, as under given circumstances it may easily enter into the realm of possibility that we shall feel ourselves called upon to give to our neighbors the support which he has thus recognized in advance to be just and opportune," and he emphasized the importance of the speech in his correspondence with the Swedish representatives in London, Paris and St. Petersburg.[26]

III

The most important foreign influence on the Danish cabinet in the formulation of its policy, was the favorable attitude of the Swedish government. The basic idea of the March Patent, the separation of Holstein from the rest of the monarchy, had been recommended since 1861 by Count Manderström, the Swedish minister for foreign affairs.[27] During the preparation of this document, Count Hamilton, the Swedish minister at Copen-

[23] *Ibid.*; S. Clason, "Skodsborgsmötet och Ulriksdalkonferens," *Historisk Tidsskrift* (Stockholm), 1914, p. 76.

[24] H. Koht, *Die Stellung Norwegens und Schwedens in deutsch-dänischen Konflikt*, p. 101. London *Times* and Augsburg *Allgemeine Zeitung* for the end of July and first part of August 1863.

[25] Paget to Russell, Copenhagen, July 29, 1863, No. 170, (Record Office, London).

[26] Manderström to Hamilton, Aug. 1, 1863, Clason, "Skodsborgmötet och Ulriksdalkonferensen," *Historisk Tidsskrift* (Stockholm), 1914, p. 76.

[27] Cf. p. 37 above.

hagen, had been in frequent consultation with some of the Danish ministers and had discussed with them plans for the Scandinavian union.[28] In February 1863, at the special request of Hall, Manderström had opened a diplomatic campaign to prepare the British and French governments to favor the Danish action.[29] In April, he expressed to the Danish minister at Stockholm his satisfaction at the coincidence of the principles that had guided the Danish government with those of the Swedish cabinet.[30] To the British minister, on the other hand, he expressed the opinion that the March Patent did not entirely establish that complete administrative separation which was contemplated in his dispatch of February 22 and "appeared doubtful about the advisability of the *proprio motu* character of the decree as well as about its satisfying Germany, to say nothing of the Danish Parliament."[31]

Nevertheless, after the resolution of the Frankfurt Diet on July 9, Manderström acted again in support of Denmark. In dispatches to London and Paris on July 19, although disclaiming knowledge of the terms of Hall's reply, he expressed his approval of the Danish point of view and called the attention of the British and French governments to the danger to the peace of the North which lay in the aggressive tendencies of Germany. Sweden, he declared, might easily be drawn by the force of events to take part in the conflict, since her own vital interests would hardly permit her to look on calmly while her neighbor was being crushed on pretexts which might later endanger her own independence.[32]

Three days later, on July 22, King Charles XV was the guest of the King of Denmark at the latter's palace of Skodsborg.[33]

[28] *Sveriges Historia*, XII, pp. 322 f.; Krieger, *Dagbøger*, II, pp. 284 f.

[29] Koht, *Die Stellung Norwegens und Schwedens im deutsch-dänischen Konflikt*, pp. 96 f. Clason, "Skodsborgsmötet och Ulriksdalskonferensen", in *Historisk Tidsskrift*, (Stockholm), 1914, p. 68.

[30] Neergaard, *Under Junigrundloven*, II, pp. 636 f.

[31] Jerningham to Russell, April 6, 1863. *Denmark and Germany No. 2, 1864*, No. 29.

[32] Manderström to Wachtmeister and Adelsvärd, July 17, 1863, *Historisk Tidsskrift* (Copenhagen) 3R III, p. 758.

[33] Except where specially noted, the following account of the meeting at Skodsborg and the subsequent negotiations to p. 68 is based upon, Clason,

King Charles was accompanied by his brother, Prince Oscar, like himself, an enthusiastic 'Scandinavian,' but by none of his responsible ministers. After luncheon, the two monarchs conversed together for a time and at about four o'clock Hall, the Danish minister for foreign affairs, who had been summoned from Copenhagen by telegraph, arrived and went at once to King Charles with whom he talked quite alone for about an hour, until dinner. As they arose from the table after dinner, the King of Sweden whispered to Count Hamilton: "Well, I've talked with Hall and everything is arranged between us." To Hamilton's questions about the agreement, the King merely answered: "You'll find that out from Hall, and don't be uneasy about it, for it was agreed upon by me and Manderström before I left." Later in the evening, King Charles and his suite returned to Sweden.

The substance of what Hall told Hamilton was that King Charles had advised the Danish government not to wait for the time limit of six weeks to expire but to reject at once the demand of the Confederate Diet for the withdrawal of the March Patent. He suggested that Federal Execution should not be resisted in Holstein but that Denmark reply to it by a blockade of the German ports. If this advice were adopted and the Germans carried out the Execution in consequence, King Charles would come at once to the defence of Schleswig with 20,000 Swedish and Norwegian troops. Hall, of course, thankfully received this offer and said that he would order the Danish minister to Sweden to return to his post at once in order to work out the details of the alliance.

This interview was followed by secret negotiations between the two governments. Manderström's plan seems to have been that, as Sweden could hardly avoid giving Denmark material aid in the defense of Schleswig, the time was ripe for the conclusion of a formal alliance. Although King Charles told Hamilton that he was in agreement with Manderström on several points, his enthusiasm had carried him beyond what his minister

"Skodsborgsmötet och Ulriksdalskonferensen," in *Historisk Tidsskrift* (Stockholm) XXXIV, (1914), pp. 61-107.

wished. The latter was trying to bring about the diplomatic intervention of Great Britain and France and therefore did not want the Danish reply to the Diet at Frankfurt to be rushed, he objected to armed resistance to the Execution and so insisted on giving up the idea of blockading the German ports as an answer to the occupation of Holstein, and he wished the official initiative for the alliance negotiations to be taken by Denmark. When these points had been arranged it became possible to proceed with the discussions of the other details.

Manderström, who managed the negotiations for Sweden, seems to have been ready to accept a defensive alliance in the widest sense if, before its conclusion, the administrative separation of Holstein from the rest of the monarchy were made more complete, for example by moving the customs frontier to the Eider, and if the same rights and liberties enjoyed by the people of the kingdom were extended to all of the inhabitants of Schleswig. From this point of view, the treaty to be concluded would be the first step toward the accomplishment of the Scandinavian Union. Hall, however, although not discouraging the idea of the union, wanted first of all a definite treaty which would assure to Denmark the support of Sweden in the defense of Schleswig, as King Charles had promised. Such a treaty, he argued, by showing the Germans what the continuation of an aggressive policy would mean, would give them pause and so render war less likely. This basis was accepted by Manderström and, with a few minor exceptions, he approved the draft of the Danish reply to the Diet.

The Swedish minister must share the responsibility for the intransigent attitude of the Danish government. But Palmerston's speech, supposed assurances from Bismarck,[34] and an optimistic view of the situation in Germany and in Europe all

[34] "Eurer Excellenz glaube ich nicht unterlassen zu dürfen...zu benachrichtigen, dass Sr. Majestät der König von Dänemark vor einigen Tagen bei einem kleinen Diner, welche in Scodsborg stattfand,...sich gegen einem Seiner hohen Beamten nach der Tafel folgendermassen geäussert hat: 'Herr von Bismarck hat mir sagen lassen, dass, so lange er preussischer Minister sei, kein preussischer Soldat meine Staaten betreten wurde.'" This was told to Balan by the official himself. Balan to Bismarck, "vertraulich," June 3, 1863. Bismarck naturally denied having given such assurances. Bismarck to Balan, June 5, 1863, (Berlin Archives).

coöperated in creating the bellicose mood that prevailed in Copenhagen.[35]

Details of the treaty were discussed at Copenhagen by Hall and the Swedish minister, Count Hamilton. On August 25, Manderström met Hamilton at Malmö where he approved the draft, and on the 29th, he paid a hasty visit to Copenhagen where he had a meeting with Hall at Count Hamilton's house. The two statesmen seem to have been agreed as to the main points.[36] There are two drafts of the treaty known, one Danish, dated August 23, and one Swedish without definite date. In the first article the King of Sweden and Norway promised to aid the King of Denmark in the defense of those territories not forming part of the German Confederation against any attack arising out of the existing controversy between Denmark and the German Confederation. The second provided that the King of Denmark might claim this aid as soon as there was danger of an attack on those parts of the monarchy. The Danish draft added that the occupation of Holstein by the troops of the confederation should be regarded as such a danger, while the Swedish draft contained the limiting clause, ''for carrying out a federal resolution which does not exclusively concern that duchy's internal administration and legislation.'' The remaining clauses dealt chiefly with the command, equipment and support of the auxiliary corps.[37]

That the real obligations of this treaty fell upon Sweden-Norway was due to the 'Scandinavian' idea that the defense of the Eider frontier was an interest of the 'North.' Charles XV, Manderström, Hamilton, and Hall were united in a more or less vague idea of the future development of a Scandinavian union formed by a permanent alliance of the three kingdoms or, as Charles XV sometimes dreamed, by uniting the three crowns on his own head.

It had been intended from the beginning that before the final conclusion of the treaty, Count Hamilton should take the draft

---

[35] Cf. p. 59 above.

[36] Cf. Krieger, *Dagbøger*, II, p. 314. ''M. var enig i det af Hamilton omskrevne Vedelske Udkast.''

[37] Danish draft in *Historisk Tidsskrift* (Copenhagen) 3R., III, pp. 736 ff.; Swedish draft in Clason, *op. cit.*, pp. 106 f.

to Stockholm for a consultation on the technical details with the military chiefs. In the beginning of September, his presence in Stockholm was felt to be all the more necessary as some of the Swedish and Norwegian ministers had begun to oppose the treaty. At this time, the situation in Sweden with reference to the alliance question was as follows. The King and Manderström, the minister for foreign affairs, with the coöperation of Count Hamilton, the minister at Copenhagen, were in agreement with the Danish President of the Council on a treaty, some details of which were under negotiation, which should provide for Swedish support on the Eider in case Holstein were occupied by German troops for reasons going beyond the federal position of Holstein. De Geer, the Swedish Minister President, was in general agreement with the idea, most of the other ministers somewhat less favorable, and the finance minister, Gripenstedt, definitely opposed.

The problem was discussed at great length by the Swedish king and his chief ministers at Ulriksdal on September 8. The opposition to the treaty was based especially on the belief that it was likely to involve Sweden-Norway in war, that the attitude of Great Britain and France toward this war was uncertain and that it would be extremely rash to enter on a war without being able to count on the support of at least one Great Power. The decision of the conference was a compromise between the view of Gripenstedt that the alliance should not be concluded and that of the King, Manderström and Hamilton that it should be concluded at once. It was agreed that the minister for foreign affairs should consult the British and French governments on the question; but it was not settled what action should follow the receipt of the replies.

The Ulriksdal conference does not mark a definite turning point in Swedish policy in the sense of a definite abandonment of the treaty negotiations. The King, against whose personal intervention in the negotiations, the opposition had been especially directed, felt that his royal honor was involved and seems to have believed that he could still have his own way.[38]

[38] He told the Prussian minister: "Ne faites pas attention à tous ces ministres et vieux militaires, qui me font de l'opposition, je me moque de ces gens-là et je le

Manderström and Hamilton took the opposition more seriously but they too did not abandon hope of carrying through the treaty project.

The British and French governments, however, gave them no encouragement.[39] Russell, who was alarmed at the possibility that Denmark, on the ground that the Diet was overstepping its competence by including the question of Schleswig in its deliberations, would resist the Execution by force and that Sweden-Norway would support this resistance,[40] was continuing his efforts to prevent the dispute from resulting in war. The situation seemed the more serious as Austria and Prussia showed no signs of willingness to restrain the action of the Diet,[41] and as the attempts to secure a more conciliatory attitude at Copenhagen were unsuccessful.[42] In a dispatch to Berlin, he pointed out that there was a material difference between the political bearing of a military occupation of territory which was solely a portion of the German Confederation and that of the invasion of a territory, which, although part of the German Confederation was also a portion of the territory of an independent sovereign, whose dominions were counted as an element of the balance of power in Europe. "By the invasion of Holstein for the purpose of compelling the King of Denmark to acknowledge certain rights claimed for Schleswig as a result of the negotiations of 1851-1852, the Diet will be entering upon a grave European question as to which they have no exclusive competency of decision and to which it belongs quite as much to every other European Government to form an opinion and pronounce a judgment."[43] To

---

jetterai par la fenêtre, s'ils ne font pas ce que je leur demande. Je trouverai de l'argent et des troupes pour défendre le Schleswig. J'ai donné ma parole de le faire et je le ferai...." Rosenberg to King William, No. 76, September 14, 1863, (Berlin Archives).

[39] Koht, *Die Stellung Norwegens und Schwedens im deutsch-dänischen Konflikt*, pp. 126 ff.

[40] Russell to Bloomfield, July 31, 1863, *Denmark and Germany, No. 2, 1864*, No. 99.

[41] Bloomfield to Russell, Vienna, August 6; Lowther to Russell, Berlin, August 29, September 4, 1863. *Ibid.*, Nos. 107, 116, 119.

[42] Cf. p. 62 above.

[43] Russell to Lowther, August 31, 1863. *Ibid.*, No. 117.

emphasize this warning, he turned to Paris and tried to persuade the French government to join with Great Britain in attempting to avert the conflict. M. Drouyn de Lhuys, the French minister for foreign affairs replied that he thought that an offer of good offices would be useless and that he had no inclination to place France in the same position with reference to Germany as she had been placed with regard to Russia as a result of the intervention in favor of Poland. If England and France were to address formal notes to Austria and Prussia, "they must be prepared to go farther and to adopt a course of action more in accordance with the dignity of two Great Powers than they were now doing in the Polish question."[44] In their replies to Manderström's notes a few days later, both powers refused to commit themselves in advance to any line of policy.[45]

In view of these non-committal replies, Manderström seems to have realized that he might have to retreat from the position he had taken; but the negotiations with Denmark were not abruptly broken off. In a dispatch of October 5, he discussed the situation at length and declared that he no longer saw the same need as before of a Danish-Swedish alliance but he recognized that if the Danes still wished it, Sweden must go on with the negotiations. The treaty, he insisted, must be purely defensive and limited to the present situation; that is, to the consequences of the refusal of the King of Denmark to withdraw the March Patent. Nevertheless, the dispatch contained the assurance that with or without a treaty, if the Germans attacked Schleswig, Denmark could count on the same support from Sweden as before.[46]

Hall had known since the middle of September that the alliance project was meeting opposition in Sweden.[47] He was disappointed at the tone of Manderström's note, but he seized at the one straw offered him and urged that the negotiations be

---

[44] Russell to Grey, September 16; Grey to Russell, Paris, September 18, 1863, *Ibid.*, Nos. 125, 126; *Cambridge History of British Foreign Policy*, II, p. 560.

[45] Koht, *Die Stellung Norwegens und Schwedens im deutsch-dänischen Konflikt*, pp. 126 ff.

[46] Manderström to Hamilton, October 5, 1863; *ibid.*, appendix V.

[47] Cf. Krieger, *Dagbøger*, II, p. 317; and Clason, *op. cit.*, p. 102.

continued. The appearance that they were still going on might be enough to give support to his policy.[48]

IV

In the meantime, on August 27, the Danish reply to the demands of the German Confederation[49] had been laid before the Diet and referred to the usual committee. Not until more than a month later, on October 1, was it finally voted that, as the Danish government had not fulfilled its obligations with regard to the constitutional relations of Holstein and Lauenburg, the decrees of the Diet were to be enforced by Federal Execution. Hanover and Saxony were called upon to provide the commissioners and troops for the occupation of the duchies and Prussia and Austria to prepare a force in reserve.[50]

It was not merely to meet the contingency of Federal Execution that Hall, the President of the Danish council, had desired the speedy completion of the Dano-Swedish alliance. He had counted on it in overcoming the opposition in Denmark to a new constitutional arrangement for Denmark and Schleswig.[51] Despite his disappointment, Hall decided to go ahead with the new constitution. At the opening session of the *Rigsraad* on September 28, just three days before the passage of the decree of Federal Execution by the Diet at Frankfurt, the speech from the throne contained the statement:

As was announced at the last session, there will be laid before the Rigsraad, the draft of a new constitution for the common affairs of the Kingdom and of Schleswig, which rests on the same basis as all the at present existing constitutional laws. It is our intention to give the Rigsraad such strength as will not only enable it to fullfil the great demands which the immediate future may impose on it, but also to put it in a position, in the course of time, to bear the weight of our whole constitutional development. The attached temporary provisions, which are made necessary by the special position of

[48] Koht, *op. cit.*, pp. 147 f., and appendix VI.

[49] See pp. 58 f. above.

[50] Protocol of the 29th session of the Diet, October 1, 1863, *Das Staatsarchiv*, V, No. 909.

[51] Draft, Hall to Hamilton, Copenhagen, August 31, 1863. Geheimregistratur 1863, No. 2299, (Copenhagen Archives).

Holstein and Lauenburg, will point out the way in which the relation of these lands to the rest of the monarchy can be arranged with the coöperation of the people and in accordance with their interests and wishes.

The long strife between Denmark and the German Confederation seems to be approaching a crisis. Now that the Princes of Germany[52] have themselves solemnly acknowledged aims whose successful carrying out would necessarily presuppose for our Federal lands such a modification in their relations to the rest of the monarchy as was laid down in Our Royal Proclamation of March 30 of this year, we will not give up hope of an agreement....

Should that hope not be fulfilled, it will be notorious that [the conflict with Germany] is not concerned with the Federal rights of Our German Federal Lands but with the independence of Our Danish Monarchy. That, We are firmly determined to vindicate against any attack and We are sure that We will not stand alone. But above all We count upon Our loyal people's love of Fatherland and freedom.[53]

In the draft, which passed its third reading on November 13th,[54] the policy which had been foreshadowed by the March Patent reached its logical conclusion. The November Constitution established in legal form, the organization of the monarchy which, eight months before, had been created by royal fiat. Many of its provisions were the same as those of the existing Constitution of October 1855. What was new besides the formal establishment of the constitution as common to Schleswig and the kingdom, was the regulation of the relations of that constitutional unit to the German Federal lands of the monarchy and the composition and the powers of the Rigsraad for Denmark and Schleswig.

The Rigsraad was changed from a unicameral to a bicameral body. The *Folkthing*, the lower house, was to contain 101 members for the kingdom and 29 for Schleswig; the *Landthing*, besides the royal princes and 25 appointed members (19 from the kingdom and 6 from Schleswig), 40 members elected by the kingdom and 10 by Schleswig.[55] Of especial importance was the

[52] During the 'Congress of Princes' at Frankfurt.

[53] Neergaard, *Under Junigrundloven*, II, p. 718 f. Cf. Thorsøe, *Kong Frederik den Syvendes Regering*, II, 956 and also Paget to Russell, Oct. 1, 1863; in *Denmark and Germany, No. 3, (1864)*, No. 145.

[54] All but one of the members of the Rigsraad took part in the final vote; 38 votes in favor were needed; 40 voted for, 16 against. Neergaard *Under Junigrundloven*, II, p. 777.

[55] *Ibid.*, 720 ff.

provision that the validity of laws for the common affairs of the
monarchy passed by the *Rigsraad* and sanctioned by the king
was no longer dependent upon the concurrence of any other
legislative body unless this concurrence were expressly provided
for in the law itself. If the *Rigsraad* passed a law concerning the
common affairs which normally included Holstein, but without
the specific provision that it should be invalid unless a similar
measure were passed in Holstein, the law thus passed would be
valid in Denmark and Schleswig even though the Estates of
Holstein rejected it. For example, if the *Rigsraad* voted an
appropriation for naval construction and the Estates of Holstein
refused to pass a complementary law, the quota of expenditure
normal to Schleswig and Denmark would be used without regard
to Holstein. From the point of view of the independence of the
non-federal parts of the monarchy, there was much justification
for this arrangement. Otherwise the obstructive attitude of the
Holsteiners could continue to make legislation for the common
affairs of the monarchy impossible. But at the same time, the
new constitution made possible the exclusion of Holstein from
those common affairs and legally established the Eider-Denmark
which it had been one of the objects of the negotiations of 1851-52
to prevent. The significance of this constitution for the internal
history of Denmark is completely overshadowed by its international aspects. The negotiations between Denmark and the
Great Powers up to the outbreak of war in February 1864 turned
upon it and it served as the pretext for the war. For that reason
it is necessary to consider in more detail than in the case of the
March Patent, whether it really involved a violation of the
obligations that Denmark had undertaken in the negotiations
of 1851-52 on which the international position of the monarchy
now rested.

The new constitution did not involve the 'incorporation of
Schleswig' with the kingdom of Denmark in the sense of an
amalgamation of the local institutions of the duchy with those
of the kingdom,[56] for no change was made in the specific local

[56] Cf. the pungent comment of Lord Robert Cecil (later Lord Salisbury) in
"The Danish Duchies," in his *Essays in Foreign Policy*, pp. 125.

institutions of Schleswig[57] or in the list of affairs that had been declared to be 'common' to the monarchy as a whole. But 'incorporation' as used in the notes exchanged in 1851-52 had a more technical meaning.

An Austrian note of September 9, 1851, states that ''The idea of separating Holstein still more from the other provinces of the monarchy, in order more closely to unite Schleswig with the Kingdom of Denmark, is repugnant to the principle of the integrity of the monarchy. ... The Duchy of Schleswig has always been an intermediate link between Denmark and Holstein-tein.... ''[58]

The principle of the Eider-Denmark embodied in the November Constitution was certainly incompatible with the position of Schleswig as an intermediate link between Denmark and Holstein. But, in any case, the Danish government had promised not merely ''not to incorporate Schleswig with the Kingdom'' but also that no steps ''tending towards that end should be taken.'' There was much justification for the view that the new constitution was a step leading to the complete incorporation of Schleswig. The speech from the throne had announced the intention of the government to give to the Rigsraad such strength that ''in the course of time it will be in a position to bear the whole of our constitutional development.''[59] ''These most imprudent words,'' which were supposed to be due to the influence of Orla Lehmann were those which to public opinion both in and outside of Denmark gave the whole institution its character. Taken in conjunction with the known views of the ministry and of many members of the *Rigsraad,* and with the statements of the in-

[57] Considerable opposition in the *Rigsraad* to the new constitution was caused by rumors that the ministry intended even to increase the powers of the local organs in Schleswig. Neergaard, *Under Junigrundloven,* II, p. 763.

[58] This meaning of incorporation was not specifically accepted by the Danish government but seems to have been clearly understood at Copenhagen during the negotiations. Cf. Krieger, *Dagbøger,* I, pp. 140-142. As the Annex to the Austrian dispatch of December 26, 1851 was formally adopted as the correct interpretation of the Danish intentions as set forth in the note of December 6, we are justified in interpreting it in the light of the dispatch of September 9, to which that of December 6 was the reply.

[59] Neergaard, *Under Junigrundloven,* II, pp. 718 f.

fluential Copenhagen press[60] they were justifiably interpreted as indicating the purpose of uniting the institutions of Denmark and Schleswig.

Even assuming that the November Constitution involved neither the 'incorporation' of Schleswig nor a step leading thereto, the fact remains that it marks the definite abandonment of the 'Whole State' policy consecrated by the agreements of 1851-52. Count Bluhme, who as minister for foreign affairs had carried on the final negotiations, argued in the debates in the *Rigsraad* that the new constitution actually was a violation of Denmark's obligations[61] and this is now generally admitted by Danish historians.[62]

The Hall ministry was not blind to the fact that there was danger in the path it had chosen, but it was possessed by an optimism that threw into high light the bright points of the situation.[63] The real danger to Denmark, the ministry declared, lay in the confusion of the question of Schleswig with that of Holstein. From the moment, however, that Germany took a step toward Federal Execution, the question would stand out with its legal limits clearly marked. Any attempt on the part of the Confederation to extend its action to Schleswig would lead it into a sphere ''where it is sure to meet that European intervention which so far, it has succeeded in averting.... Under these circumstances, the Confederation, especially in the present conjuncture of European politics, will scarcely go farther than to make protests and reservations and these methods will hardly have any telling effect or find any substantial response on the part of the Powers....''[64]

The Danish government deliberately took the step of bringing to a head the conflict with Germany but it did not foresee and

[60] Neergaard, *Under Junigrundloven*, II, 725 ff.

[61] Thorsøe, *Kong Frederik den Syvendes Regering*, II, pp. 890 f; Neergaard, *Under Junigrundloven*, II, pp. 769 ff.

[62] Cf. Neergaard, *op. cit.*, II, pp. 617 ff, 722 ff.; Rubin, *Maend og Bøger*, p. 95; Arup, *Rids af Danmarks Historie til Brug ved Universitets Undervisning*, p. 61.

[63] Neergaard, *Under Junigrundloven*, II, pp. 764 f.

[64] Ministerial report to the King, Sept. 24, 1863; *Ibid.*, pp. 717 ff.

could hardly have foreseen the change in the situation brought about by the events immediately following the passage of the constitution.

V

On November 15, two days after the passage of the constitution and before it had received his formal approval, King Frederick VII, the last male in the direct line of the Danish royal house, died suddenly at Glücksburg in Schleswig. In accordance with the Treaty of London of 1852 and the Danish law of succession of 1853, he was succeeded by Prince Christian of Schleswig-Holstein-Sönderburg-Glücksburg as King Christian IX.

The new king came to the throne at a moment of crisis for Denmark and his personal difficulties were increased by the fact that he followed a ruler, who, in spite of many faults, was very popular with his Danish subjects. King Christian, then in his forty-sixth year, was not well known to his people. Since 1856, he had been a member of the Privy Council [Geheimestatsraad] but had had practically no influence on the course of government. He and his wife had shown their loyalty to the state in the difficult days of 1848, but, at the same time, birth, upbringing, and family connection linked them closely to the German population of the duchies. For this Prince, brought up in the tradition prevailing before 'Forty-eight,' it was only natural to combine Danish and German sympathies. As he might be regarded as having a mandate from the Danish King and Diet and from the European Powers to hold the monarchy together, he opposed all separatist tendencies, whether Eider-Dane or Schleswig-Holstein. This point of view, added to his conservative cast of mind, brought him close to the 'Whole State' party and in its ranks were to be found his political confidants. The National Liberals regarded him as an opponent and their press often commented on his supposed lack of national feeling. As the tendency of the government policy had become more markedly Eider-Danish, the Prince, whose position and nature forbade him to step into the active opposition, took a more and more passive attitude. Those who knew him well, liked and honored him, but his lack of ability to impress the crowd and his reluctance to seek popularity, made it difficult for him at first to overcome the prejudice against him and to stand the contrast with the jovial Frederick VII.[65]

Immediately on his accession, King Christian was faced by the problem created by the passage of the new constitution. Should he or should he not give it his sanction? From the beginning, he was left in little doubt as to the attitude of his capital. Shortly before noon on November 16, Minister President Hall announced from the balcony of Christiansborg Palace the death of King Frederick VII and the accession of Christian IX. Half-hearted cheers for the new monarch were followed by loud shouts of: "The Constitution of November 13!" "Hurrah for the Constitution!" "Three cheers for the Hall Ministry!" Similar scenes took place when the garrison and the civic guard took the oath of loyalty. The next day, delegates from various civic bodies called to pay their respects and to urge the King to complete the work of his predecessor by signing the new constitution. "Answer! Answer! Yes or no?" shouted the crowds outside the palace.[66]

King Christian was in a situation of unusual difficulty. If he refused to sign the constitution, he would alienate a numerous and influential element among the Danes; if he did sign, he would add to the already existing complications in Denmark's relations to the duchies and to Germany. Frederick VII's title to the whole Danish Monarchy had been unquestionable. But his successor's right to the duchies was denied by the Schleswig-Holstein party in the duchies and by their sympathizers in the rest of Germany. Even more important was the question as to what attitude Austria and Prussia would take if an act violating the agreements of 1851 were consummated.

---

[65] Neergaard, *Under Junigrundloven*, II, pp. 871 f.; M. Rubin, *Mænd og Bøger*, pp. 94 f.

[66] Neergaard, *Under Junigrundloven*, II, pp. 874 f.; G. Brandes, *Levned*, I, p. 157; Paget to Russell, November 18, 1863, (Record Office, London); Balan to King William, November 16, 1863, (Berlin archives); Dotézac to Drouyn de Lhuys, November 18, 1863, (Paris Archives).

On November 15, the day of King Frederick's death, Balan, the Prussian minister, had communicated to Hall a note dated November 13, protesting against the proposed constitution.[67] From Berlin, Quaade, the Danish minister, telegraphed on November 17 that "under present circumstances, the sanction of the new Constitution will have the most fatal effect upon the action of the Confederate Diet. The young Augustenburger is said to be in Frankfurt and the Diet already busying itself with the succession question. The Execution at present will mean a double danger. Bismarck does not indeed demand that the sanction never be given. He only advises that we wait as long as possible and do not carry out the decision now."[68] The British foreign secretary expressed the opinion that if the King wished the proposed British mediation to be successful, it would be advisable to suspend his signature until the international question was settled.[69] A warning from Gorchakov probably arrived too late to have had any influence on the King's decision, but it was well known at Copenhagen that the Russian cabinet was unsympathetic toward the Eider policy.[70] On the other hand, Count Hamilton is said to have been ordered by the Swedish government to advise the King to give his sanction without

---

[67] Bismarck to Balan, November 13, 1863; Bismarck, *Die gesammelten Werke*, IV, No. 151; Balan to Bismarck, No. 252, November 15, 1863, (Berlin Archives).

[68] Neergaard, *Under Junigrundloven*, II, p. 878.

[69] Russell to Paget, telegram, November 17, 1863, 11:10 A.M. (Record Office, London). On the other hand the King of Sweden told the French minister at Stockholm: "Il [Christian IX] a, de suite, télégraphié à son gendre, le Prince de Galles, pour le prier de lui transmettre l'avis de Lord Palmerston. Le 18, le Prince a répondu que Lord Palmerston engageait le Roi à donner sa sanction sans delai." Fournier to Drouyn de Lhuys, No. 37, November 30, 1863, Très confidentielle, (Paris Archives).

[70] Neergaard, *Under Junigrundloven*, II, pp. 879 f. Krieger, *Dagbøger* II, p. 346, (19 November), notes: "...igaar telegrapherede O. Plessen, at man endelig ikke maatte stadfæste Grundloven,.... .—For seent!" The King of Sweden told the French minister that Gorchakov had telegraphed already on November 16. Fournier to Drouyn de Lhuys, No. 37, November 30, 1863, (Paris Archives). This seems too early a date. According to Redern's telegram to Bismarck, No. 131, November 19, 1863, (Berlin Archives), Gorchakov's telegram was not sent before November 19, the date of his corresponding dispatch to Nicolai, the Russian minister at Copenhagen. Cf. *Denmark and Germany, No. 3, 1864*, No. 286.

delay,[71] and the Danish minister at Stockholm telegraphed that Count Manderström had declared to him that the death of Frederick VII would not affect the attitude of the Swedish cabinet toward the treaty of alliance.[72]

The ministry urged the King not to delay his sanction. Finally, King Christian, unable to find anyone to form a new ministry and unable to persuade Hall to take the responsibility for postponement, yielded to the pressure and, at a council shortly after noon on November 18, signed the new constitution. At the new year, it would go into effect.[73]

The coincidence of the dynastic change with the sanction of the November Constitution gave the Germans the opportunity to combine two lines of attack upon the integrity of the Danish Monarchy: the constitutional and the dynastic. King Frederick VII could have been forced to make good only the violation of the agreements of December 1851; his successor's very title to the duchies could be made to stand or fall with the observance of Denmark's obligations.

[71] Fournier to Drouyn de Lhuys, No. 37, November 30, 1863, (Paris Archives).

[72] Neergaard, *Under Junigrundloven*, II, pp. 880 f.

[73] Neergaard, *Under Junigrundloven*, II, pp. 881-887. M. Rubin, *Mœnd og Bøger*, p. 96, perhaps on the authority of information obtained from King Christian, says that Hall secured the king's signature by promising to undertake the revocation of the constitution if it should prove to be a cause for war. This probably rests on a misunderstanding.

CHAPTER III

THE AUSTRO-PRUSSIAN ALLIANCE

I

The death of Frederick VII stirred up an outburst of national excitement in Germany that soon evoked in the minds of the governments vivid memories of the enthusiasm of 1848; and the news of the sanction by his successor of the constitution for Denmark and Schleswig poured oil on the flames. The agitation quickly found a rallying point in Prince Frederick of Augustenburg, the eldest son of that Duke Christian August in whom, up to 1852, the hopes of the duchies had centered.

Prince Frederick was thirty-four years old. He had taken part with the Schleswig-Holstein army in the campaigns of 1848-50. He had later attended the University of Bonn where he had acquired the friendship of a number of men, who in 1863 were in a position to be of great service to his political ambitions: Crown Prince Frederick William of Prussia, the Grand Duke of Baden and Duke Ernst of Saxe-Coburg-Gotha. By his marriage with Princess Adelheid of Hohenlohe-Langenburg, the daughter of a half-sister of Queen Victoria, he came into close personal relations with the British court.[1] The young Augustenburger had, however, taken no part in public life up to November 1863 and was little known in Germany and the duchies.[2]

The news of the death of King Frederick reached the Augustenburg family at their estate of Primkenau in Silesia late on the afternoon of November 16. That evening, Christian August

---

[1] In conversation with Earl Russell, the Queen suggested him as a possible candidate for the throne of Greece. "The Queen thought that there would be a degree of justice in placing him on that throne, considering that we had been instrumental in depriving him of his just rights to the duchy of Holstein." *Letters of Queen Victoria*, 2nd series, I, p. 50.

[2] H. Hagenah, "1863. Die nationale Bewegung in Schleswig-Holstein," *Z. f. s.-h. G.*, LVI, pp. 315-323.

renounced his claims to the duchies in favor of his eldest son and the Prince set out at once for the court of Gotha. On his arrival there the next morning, Duke Ernst formally recognized him as Duke of Schleswig-Holstein and allowed him to organize a provisional government of Schleswig-Holsteiners whom he had taken into his own service after their banishment from the duchies.[3]

There has been much argument as to the legal and moral justification of this action of the Augustenburgs. In 1852, Christian August had promised for himself and his family not to make use of his rights to the succession. It was now argued, however, that, as Prince Frederick had been of age at the time, he was not legally included in the Duke's "family" and not subject to his authority. It was not until 1859, however, that the former made any formal protest or reservation of his rights and even then very little attention was paid to him. But there can be no doubt that the father at least, evaded his obligations. He had promised "not to undertake anything whereby the tranquillity of His Majesty's dominions and lands might be disturbed, nor in any way to counteract the resolution which His Majesty might have taken, or in future may take, in reference to the succession to all the lands now united under His Majesty's sceptre or to the eventual reorganization of His monarchy." He further promised "for ourself and our heirs and descendants, that we will faithfully fulfil on our side all that has been stipulated..., and will not allow any of ours to do or to undertake anything against it."[4] Sybel's comment is unanswerable: "What, however, could he have undertaken against this succession arrangement better suited to shatter it than the cession of claims which he was bound not to exercise to an heir whose hand was free?"[5] But in November 1863, Germany was in no mood to listen to reason and Prince Frederick became the idol of the nation.

The duchies received the news of the dynastic change with

[3] Details in Gebauer, *Herzog Friedrich VIII von Schleswig-Holstein*, pp. 61-64.
[4] Dec. 30, 1852. *Das Staatsarchiv*, VI, No. 1026.
[5] Sybel, *Die Begründung des deutschen Reiches*, III, p. 150.

outward calm. The new king's sympathies were known and many waited to see what policy he would adopt.[6] The political leaders were at first divided and uncertain as to what should be done but with the news of the signing of the constitution and an order to all officials to take the oath of allegiance to King Christian, the proclamation of Prince Frederick as Duke of Schleswig-Holstein, published in Holstein on November 18, gave the impetus to a rapidly increasing agitation in that duchy. The officials decided to refuse the oath. But in Schleswig, where most of the officials were Danish, the population remained more quiet.[7]

From Gotha, Prince Frederick[8] hurried on November 18 to Berlin to ask for the support of Prussia. His appearance there created a serious problem for Bismarck. The latter had no desire to see Schleswig and Holstein fall into the hands of the Prince. He had often said that he preferred the King of Denmark in the Duchies to a new Grand Duke, who out of fear of Prussian desire for his lands would always vote against her in the Diet.[9] Public opinion in Germany and in Prussia in favor of the Augustenburgs could be resisted; Bismarck was accustomed to that. But here the trouble was that King William seemed to waver. Even the fact that Prince Frederick was the close associate of the 'Coburgers', the liberal element against whose principles the King was standing so firmly was not enough to shake the monarch's strong sense of the legitimacy of the Prince's claims and the feeling that "Prussia had something to make up for" in the[10] Schleswig-Holstein question. The argument that must have appealed most to Bismarck: that recognition of the Prince as rightful sovereign of the duchies would block Prussia's chance of acquiring them could not yet be used on honest King William.

---

[6] C. Tiedemann, *Aus Sieben Jahrzehnten*, I, p. 288.

[7] H. Hagenah, "1863. Die nationale Bewegung in Schleswig-Holstein," *Z. f. s.-h. G.*, LVI, pp. 329-355.

[8] As Frederick never succeeded in establishing his claims, I shall continue in general to refer to him not as Duke but as Prince.

[9] Buchanan to Russell, No. 485, October 17, 1863, most confidential, (Record Office, London); Talleyrand to Drouyn de Lhuys, No. 116. Nov. 19, 1863, (Paris Archives).

[10] Memorandum by King William, Nov. 18, 1863, (Berlin Archives).

But the Treaty of London proved the trump card. Prussia had agreed to recognize the succession of Christian IX to all the lands of the Danish Monarchy. So the Prince was told by both minister and monarch that at present Prussia could do nothing for him.[11]

II

At this time, Bismarck was still regarded as the worst enemy of the national ambitions of Germany. Just before the death of Frederick VII, it was rumored in usually well-informed circles in Berlin that he had turned the whole affair over to "little Abeken" and had told him to do what he would with it so long as he took care that it did not lead to war.[12] In many ways, his policy seemed not unfavorable to Denmark. He had openly expressed his agreement with Rechberg that the Danish reply to the Diet, presented on August 27, was unsatisfactory and that the legal procedure should be allowed to take its course.[13] Secretly however, during October and the first weeks in November, he was negotiating with the British ambassador in an attempt to avert the Execution by securing adequate concessions from Denmark. He gave the appearance of favoring the British proposal of mediation to settle the Schleswig question and he supported an intrigue at Copenhagen to overthrow the Hall ministry and to effect a complete reversal of Danish policy with regard to the duchies.

While the Danish ministry, with the aid of the National Liberal majority, had been pushing the new constitution through the Rigsraad, Earl Russell had not given up hope that, through

---

[11] Jansen-Samwer, *Schleswig-Holsteins Befreiung*, pp. 686 f.

[12] *Aus dem Leben Theodor von Bernhardis*, V, p. 139.

[13] Rechberg sent an unciphered telegram from Frankfurt: "Königl. Preussischen Ministerpräsidenten v. Bismarck in Baden. Ich halte die dänische Antwort für ungenügend, die Forderungen des Bundes verneinend und im Schlüsse dessen Autorität misskennend. Wäre der Ansicht unsere Bundestagsgesandten für die Ausschuss kurzer anzuweisen, dem eingeleiteten gesetzlichen Verfahren Folge zu geben. Sind Eure Excellenz einverstanden?" The draft reply in Bismarck's hand was: "Vollkommen einverstanden, und wird Herr von Sydow morgen mit entsprechenden Instruktionen versehen sein." August 28, 1863, (Berlin Archives).

British mediation, a peaceful solution of the German Danish conflict could be found. He had failed in his preaching of moderation at Copenhagen, he had seen his advice to the Diet at Frankfurt practically disregarded, and he had been unable to secure the support of France for a more emphatic intervention.[14] As a last resort he had turned to Prussia, generally regarded as the most dangerous enemy of Denmark but for the moment in open opposition to Austria and the majority of the states represented in the Diet.

The apparent moderation of the Prussian government in the Schleswig-Holstein question had begun to make an impression on the British Foreign Secretary. Bismarck represented Austria and the south German states as pushing the Diet on, while he himself was attempting to keep their action within reasonable bounds.

He [Bismarck] said it was difficult to say when the execution would take place, but that according to a calculation he had made it would not be before the middle of October; he was himself personally opposed to the claims of Germany in Schleswig-Holstein, but that it was so popular a question in Germany and Prussia, that no minister could remain a day in power who declared himself opposed to it; all that he could do and had done was to use his influence with the Austrian and other governments in order that some modifications might be made in the proceeding to be taken against Denmark.

Some of the South German Governments, he added and more particularly Bavaria were great advocates for action on this subject, and he said M. von der Pfordten [Bavarian representative in the Diet] maintained that as war with France sooner or later was a certainty it would be better that it should take place for so good a cause as the German Duchies. . . .His Excellency [Bismarck] denied that the Diet intended to invade Holstein for the purpose of compelling the King of Denmark to recognize certain rights which the German Confederation claim as belonging to Schleswig by virtue of the arrangements of 1851-1852, and his Excellency took credit to himself for having caused the Austrian Government to modify its proposals—one of which was that Holstein should be taken as pledge for Schleswig;[15] that Count Carolyi [sic], the Austrian Minister [at Berlin] was continually urging him to action, but that he was personally indisposed to act in the matter and was continually endeavoring to restrain the others. . . . If, said M. de

---

[14] Cf. A. W. Ward, in *Cambridge History of British Foreign Policy*, II, pp. 559 ff.

[15] The dispatch says "Schleswig. . .as a pledge for Holstein. . ." but this is doubtless a slip and it should certainly read "Holstein" for "Schleswig". Cf. Buchanan to Russell, telegram, May 29, 1863, (Record Office, London).

Bismarck, there was a European conference on the Duchies, and this were proposed by England, not by France, it would be very well received.[16]

Bismarck's official dispatches were naturally more unbending[17] but in his conversations he continued to be amiable and to throw the blame on Austria. "He saw no prospect of a Federal Execution in Holstein being prevented," he said, on September 18.

...Austria had brought things to their present state in her new character as the champion of German rights in Schleswig-Holstein, and...it would now be impossible for the King to act in opposition to the sympathies of Germany, although if the occupation of Holstein should lead to war with Denmark, the maritime interests of Prussia might be seriously injured.

M. de Bismarck said he had done everything to promote moderation at Vienna and Frankfurt. In the first place he had refused to adhere to the Austrian proposals to occupy Holstein as a pledge for a satisfactory arrangement with respect to Schleswig. He had then declined to furnish Prussian troops for the occupation of Holstein, and when Hanover, where party feeling is strong against Denmark, was selected for carrying out the federal decree, the Prussian Government had insisted on Saxony being associated with her and on the troops being limited to six thousand. . . . . .[18]

At the end of September, Russell addressed a dispatch to the British representative at Frankfurt in which he sternly warned the Diet that

Her Majesty could not see with indifference a military occupation of Holstein, which is only to cease upon terms injuriously affecting the constitution of the whole Danish Monarchy; Her Majesty's Government could not recognize this military occupation as a legitimate exercise of the powers of the Confederation, or admit that it could properly be called a Federal Execution; Her Majesty's Government could not be indifferent to the bearing of such an act upon Denmark and upon European interests,

and they requested the Diet to submit the question in dispute between Denmark and Germany to the mediation of other powers, "unconcerned in the controversy, but deeply concerned in the maintenance of the peace of Europe and the independence

[16] Lowther to Russell, Berlin, September 12, 1863, No. 94, received September 14, (Record Office, London).

[17] Cf. Bismarck to Katte, Berlin, September 11, 1863; presented to Earl Russell, September 14, 1863, *Denmark and Germany, No. 2, 1864*, No. 123.

[18] Lowther to Russell, Berlin, September 19, 1863, No. 386; received September 21, (Record Office, London).

of Denmark.''[19] Copies of this dispatch were forwarded to Vienna and Berlin,[20] and in separate dispatches Austria and Prussia were reminded of their obligations under the Treaty of London of 1852, ''to respect the integrity and independence of Denmark.''[21]

In a second dispatch of the same date to Berlin, however, Earl Russell adopted a milder tone.

Her Majesty's Government take a great interest in the welfare of Denmark, and they are glad to learn that Prussia has counselled moderation in respect to the question of Holstein.

It appears to Her Majesty's Government that instead of resorting at once to a Federal Execution, the Diet ought to demand from Denmark a clear and explicit declaration of the meaning of the words 'explanations' and 'negotiation' which she has used in relation to the Royal Letters-Patent of the 30 March.

If these explanations open the way to a satisfactory arrangement all grounds for a Federal Execution will be taken away; and if they do not, the Diet can still resort to a Federal Execution.

Her Majesty's Government are willing to offer their good offices in order to bring about a conciliatory termination of these difficult affairs.[22]

Count Rechberg, the Austrian foreign minister, informed the British ambassador that ''the mediation of a foreign power between the Confederation and Holstein was not to be thought of,''[23] and the slow and formal procedure of the Diet delayed the answer from that body. Bismarck, however, entered with apparent cordiality into the viewpoint of the British government. He and the King were absent from Berlin during the first few days of October, but on the seventh of the month he had a conversation with the British ambassador, which the latter embodied in a memorandum and sent to Bismarck, who was again away from Berlin, for correction and comment.[24] ''Our

[19] Russell to Malet, September 29, 1863. *Denmark and Germany, No. 2, 1864*, No. 137.

[20] *Ibid.*, No. 138.

[21] Russell to Bloomfield and Buchanan, September 30, 1863. *Denmark and Germany, No. 3, 1864*, No. 139.

[22] Russell to Buchanan, September 30, 1863, *ibid.*, No. 140.

[23] Bloomfield to Buchanan, October 8, 1863, *ibid.*, No. 157.

[24] Bismarck, *Die gesammelten Werke*, IV, No. 132.

concern in the Danish affairs is too delicate'' Bismarck wrote to
Sir Andrew Buchanan,

> to be made the object of an authentical [sic] declaration authorized by
> His Majesty; it is not ripe for official proceedings between our Government
> and yours.....I still agree with the idea expressed in the first part of your
> account considering the favorable chance of conciliatory steps to be made
> *after* the entrance of some Hanoverian troops into the Duchy of Holstein.
> But as to the plan of arresting the Execution beforehand, after some con-
> versations I have had at Frankfort I scarcely am allowed to trust that it
> might be successful.
>
> Whatever may be the proceedings of the British Government to prevent
> the disturbance of the peace, it will be advisable to keep them free from the
> appearance of a previous intelligence with Prussia; the supposition of their
> being favored by us, might not only render them ineffectual, but probably
> influence our own conduct in a direction contrary to my personal intentions.
>
> After all there is no reason to hasten the steps that are to be made by you
> at Frankfort; the execution will not be carried forth [sic] before the end of
> next month, and in the meanwhile things may take a turn fit for more
> peaceful proposals.[25]

This letter written ''intentionally in English, in order to take
from the affair all *official* character,''[26] and Bismarck's marginal
notes to Buchanan's memorandum left little more than an empty
shell of the originally almost non-committal negotiation. In
substance Bismarck agreed that if Denmark did not resist the
Execution, ''a proposal for a mediation or for assembling a
Conference to arrange the international and Schleswig questions
would be deemed acceptable by Prussia.'' If Denmark accepted
British mediation and the British Government attempted to
effect an amicable arrangement, the Prussian representative at
the Diet would not be able to vote for it, but ''at all events [he]
will be instructed to employ his influence, in order that interference though unacceptable with regard to purely *German*
affairs, might be declined in a way acknowledging it as a friendly
overture.''[27]

It was very little, but it was more than Great Britain was
obtaining from the other parties to the dispute. Bismarck
committed himself to nothing substantial, but his method of

---

[25] Bismarck, *Die gesammelten Werke*, IV, No. 133.

[26] *Ibid.*, No. 134.

[27] *Ibid.*, p 180.

doing so was gracious and cordially confidential. Meanwhile, Sir Augustus Paget at Copenhagen was struggling with the Danish president of the Council to secure the withdrawal of the March Patent as a possible means of averting the Execution. The best he could obtain was that "although in the absence of the King it was impossible for His Excellency [Hall] to say anything positive in respect to the withdrawal of the Patent, he promised me that if it was not actually withdrawn, the Danish government would state in the reply to the Diet that they did not absolutely adhere to the Patent in its present form, and would be willing to modify it in the sense of the decree of the 8 March 1860; that is to say that its arrangements should be only provisional until the definitive position of Holstein had been settled with Germany."[28] Holstein would be permitted to retain complete control over its legislation and expenditure. The Danish government also agreed to the mediation of the powers who signed the Treaty of London, "reserving the right of explaining the basis on which they will negotiate when they are invited to do so."[29]

Bismarck in the meantime, continued his conversations with Sir Andrew Buchanan. "He would endeavor," he said on October 14,

> to soften down M. von der Pfordten's report [to the Diet], and introduce an opening into it for the acceptance of a mediation on the international question, if such a mediation having previously been accepted by Denmark, should be offered to the Diet. Various pretexts, he said, might also be found on points of form to delay the execution and if the Reichsraad [sic] at Copenhagen adopted the new constitution now under discussion for the affairs of the Kingdom and the Duchy of Schleswig, which it might do in a fortnight or three weeks, he hoped the Danish Government would then withdraw the Edict of March 30 as a preliminary to new negotiations with the Diet as to Holstein and Lauenburg, and give the Diet such satisfaction with respect to these Duchies as would enable Prussia to advocate the abandonment of the Execution.

As a summary of his views, Bismarck accepted Buchanan's minute: "If Denmark would declare to the Diet that she is

[28] Paget to Russell, Copenhagen, October 14, 1863, *Denmark and Germany, No. 3, 1864*, No. 165.

[29] Paget to Russell, telegram, Copenhagen, October 20, 1863, (Record Office, London).

ready to give them satisfaction as to the claim of Holstein and Lauenburg to accept and control their own legislation and the expenditure of all moneys raised in the Duchies, to accept the mediation of Great Britain for the arrangement of the international question, Prussia will endeavor to prevent the execution.''[30]

''My Federal Councillor [sic],'' Bismarck wrote to Buchanan the next day, ''is afraid of public opinion, but I maintain the contents of the minute you took last night trusting that the matter will be discreetly managed; I do not doubt the success especially if our confederates get no scent of 'Prussian influence' in the scheme.''[31]

Again Bismarck promised little: ''Prussia will endeavor to prevent the Execution.'' But he added to his confidences by telling Sir Andrew that at the council of October 14 he [Bismarck] had represented to King William that it was not to the interest of Prussia to support Ultra-German views in the question of the Danish Duchies,

as the King of Denmark if the Schleswig-Holstein question were once settled would probably prove a more useful ally to the King of Prussia and a better neighbor than the Duke of Augustenburg, if His Highness's friends succeeded in placing him, as they hoped eventually to do, on the Ducal throne of an independent Schleswig-Holstein. He said the King of Denmark's interest would make him cultivate the friendship of Prussia whereas a Schleswig-Holstein Duke, from a dread of the eventual absorption of his Duchy in Prussia, would be jealous of her influence in Germany and use his own to thwart her policy and check her power.[32]

In spite of the efforts of British diplomacy, the establishment of a basis for mediation was a slow and difficult process. The Danish government did not believe that a peaceful settlement was probable and made what concessions it did because, on the one hand, the British minister at Copenhagen threatened to write a dispatch emphasizing the fact that it was the obstinacy

[30] Bismarck, *Die gesammelten Werke*, IV, No. 137; Buchanan to Russell, No. 434, Berlin, October 17, 1864, most confidential, (Record Office, London).

[31] (Copy) Bismarck to Buchanan, Berlin, October 15, 1863, private, (Record Office, London).

[32] Buchanan to Russell, Berlin, October 17, 1863, No. 485, most confidential, (Record Office, London).

of Denmark that was preventing an agreement[33] and, on the other, because delay of hostilities until spring when the Danish fleet could operate more effectively was distinctly to Denmark's advantage. There was even no agreement as to the mediator. Denmark was ready to accept, with reservations, the mediation of the powers signatory to the Treaty of London; Bismarck insisted on the mediation of Great Britain alone,[34] a compliment which was not without appeal to the British Foreign Secretary.

The Danish reply to the Diet's decree of October 1 was unsatisfactory and Bismarck reacted sternly to reports that the Danish government had decided to resist the Execution by force.[35] But in other respects he continued to impress his personal moderation upon the British ambassador and the Danish minister. The latter, Quaade, seems to have been convinced of Bismarck's good faith and willingness to do what he could to realize the intentions of the Danish government if he could find the means of doing so without exposing himself to a rebuff.[36]

Indeed some of Bismarck's statements as reported by Quaade have exposed the former to the charge of deliberately leading on the Danish government to persist in a line of policy which Bismarck then treacherously used to justify his attack on Denmark. On October 7, for example, in discussing the importance of separating the questions of Schleswig and Holstein, Bismarck expressed the conviction that the German Diet had not the least intention of exercising its influence over the parts of the Danish Monarchy which did not belong to the Confederation. "He added", wrote Quaade, "that he [Bismarck] had some difficulty in comprehending my objections. He had supposed on the contrary that the proceedings of the Diet corresponded to the wishes of my Government which had desired exactly that

[33] *Denmark and Germany, No. 3*, p. 162.

[34] Quaade to Hall, Berlin, October 28, 1863, *Archives diplomatiques*, (1864), IV, p. 71.

[35] Buchanan to Russell, October 20, 1863. *Denmark and Germany, No. 3, 1864*, No. 181; Quaade to Hall, Berlin, October 21, 1863, *Archives diplomatiques*, (1864), IV, p. 58.

[36] Quaade to Hall, October 31, November 3, 1863, *Archives diplomatiques*, (1864), IV, pp. 72-78.

separation of Holstein. The Diet at present, being about to
carry out that measure, the projects of Danisation in Schleswig
would be only the easier to carry out.''[37] Quaade naturally
denied that the Danish government wished to incorporate
Schleswig with the Kingdom, but when the conversations were
renewed later in October, Bismarck occasionally threw out
similar remarks. ''The first thing necessary according to M. de
Bismarck, to obtain a solution of the serious difference which
occupies us and to avert a conflict as serious as it is imminent,
is to draw a line of demarcation clearly and precisely between
the federal and the international parts of the dispute, and at the
same time, reducing the federal question to its smallest possible
dimensions. There would result from acting in this way a *de
facto* situation consisting of an Eider-Holstein and an Eider-
Denmark. . . . . . .''[38] That such statements of Bismarck's
really were responsible in any great degree for the policy of the
Danish government need not be seriously considered. That
Government had adopted its policy before they were made and
had no intention of modifying it. The conditions that Bismarck
laid down in the same series of conversations as essential for the
success of his moderating efforts were disregarded and no real
weight was laid on his reiteration of the fact that if the conflict
resulted in war, Prussia would not stand aside.[39]

During these same weeks in October, Bismarck supported an
attempt of a somewhat different nature to avert the Execution.
Baron Blixen Finecke, a ''gifted, active and impulsive, but
mercurial'' personality, occupied an unusual position in Danish
politics.[40] With estates in Denmark and Sweden, he was equally
at home in both countries, and his marriage with a sister of Prince
Christian of Glücksburg brought him into close relationship with

[37] Quaade to Hall, Berlin, October 8, 1863, *Archives diplomatiques*, (1864),
IV, pp. 54 ff.
[38] Quaade to Hall, Berlin, October 28, 1863, *Archives diplomatiques*, (1864),
IV, pp. 68 f.
[39] *E. g.*, Quaade to Hall, Berlin, October 8 and 21, 1863, *Archives diplomatiques*,
(1864), IV, pp. 56, 58.
[40] Cf. Aage Friis, ''Blixen Finecke og Bismarck'' in *Danske Magazin*, 6
ser., II, pp. 365-387.

royalty. He had dabbled in politics in the 1850's and, for a few months in 1860, had held the portfolios of minister for foreign affairs and for Schleswig in the shortlived Rottwitt Cabinet. The basis for his friendship with Bismarck had been laid during their student days at Göttingen. They had had some political correspondence on various occasions and in the summer of 1857, Bismarck had been Blixen Finecke's guest in Sweden.

Before Bismarck's appointment as Prussian Minister President, Blixen Finecke had favored a vigorous Eider-Danish policy at the risk of war with Germany. He then changed, not his aims, but his views as to tactics. He believed that Bismarck's policy really was ''to fill out Prussia's thin body,'' to break up the old Confederation and to create a new one with Prussia as the dominant power. He realized Bismarck's aversion to Schleswig-Holstein enthusiasm as the counterpart of German and Prussian Liberalism. He hoped to secure Prussian support for the Eider policy by satisfying Prussian ambitions in Holstein and thus leaving Bismarck, with a friendly Denmark in his rear and with an understanding with Napoleon III., to fight it out with Austria and whatever other elements in Germany might oppose the new order.[41] As the relations between Denmark and Germany became more dangerous in the late summer of 1863, Blixen Finecke was more and more convinced of the futility of the Dano-Swedish alliance negotiations. In view of the critical situation, he decided to take advantage of his personal relations with Bismarck to ward off the danger to which, he believed, Denmark was exposed. In a letter on October 3, he asked if Bismarck would be in a position to prevent the Federal Execution and to turn the question over to negotiations for solution if the Danish Government— the present or a new ministry—at once withdrew the March Patent and its consequences and, at the same time, voluntarily made concessions to the Germans of Schleswig. ''If you could say to me in a few words, which I could show the King, that under those circumstances you would be willing and in a position to

[41] Neergaard, *Under Junigrundloven*, II, p. 752.

stop the Execution, you would—I am convinced—be able to reckon definitely on such concessions.''[42]

These proposals, the substance of which had reached Berlin on the afternoon of October 3 in a telegram from the Prussian chargé at Copenhagen, seem to have made an impression on King William.[43] Bismarck's reply was sent on October 10 from Baden and was received by the Baron on his return to Copenhagen from a visit to King Frederick at Glücksburg in Schleswig.

If the proclamation of March 30 is revoked; if the new arrangements, which, according to the statements of the Ministry, will make it no longer indispensable, do not introduce new complications; if, in addition, the indicated amelioration of the position of the Germans in Schleswig comes to pass; I will vote against the execution and believe that I can put through my views, no matter how warmly Austria and her friends try to carry it out. If the conditions precedent fail, I lose all basis for carrying out my moderate views, and the Confederation is already so far advanced in the matter that even the English mediation will be unable to achieve a practical success.

Bismarck concluded with the expression of the pleasure he would feel if he could negotiate officially with his friend.[44]

According to a telegram of Schlözer the Prussian chargé, the Hall Ministry was shaken as a result of Bismarck's letter to Blixen Finecke. ''Spurred on by the Minister of the Interior,[45] it is straining every nerve to maintain itself.... If the German Confederation presses on calmly and firmly and if our official press comes out for the Execution, Hall's game will be thwarted and there will be a possibility of realizing the plans of Baron Blixen Finecke.''[46]

[42] A. Friis, ''Blixen Finecke og Bismarck'' in *Danske Magazin*, 6 ser., II., pp. 382 ff.

[43] Schlözer to Bismarck, telegram, Copenhagen, October 3, 1863; 2:49 P.M., received, 5:55 P. M., No. 228, (decypher), (Berlin Archives). On a list of dispatches received, King William underlined the number of this telegram and added in pencil: ''Erscheint sehr wichtig. Nicht von der Hand zu weisen....''

[44] A. Friis, ''Blixen Finecke og Bismarck,'' *loc. cit.*, pp. 384. The original contains two unessential paragraphs which are not in the draft in the Berlin Archives as printed in Bismarck, *Die gesammelten Werke*, IV, No. 135.

[45] Orla Lehmann.

[46] Schlözer to Bismarck, telegram, Copenhagen, October 20, 1863; 9:40 A. M., received 12:12 P. M.; No. 234, (decypher). Cf. dispatches Nos. 236, 237, (Berlin Archives).

The *Norddeutsche Allgemeine Zeitung*, therefore, on October 22, contained a vigorous article on the attitude of Denmark and Schlözer was instructed not to make any secret at Copenhagen of its semi-official character.[47] The intrigue, however, failed in spite of Bismarck's support. Blixen Finecke showed Bismarck's letter to Hall and to other Copenhagen politicians as well as to the British minister but the cabinet soon recovered its balance.[48]

At the beginning of November, the Danish government seemed ready to make a slight concession with reference to the control of Holstein over the normal budget. When the matter was referred to a hostile committee by the Frankfurt Diet, Bismarck adopted a passive attitude and excused himself to the British ambassador on the grounds that the concession was inadequate and that he had done all that he could.[49]

When it began to appear likely that the Danish *Rigsraad* would pass the new constitution, Bismarck directed the Prussian minister at Copenhagen to warn the Danish government against it as a violation of the agreements of 1851-52 which would prejudice the proposed British mediation and make a peaceable solution less likely.[50] Count Bernstorff at London was ordered to ask the British government to support these representations.[51] Although Bismarck's dispatch reached Copenhagen only after

[47] Marked copy of the *Norddeutsche Allgemeine Zeitung*, and Bismarck to Schlözer, draft telegram, October 21, 1863, (Berlin Archives).

[48] Neergaard, *Under Junigrundloven*, II, p. 754; Paget to Russell, Copenhagen, October 20, 1863, Most confidential. (Record Office, London); Schlözer to Bismarck, Copenhagen, October 20 and 21, 1863, Nos. 236 and 237, (Berlin Archives).

[49] Cf. Neergaard, *Under Junigrundloven*, II, p. 761; Bismarck, *Die gesammelten Werke*, IV, Nos. 144, 146, 156; Buchanan to Russell, Berlin, No. 502, November 14, 1863 (Record Office, London) extract in *Denmark and Germany, No. 3*, pp. 204 ff.

[50] Bismarck to Balan, November 13, 1863; Bismarck, *Die gesammelten Werke*, IV, No. 151.

[51] Bismarck to the Foreign Office, telegram, Letzlingen, November 11, 1863: "Bitte, an Graf Bernstorff telegraphiren, wie Geheimer Rath Abeken mir geschrieben hat, dass die Vermittlung und Erhaltung friedlichen Beziehungen Aussicht auf Erfolg verlieren, wenn Dänemark mit Einverleibung Schleswigs vorgeht....;" draft telegram to Bernstorff, No. 467, November 12, 1863, (Berlin Archives). Cf. Bismarck, *Die gesammelten Werke*, IV, No. 152.

the constitution had passed its third reading, Herr von Balan was informed that "the possibility was taken into account that the instructions might arrive after the adoption by the Rigsraad. It still lacks the Royal sanction. Make use of the instructions."[52] Before this could be done, King Frederick was dead, but Bismarck transferred the pressure to his successor and requested both Great Britain and Russia to use their influence to prevent King Christian from causing new complications by over hasty action.[53]

It may be true as claimed by his opponents, that Bismarck preferred to see the duchies under the rule of Denmark than under that of the Prince of Augustenburg since it would be easier in the future to find a pretext for taking them away from Denmark than from a German sovereign. It is certainly true that in the existing state of the German Confederation, the creation of a new German dynasty would be likely to add to the opponents of Prussia in the Diet. A safer interpretation of Bismarck's action is that he was confident that the King of Denmark would be unable to follow the advice given him and that it would help Prussia's game to have the Powers believe in his unwillingness to upset the existing arrangements. At the very time that he was putting pressure on King Christian not to consummate by his sanction of the constitution the violation of Denmark's obligations, Bismarck began cautiously to bring forward the policy that was to give him his success: the insistence on the interdependence of the Danish fulfilment of the promises of 1851-1852 and the Prussian recognition of the binding force of the Treaty of London.[54]

The fate of the duchies depended not on King William being able to resist Bismarck but on Bismarck being able to restrain the King from hasty action that might have led to serious intervention by one or more Great Powers. For it was the Great Powers on whom Bismarck fixed his attention and according to their attitude he shaped his tactics. "The Schleswig-Holstein

---

[52] Draft telegram to Balan, No. 290, November 14, 1863, (Berlin Archives.)

[53] Bismarck, *Die gesammelten Werke*, IV, No. 157; Buchanan to Paget, telegram, November 17, 1863, reported in Buchanan to Russell, No. 507, November 17, 1863, (Record Office, London).

[54] Bismarck, *Die gesammelten Werke*, IV, Nos. 160, 161, 164.

question," he once remarked to Lothar Bucher, "was a nut on which we might well have broken our teeth. Denmark didn't worry me; I counted on her making blunders and it was only a question of creating a favorable situation. Austria had to be brought to see that she would dissipate all sympathy in Germany if she didn't go with us; Russia had to be reminded of the services we rendered when Austria wanted to mobilize Germany against her; England had to be isolated so that she would confine herself to threats, as she always does when no one will pull the chestnuts out of the fire for her. The individual actions were, in themselves, trifles; to see that they dove-tailed was the difficulty."[55] The skill with which Bismarck made them dove-tail and his genial handling of the international situation justify him in regarding the Schleswig-Holstein question as his diplomatic masterpiece.[56]

III

Bismarck's first great triumph was to secure the coöperation of Austria. If the two German Great Powers were united in the question, other Powers would think long before venturing armed intervention. Prussia had experienced from 1848 to 1850 what it meant to be one against four; two against three was a much better situation.[57] Bismarck not only got Austria on his side, but he dragged her after him through the tortuous paths of his policy.

Since Bismarck had been in office as Minister President, Austro-Prussian relations had often been strained. The climax was reached after William I had refused to accept Francis Joseph's invitation to the Congress of Princes at Frankfurt in August 1863.[58] When it was seen that the Austrian scheme was leading to absolute fiasco the cabinet of Vienna began to swing

[55] "Aus Bismarcks Leben. Nach Mittheilungen von Lothar Bucher u. a." in Poschinger, *Bismarck-Portfeuille*, III, pp. 114 f.

[56] M. Busch, *Bismarck, Some Secret Pages from his History*, II, p. 337.

[57] Friedjung, *Kampf um die Vorherrschaft in Deutschland*, I, 76.

[58] Cf. R. H. Lord, "Russia and Prussia in 1863," in *American Historical Review*, October 1923; J. Redlich, *Das Oesterreichische Reichs- und Staatsproblem*, II, pp. 766 ff.

away from the minor states and towards the conservative policy of Prussia.[59] Schmerling's policy of making unified Austria the leader of a unified Germany had failed. His star began to sink and the control of affairs passed to his rival, Count Bernhard von Rechberg. The basis of his policy was to maintain the map of Europe in its existing state and he desired to return to the Metternichian system of close coöperation with Prussia.[60]

The chief motive of the Austrian change of front was fear of France. On November 1 an Austrian Council of Ministers had debated the question of what Austria would do in case France, with which power Rechberg did not desire to coöperate, continued her attempts to secure the reconstitution of the Kingdom of Poland[61] but the blow fell sooner than was expected. In his speech from the throne on November 5 to the *Corps Legislatif*, Napoleon III pronounced the phrase: ''The Treaties of 1815 have ceased to exist'' and announced his intention of inviting the Sovereigns of Europe to meet in Congress at Paris to ''regulate the present and secure the future.''[62] The Austrians were not ignorant of Napoleon's views on the reconstruction of Europe and they had every reason to fear that ''the Congress speech'' was the prelude to the loss of Galicia and Venetia.[63]

The Austrian statesmen had little confidence in their own military strength.[64] Russia had been alienated by Austrian ingratitude in the Crimean War and still more in the Polish crisis of the past year; Great Britain, Austria's best friend, was not a strong military power; the only possible ally was Prussia.

It is true that the first reports to reach Vienna after Napoleon's speech were not entirely unfavorable. Count Mülinen, the chargé d'affaires, gained from Drouyn de Lhuys and others, the

---

[59] ''Wenn Ihr es so haben wollt, mit Preussen können wir uns auch verständigen,'' Rechberg said to Beust at the Nuremberg Conference. Beust, *Aus drei Vierteljahrhunderten*, I, p. 336.

[60] Friedjung, ''Graf Bernhard von Rechberg,'' in *Historische Aufsätze*, pp. 313, 314. Cf. F. Engel-Janosi, *Graf Rechberg*, pp. 124, 143ff.

[61] Schlitter, ''Die Frage der Wiederherstellung Polens im Osterreichischen Ministerrat 1863,'' in *Oesterreichische Rundschau*, LVIII (1919), pp. 63-69.

[62] *Das Staatsarchiv*, V, Nos. 916, 918.

[63] Cf. A. Stern, *Geschichte Europas*, IX, pp. 164, 181.

[64] Schlitter, *op. cit.*; Vogt, *Die Hessische Politik*, p. 15.

impression that France was willing to coöperate with Austria to settle *all* questions, even the Danish. "The continuance or abandonment of the entente still rests in Austrian hands, but Napoleon will undoubtedly want a secret understanding for eventual action."[65] Prince Metternich, the ambassador, who had hurried back to his post, telegraphed that his first impression was that the new plan was not based on definite unpleasant objects, but was intended as an escape from an untenable position. "They expect some conditional adhesions and many refusals; they realize our objections but hope to reach an agreement as to the direction to be given the Congress if it succeeds and for action *à deux* if it fails."[66] Count Rechberg had no desire to coöperate with France alone,[67] and he began to sound Prussia for an understanding on the Congress question.[68]

Bismarck at first received the Austrian advances coldly. He welcomed the opportunity to put pressure on Austria and to improve the diplomatic position of Prussia.[69] His wrath at the Austrian attempts at the reform of the Confederation was not turned away by the last note which Count Karolyi, the Austrian minister had read to him on the subject. He accused Austria of trying to frighten Prussia by the threat of an Austro-French alliance,[70] and refused to enter into confidential communications

[65] Mülinen to Rechberg, No. 46B, November 7, 1863, (Vienna Archives).

[66] "Mein erster Eindruck ist dass der neue Plan nicht auf bestimmte unangenehme Ziele sondern vorerst auf Umänderung eine nicht durchzuführenden Situation berechnet wurde. On s'attend à quelques adhésions conditionelles et à beaucoup de réfuses; on prévoit nos objections avec l'espoir de s'entendre sur la direction à donner au Congrès s'il réussit et à l'action à *deux* s'il échoue...." Télégramme, Prince Metternich, Paris, November 11, 1863. Nuit, Chiffre, No. 98. (Vienna Archives).

[67] Schlitter *op. cit.* and telegram, Rechberg to Metternich, referred to in Metternich to Rechberg, telegram No. 98, Paris, November 10, 1863, (Vienna Archives).

[68] "....Graf Rechberg wünscht sehnlichst zu erfahren, wie andere grossmächte diesen vorschlag auffassen...." Werther to Bismarck, Telegram No. 291, November 7, 1863, (Berlin Archives). Cf. Hengelmüller, "Graf Alois Karolyi," in *Deutsche Revue*, August 1914, pp. 225 ff.

[69] Draft telegram, Bismarck to Goltz, No. 443, November 8, 1863, and Goltz to Bismarck, Paris, November 6, 1863, No. 300, (Berlin Archives).

[70] Karolyi to Rechberg, No. 106 A. B., Berlin, November 7, 1863, (Vienna Archives); Bismarck, *Die gesammelten Werke*, IV, No. 155.

with her. He did tell Count Karolyi that if it had not been for the Austrian reform project, his first idea would have been to advise King William to meet Francis Joseph personally to discuss the French Congress and to meet it with an alliance of the Three Eastern Powers. Now he could not take any initiative.[71]

The Austrians realized that the possibility of an *entente* with Prussia depended upon the complete abandonment of the anti-Prussian policy involved in the Congress of Princes while Prussia would probably not give up her anti-Austrian policy in the *Zollverein*.[72] They had to swallow their pride and when the Schleswig-Holstein crisis burst upon them, they were glad to learn from Under Secretary Thile that Prussia intended to remain on the basis of the Treaty of London and would not encourage the claims of its opponents.[73] The rapprochement then came speedily and completely.

[71] " . . . his reason for thus abstaining from entering into confidential communications with Austria, he said applies to all other questions and is the natural consequence of the manner in which Austria has behaved to Prussia with respect to Federal Reform. The Prussian Government being unwilling to take the initiative in renewing any common action with her in the treatment of political affairs. . . . . " Buchanan to Russell, No. 502, November 14, 1863. " . . . The Austrian Minister has asked whether Prussia would concert common action with Austria, and Bismarck answered that the proposal for such action must come from Vienna, as Austria menaced Prussia with a French alliance on the 3rd inst. . . . " Buchanan to Russell, No. 506, November 15, 1863. (Record Office, London). Hengelmüller, "Graf Alois Karolyi," in *Deutsche Revue*, August 1914. "Ew. Excellenz sagen dass Rechberg unsere Standpunkt in der Congress Frage völlig übereinstimmend mit dem seinen finde. Woher kennt Graf Rechberg unsere Standpunkt? Das Telegram No. 492 an Ew. Excellenz erhielt keinen Auftrag zur Mittheilung des Inhalts." Draft telegram, Bismarck to Werther, No. 495, November 15, 1863, (Berlin Archives). A decyphered copy of this telegram is in the Austrian Archives, *Varia de Prusse, 1863.* Karolyi to Rechberg, No. 108 A-D. Vertraulich. November 13, 1863, (Vienna Archives).

[72] Karolyi to Rechberg, No. 109 A. E. Vertraulich, November 21, 1863, (Vienna Archives).

[73] "Nachdem Herr von Bismarck seit zwei Tagen nicht zu sprechen ist, konnte Herr von Thile mir bloss eröffnen dass Preussen auf den Londoner Vertrage stehe und die gegnerischen Ansprüche nicht ermuthigen werde." Telegram, Karolyi to Rechberg, *chiffre*, No. 44, November 20, 1863, (Vienna Archives).

IV

The first meeting of the German Federal Diet after the dynastic change at Copenhagen took place on November 21. The Danish plenipotentiary formally notified the assembly of the death of King Frederick VII and presented his new credentials. Herr von Mohl, the representative of Baden, in accordance with the authorization of his government, then announced the accession of Duke Frederick VIII to the throne of Schleswig-Holstein and protested against the further presence of a representative of the King of Denmark. As had been arranged between Bismarck and Karolyi the night before, Austria and Prussia succeeded in having the question referred to the Committee for Holstein and Lauenburg.[74]

At the next session, on November 28, Herr von der Pfordten, the Bavarian minister, recommended on behalf of the majority of the committee that the vote of Holstein-Lauenburg be suspended, pending a settlement of the succession question. The minority, the representatives of Austria and Prussia, read a declaration that their governments regarded themselves as bound by the treaty which had been signed at London on May 8, 1852 "after certain preliminary conditions had been settled with Denmark in 1851 and 1852." These agreements, they declared, formed an inseparable whole of which the conclusion was the Treaty of London. When the Crown of Denmark fulfilled the preliminary agreements, Austria and Prussia would be ready to carry out their part of the bargain. But regardless of the Treaty of London, they regarded King Christian IX as indisputably entitled to the succession to Lauenburg and his representative, therefore, should be allowed to sit for that duchy. In the vote that followed, the majority report was adopted and the two Great Powers accepted their defeat.[75]

The Austro-Prussian declaration had been adopted after several days of negotiation between Bismarck and Karolyi and

---

[74] Protocol of the 37th session of the Diet, *Das Staatsarchiv*, VI, No. 1033. Hengelmüller, "Graf Alois Karolyi," in *Deutsche Revue*, June 1915, p. 296.

[75] Protocol of the 39th session of the Diet, *Das Staatsarchiv*, VI, No. 1035.

was a distinct victory for the former's policy. Rechberg and
Karolyi had at first insisted on the necessity of Austria and
Prussia acting together at Frankfurt on the basis of the Treaty
of London. Whether Denmark had or had not lived up to the
obligations, on the security of which the German Great Powers
had signed the treaty, made no difference; it remained binding
on Austria and Prussia and they had only the right *subsequently*
to demand the fulfillment by Denmark.[76] Bismarck, however,
upheld the thesis of the solidarity of the Treaty of London with
the previous engagements: "No fulfillment of the Danish
obligations of 1851-52, no Treaty of London."[77] Austria, which
had nothing to gain in Schleswig-Holstein, preferred not to leave
any loopholes, but dared not risk endangering Bismarck's position
with his King. If he were forced out of office, Prussia would go
into the arms of 'the Revolution' and then Austria would have
to follow or completely give up her position in Germany.

At the same time, Bismarck joined with the Austrian Cabinet
in pressing upon the Diet the importance of carrying out the
Execution as soon as possible on the basis already voted. This
question was the more urgent as the minor states were showing
a desire to change the Execution, which they regarded as a tacit
recognition of Christian IX as Duke of Holstein, to an *occupation*
of the duchy to sequester it until it could be turned over to its
rightful sovereign.[78] In a second session of the Diet on November
28, this was actually proposed, but, as usual, referred to the
committee on the affairs of Holstein and Lauenburg. Bismarck
and Karolyi had agreed that Austria and Prussia could submit
to being outvoted on the question of the admission of the Danish
representative to the Diet. But changing the basis of the
Execution was something that might seriously endanger their
relations to the other Powers, and Bismarck proposed, therefore,
that identic notes be sent to all the German states warning them

[76] Thile's memorandum of conversation with Karolyi, Berlin, November 19
1863, (Berlin Archives). Hengelmüller, "Graf Alois Karolyi," in *Deutsche Revue*,
June 1915, p. 296.

[77] Karolyi to Rechberg, telegram, No. 46, November 23, 1863. (Vienna
Archives).

[78] Cf. Bismarck, *Die gesammelten Werke*, IV, nos. 168, 170, 171.

of the danger of following out their policy. In case this did not have the desired result, Austria and Prussia would have to forestall the action of the Confederation by themselves occupying Holstein.[79]

The firmness of the two Great Powers had its effect. At the session of the Diet on December 7, their motion that the Execution be carried out without further delay was adopted, but by a majority of only one vote.[80]

V

The March Patent ostensibly the motive for the Execution, had been revoked on December 4,[81] but in the prevailing excitement this fact was disregarded. On December 24, the troops of Execution entered Lauenburg and Holstein. As had been arranged, the Danish garrisons retired before them and by the last day of the year, the two duchies were in German hands.

In Lauenburg, the people on the whole remained loyal to King Christian but in Holstein, as the Danes retired, the populace declared enthusiastically for the Prince of Augustenburg.[82] On December 30, the Prince arrived in Kiel and took up his residence there.[83] The Federal commissioners bowed to the *fait accompli* and left the unrecognized "Ducal" government undisturbed.

Austria and Prussia had succeeded in imposing their will on the Diet in carrying the vote for Execution but, in the storm of indignation that followed, it became more and more doubtful whether, in the future, a majority could be obtained for any

[79] Hengelmüller, "Graf Alois Karolyi," in *Deutsche Revue*, June 1915, pp. 298 ff.

[80] Protocol of the 40th session of the Diet; *Das Staatsarchiv*, VI, No. 1036.

[81] This had been strongly urged by the British government, and as, now that the November Constitution had been passed, the Danes no longer felt any special need for the Patent, they made the concession.

[82] Jansen-Samwer, *Schleswig-Holsteins Befreiung*, pp. 160 ff.

[83] King William had expressly warned the Prince against creating difficulties for the Federal authorities by going in person to the duchy. But lest he appear faint-hearted in the face of the popular demand for his presence, he decided to take the risk of offending the King. He was confirmed in his decision by the advice of the Court of Baden and especially by the Crown Prince and Princess of Prussia. Gebauer, *Herzog Friedrich VIII*, p. 80.

policy that continued to imply the recognition of the Treaty of London. Not only the people of Germany, but the governments of the 'Middle States' as well were upholding the claims of the Prince of Augustenburg. It seemed for a time as if, under the leadership of Bavaria, Saxony and Wurtemberg, the conduct of the Schleswig-Holstein question might be snatched from the hands of the two Great Powers unless they bent their policy to the will of the nation.

Federal Execution might safeguard the rights of Holstein but could not exert any influence upon the position of Schleswig. It was, however, the question of Schleswig, the international question, which was the danger spot in the relations of Germany with the Great Powers who upheld the principle of the integrity of the Danish Monarchy, and Austria and Prussia could not afford to let the situation escape from their control. If Federal troops stood on the Eider, there would constantly be danger that they would cross it to tear up the Treaty of London and would thus bring on foreign intervention. In order to forestall this danger, Austria and Prussia decided that the Eider must be crossed in support of the Treaty of London. If the Diet could be brought to accept this policy, so much the better; if not, Austria and Prussia must act in their capacity as European Great Powers.

At the session of the Diet on December 28, the Austrian and Prussian representatives proposed that the Confederation occupy Schleswig as a material pledge for the fulfilment of the Danish obligations of 1851-1852. It was soon clear, however, that there was little likelihood of a majority being obtained for this.[84]

The procedure to be followed by Austria and Prussia in case of defeat in the Diet was arranged during the first weeks of January and a protocol for common action was signed by Bismarck and Karolyi on January 17. With one exception, the six articles adopted were those of the text drafted by Rechberg, but the one exception shows how Bismarck gave the policy adopted in harmony with Austria the slight turns that were necessary to

[84] A preliminary test of strength, the vote on January 2, 1864, on an Austro-Prussian motion that the Prince of Augustenburg be expelled from Holstein, showed the Great Powers in a hopeless minority in the Diet.

the carrying out of his policy. Rechberg's version of Article V provided that in case of hostilities with Denmark and the consequent abrogation of the existing treaty relations between the German Powers and Denmark, the Courts of Austria and Prussia reserved the right to regulate the relations of the duchies on another basis than that of the agreements of 1851-1852. Only by mutual agreement would they declare themselves released from the principle of the maintenance of the integrity of the Danish Monarchy and from the obligation to recognize the succession of King Christian to all of its parts as provided by the Treaty of London. Such a clause, of course, would have insured Austria against Prussian attempts to secure the duchies for herself. Bismarck, however, proposed the variant that in case of hostilities with Denmark, the future relations of the duchies and especially the question of the succession would be settled only by mutual agreement. This left open the question of the denunciation of the Treaty of London and, though at first, Karolyi objected, he was finally authorized to sign. The Austrian Government was convinced by Bismarck that King William would refuse to be bound further and was comforted by the thought that in case of future complications, the provision that the future of the duchies should be settled only by mutual consent gave sufficient hold on Prussia.[85]

On January 14, the Austro-Prussian motion for the occupation of Schleswig as material pledge for the fulfilment by Denmark of the obligations of 1851-1852 was rejected by the Diet. Thereupon, the Austrian and Prussian representatives announced that their governments intended to act on their own account. On

---

[85] For details of the negotiations which led up to this agreement, cf. von Sybel, *Die Begründung des deutschen Reiches*, III, pp. 207-214 and Hengelmüller, "Graf Alois Karolyi" in *Deutsche Revue*, July 1915, pp. 78-85. According to Friedjung, *Der Kampf um die Vorherrschaft in Deutschland*, I, p. 80, the agreement was reached on January 16. Because of the difficulty with regard to Article V, the actual signature did not take place until January 17, 12:30 P. M. Karolyi to Rechberg, No. 8 A-B, January 17, 1864. Rechberg telegraphed to Karolyi at 7:45 P. M. on January 16 authorizing him to sign the agreement and stating that Austria had no objection to dating it January 16. (Vienna Archives). The other points had been accepted some days before so that the ultimatum to Denmark could be ordered as soon as the report of the action of the Diet was received.

January 16, the Ministers of the two Powers at Copenhagen presented an ultimatum demanding the withdrawal of the November Constitution within forty-eight hours. The reply was a refusal; diplomatic relations were broken off. In spite of the presence of the Federal army the Austro-Prussian forces which had been gathered in readiness, marched into Holstein and advanced towards the frontier of Schleswig. On the morning of February 1, the allied troops began to cross the Eider into Schleswig.

VI

The Austrian and Prussian governments were acting in the closest harmony but their ultimate aims were very different. The national excitement in Germany made it impossible for Francis Joseph, who regarded himself as the first among the German princes, to stand aside when a German interest was at stake. Rechberg, who was directing Austrian policy, wished to see the Schleswig-Holstein question settled with as little change in existing arrangements as possible and Austria's objective remained the consolidation of the Danish Monarchy on a conservative basis.

It was necessary to give some satisfaction to German public opinion but it was hoped that this could be limited to the restoration of the old real union of Schleswig and Holstein, leaving them united in personal union with the crown of Denmark under the beneficent ægis of the Treaty of London. National movements, whether Danish or German were not in favor at Vienna. Schmerling, advised that the Prince of Augustenburg should not be too sharply rejected and that Austria should not give up her coöperation with the 'Middle States' but Francis Joseph had been convinced by the failure of the Congress of Princes at Frankfurt that Schmerling's German policy was impossible. For the time being, Rechberg's policy in foreign affairs held the emperor's confidence.[86] Rechberg, to be sure, was a little suspicious that

---

[86] Friedjung, *Der Kampf um die Vorherrschaft in Deutschland*, I, pp. 74 f; Redlich, *Das österreichische Reichs- und Staatsproblem*, II, p. 384.

Bismarck still had unrevealed, ulterior aims. He told the Hessian minister at Vienna that he would not permit Prussia to annex the duchies and even spoke of the alliance with Prussia as "merely ephemeral." He expressed some doubt as to whether, in a conflict with a non-German Power, Austria would have Prussia as an ally, though he was rather scornful of the lesser German states and preferred the conservative policy of coöperation with Prussia on the basis of respect for existing treaties.[87]

Prussia, however, was in a position to profit by a change in the *status quo*. Even if King William were proof against the temptation of the annexation of the duchies to Prussia, a German duchy of Schleswig-Holstein would, from its very geographical location, be in Prussia's sphere of influence. The Prussian sovereign had little to fear from the application of the principle of nationality. He was eager for the abandonment of the Treaty of London and of the integrity of the Danish Monarchy. So was his Minister President.[88] But Bismarck, unlike his master, was convinced that the time had not yet come and that, if it were to come at all, the situation must be carefully prepared. The struggle was a hard one and at first Bismarck could obtain from King William merely the concession that Prussia would not declare herself free from her treaty obligations until the November Constitution went formally into effect on January 1, 1864. Even for that he had to use the threat of resignation.[89] The King, who urgently felt the need of Bismarck's support for his internal policy and who was more and more upset by the revolutionary aspect which the Augustenburg agitation was taking on, was held to his minister's policy of caution.[90]

[87] E. Vogt, *Die hessische Politik in der Zeit der Reichsgründung, (1863-1871)*, pp. 20 f; Friedjung, *Der Kampf um die Vorherrschaft in Deutschland*, I, pp. 74 f; Redlich, *Das österreichische Reichs- und Staatsproblem*, II, pp. 767 f.

[88] *Aus dem Leben Theodor von Bernhardis*, V, p. 195; Von Sybel to Robert von Mohl, December 4, 1863, in Heyderhoff and Wentzcke, *Deutscher Liberalismus im Zeitalter Bismarcks*, I, p. 193.

[89] Cf. *Anhang zu den Gedanken und Erinnerungen von Otto Fürst von Bismarck*, I, pp. 86 f.

[90] Cf. *Kaiser Wilhelms I. Briefe an seine Schwester Alexandrine und deren Sohn Grossherzog Friedrich Franz II*, No. 60.

The King's attitude was very useful to Bismarck, however, in forcing the Austrian policy to adopt the modifications he wished to impose on it. To Count Karolyi, the Austrian minister at Berlin, Bismarck appeared as the best support of the Treaty of London.[91] If the compromises to which he won the King were not accepted by Vienna, Bismarck would fall from power and the consequences for Austria might be disastrous.[92]

Although to the Austrian minister, Bismarck appeared in agreement with Austrian policy, to King William he represented himself as differing mainly in method. Even after the first of January, he argued against immediate denunciation of the Treaty of London. Such action, he insisted, would be in the interest not of Prussia but of the Augustenburg succession. He disputed the right of the Diet at Frankfurt to give the decision in a succession question and claimed that the rights of the Augustenburg House applied only to portions of Holstein. If Prussia denounced the Treaty of 1852, Austria would abandon her and leave her, single-handed, to face a conflict with the other signatory Powers. It would, therefore, be advisable to follow the path indicated by the Austro-Prussian motion for the occupation of Schleswig and to keep in mind as the "provisional" aim of Prussian policy the personal union of the united duchies with Denmark and the establishment of Rendsburg as a Federal fortress. Faced by the unanimous opinion of the ministry, the King decided, "for weighty reasons of expediency," not to yield to the ardent advice of the Crown Prince and to his own personal desire for immediate denunciation of the Treaty of London and support of the Augustenburg claims. He insisted, however, that if the occupation of Schleswig led to war with Denmark, the aim of his policy should be no longer the program of 1852 but the

---

[91] Karolyi to Rechberg, No. 7B, January 16, 1864, (Vienna Archives).

[92] Rechberg had much less confidence in a "ministry of the left," than he did in Bismarck. Cf. his opinion expressed in a council on May 19, 1863, in Redlich, *Das österreichische Reichs- und Staatsproblem*, II, pp. 767 f. Bismarck recognized the hold that this gave him. Cf. his letter to Goltz, Bismarck, *Die Gedanken und Erinnerungen*, II, p. 3, and his remarks to Hohenthal, the Saxon Minister in Hessell, *König Albert von Sachsen als Kronprinz*, II, p. 164.

complete separation of the duchies from Denmark and their annexation to Germany.[93]

Bismarck had already made up his mind that the result of the war should be the annexation of the duchies not to Germany but to Prussia. On New Year's eve, in the intimacy of the family circle, he disclosed his real policy. ''The 'up ewig unge-deelt'[94] must some day be Prussian. That is the goal toward which I am steering; whether I reach it rests in God's hands. But I could not take the responsibility for letting Prussian blood be shed just to create a new 'middle state' which would always vote with the others against us in the Diet.''[95]

It was apparently not until a council meeting on February 3, however, after hostilities had actually commenced, that Bismarck revealed his secret to the King. In discussing the draft of an Austro-Prussian identic note to England, His Majesty objected to the phrase that Prussia, in proceeding with the occupation of Schleswig, did not have the intention of abandoning the principle of the integrity of the Danish Monarchy. Bismarck replied that, out of regard for Austria, it would be impossible to make last minute changes but that he would never have recommended the draft if he had been of the opinion that by it Prussia was permanently and definitely bound to maintain the integrity of the Danish Monarchy. He was far from wanting to maintain that integrity. He looked, rather, to the union of the duchies of Schleswig and Holstein with the Prussian monarchy as the ultimate goal of the warlike operations that had just begun. He had often expressed the opinion that the present hostilities would probably lead to a general European war. If, as was to be hoped, Prussia was successful, Schleswig and Holstein must be kept in mind as suitable compensation. He must, therefore, stand definitely against favoring the Augustenburg claims which would place a permanent obstacle in the way of the acquisition

---

[93] Protocols of the Crown Councils of January 2 and 3, 1864. Stern, *Geschichte Europas*, IX, pp. 582 ff. Cf. Jansen-Samwer, *Schleswig-Holsteins Befreiung*, p. 193.

[94] Schleswig-Holstein.

[95] Keudell, *Fürst und Fürstin Bismarck*, p. 140.

of those lands by Prussia and would materially strengthen the 'Middle State' group in Germany, which was necessarily hostile to the development of the Prussian state. If the complications led to a breach with England, France would probably offer Prussia an alliance and, in case this were refused, come to an understanding with England. If Prussia had to face such dangers, the establishment of the Augustenburg dynasty in the duchies would not be a satisfactory equivalent. King William finally accepted the proposed note as recommended but what the Minister President had set forth as the object of the war, he wrote on the margin of the protocol of the council proceedings, was not the only aim of Prussian policy but merely one of the possible eventualities.[96]   Prussian policy, like Austrian, continued

[96] Protocol of the council of February 3, 1864, No. 53. Through the kindness of the Prussian Ministry, I was permitted to consult the original protocols in the archives of the Ministry of State. The pertinent sections have since been published in Stern, *Geschichte Europas*, IX, pp. 582-586. It is difficult to reconcile some of the details of Bismarck's testimony with the evidence of the protocols. In the *Gedanken und Erinnerungen*, II, pp. 8 f., Bismarck says: "Die Abstufungen, welche in der dänischen Frage erreichbar erschienen und deren jede für die Herzogthümer einen Fortschritt zum Bessern im Vergleich mit dem vorhandenen Zustande bedeutete, gipfelten m. E. in Erwerbung der Herzogthümer fur Preussen, wie ich sofort nach dem Tode Friedrichs VII in einen Conseil ausgesprochen habe. Ich erinnerte den König daran, dass jeder seiner nächsten Vorfahren—selbst seinen Bruder nicht ausgenommen—für den Staat einen Zuwachs gewonnen habe, Friedrich Wilhelm IV. Hohenzollern und das Jahdegebiet, Friedrich Wilhelm II. Polen, Friedrich II. Schlesien, Friedrich Wilhelm I. Altvorpommern, der Grosse Kurfürst Hinterpommern und Magdeburg, Minden u. s. w., und ermunterte ihn, ein Gleiches zu thun. In dem Protokolle fehlte diese meine Aeusserung. Der Geh. Rath. Costenoble, der die Protokolle zu führen hatte, sagte, von mir zur Rede gestellt, der König hätte gemeint, es würde mir lieber sein, wenn meine Auslassungen nicht protokollarisch festgelegt würden; Seine Majestät schien geglaubt zu haben, dass ich unter bacchischen Eindrücken eines Frühstücks gesprochen hätte und froh sein würde, nichts weiter davon zu hören. Ich bestand aber auf der Einschaltung, die auch erfolgte. Der Kronprinz hätte während ich sprach, die Hände zum Himmel erhoben, als wenn er an meinen gesunden Sinnen zweifelte; meine Collegen verhielten sich schweigend." A number of parallel versions have been printed and analyzed by Pahncke, *Die Parallel-Erzählungen Bismarcks zu seinen Gedanken und Erinnerungen*, pp. 110 ff. Bismarck, *op. cit.*, II, p. 11, dates this council in December; Keudell and others think that Bismarck is referring to the Council of January 2 and 3, 1864; Keudell, *Fürst und Fürstin Bismarck*, pp. 142 f. and note. It is difficult to maintain this date as against the clear evidence of the protocols. On the other hand, Bismarck states that the Crown Prince was present

on the basis of respect for the Treaty of London, but it was so shaped that it could lead to the abrogation of that treaty.

at the council meeting. According to Philippson, *Kaiser Friedrich III*, p. 142, the Prince joined army headquarters on January 31. He was present, however, at the meeting on January 29, of which that of February 3 was a continuation and it is possible that on that occasion, Bismarck began the disclosure of his aims. In a letter to Bismarck on April 17, 1864, (Phillippson, *op. cit.*, p. 152), Frederick William wrote: "...wenn ich nicht etwa aus einigen Andeutungen auf gewisse Hintergedanken schliessen soll, die mann Ihnen beilegt, und mit denen allerdings manche Ihrer früheren Aeusserungen, namentlich in den letzten Konseils, denen ich vor meinen Abgang zur Armee beiwohnte übereinstimmen scheinen. Ueber diese Hintergedanken einer preussischen Vergrösserungspolitik...." If the Crown Prince had actually heard the speech Bismarck says he made, or if he had seen the protocol of the meeting of February 3, his letter to Bismarck would hardly have referred to Bismarck's intentions in such indefinite terms. The protocol does not, to be sure, contain Bismarck's historical summary but it does report the main points and arguments and is not, of course, intended to be a verbatim report. On the basis of the protocols, I agree with Stern that it was probably on February 3 that Bismarck disclosed his policy to the King. R. Sternfeld, "Der Preussische Kronrat von 2/3 Jan. 1864" in *Historische Zeitschrift*, CXXXI, pp. 72-80 dissents from Stern's opinion. The Crown Prince's diary throws little new light on this problem. The entries for January 2, 3, 4, 6, 29, tend to confirm Stern's view; that for April 16, Sternfeld's. Kaiser Friedrich III., *Tagebücher von 1848-1866*, pp. 231f., 236, 334.

CHAPTER IV

THE INTERNATIONAL SITUATION ON THE EVE OF THE WAR

I

In 1848-1850, Denmark had been rescued from the attacks of Germany by the intervention of Great Britain and Russia. In 1864, no effective intervention took place, notwithstanding the fact that, in the meantime, in 1852, the Powers had recognized by formal treaty the importance of the integrity of the Danish Monarchy as an element of the European Balance of Power. This difference in the attitude of the Powers was due to changes in the general international situation which Bismarck knew how to exploit in masterly fashion.

During the summer of 1863, the international situation had been favorable to Denmark. The two German Great Powers were divided. Austria was grouped with Denmark's friends, France and Great Britain. Prussia stood with Russia, which, while not as friendly to Denmark as in the past, was interested in the maintenance of the *status quo*. At the end of the year and throughout the war, the grouping of the Great Powers favored Prussia. Austria, Russia, and Great Britain were suspicious of France. Outwardly, Prussia stood with this group but her relations with France were cordial and confidential. France was cool to Great Britain and almost hostile to Austria. In opposition to France, Great Britain stood with the Eastern Powers; in the Danish question, she was isolated.

This grouping had begun to form as a result of the failure of Austria and Great Britain to support Napoleon's policy in the Polish question to the limit; it was crystallized by Napoleon's Congress proposal at the beginning of November 1863.

II

In November and December 1863, the foreign policy of France was based on the Emperor's proposal of a great Congress of Sovereigns of Europe meeting at Paris "to settle the present and to secure the future."[1] Such a congress was an old element in Napoleon's ideology,[2] but while both before and after 1863, he attempted to bring about congresses, it was more for the prevention of imminent wars than for the general application of the *idées Napoléoniennes* to the map of Europe. None of these congresses ever met, yet this proposal of November 1863 exercised an influence on the grouping of the Powers and on succeeding events that raises its importance far above that of any of the other proposed congresses.

Of course, to a certain extent Napoleon's *"coup de théâtre"* of November 5, 1863, was an attempt to escape from the *impasse* to which his Polish policy had brought him. Yet at times he seems to have believed sincerely that the opportunity had come for a peaceful and permanent settlement of the questions which were troubling Europe. As in so much of Napoleon's foreign policy there was in this plan a curious mixture of Utopia and Machiavelli, and at first, at least, the former seems to have predominated. As Prince Metternich, the Austrian ambassador, expressed it: "He has placed himself upon a pedestal, on which he admires himself and on the base of which he has inscribed 'raprochement de ma dynastie avec les autres—entente amicale— et *impartialité poussée jusqu'à l'abnégation'* ".[3] Lord Cowley, the British ambassador wrote later that it would be unfair to doubt that Napoleon really believed in the success of the Congress[4] and Lord Dufferin, who visited the Emperor at Compiègne wrote that Napoleon's predominant feeling was astonishment at

---

[1] *Archives diplomatiques*, (1863), IV, p. 188.

[2] Cf. F. A. Simpson, *Louis Napoleon and the Recovery of France, 1848-1856*, p. 41.

[3] Metternich to Rechberg, No. 49 A-B., November 17, 1863, (Vienna Archives).

[4] Cowley to Russell, No. 1160, Most confidential, Paris, December 15, 1863, (Record Office, London).

the mistrust of him in England, "real bona fide surprise;. . . . . None of those about him whom we imagine he most trusts seem really in possession of what the French call 'le fond de sa pensée,' and I confess I could not feel certain whether the regret he expressed at our rejection of his Congress was real or assumed. The Frenchmen I talked to seemed to consider his design had been serious and had not yet recovered their astonishment at discovering he was in earnest, for they had at first imagined it had been simply a parade to cover his retreat from the Polish difficulty."[5] The other Powers, however, had little confidence in Napoleon's impartiality or abnegation. Their indignation and alarm, especially at the statement that "the treaties of 1815 have ceased to exist" led to an exchange of views as to how the Congress could be averted.[6] As the Power which could least

[5] Dufferin to the Duke of Argyll, December 20, 1863, Lyall, *Dufferin*, I, 135-139.

[6] "Le Comte de Bernstorff me télégraphie: 'J'apprends de source certaine et très confidentielle que la Reine...trouve la démarche fort impertinente.' Le Baron Werther télégraphie: 'Le Comte de Rechberg craint le Congrès dont il désapprouve le principe, espérant que le projet en échouera devant un refus de l'Angleterre.....' " Copy of draft telegram, Bismarck to Redern, No. 427, November 7, 1863. Gorchakov seems not to have been averse to the idea. "Le Prince Gortchakoff m'assure qu'aucune entente, pas même un échange d'idées n'avait eu lieu entre la France et la Russie au sujet du Congrès. Toutefois le Vice-Chancelier m'a donné à entendre très confidentiellement, que la Russie, ayant déjà au mois d'Avril dernier mis en avant l'idée d'un congrès, qui aurait à examiner l'ensemble de la situation politique, ne saurait s'y opposer aujourd'hui." Redern to Bismarck, telegram No. 129. November 11, 1863. 3:30 P. M. When the telegraphic report of Napoleon's speech reached him, Gorchakov was "bei einer Partie Whist mit denjenigen intimen Personen, welche stets seine Abendgesellschaft bilden. Durch eine jener Personen, erfahre ich dass der Fürst bei dem Lesen jener Depesche sehr unverholen seine Freude uber die Congress Vorschlage mit den Worten: 'Je m'y associe de grand coeur' ausgesprochen und mehreremale hervorgehoben hat wie gelegen und genehm ihm derselbe sei." Redern to Bismarck. No. 130. November 12, 1863. Vertraulich. Tsar Alexander, however, exclaimed: "Der Streich ist doch zu stark." Ausszug. Aeusserung Sr. Majestät des Kaisers von Russland gegen den Oberst u. Flügeladjutanten Freiherrn von Loën. November 16, 1863. (Berlin Archives). Russell's first impression was not unfavorable, but Palmerston seems to have opposed it from the beginning. ". . . .My own impression is that Congress is practicable, but that they must soon arrive at the question of War or no War. Is it easier to take that question in a Congress or by common diplomatic means?. . . . . ." Draft telegram, Russell to Cowley, sent November 7, 1863, 2:30 A. M., (Record Office, London). Cf. Ashley, *Palmerston*, II, pp. 236 ff.

easily be affected materially by Napoleon's resentment, the decisive rejection was left to Great Britain and Earl Russell's note of November 25, made the Congress impossible.

The flat refusal, and especially the fact that it was published in London before it was received by the French government,[7] was felt by Napoleon to have been a bitter insult. It increased the coolness between the two governments with serious consequences for the Schleswig-Holstein question.

The congress proposal accelerated the change in the grouping of the Great Powers which had begun with the failure of the diplomatic campaign in the Polish question. Napoleon turned away from Great Britain and Austria, and towards Prussia and Russia. As it became clearer that a general understanding of the Powers was impossible, he devoted his efforts to the formation of a system of alliances for France.

III

As early as June 8, 1863, Napoleon III seems to have been ready to restore the confidential relations with Prussia which had been disturbed by Bismarck's support of Russia in the Polish question[8] and at the end of August, Count Goltz, the Prussian ambassador at Paris wrote to Bismarck that he and "Caesar" were "one heart and one soul."[9] In the first weeks of November, the question of a Franco-Prussian *entente* was again taken up.

In his first conversation with Count Goltz about Napoleon's speech from the throne, Drouyn de Lhuys, Napoleon's minister for foreign affairs, hinted at a desire to coöperate with Prussia at the Congress, or even if the Congress did not meet. "As far as Prussia in particular is concerned," he said, " . . . .it seems that our proposition is of a nature to facilitate your escape from

---

[7] It appeared in the Gazette on November 27, but was not read to Drouyn de Lhuys by Lord Cowley until November 28.

[8] Cf. Prince Henry VII of Reuss's notes of his interesting conversation with Napoleon, Fontainebleau, June 8, 1863. H. Oncken, *Die Rheinpolitik Kaiser Napoleons III*, I, pp. 17-21.

[9] Paris, 31 August 1863, Kohl, *Bismarck Jahrbuch*, V, p. 219.

the difficulties against which you are struggling in the interior and in Germany. Beyond that it could serve us to make closer our relations, which have never been bad, but which have been chilled because we have been discussing the question of Poland alone, on which question we are not in agreement. You will recall that I have several times expressed the desire of doing something with you: perhaps the moment has arrived...."[10] A few days later, he spoke more definitely: "......if Russia and Prussia, or even Prussia alone and some of the second rate Powers consented to join with us, their deliberation could lead to important results."[11]

For Bismarck's policy, the break-up of the Anglo-Austrian-French *entente*, and especially the coolness between France and Austria which the congress proposal called forth, was of inestimable value, and he hastened to express to the French ambassador, his personal agreement with the idea of the Congress. The action of France in the Polish question had, to be sure, given the Prussian government cause for anxiety and had disturbed the pleasant impressions which the King had brought back from his visit to Compiègne in 1861. Bismarck hoped, however, that full confidence would soon be restored as he, personally, had complete confidence in the frankness and amicable intentions of the Emperor.[12]

King William, who received Napoleon's invitation from the hands of the French ambassador on November 13, expressed his

---

[10] "Pour ce qui concerne en particulier la Prusse...il me semble que notre proposition soit de nature a vous faciliter de sortir des difficultés contre lesquelles vous luttez à l'intérieure et en Allemagne. Elle pourra en outre, nous servir a reserrer no relations, qui n'ont jamais étés mauvaises, mais qui cependant avaient étés refroidies parceque nous ne discutions que la question de Pologne seule, sur laquelle nous n'étions pas d'accord. Vous vous rappelerez que je vous ai plusieurs fois exprimé le désir de faire quelque chose ensemble avec vous: peut-être que ce moment est arrivé..." Goltz to Bismarck, No. 306, November 8, 1863. Confidentielle, (Berlin Archives). Sybel, "Napoléon III", in *Kleine historische Schriften*, III, pp. 605 f.

[11] Goltz to Bismarck, No. 311, confidential, Paris, November 14, 1863, (Berlin Archives).

[12] Bismarck to Goltz, November 8, 1863. Bismarck, *Die gesammelten Werke*, IV, No. 150.

agreement with the Congress in principle and merely suggested that a preliminary agreement of the Great Powers and a meeting of the chief ministers instead of the Sovereigns would be more expedient. The treaties of 1815 in so far as they had not been modified by treaty, he regarded as still in full force. His formal reply maintained these points of view.[13] The suggested modifications, of course, would have deprived the Congress of part of the glamor with which Napoleon desired to surround it, but the cordial tone of the King's letter and especially the mention of his visit in Compiègne made Napoleon regard it as the most satisfactory of the replies from the Great Powers.[14]

The death of the King of Denmark and the consequent development of the Schleswig-Holstein question offered the French government not only a useful illustration of the need for a Congress but also a definite point of *rapprochement* with Prussia. "Acceptance of the Congress promptly and without reservations," said Drouyn de Lhuys on November 16 to Count Moltke-Hvitfeldt the Danish minister, "will be very desirable. It will be pleasing to the Emperor and will be a happy inauguration of the relations between his Majesty and King Christian. If the Congress meets..., your question will be discussed and you may be sure of our support."[15] "We regret sincerely the death of the King", Drouyn de Lhuys telegraphed that evening to the French minister at Copenhagen. "Say to King Christian that the best way of inaugurating his relations with the Emperor would be to accept without delay, and without hesitation, the invitation of his Majesty. Before Germany, Denmark loses her case; before Europe, she may win it. Her interest then, is to refer it to a European Congress."[16] And again on November 26,

---

[13] Bismarck, *Die gesammelten Werke*, IV, No. 153; *Das Staatsarchiv*, V, No. 975.

[14] Goltz to Bismarck, No. 322, Compiègne, November 23, 1863; confidential, (Berlin Archives); Metternich to Rechberg, No. 54-B, November 27, 1863, (Vienna Archives).

[15] Moltke-Hvitfeldt to Hall, telegram, November 16, 1863, (Copenhagen Archives).

[16] Drouyn de Lhuys to Dotézac, telegram, Paris, November 16, 1863, 6 p. m. (Paris Archives).

Count Moltke-Hvitfeldt found that the French minister showed the "same sympathetic disposition to our cause, which he has always evidenced and the sincerity of which I cannot doubt. But", he found it necessary to add, "I am not the only one who is satisfied with the attitude of the imperial Government... Count Goltz had had a long conversation with the Emperor on our question and has told several people that he has every reason to be contented with the way in which His Majesty has expressed himself....."[17]

If the Danish minister had known what Drouyn de Lhuys and Napoleon had been saying to Count Goltz, he would have been anything but convinced of the sincerity of their dispositions towards Denmark. The Prussian ambassador, too, had seen Drouyn de Lhuys on November 22 and had given his personal opinion of the various phases of the conflict. The French minister did not at this time take up Goltz's remarks that France had less interest than any of the other Great Powers in the maintenance of the order of succession established by the Treaty of London, that this question offered France an opportunity to show at the same time her sympathy for a national cause and her respect for old established rights, and that the plan for a Scandinavian Union could be realized only after the separation of the German territories from Denmark. He answered briefly that while, on the one hand, France could not arbitrarily declare herself free from the obligations of a treaty which had been signed but twelve years before, yet, on the other hand, great weight ought to be laid on the wishes of the German nation and, if the Congress met, France would make a sincere effort to pay due respect to both points of view.

Later in the day, when Count Goltz presented the King's letter to Napoleon at Compiègne, where he was the Emperor's guest, the latter spoke plainly of his desire for an *entente* with Prussia. "I have nothing to demand from you, but you cannot conceal from yourselves the fact that you cannot continue in your present situation. Prussia is surrounded by a crowd of small

<hr/>

[17] Moltke-Hvitfeldt to Hall, November 23 and November 26, 1863, (Copenhagen Archives).

states which hamper its action without adding to its strength. I had hoped that the meeting of the Sovereigns would give the opportunity of establishing an understanding between us on this as well as on the other great questions.''[18]

The next day Goltz brought Drouyn de Lhuys a copy of Bismarck's circular of November 20,[19] and after a perfunctory discussion of the dispatch spoke of the division of Schleswig according to nationalities, leaving the Danish part unconditionally to the Kingdom, as a solution which might now be acceptable to Germany. In reply to this Drouyn de Lhuys expressed the opinion that if such a separation according to nationalities, especially in view of the possibility of a closer union of the Scandinavian lands, were to be put through the Congress, it would be better not to create a new small duchy out of the German section, but to give this territory to Prussia,[20] which would administer it well and would probably know how to make it of use for increasing her maritime power.'' When he hinted at compensation, Goltz answered that Prussia had no provinces to give away, whereupon Drouyn de Lhuys hastened to remark that he was not thinking of territorial cessions. Compensation could mean perhaps a money indemnity to Denmark, giving the Duke of Augustenburg a distinguished position in Prussia, or services to other Powers in other questions.''[21]

---

[18] Goltz to King William, Compiègne, November 23, 1863, (Berlin Archives). See Appendix IV. Sybel, III, p. 167, erroneously places the conversation on November 23. Brandenburg, *Untersuchungen und Aktenstücke zur Geschichte der Reichsgründung*, p. 400, says: ''Daher suchte Napoleon gleich nach dem Tode des dänischen Königs in der Frage der Herzogthümer Fühlung mit Preussen zu gewinnen und eine gemeinsame Aktion aller deutschen Staaten zu hintertreiben.'' Rather, the death of the King of Denmark occurred while Napoleon was seeking closer relations with Prussia.

[19] Cf. Bismarck, *Die gesammelten Werke*, IV, No. 161.

[20] In conversation with Talleyrand, on November 18, Bismarck had shown his opposition to the Augustenburg claims. ''Pour la Prusse,'' m'a dit M. de Bismarck, ''je préfère le Roi de Danemark à Kiel et à Altona, qu'un Duc de Holstein, qui, par peur de notre voisinage se croira obligé, comme tant d'autres Princes de nous faire de l'opposition a Francfort....'' Talleyrand to Drouyn de Lhuys, No. 116, November 19, 1863. Marked: ''Cabinet 21 Novembre 1863.'' (Paris Archives).

[21] Goltz to Bismarck No. 34, Compiègne, November 23, 1863, (Berlin Ar-

After dinner on the evening of November 24, Goltz had a final chat with Napoleon.   In the Schleswig-Holstein question, the Emperor declared that, while his sympathies were on the side of nationality, he would remain neutral.   The conflict, however, showed clearly the need for the Congress.   He was, he said, completely satisfied with the King of Prussia's letter and was sincerely grateful for it, but he had little hope, in view of the attitude of most of the Great Powers, that the meeting would produce any important results.   It remained for him to take into consideration the forming of new alliances and he wished one with Prussia.[22]   Goltz welcomed the idea put implied that the time was not yet ripe.   ''Agreement in almost all European questions—from which I except only the Polish—will of itself lead to this goal.   It is a question of time, I might say a question of temperament: one of us wants to steer directly towards it, the other believes that the object can be more surely attained by a cautious attitude and a gradual rapprochement.''   He noted with delight, however, that Napoleon not only did not rebut his statement that on the basis of its present policy France could ally itself with England,[23] Russia, or Prussia, but never with Austria, but also agreed with the statement that as the existence of Austria rested only on treaties, that Power could not tolerate a policy based on the principle of nationality.[24]

After the British rejection of the Congress, Napoleon increased his efforts to bring about an alliance with Russia and Prussia.   To Goltz, Drouyn de Lhuys expressed himself as well satisfied with the Russian reply to Napoleon's invitation and pretended that the position of France was better than before the Congress proposal.[25]   France had shown her pacific and conciliatory tendencies and she had been able to ascertain which powers

chives). Sybel, III, p. 167, makes no distinction between the two separate conversations. The chronology in Goltz's dispatch is, however, perfectly clear.

[22] Hierauf bliebe vorzugsweise die Bildung eines Allianz-Systems ins Auge zu fassen und ein solches würde er wünschen mit Preussen einzugehen.

[23] This was before the publication of Russell's note on the Congress.

[24] Goltz to Bismarck, No. 323, Compiègne, November 24, 1863 (Berlin Archives).

[25] Goltz to Bismarck, telegram, No. 325, November 28, 1863; 5:10 P. M. (Berlin Archives)

had views coinciding with hers. "If you now have something to whisper in our ears, we shall listen to you attentively. If we on the other hand wish an understanding with you on any question we shall not hesitate to tell you so."[26] Baron Budberg's audience to present the Tsar's letter to Napoleon occurred on November 30 and in general had a stormier course than that of Goltz on November 22.[27] But to Budberg Napoleon spoke as he had to Goltz of a new system of alliances: that he had attempted an alliance with England and Austria which had failed and that he now desired to revert to a combination which he had always preferred—an alliance between France, Russia, and Prussia.[28] Napoleon suggested that it would not be incompatible with Russian interests to grant Poland independence and to take Eastern Galicia or the Danubian Principalities in exchange. Budberg, however, declared that on this question there was no possibility of agreement and he left the audience with the conviction that Napoleon would begin a war in the spring probably against Austria.[29]

Goltz believed that the time had come when it would be necessary for Prussia to take a definite position,[30] and warned his government that if the attitude of the two Great German Powers, as foreshadowed by their identic vote of November 28 at the Diet,[31] should develop into a complete solidarity, Prussia would soon take, in the eyes of Napoleon, the position of Austria "which now seems to be the object of his first attack." To Goltz, the Schleswig-Holstein question more than any other seemed suited to vigorous action on the part of the Prussian government. He wished to see Prussia place itself at the head of the national movement in Germany, lead in this way "the mod-

[26] Goltz to Bismarck, No. 326, Paris, November 29, 1863, confidential, (Berlin Archives).

[27] Cf. pp. 116 f.

[28] Napier to Russell, No. 825, St Petersburg December 31, 1863, most confidential (Record Office, London).

[29] Goltz to Bismarck, No 327, December 1, 1863, most confidential, Appendix IV (2), pp. 296 f.

[30] Goltz to Bismarck December 1, 1863, Kohl, *Bismarck Jahrbuch*, V, p. 230.

[31] Cf. p. 99 above.

erate elements in its own land in a sounder direction,'' and with the middle and small states follow a policy in opposition to Austria.[32]

Bismarck, however, preferred the policy of coöperation with Austria. He wanted to settle the Schleswig-Holstein question not in accordance with National, Liberal methods, but in the interests of the conservative, monarchical Prussian policy. ''The more sensible and moderate elements,'' he answered,

> form a constantly diminishing minority in the movement which is sweeping through Germany. To attain even a temporary community of action with the real leaders of it, I regard as impossible, because incompatible with the existence of an orderly state of affairs in Prussia. I believe, therefore, that we ought to lay more weight on our alliances with the other Great Powers than on agreement with the present direction of public opinion, and believe rather in directing our policy toward open conflict than toward open alliance with the national and revolutionary movement which is preparing. I cannot, therefore, advise his Majesty to sacrifice to the impression which our conduct may make on the public, any prospects of European alliances.[33]

It is true, of course, that Napoleon had often spoken in favor of the annexation of Schleswig and Holstein to Prussia and that in coöperation with France, it might have been easier for Bismarck to secure this than by an alliance with Austria, which Power he knew would oppose it. On the other hand alliance with France might well have been the prelude to a general European war, in which Prussia would take the lion's share of risk. Alliance with Austria and the maintenance of a conservative policy and action based on recognized treaty rights, offered the possibility of carrying through the war against Denmark without serious outside intervention. There was no reason for him to trust Napoleon,[34] and it was a safer policy not to antagonize Austria, Russia and Great Britain by an open association with France. It would still be possible that by skilful diplomacy, he could keep Napoleon friendly. ''I do not wish,'' Bismarck told

---

[32] Goltz to Bismarck, No. 328, December 1, 1863, (Berlin Archives).

[33] Bismarck to Goltz, No. 497, December 20, 1863, Bismarck, *Die gesammelten Werke*, IV, No. 191. Cf. Bismarck to Goltz, December 24, 1863. Kohl, *Bismarck Jahrbuch*, V, pp. 232-233; Bismarck, *Gedanken und Erinnerungen*, II, pp. 1-8.

[34] Bismarck's marginalia to Goltz's letter; Kohl, *Bismarck Jahrbuch*, V, p. 241.

the French ambassador that he had said to the King, "to throw down the gauntlet into darkness and without knowing who will pick it up. I cannot expose myself at one blow to the polite observations of France, to the violent recriminations of England, to the paternal admonitions of Russia, and, finally, to be coolly abandoned by Austria, who may well be tempted to show herself moderate at our expense. I shall not, then, take a step without her and without her sharing our risks and perils."[35] But even if Bismarck, personally, had wished for the French alliance it would have been extremely difficult to bring King William to accept it.[36] He still looked with horror upon the idea of an alliance with France and wished sincerely to remain on good terms with Francis Joseph.

To keep on good terms with all the Great Powers was not easy, but Bismarck succeeded in doing it. The possibility which it afforded him of balancing between France on the one hand and England, Russia and Austria on the other and of swinging easily from side to side was of great value in carrying out his policy.

The French proposal of a Congress to be held in Paris even without the participation of Great Britain, which was communicated to the Powers by a circular dispatch of Drouyn de Lhuys on December 8,[37] gave Bismarck an opportunity to consolidate

[35] Talleyrand to Drouyn de Lhuys, No. 125, December 11, 1863, (Paris Archives).

[36] Bismarck's statement: "Da ich aus Eurer Majestät allerhöchster Randbemerkung zu meinem gestrigen Schreiben in Betreff des französischen Vorschlage von Neuem ersehe, dass Allerhöchstdiesselben nach wie vor die bestehenden guten Beziehungen zu England, Russland und Oestreich erhalten wollen, und dass der Gedanke einer französischen Allianz Eurer Majestät fern liegt," should not, I think, be interpreted as meaning that Bismarck favored such an alliance, but merely as holding up before the King the alternative of a policy to which he (the King) was fundamentally opposed as a scarecrow to hold him from yielding to the Augustenburg influences, which would mean a breach with the other three Powers. *Anhang zu den Gedanken und Erinnerungen von Otto Fürst von Bismarck*, I, p. 94. At the head of Goltz's dispatch of November 24, 1863, (cf. p. 118 above), King William had scrawled: "Was soll es heiss—dass Gf. Goltz immer von einer möglichen französ Preuss-Allianz spricht? Dazu ist er von mir *nie* autorisirt worden!"

[37] *Les Archives diplomatiques*, (1864), I, p. 79. It is curious to note that French writers date this December 18. *Les Origines diplomatiques de la guerre de 1870-71*, I, p. 2; Muret. "La Politique Française dans l'affaire des Duchés," p.

his relations with the other Powers and, at the same time, to adopt a more cordial attitude than they towards France.[38] He took a leading part in establishing an understanding among the governments that they would decline a general congress of the sovereigns and suggested that instead they agree to accept a conference at Paris, to which Great Britain should be invited, to deal with the Danish question only. Bismarck had no real desire to see even this question settled by a conference but he regarded the proposition as a means of cultivating the favorable dispositions of Napoleon in the Schleswig-Holstein question and of using them as a means of putting pressure on Great Britain. As he wrote to the Prussian ambassador at Paris,

until we can forecast more clearly the form which the relations of the Great Powers to each other will take as a result of the conflict with Denmark, it will be necessary for us to keep the congress question in flux, to cultivate our relations with France on that basis and to employ the favorable dispositions of the Emperor Napoleon as a means of pressure on England and its attitude towards Danish affairs.

It is in this sense that your Excellency will understand the proposal which we have directed to London, Petersburg and Vienna concerning a conference on Danish affairs. In spite of the detailed responses which we have received from Vienna, Petersburg and London, it is not at all probable that a definite declaration of willingness to attend will follow quickly; it does not seem to me certain that it will follow at all. If it should, we would admit to negotiation only the international side of the German-Danish question, not the federal one of Holstein, and would thus retain the final conclusion in our own hands. .... Should the conference come to pass, I should look upon it less as a means of solving the Danish question than as the terrain on which the alliances for the presumably impending European war would form themselves. That would not exclude our striving at the same time to secure the arrangement of the Danish question that would be most favorable to the interests of Prussia.

In the present stage of the congress question, it is for us I repeat, to retain our good relations with France and to utilize these where possible against the Danophil tendencies of England.[39]

154. Drouyn de Lhuys told the British ambassador that the project was largely Napoleon's personal policy. Cowley to Russell, December 15, 1863, No. 1161, (Record Office, London).

[38] Cf. Talleyrand to Drouyn de Lhuys, Berlin, December 17, 1863, Appendix IV, pp. 297 ff.

[39] Bismarck to Goltz, December 20, 1863, Bismarck, *Die gesammelten Werke*, IV, No. 191.

Bismarck held up before the British ministers the spectre of a new Confederation of the Rhine forming in southern and western Germany to force the two Great Powers to adopt the national policy against Denmark. To the British ambassador at Berlin, Bismarck spoke of the critical condition of Germany, observing that Baden was drifting rapidly to revolution.

He would not be surprised if Austria and Prussia were called upon ere long to contend with a new Confederation of the Rhine established under the protection of the Emperor of the French, and he asked what support Austria and Prussia might expect from England in such an eventuality, adding that it might be necessary soon that they should know upon what assistance they could calculate, for if Prussia did not see her way clearly in her resistance to the democratic influences which were now driving the country towards war with Denmark, she might be carried away by the stream and the King might yield to the entreaties of those who wish him to place himself at the head of the popular movement of the day. ....[40]

A few days before, he had telegraphed a similar appeal to the Prussian ambassador at London,

Reports from Paris give rise to the fear that with the complete failure of the congress idea, Napoleon is preparing a revolutionary war for next spring, to begin by a rising in Galicia. A conference at Paris without England is as little adapted to assure peace and is contrary to our [good] relations with England. If England wishes peace maintained, would Lord Russell regard as a suitable means the participation of England in a conference of ministers to be held at Paris on the Danish question alone? The impression of the complete fiasco of Napoleon's congress idea would thus be avoided. Questions dangerous to the peace of the Great Powers; i. e., Poland, Italy and the Eastern Question remain excluded. ....[41]

Goltz's warning reports from Paris may perhaps have made Bismarck believe that there was danger from France in case Napoleon's ideas were not given due consideration. But the visit of General Fleury in Berlin on his return trip from Copenhagen gave Bismarck an opportunity to learn more definitely from one of the Emperor's confidential agents what his real attitude was. What was perhaps more important, it gave him a chance to impress upon Naploeon that his, Bismarck's, personal

---

[40] Buchanan to Russell, December 21, 1863, No. 264, confidential, (Record Office, London). The conversation took place on December 20.

[41] Bismarck, *Die gesammelten Werke*, IV, No. 186.

policy was more in accordance with the former's views than that
which he was compelled for the present to adopt, and to dangle
before the Emperor, brilliant prospects for the future. Goltz,
who was opposing Bismarck's policy at this time was not a
satisfactory channel for confidential communication of this
nature.[42]

The mission of General Fleury to Copenhagen and Berlin
presents a good example of the secret, personal diplomacy of
Napoleon III and of the methods by which Bismarck manipulated
the Emperor. Ostensibly, General Fleury's mission was the
same as that of the envoys of the other Great Powers: to congratulate King Christian on his accession and confidentially to
put pressure on Denmark to fulfill her obligations. But the
secret object of the mission was to make another attempt to
secure the combination which Napoleon had been trying to
bring about: an alliance of France, Prussia and Russia.

At Copenhagen, General Fleury made overtures to M. d'Ewers,
the Russian Envoy, for a better understanding between France
and Russia,[43] and then went to Berlin to make a last attempt with
Bismarck.[44]

---

[42] "Il [Goltz] s'échauffe mal à propos," me disait le Bon de Bismarck, "et
s'entête à voir une offense a l'honneur allemand dans une conférence réunie à
Paris sur les affaires du Schleswig-Holstein. J'ai été obligé de lui écrire une lettre
particulière, où je lui donne à entendre qu'il serait impossible à [sic] Ministre des
Affaires Etrangères de conserver à Paris un ambassadeur qui ne s'identifierait pas
avec sa politique extérieure." Talleyrand to Drouyn de Lhuys, Berlin, December
22, 1863. No. 131, (Paris Archives). Cf. Bismarck's well-known letter to Goltz,
December 24, 1863; Bismarck, *Gedanken und Erinnerungen*, II, pp. 1-8; Kohl,
Bismarck Jahrbuch, V, pp. 232-238.

[43] "I have seen a letter from M. d'Ewers to Prince Gortchakoff marked 'Secret'...M. d'Ewers states that General Fleury plainly originated overtures for a
(Note 43 continued on next page).

---

[44] Fleury, *Souvenirs*, II, p. 278. The interpretation usually given to the
phrase "j'étais munis d'instructions secrètes pour Berlin, où je devais tenter un
dernier effort auprès de M. de Bismarck" in the sense of a last effort to prevent the
war, seems to me, in spite of the context, untenable, except, perhaps, with the
saving clause "in order to pave the way for the Congress." It is rather, I think,
to be interpreted as a last attempt to secure the Prussian alliance; "last" in the
sense of the last of the series of attempts made during November and December.
Cf. Frahm, "Die politische Lage beim ausbruch des deutsch-dänischen Krieges,"
in *Historische Vierteljahrschrift*, XVI (1913), p. 527.

The account of General Fleury's mission in Berlin as given in his memoirs,[45] and especially his condensed telegraphic summary of his conversation with Bismarck, is tantalizingly unsatisfactory in its details. But it fits clearly enough into the story of Franco-Prussian negotiations. The first long conversation opened with a discussion of the Danish constitution and the situation in Copenhagen, but then turned to broader questions. Bismarck insisted now that the Congress must be limited to the question of the Duchies. A Congress, even one limited to the Powers signatory to the Treaty of London, would be impossible if it were intended to deal with affairs in general. Prussia and Russia would not come any more than would England and Austria.

"Rather die," said Bismarck, "than permit discussion of our possessions in Posen. I would rather cede our Rhenish provinces."[46]

better understanding between France and Russia. He stated with that confidence which characterizes upstart Frenchmen that the national pride of Russia must now be satisfied; that although there had been some expressions unacceptable to Russia in the Emperor's speech, full justice had been rendered to Russia in that passage in which her services to France were recognized in the question of Savoy and Nice; nothing now divided the two Governments; but as the last advantage had remained with Russia, it was for her to make the first advances. 'Let your Emperor,' said General Fleury, 'send some [one] in his confidence to Paris. Our Sovereign will immediately send some one in his confidence to St. Petersburg— myself for instance. We shall then soon come to an understanding.'

"Opposite the passage respecting Savoy and Nice Prince Gortchakoff had written 'quel aveuglement cinique.'

"M. d'Ewers received the expressions of General Fleury with great caution. At the top of the sheet, in the handwriting of the Emperor, I observed 'I entirely approve the reserve of M. d'Ewers on this occasion'...." Napier to Russell, No. 828, December 31, 1863, secret and confidential, (Record Office, London).

[45] Fleury, *Souvenirs*, II, ch. LXIV, *Les Origines diplomatiques de la guerre de 1870-71*, I, No. 1. Bismarck's explanations to the Russian and Austrian ambassadors cannot, of course, be taken as giving a true picture of what occurred.

[46] The dispatches of the French Ambassadors in Berlin have given other examples of Bismarck's use of casual remarks of this nature to suggest to France the possibility of territorial gains. *E. g.*: "Quant à moi," ajouta M. de Bismarck, "s'il me fallait opter, je préferais voir la France s'emparer de la Belgique, étendre même au delà ses frontières que la Prusse renoncer aux avantages territoriaux que lui a fait le partage de la Pologne." Talleyrand to Drouyn de Lhuys, February 23, 1863 (quoted without reference in Ollivier, *L'Empire libéral*, VI, p. 116); December 17, 1863, (Paris Archives).

But he would do his best to have the interested Powers come to the special Congress, which should meet in Paris as a satisfaction to Napoleon.

This, he implied, would be the first step toward a future Franco-Prussian entente,

the bridge,[47] by which to make the King pass, who is very fearful of his family of princes and princesses, very sentimental toward Austria in the German question, still quite on edge about the question of Poland and French opinion on that subject. Bismarck himself would lose all his strength in Germany by separating from Austria in the German Question.

Nothing then possible later, if we do not start with the Danish question. Everything will rise from that and the situations will shape themselves.

As for projects of aggrandisement, of preponderance at the expense of Austria, that is understood.[48] As for the Rhine frontier, the word has been pronounced. Should it be accentuated?

But to arrange with the King, in fine to form an alliance, there is no other chance than the Danish Congress.

As for Russia, nothing to be done with a crash, as the Emperor thinks. The reconciliation ought to come about of itself, by sending another ambassador in place of Montebello, who no longer has any authority.[49]

[47] "....The Russian Minister at Berlin reports the substance of a conversation between General Fleury and M. de Bismarck related by the latter. The General, in speaking of the proposal for a limited conference of certain powers at Paris on the Danish Question alone, observed to M. de Bismarck, 'This is a golden bridge which you raise for England to pass out of her isolation.' M. de Bismarck says that he did not 'take any notice of this remark, but he thought in his heart that the bridge was cast rather upon the Seine than upon the Thames.' " Napier to Russell, No. 828, December 31, 1863, secret and confidential, (Record Office, London).

[48] On his arrival in Berlin, Fleury found the following telegram from Napoleon: "...Je n'ai pas d'autres instructions à vous donner. Si la Prusse se met à la tête des petits Etats de l'Allemagne, elle prendra sa revanche du congrès de Francfort; mais pour que nous la soutenions, il faut qu'elle s'entend avec nous." Fleury Souvenirs, II, p. 281. Döhler, Napoleon III und die deutsch-dänische Frage, p. 37, regards this as a warning against common action with the Middle States. Such an interpretation seems to me absurd; the message rather suggests such a course. Fleury says, op. cit., II, p. 283: "Sauver le Danemark de la guerre, tout en soutenant les prétentions d'agrandissement de la Prusse en Allemagne en échange des concessions promises à la France, telle était la politique de l'Empereur."

[49] "Comte Walewski m'assure tenir de source authentique que Général Fleury aurait rapporté de Berlin proposition de la Prusse de servir d'intermédier pour ramener l'ancienne intimité avec la Russie et insinuer de servir les intérêts de l'Empereur en Italie s'il consent à laisser la Prusse s'annexer Kiel et les Duchés et de donner le Danemarc à la Suède. L'Empereur aurait refusé de s'engager mais laissera faire la Prusse pour se donner un droit de compensation. Lord Cowley m'en a aussi parlé comme d'une affaire à laquelle poussent le Comte Morny et M.

The result was all that Bismarck could have desired.

"We have done on the side of Denmark all that we could do," was Napoleon's telegraphic reply. "In regard to the congress limited to Denmark, answer that you will refer the matter to your government. Don't talk about the Rhine and calm him about Posen."[50]

Napoleon did not accept the plan for a conference limited to the Danish question as an adequate substitute for his greater idea.[51] He still seems to have hoped that the increasing danger of war would lead the other Powers to accept the Congress. If it did not, he was prepared to sit back and let matters come to a head, trusting that the future might bring about developments more to his liking, hoping that something might turn up advantageous to France.

He continued, therefore, to encourage Prussia to adopt an active policy. On January 6, Drouyn de Lhuys reminded Count Goltz of their conversations of the previous November at Compiègne and repeated the opinion he had then expressed that the best solution of the Schleswig-Holstein question would be the annexation of Denmark to Sweden and of the duchies to Prussia. At a court ball, that same evening, the Emperor, too, spoke of his preference for a far-reaching settlement.[52] About a week later, Drouyn de Lhuys again discussed the situation with Goltz. He expressed his concern that Denmark would not voluntarily evacuate Schleswig and that the first cannon shot would be the signal for a general European war. It was curious, he remarked, that the two most conservative governments of Europe, the Prussian and the Austrian, should start a war, while France, which was so often suspected of such an intention, should

Fould." Metternich to Rechberg, No. 2, January 9, 1864. Cf. Bismarck's commentary in Karolyi to Rechberg, No. 11B, January 24, 1864. (Vienna Archives). Cf. p. 314 below.

[50] Fleury, *Souvenirs*, II, p. 285, *Les Origines diplomatiques de la guerre de 1870-71*, I, No. 2.

[51] Muret, "La Politique française dans l'affaire des Duchés," in *Revue d'histoire moderne et contemporaine*, XVI, pp. 137-169, 300-333.

[52] Goltz to Bismarck, No. 6, Paris, January 7, 1864, (Berlin Archives); extract in Hähnsen, *Ursprung und Geschichte des Artikels V des Prager Friedens*, I, pp. 17 f.

be avoiding any intervention in the conflict. "He attempted in the further course of his remarks," Goltz reported to King William, "to show that Prussia, which, aside from the establishment of the Zollverein, had not for a long time had any outstanding success to its credit, must now undertake an independent and decisive course of action to maintain its position. He followed this with the repeated expression of the wish he has so often indicated to me for our alliance with France and said that this latter Power did not seek conquests, but if everyone else was aggrandized, France could naturally not look on passively."[53]

Goltz gained the impression from these remarks of Drouyn de Lhuys that the French minister regarded a European war as inevitable and that the Imperial Government intended to give Prussia the choice between an alliance with France or a war against her. He did not yet grasp the true import of Bismarck's policy nor did he, apparently, know the details of Bismarck's conversations with General Fleury and with the French ambassador at Berlin. He replied to Drouyn de Lhuys that he did not think it right or expedient to call an alliance into being without special occasion.

If the Congress had met, we might perhaps have come to it, but as matters now stood, we should, if we concluded an alliance with France, expose ourselves also to unjustified suspicions. In Germany, especially, people would not fail to charge that we were aggrandizing ourselves at the expense of our German allies and that we intended to turn over the left bank of the Rhine to France. I should, therefore, regard it as a more correct line of policy to follow out with firmness and vigor a question of such great importance to Prussian and German interests as that of Schleswig-Holstein, in the measure of those interests and, in that way, to determine who were our true friends and who our real foes. If this line of policy should lead to an alliance with France, it would be very popular in Germany and no one could accuse us of betraying German interests and this would not exclude the possibility of counter services by us to France.[54]

Bismarck, however, assured Talleyrand that he had impressed upon King William the importance of securing, if possible, the

---

[53] Goltz to King William, No. 19, Paris, January 14, 1864, (received January 17), (Berlin Archives). Extract printed in Oncken, *Die Rheinpolitik Kaiser Napoleons III*, I, pp. 24 f.

[54] *Ibid.*

support of the Emperor Napoleon and kept dangling before the French ambassador the prospect of a civil war in Germany.[55] Both Napoleon and his minister were nevertheless more and more disturbed by the continued close coöperation of the two German Great Powers. Reports were reaching Paris that, in return for support in the Schleswig-Holstein question, Prussia had guaranteed to Austria the possession of her non-German territories.[56] The French diplomats were instructed to verify this[57] and Drouyn de Lhuys formally asked Goltz whether it was true.[58] The categorical denial was accepted and Napoleon continued his watchful waiting.[59]

IV

In 1848-1850, Nicholas I had intervened in the German-Danish struggle as the 'conservative policeman' of Europe. But after the disasters of the Crimean War, Russian foreign policy became cautious and unassertive. Occupied with constructive reforms at home and desirous of letting his Empire recuperate from the collapse to which the policy of Nicholas had brought it, Alexander II wished to avoid as far as possible any international adventures. In 1863, Russia had been strained still further by the necessity of crushing the revolt in Poland. The Empire, roused by the threatened intervention of France, England and Austria, had indeed shown signs of defensive strength but was not yet in a position to adopt the vigorous offensive policy that would have been required by armed intervention in favor of Denmark.[60]

[55] *Les Origines diplomatiques de la guerre de 1870-1871*, I, Nos. 38, 39, 63, 90, 129, 152.

[56] *Ibid.*, Nos. 45 and 87.   [57] *Ibid.*, Nos. 45 and 114.

[58] Goltz to Bismarck, telegram No. 36, January 27, 1864, 5:40 P. M., received 8 P. M.; Goltz to King William, No. 37, January 28, 1864; (Berlin Archives).

[59] Bismarck to Goltz, draft telegram, No. 31, secret, January 27; Goltz to Bismarck, No. 43, confidential, February 1, 1864; (Berlin Archives).

[60] "I need not enlarge upon the diminution of Russian Power. Your Lordship is well aware to what extent, and by what agencies, this Empire has been reduced to a state of comparative prostration, from which the patriotism of its people can now only arouse it for defensive purposes in a national cause." Napier to Russell, No. 33, confidential, January 11, 1864, (Record Office, London).

Moreover, the attitude of Russia toward the two states principally involved, had undergone a change. Bismarck had shown his friendliness to Russia at the time of the Crimean War, and, when he had become Prussian Minister President, had earned the gratitude of Russia and especially of Tsar Alexander by his vigorous and ostentatious action in the Polish crisis.[61] Denmark, however, had joined with the 'Western Powers' in protesting to Russia in favor of the Poles.[62]

The Russian government still desired to see the integrity of the Danish monarchy maintained. It had no more desire in 1863-1864 than before to see a German fleet in the Baltic based on Kiel nor to see Denmark so weakened by the loss of the duchies that it would join with Sweden-Norway in a Scandinavian union and thus place the entrance to the Baltic in the hands of a single fairly strong power. But Russia did not understand, nor had she sympathy with the national ambitions of the Eider Danes. Even in 1850, when Russia was exerting herself in the interest of Denmark, this had been clearly shown. ''What difference does it make to you,'' Nesselrode had said to the Danish minister, ''that the Duchies have a common bank and that the lunatic asylum belongs to them in common?''[63]

Although it sympathized with King Christian personally, the Russian government disapproved of the democratic tendencies of Denmark. Gorchakov and Tsar Alexander made no secret to the Danish government of the facts that they regarded the November Constitution as a violation of Denmark's obligations

[61] Cf. R. H. Lord, ''Bismarck and Russia in 1863'' in *American Historical Review*, XXIX, pp. 24-48.

[62] Neergaard, *Under Junigrundloven*, II, 658-664. Napier to Russell, No. 33, confidential, January 11, 1864. (Record Office, London). ''While the Government and the nation would be little inclined to an active policy abroad, and little capable of undertaking it with effect, we must remember that the Government and the Court are bound by peculiar ties of intimacy and gratitude to Prussia, in consideration of the great services rendered by that state to Russia in regard to Poland. It would be considered an act of ingratitude and baseness here to turn against Prussia, and particularly against the Government of M. de Bismarck, when their efforts and sacrifices in the Russian cause are so fresh on the recollection and so marked by the blame of Europe.''

[63] O. Plessen to Moltke, No. 36, June 8, 1850, (Copenhagen Archives).

and that Denmark could not count on their support as long as there was persistence in the policy it involved. Russia had advised King Christian not to sanction the constitution. When Count Otto Plessen, the Danish minister, tried to justify the policy of the King and government, Gorchakov frankly expressed his disapproval.

"You talk to me so often," he said, "of the necessities of your domestic politics; but I who am called upon to direct the policy of Russia, have to take account also of the necessities of domestic politics of those with whom you are in conflict," and he added: "It is impossible for me not to find, that by this last act, the Royal sanction, you have failed to respect your engagements to Germany." Plessen's rejoinder, that Germany had failed to respect her engagements by attempting to extend her action to the non-German parts of the Danish Monarchy, was coolly received and was appreciated, he writes, "as an observation that I could not maintain before an impartial tribunal."[64] This attitude was confirmed and emphasized by the Tsar when Plessen had an audience to present his new credentials.

"Not only from my personal sympathies—they are of long standing and the King knows it—but also from my very sincere interest for Denmark," said the Tsar,

I will do what I can. But you know that already for some time we have found that in your policy toward Germany, you have been drawing the cord too tight. We shall be consistent.... If unhappily war should break out between you and Germany, I cannot take part in it; you know our situation, you ought to understand. .... I don't want to say anything painful to you; we are merely consistent; we have often warned you. .... I admit that the movement against you in Germany has at present in part a revolutionary basis; but on your part, too, there are also—don't take it amiss that I speak of it—symptoms of exaggerated tendencies. .... All that I can do, I will do.[65]

With the Prussian minister, Gorchakov was more reserved. He at first evaded an answer to the request that Russia put pressure on the King of Denmark not to sanction the new

[64] O. Plessen to Hall, No. 68, November 24, 1863, (Copenhagen Archives).

[65] O. Plessen to Hall, No. 72, December 10, 1863, (Copenhagen Archives). The audience took place on December 9.

constitution, pointing out the dangers to Christian's position, should he fail to do so. But he finally gave his consent and later read to Count Redern a sharp note which he had despatched to Copenhagen.[66] When the news came that King Christian had signed he expressed his regret at this action.[67] For the months of November and December 1863, the Prussian archives throw little direct light on Gorchakov's relations with Bismarck.[68] There is no reason to assume, however, that these relations were at all discouraging to Bismarck, whose moderate attitude in regard to the Treaty of London and in opposition to the liberal and national agitation in Germany was bearing good fruit.[69]

V

The British government was greatly disturbed by the news of the death of the King of Denmark[70] and the consequent excitement in Germany. Two days before, Lord Russell had temporarily abandoned his attempts to arrange a mediation between Denmark and Germany,[71] but he now again brought his pen into action in

[66] Count Redern attributed this action partly to the influence of the Danish Minister "welcher in der Sanction der Gesammt-Verfassung eine Gefährdung der Gesammt-Monarchie erblickte." Redern to Bismarck, November 20, 1863, (Berlin Archives).

[67] Redern to Bismarck, telegram No. 131, November 19, 1863; dispatch November 20, 1863, (Berlin Archives). Cf. Napier to Russell, November 20, 1863, *Denmark and Germany, No. 3, 1864*, No. 286.

[68] Redern to Bismarck, No. 130, *höchst vertraulich*, December 1, 1863, (Berlin Archives). Gorchakov said to Redern: "J'en ai dit deux mots à Mr. d'Oubril. Il communique tout à Monsieur de Bismarck. Nous n'avons pas de secret pour vous et je ne vous cache rien." Next to this there is a marginal note in King William's hand: "Wie lauten die—2 mots?"

[69] "It is thought here of the highest importance to support M. de Bismarck in every way. He is considered the only bulwark against war with Denmark and revolutionary agitation." Napier to Russell, telegram, St. Petersburg, December 23, 1863, (Record Office, London). Cf. Napier to Russell, December 1, 1863, *Denmark and Germany, No. 3, 1864*, No. 359.

[70] Bernstorff to King William, No. 398; to Bismarck No. 399, November 16, 1863; to King William, No. 404, November 20, 1863, (Berlin Archives).

[71] Russell to Buchanan, November 13, 1863, *Denmark and Germany, No. 3, 1864*, No. 224; Bernstorff to Bismarck, telegram, November 17, 1863, (Berlin Archives).

an effort to secure time for a peaceful settlement. To Berlin and Vienna he expressed the hope that the news of the change of dynasty would induce the Diet to delay the carrying into effect of the Federal Execution to allow the new King of Denmark to consider his position and to form his ministry.[72] Two days later, he offered British mediation on the international question at issue: the relations of Schleswig to Denmark proper and to the German Confederation and the position of Holstein in the Danish Monarchy.[73] In the meantime, he had to consider the question of the new Danish constitution and telegraphed to Sir Augustus Paget at Copenhagen that while Her Majesty's government was very unwilling to interfere in the matter, if the King wished the mediation to be effectual, he might suspend his signature until the international questions were settled.[74] These first efforts, however, led to no result[75] and with the news of the proclamation of the Prince of Augustenburg, Russell changed his tactics. He had at first tried to delay the Execution; he now urged that it be carried out as quickly as possible because it would imply a recognition by the Diet of Christian IX as Duke of Holstein.[76]

The next day he shifted again. A dispatch from Vienna stated

[72] Russell to Buchanan, telegram, November 16, 1863, 6.00 P. M., (Record Office, London); to Buchanan and Bloomfield, November 16, 1863, *Denmark and Germany, No. 3, 1864*, No. 235.

[73] Russell to Malet; to Paget, November 18, 1863, *Denmark and Germany, No. 3, 1864*, Nos. 239, 237; Russell to Buchanan, November 18, 1863, telegram, 1:40 P. M., (Record Office, London); Buchanan to Bismarck, Berlin, November 18, 1863, confidential, (Berlin Archives).

[74] Russell to Paget, telegram, November 17, 1863, 11:10 A. M. (Record Office, London). On November 17, Russell told the Danish minister in London, however, "que si d'un côté il serait peut-être sage pour Sa Majesté d'attendre un peu avant de sanctionner cette mesure et pour le motif allégué par M. de Bismarck, d'un autre côté il se pourrait qu'une pareille hésitation de la part du nouveau Roi fût mal accueillie en Danemark et entachât d'inpopularité les premiers actes du nouveau Souverain. ...D'ailleurs la question constitutionelle dont il s'agissait était, selon le ministre, une affaire de politique intérieure...." Bille to Hall, No. 94, November 18, 1863, (Copenhagen Archives).

[75] Cf. Russell to Paget, telegram, November 18, 1863. 2:15 P. M., (Record Office, London); Hall to Paget, November 20, 1863, *Denmark and Germany, No. 3, 1864*, No. 384, enclosure.

[76] Bernstorff to Bismarck, November 22, 1863, Sybel, *Die Begründung des deutschen Reiches*, III, p. 163.

that Rechberg said that the signing of the constitution made Execution inevitable and one from Berlin that, while Bismarck would urge the Diet to accept the proffered mediation, the Execution should be carried out immediately if the Diet refused.[77] But as the situation was developing in Germany, Russell began to suspect that Execution might be used merely as a means of getting possession of Holstein until the Diet made up its mind on the succession question and that the Danes fearing this, would offer armed resistance. Notes were therefore sent to the German states which were parties to the Treaty of London, and to Copenhagen and Frankfurt, saying that the British government expected that Christian's right of accession to all the territories of the Danish Crown would be acknowledged, and to Berlin and Vienna warning against the use of Federal Execution to enforce the international obligations.

It seems to her Majesty's Government that the course which at the present crisis the Diet should pursue would be to require Denmark to withdraw the Letters-Patent of the 30th of March, and to comply in Holstein with the demands of the Diet as regards that Duchy, intimating, at the same time, that if Denmark should refuse to make these concessions, the threatened Federal Execution should be carried into effect. The Diet might at the same time, require that questions of an international character should be referred by both parties to the Powers who were parties to the Treaty of May 1852. Her Majesty's Government considers that if the Diet were to adopt this course war might be averted; and they trust that in the present perilous state of affairs, Austria and Prussia will act together and afford by so doing the best chance of averting from Germany the danger of a Democratic revolution.[78]

"The line of policy to be pursued by Her Majesty's Government in the questions at issue between Denmark and Germany is perfectly clear," Russell wrote on December 1. "That policy is to advise Austria, Prussia and the other Powers who signed the Treaty of London to adhere to their engagements and to advise

[77] Bloomfield to Russell, November 19, 1863, received November 23; Buchanan to Russell, November 21, 1863, received November 23, *Denmark and Germany, No. 3, 1864*, Nos. 258, 261.

[78] Russell to Bloomfield, *et al.*, November 23, 1863; Russell to Bloomfield, November 23, 1863, *Denmark and Germany, No. 3, 1864*, Nos. 274, 275.

Denmark to observe all the engagements which she has taken to Germany.''[79]

With the Germans, and especially Bismarck, he engaged in a war of notes reiterating his opinion that the engagements of 1851-52 afford no valid excuse for failing to observe the Treaty of London. To Denmark, he expressed his regret that the King had signed the constitution although, ''it is possible that in the circumstances this step could not be avoided,'' and he recommended that the King issue a proclamation ''assuring his subjects of German race that they will enjoy equally with the Danes the privileges of freedom and his Royal protection.''[80]

VI

In accordance with custom, special envoys were sent to congratulate the King of Denmark on his accession to the throne. In order to strengthen the position of Austria and Prussia in maintaining the Treaty of London against the clamor of public opinion in Germany, Gorchakov proposed that these envoys be secretly instructed to urge upon the King the necessity of modifying the November Constitution. It was his original intention that this pressure be applied by all of the Powers signatory to the Treaty of London, but as the Emperor of Austria and the King of Prussia had refused to receive the envoy sent to notify them of King Christian's accession and in consequence did not intend to reply by envoys to Copenhagen, the plan was correspondingly modified. The British and French governments, however, accepted the plan; the former enthusiastically,[81] the latter, less warmly, because of its desire for a European Congress.[82]

As Russian envoy, Councillor Ewers was selected. At the time of the first Schleswig-Holstein war, he had been secretary of the legation at Copenhagen and since then had been in the Foreign

---

[79] Russell to Paget, December 1, 1863, *Ibid.*, No. 338.
[80] Russell to Paget, November 20, 1863, *Ibid.*, No. 250.
[81] Russell to Napier, December 2, 1863, *Ibid.*, No. 346.
[82] See pp. 111 ff. above.

Office at St. Petersburg, where he had been entrusted with the details of the German-Danish question.[83] The British government chose Lord Wodehouse, a former Under-Secretary of State for foreign affairs, whose attitude had been violently pro-Danish. In the spring of 1863, he had bitterly attacked Lord Russell's attempts to settle the question; but at this time he seems to have modified his views.

"The choice of Lord Wodehouse is remarkable," the Saxon minister at London commented. "It was he who only last session attacked Lord Russell's policy of mediation in a speech which nobody could say was impartial. The ambition to obtain some practical result, the extreme importance attached here to a peaceful settlement of the Danish dispute, the reaction of public opinion in favor of Germany, and perhaps the regard for the Queen, may possibly have toned down the harsh views of the former Under-Secretary of State. 'The Devil is not so black as he is painted,' he said yesterday to Count Bernstorff. 'I shall preach peace to the Danes, and advise them to make every concession to the German Powers which does not imply an absolute impossibility.' "[84] General Fleury, the French envoy, was aide-de-camp and close personal friend of the Emperor Napoleon, but hardly an expert on the Schleswig-Holstein question.

Both Ewers and Wodehouse travelled to Copenhagen via Berlin. The former's instructions were drawn in general terms. They pointed out that Austria and Prussia had declared their intention of abiding by the Treaty of London and that it was important, therefore, that those Powers be supported in the attempt to secure the recognition of that document by the Diet. "Equity, as well as the clear interest of Denmark itself,

---

[83] Neergaard, *Under Junigrundloven*, II, p. 932. The ardent National Liberal, Krieger, characterizes him as "en hensynsløs kold Tydsker." Krieger, *Dagbøger*, III, p. 12.

[84] Vitzthum von Eckstädt, *St. Petersburg and London*, II, pp. 266 f. letter of December 7, 1863. " . . . .Schlechteste Wahl die man treffen konnte obgleich er mir versichert, dass er versöhnlich sein werde." Bernstorff to Bismarck, telegram, No. 431, December 5, 1863. 7 P. M., (Berlin Archives).

demand imperiously a modification of the Constitution of November 18.''

The Russian government claimed to be far from intending to impose upon King Christian the obligation of revoking a law to which he had given his sanction. It left to the Cabinet of Copenhagen entire latitude in the choice of its means of re-assuring the German Confederation and the Duchies of a sincere intention of not violating its promise in regard to the non-incorporation of Schleswig, and of offering a satisfactory guaranty of its intention to execute loyally the terms of the Royal Proclamation of January 28, 1852. Finally, Ewers was instructed to make clear to the Danish ministry that in case it refused to adopt the policy of conciliation recommended by the Powers, they, for their part, would decline any responsibility for the consequence of such refusal.[85] Of Ewers' interview with Bismarck, little is known, except that it was not difficult for Bismarck to reach an agreement with him.[86]

Wodehouse's preliminary instructions stressed the binding force of the Treaty of London and drew a sharp distinction between the obligations defined by that document and those of Denmark contained in the exchange of notes of 1851.

''It is not my purpose either to point out how these engagements have been observed or to affirm that any of them have been violated,'' wrote Russell. ''It will be for the ministers of Austria and Prussia to make their complaints on this head. . . .

[85] Memorandum destiné à servir d'instruction au Conseiller d'Etat actuel Ewers, (Berlin Archives). As our knowledge of the text of this instruction comes from the copy given to the Prussian government it is impossible to say that there were no other more confidential ones. It seems probable, however, that there were not. Later, when Lord Wodehouse suggested the definite advice to the Danish government that the constitution be revoked as regarded Schleswig, ''Ewers said 'that although he was not directed to give such advice to the Danish government ...such a step would be in conformity to the spirit of his instructions'....On further consideration, M. d'Ewers referred to his Government for instructions....'' Wodehouse to Russell, December 19, 1863, *Denmark and Germany, No. 4, 1864,* No. 504.

[86] Sybel, *Die Begründung des deutschen Reiches,* III, p. 185. Ewers' statement that Bismarck had given him a definite assurance that he intended to abide by the Treaty of London apparently refers to his return journey from Copenhagen. Cf. Redern to Bismarck, No. 8, January 16, 1863, (Berlin Archives).

The result to be arrived at is the fulfilment of the Treaty of May 8, 1852 and of the engagements entered into by Austria, Prussia and Denmark, in 1851-52. The mode of arriving at that result cannot yet be laid down. Patience and impartiality on the part of the Great Powers will conduce greatly to that end, and will contribute in the same proportion to the maintenance of the peace of Europe.''[87]

Wodehouse arrived in Berlin on the evening of December 11, and on the next day had a long conversation with Bismarck.[88] He attempted to shake Bismarck's claim that the observance of the Treaty of London by Austria and Prussia depended on the fulfilment by Denmark of her promises of 1851-52, but to no avail.[89] In regard to the November Constitution, said Bismarck, there could be no compromise. Before January 1 the Constitution must be declared to be inapplicable to Schleswig, otherwise the German Powers would hold themselves released from all their engagements to Denmark including the Treaty of 1852. Wodehouse also tried to impress the British point of view on King William and on Count Karolyi, the Austrian minister, but found that in regard to the Treaty of London, their language hardly differed from that of Bismarck.[90] Wodehouse took with him

[87] Russell to Wodehouse, December 9, 1863, *Denmark and Germany, No. 3, 1864*, No. 394. The British Archives contain no secret instructions to accompany this. It seems, however, that the British government was prepared to accept mere personal union of the Duchies with Denmark as a solution of the problem. *Aus dem Leben Theodor von Bernhardis*, V, pp. 346, 277. Wodehouse spoke to Bismarck of personal union, but only in reference to Holstein. This passage is omitted from the dispatch as published in the Blue Book. It follows after line 2 on p. 376, *Denmark and Germany, No. 3, 1864*, No. 434; Wodehouse to Russell, No. 3, December 12, 1863, (Record Office, London).

[88] Wodehouse to Russell, No. 3, December 12, 1863 (Record Office, London). A large part of this dispatch has been published; *Denmark and Germany, No. 3, 1864*, No. 434.

[89] "... I regret to be obliged to add that my observations appeared to make little impression on M. de Bismarck, and that I fear from his language that the Prussian Government will not hesitate to repudiate the Treaty, if they do not obtain from Denmark the satisfaction they require as to the engagements of 1851-52." Wodehouse to Russell, No. 3, December 12, 1863, (Record Office, London).

[90] Wodehouse to Russell, No. 6, December 13, 1863 (Record Office, London). Wodehouse to Russell, December 13, 1863, *Denmark and Germany, No. 3, 1864*,

from Berlin a memorandum of the demands of Austria and Prussia on Denmark.

The Austrian and Prussian Governments require that the Danish Government shall carry out the engagements of 1851-52; so that, apart from the Federal ties which concern only Holstein, Schleswig shall not be more closely connected with the Kingdom of Denmark than Holstein. They therefore consider that the Constitution of November 18, 1863, is a violation of the engagements of Denmark, and they require that measures will be taken before January 1 by the Danish Government to prevent that Constitution being carried into effect as regards Schleswig. When such measures shall have been taken they expect to receive from Denmark propositions as to the manner in which the engagements of 1851-52 are to be fulfilled.[91]

This "most meagre document"[92] was hardly adapted to lead to a settlement of the questions at issue and there is no reason to suppose that Bismarck intended it should.[93] The Danish govern-

No. 435. Bismarck had suggested that the British envoy have an audience with the King. "Bismarck is anxious for immediate arrival of special envoy to Copenhagen, as it is essential in order to counteract the daily influences to which the King is exposed that a representation from her Majesty's Government should be made without delay to His Majesty with more authority than usual as to the propriety of Prussia observing the Treaty of London...." Buchanan to Russell, telegram, private and confidential, December 4, 1863, reported in No. 560 (Record Office, London).

[91] *Denmark and Germany, No. 3, 1864*, No. 439, inclosure. This memorandum was approved by King William and by Count Karolyi. Wodehouse to Russell, December 13, 1863. *Ibid.*, No. 436. "Count Rechberg sends no special instructions to Count Karolyi but has authorized him to concert with M. de Bismarck as to the proposals which Austria and Prussia may consider it advisable to submit to Lord Wodehouse. His Excellency leaves the affair entirely in the hands of the Austrian Minister in Berlin. ...." Bloomfield to Russell, telegram, December 10, 1863, reported in No. 603 (Record Office, London).

[92] In conversation with Buchanan on December 15, Bismarck admitted that the memorandum for Lord Wodehouse was a "most meagre document" but excused himself on the ground of having explained fully orally to Wodehouse the arrangements which would be required. Buchanan to Russell, No. 600, Postscript, December 16, 1863 (Dispatch dated December 13); Buchanan to Russell, No. 590, confidential, December 13, 1863 (Record Office, London).

[93] "Si l'Angleterre veut savoir,' m'a dit le Ministre [Bismarck] à quel prix nous reconnaîtrons le Roi de Danemark et nous renouerons avec lui de bons rapports de voisins et de Confédérés, je dirai que nous prendrons pour bases les conditions constitutionelles agrées réciproquement en 1851. J'admets qu'elles sont d'une exécution peu pratique et que c'est à peu près la quadrature du cercle que nous demandons au Cabinet de Copenhague de résoudre...." Talleyrand to Drouyn de Lhuys, No. 125, December 11, 1863 (Paris Archives).

ment had known since the middle of November that Prussia regarded the constitution as a violation of the Danish obligations. It was very doubtful whether in the present state of feeling in Copenhagen it could be revoked. Bismarck bluntly recommended a *coup d'état*: ''Germany would never be on good terms with Denmark as long as the present democratic institutions of Denmark were maintained.''[94] But Christian IX was not the man for a *coup d'état* nor was an Englishman likely to advise one. Above all, the last sentence of the memorandum contained the rock on which all the previous negotiations had been wrecked: Germany could always declare that the new Danish proposals were unsatisfactory.[95] What Wodehouse had wished to obtain was a clear and definite expression of the views of Germany and he had failed[96] in this as he had failed to hold Prussian policy unconditionally true to the Treaty of London.

Lord Wodehouse arrived at the Danish capital on the morning of December 15, and after a conference with Sir Augustus Paget, had a preliminary talk with Hall. ''I impressed strongly upon his Excellency,'' he reported,

that if Austria and Prussia were bound in good faith to carry out the Treaty of 1852, without reference to any other engagements not contained in that Treaty, Denmark was on her part bound to fulfil her engagements to Germany; and I did not conceal from him my opinion that the Constitution recently signed by the King might be regarded as at variance with the promise made by Denmark in Annex No. 2 to the despatches of December 6, 1851, to Vienna and Berlin, that Schleswig should not be incorporated with Denmark, and that no steps should be taken tending to such incorporation.

I pointed out to him also that if on the one hand Her Majesty's Government would never counsel the Danish Government to yield anything inconsistent with the honour and independence of the Danish Crown and the integrity of the King's dominions, so, on the other, we had a right to expect

---

[94] Wodehouse to Russell, December 12, 1863, Buchanan to Russell, December 10, 1863. *Denmark and Germany, No. 3, 1864*: Nos. 434, 414.

[95] Buchanan to Russell, December 4, 1863; *Ibid.*, No. 461.

[96] Bismarck told the French Ambassador that he had replied to Wodehouse: ''Vous êtes un homme d'affaires trop distingué pour vous attendre à une réponse de ma part. Si j'avais à vous vendre un cheval de deux cents louis, je ne vous confierais pas que je finirais par vous le céder pour cent car vous ne m'en offririez alors que quatre-vingt.'' Talleyrand to Drouyn de Lhuys, No. 126. December 15, 1863. (Paris Archives).

that the Danish Government would not, by putting forward extreme pretensions, drive matters to extremities.

Hall, however, showed no disposition to yield and hinted that if concessions to Germany were made, it was not probable that it would be by the advice of a ministry of which he was the head.[97]

The first few days of Lord Wodehouse's stay in Copenhagen were occupied with formal visits, with negotiations with the Russian and French envoys as to the procedure to be adopted in giving their advice to the Danish government, and with the ceremonies incidental to the funeral of Frederick VII at the cathedral of Röskilde. Lord Wodehouse wished the *démarche* to be in the form of a joint communication from the representatives of Great Britain, Russia, France and Sweden. M. d'Ewers was authorized to take part in this and to coöperate closely with the British envoy. General Fleury, however, was instructed to act separately. He was ordered, he said, to tell the Danish government explicitly that if Denmark became involved in a war with Germany, France would not come to her assistance;[98] to advise in general terms moderation and concessions to Germany; but to state that the Emperor Napoleon would not consent to any formal negotiations on the German-Danish question except in a European Congress. Count Hamilton, the Swedish minister, was not authorized to put pressure on Denmark.[99]

On Sunday, December 20, Lord Wodehouse and M. d'Ewers were received by Hall. At the request of the Russian envoy, Lord Wodehouse took the lead in presenting the views of the two powers. He informed Hall of the substance of his conversations with Bismarck and gave him a copy of the memorandum of the demands of Austria and Prussia. He went on to say that

[97] *Denmark and Germany, No. 4, 1864*, No. 451.

For the time being, the burning question was whether the Federal Execution, the formal announcement of which coincided with the arrival of Lord Wodehouse, would lead to a collision between the German and Danish troops. On this point, at least, the advice of the friendly Great Powers was followed; the Danish troops were withdrawn from Holstein and war was temporarily avoided.

[98] Cf. Cowley to Russell, Paris, December 29, 1863, *Ibid.*, No. 551.

[99] Wodehouse to Russell, No. 13, December 16, 1863; telegram, December 17; No. 19, December 19 (Record Office, London). Published in part in *Denmark and Germany, No. 4, 1864*, No. 504.

Her Majesty's Government were of the opinion that the Constitution of November 13 was a violation of the promise of Denmark not to incorporate Schleswig with the kingdom and not to take steps which would tend thereto. M. d'Ewers expressed his entire agreement with Lord Wodehouse's point of view and urged that the constitution be revoked.[100] They were followed by General Fleury, who supported their advice about the constitution but confined himself to general observations and to emphasizing the plan for a Congress.[101] Finally, Sir Augustus Paget came to back up the arguments of Lord Wodehouse and M. d'Ewers.[102] Hall was obdurate. He refused to consider the revocation of the constitution. On the next day, the Danish ministers burned the bridges behind them by dissolving the *Rigsraad*, the only body which could legally carry out the repeal.

The royal message which, on December 21, announced to the *Rigsraad* the formal closing of its session, made no direct reference to the events of the preceding day. The new constitution, it stated, opposed no obstacle to an agreement between the *Rigsraad* and the Estates of Holstein for a constitutional union of the whole monarchy. "It must, therefore, be in consequence of some misunderstanding that certain Powers have seen a reason for its being left incomplete, however willing they may be to fulfill unconditionally the obligations of a treaty." The King appealed to the people for loyalty and coöperation in the stormy days that lay before them and expressed the hope that against further German schemes, Europe would know how to uphold the undivided inheritance of the whole Danish Monarchy, the unmodified existence of which had been recognized as necessary for the maintenance of European peace.[103]

---

[100] *Denmark and Germany, No. 4, 1864*, No. 507.

[101] *Ibid.*, No. 508; Krieger, *Dagbøger*, III, p. 23. C. N. David, "Optegnelser om Aarene 1863-1865," in *Historisk Tidsskrift*, (Copenhagen) 1914, p. 57.

[102] Paget to Russell, No. 318, December 22, 1863. Extract published in *Denmark and Germany, No. 4, 1864*, No. 509.

[103] Translation in *Denmark and Germany, No. 4, 1864*, p. 422.

VII

As a matter of fact, in the council which followed the *démarche* of the foreign envoys, the Danish ministers had merely adhered to a decision made almost a week before. They had already learned from the correspondence of their representatives abroad that Denmark would be urged to revoke or suspend the new constitution and the actual interviews added nothing essential. On December 16, the day after Hall's first brief talk with Lord Wodehouse, the council of ministers formally advised King Christian that a peaceful solution of the conflict with Germany was very improbable. On the one hand, the strained relations of France and England which had resulted from the latter's rejection of the Congress, would make mediation most unlikely and, on the other, German opinion on the question had become so hot that it would be impossible for Austria and Prussia, even with the best of will, to negotiate on any basis acceptable to Denmark. There were two points on which Denmark must be unyielding: the rights of the king under the Treaty of London and the independence of the non-federal parts of the monarchy. If this basis were accepted, it would still be possible to negotiate for a constitution which should include all four parts of the monarchy. The existence of the November Constitution would be no bar to such negotiation, for to secure its results would merely require their acceptance by the new *Rigsraad* for Denmark and Schleswig and by the Estates of Holstein. In any case, the wishes of the foreign Powers for the suspension or revocation of the November Constitution could not be fulfilled. Leaving out of account the procedure of constitutional amendment and other difficulties of a practical nature, such an action would only give rise to the most serious consequences. It would have no influence on the attitude of Germany for it was not really the constitutional question but the very existence of the Danish Monarchy on which the conflict turned. Such a decision, moreover, would have a most unfortunate effect on the internal situation in Denmark, particularly upon that section of the population "which, through its intelligence and its general position in the community, will always have a determining influence on the public mind and which has gratefully rallied to the new constitution as the fulfilment of the legitimate wishes of the Danish people.'' The more threatening the external situation became, the report concluded, the more necessary was the intimate adherence of the nation to the policy of the royal government and such adherence would the sooner bring the foreign Powers to recognize their duty to support Denmark.[104]

In his answers to Wodehouse, Ewers, and Paget, Hall stressed the considerations of domestic policy. ''He was but too sensible,'' the former reported, ''of the dangers with which Denmark was menaced if she rejected our advice, but the danger of accepting it seemed to him still more serious. At present, the King and his people were united and this cordial union of the King and people was a tower of strength. But if the constitution were revoked, this great advantage would be lost.''[105] It is true that with the exception of a small group of conservative 'Whole State' men, the spokesmen of all the Danish parties approved the national policy of the government and were willing to see it followed to the bitter end.[106] Hall knew, however, that the King did not really approve the policy he was following and his argument probably represents rather an attempt to influence the Powers than an expression of his own point of view. Hall's other main argument represents better his own and his associates' reasoning and carries more weight than that based on the intimate union of King and people. Even if the constitution were revoked, he asked, what would be the advantage to Denmark? There was no promise given that the Powers would support her if Germany continued her aggressions; there was no prospect even of the Execution being arrested. The revocation of the March Patent had been asked for; the concession had been made but had not averted the Execution. If the constitution should be

[104] Neergaard, *Under Junigrundloven*, II, pp. 957-962.

[105] Wodehouse to Russell, December 21, 1863, *Denmark and Germany, No. 4, 1864*, No. 507.

[106] Neergaard, *Under Junigrundloven*, II, pp. 594 ff.; the feeling in National Liberal circles is shown in Krieger, *Dagbøger*, III, passim.

annulled, what security did Denmark have that this would be the last concession demanded of her?[107] On the margin of a British dispatch which contains this question, Bismarck has written the answer: "None."[108]

None of the responsible ministers seems to have left an adequate explanation of their decision. Monrad, writing many years later, compared the action of the ministry to that of an animal which, long followed by the hounds, suddenly turns to fight to the death. "The ministry had long been hunted; they had tried in vain to reach an agreement; they were tired of it and felt that the people were tired of it and were beginning to be impatient of the eternal and fruitless negotiation, of the years of insecurity and uncertainty. They were possessed by the feeling: 'Now the thing must be ended, now we must call a halt, now we must make or break.' There is a courage born of desperation that sometimes conquers but oftener succumbs. Such courage inspired the ministry."[109] Madvig, who was president of the *Rigsraad* and in close touch with the cabinet wrote in 1865: "...With the vague hope of a more placable attitude [on the part of the Powers] and of mediation, we were to give up the whole of our constitutional basis for the common affairs of the monarchy and cast ourselves entirely defenseless into the worst confusion of negotiations. ...."[110]

In the past, Hall's policy had not been over-bold. He had come to regard the closest possible connection between Schleswig and the kingdom as essential for the independence of the Danish state and for the national development of its people. He had not, however, shared the sanguine hopes of many of his associates that this aim of his policy could be attained without regard for the other factors in the situation. In the eyes of many Danes,

[107] Paget to Russell, December 22, 1863, *Denmark and Germany No. 4, 1864*, No. 509. Cf. Krieger, *Dagbøger*, III, pp. 19, 23; Monrad, *Deltagelse i Begivenhederne 1864*, pp. 48 f; Madvig, *Den nationale Politik og det danske Monarchie*, pp. 125 f.

[108] Marginal note on a copy of Russell to Buchanan, December 31, 1863 (Berlin Archives).

[109] Monrad, *Deltagelse i Begivenhederne 1864*, p. 49. This was written in 1880.

[110] J. N. Madvig. *Den nationale Politik og det danske Monarchie*, p. 126.

he had paid entirely too much attention to the attitude of the Germans and to the wishes of the other European Powers.[111] It is not easy to reconcile his action at the decisive moments in November and December 1863 with his usually moderate and judicial attitude. Perhaps Neergaard is right in suggesting that since the sudden death of Frederick VII, Hall was governed by a sort of fatalistic belief that a serious crisis was inevitable and that he had come to regard himself less as a leader who could choose his paths and direct his country's policy toward a definite goal, than as an instrument in the hands of a mightier power.[112]

Probably Hall and his colleagues, convinced as they were of the justice of their position, could not bring themselves to believe that they would be abandoned to their foes.[113] The special envoys of the Powers, had, to be sure, declared that if Denmark refused to follow their advice, she would be left to bear the consequences of her refusal. Yet, would this actually be the case if the Germans tried to change the Execution into sequestration of Holstein for the Prince of Augustenburg; if they attacked the non-federal parts of the monarchy; if the independence and integrity of the monarch were really endangered?

There was no reason to hope for a change in Russian policy.[114] In England, however, public opinion, especially as represented by the most influential London newspapers, was loud in favor of Denmark. Even while putting pressure on the Danish government by threatening to leave Denmark in the lurch, Earl Russell had not abated his activity in preaching to the German states the sanctity of treaties and the dire consequences that might ensue if the integrity of the Danish monarchy were menaced.[115] To the

[111] C. St. A. Bille, ''Carl Christian Hall,'' in Bricka, *Dansk Biografisk Lexikon,* VI, p. 497.

[112] Neergaard, *Under Junigrundloven,* II, p. 883. Erik Arup has interpreted Hall's policy after the death of Frederick VII as an attempt to create a domestic crisis for the purpose of bringing about a 'Scandinavian' revolution. ''David og Hall. Krisen i Danmarks historie 1863'' in *Scandia* I (February 1928), pp. 166-179. His argument is not convincing.

[113] Cf. Monrad, *Deltagelse i Begivenhederne 1864,* p. 50.

[114] Cf. Krieger, *Dagbøger,* III, pp. 14, 23.

[115] Cf. *Denmark and Germany, No. 3, 1864,* Nos. 446, 447, 503, 519.

Danish minister at London, Lord Palmerston denounced in vigorous terms the "bad faith of Germany" respecting the Treaty of London. He was not ignorant, he said, of what Germany wanted: it was the dismemberment of Denmark. He related, *à propos* of this, that Herr von der Pfordten, the Bavarian representative at Frankfurt, had declared openly that it was necessary to seize the present opportunity of finishing once for all with Denmark; "but," he had added, "fortunately, Herr von der Pfordten is not Providence."[116] Earl Russell's support of the Russian pressure was explained by Bille, the Danish minister to England, as probably due to the consideration that it was much easier to force a weak state like Denmark to yield than Great Powers, like Austria and Prussia.[117] At least once in the past an unfavorable action of Russell's, the 'Gotha dispatch' of September 1862, had been repudiated by Parliament and country and this might happen again, for even if the Whig ministers persisted in their policy of non-intervention, there was no certainty that they could, after the opening of Parliament, maintain themselves in power. The Tories were even more favorable to Denmark than were the Whigs.[118]

The British representatives in Copenhagen, Sir Augustus Paget and Lord Wodehouse, believed that Hall still hoped for eventual aid from Sweden and France. "I have ascertained in a positive manner," Sir Augustus telegraphed on December 12,

[116] T. Bille to Hall, London, December 2, 1863, No. 102 (Copenhagen Archives).

[117] T. Bille to Hall, London, December 11, 1863, No. 105 (Copenhagen Archives).

[118] A. F. Krieger notes in his diary on December 20: "T. Bille er selvfolgelig ivrig i at fraraade Eftergivenhed; City vil tvinge Russell til at give efter eller til at gaae af, Brunnow [Russian Ambassador in London] troer ikke, at Preussen tør gaae ind i Slesvig." *Dagbøger*, III, p. 23.

Bille reported in a dispatch of December 23, 1863, received January 1, 1864: "Le parti Tory ou conservateur a l'intention, selon ce qu'on dit, de faire de notre question leur cheval de bataille à la prochaine session du Parlement et le parti espère de pouvoir renverser le Ministère en l'accusant d'avoir mal mené notre question en ne soutenant pas comme on aurait dû le Danemark vis à vis de l'esprit d'aggression dont l'Allemagne a été de plus animé contre nous." (Copenhagen Archives).

that the Swedish Government informed the Danish Government in October that if Denmark was attacked in Sleswig, she would be assisted by another Power besides Sweden,—and that in the above event, with or without a treaty, Sweden would support her to the utmost of her means. This communication has been repeated today, but at the same time I am assured most positively that Sweden is not bound by any treaty with Denmark, and is doing everything to induce the Danish Government to avoid hostilities and to come to an arrangement.....[119]

In his dispatch explaining this telegram, Paget describes how he was waiting at the ministry of foreign affairs to see Hall, when Count Hamilton, the Swedish minister, entered and their conversation turned to the present situation. He was not, he told Count Hamilton, informed of the proposals to be brought by Lord Wodehouse but believed that the latter was to try to get from Bismarck a precise statement of the demands of the German Powers.

As I was convinced that whatever might be the pretentions of Germany, Her Majesty's Government would not be a party to any proposal which was not just and equitable, I could not but be of opinion that the only course open to the Danish Government was to at once adopt the advice which might be suggested to them by the Powers interested in the welfare of the Danish Monarchy. Personal considerations and extreme Danish views must now give way, I said, to the all important object of maintaining peace and saving, if that were still possible, the Danish Monarchy from the violent shock which threatened it. The position of Denmark was one of isolation and if the Danish Government did not listen to reasonable proposals, although they might not be in conformity with the views and policy which had recently been followed, they would incur a very heavy responsibility.

Count Hamilton replied that, if the proposals to be made to Denmark were at all acceptable, he was quite of opinion that the Danish Government would do well to adopt them, but there were certain things which he thought the Danish Government should rather incur the risks of war than agree to. Denmark, he added, was not quite in the isolated position which I imagined, for if a war broke out she would be assisted by more Powers than one. I asked who these Powers were, for I presumed, I said, that since Sweden had denounced the Treaty, she was not one of them. Count Hamilton replied by drawing a paper from his pocket, an extract of a despatch, which he read to me. It was to the effect which I have already reported, namely, that if Denmark was attacked in Sleswig she would be supported by another Power besides Sweden, and that Sweden with or without a Treaty would come to her assistance with all her means.

[119] Paget to Russell, 5 P. M., December 12, 1863. Reported in dispatch No. 304 (Record Office, London).

Deriving the impression that this was a despatch just received by Count Hamilton, and that he was now for the first time about to communicate it to the Danish Minister, I suggested to him whether under present circumstances it would not be advisable to withhold the communication because I was afraid the promise of support therein held out would make the Danish Government less amenable to reason.

Count Hamilton replied that the contents of this despatch was no news for the Danish Government,—as he had communicated it as long ago as the month of October. What had in part given rise to its being written was something which had passed between M. de Bismarck and M. de Järta, the Swedish Minister at Berlin, in September last to the effect that if Sweden made a treaty of Alliance with Denmark, the German Powers would object to her being admitted to the negotiations on the international questions;— and his Government was therefore desirous of reassuring Denmark that whether there was a Treaty or not the forces of Sweden would be at the disposal of Denmark in the contingency alluded to—namely, an attack on Sleswig.

I said that I thought the allusion to France, for no other Power could be meant, was calculated to make the Danes very obstinate,—and I asked what reasons the Swedish Government had for supposing that that Power would assist Denmark; whether in short what was said to the Danish Government in Count Manderström's despatch was founded on something more than general surmises as to the possible line which it might be supposed the interest of France would induce her to take in the event of a war between Denmark and Germany.

Count Hamilton replied that of course no one could answer absolutely and positively for the particular conduct which, at a future moment, it might suit the Emperor of the French to adopt,—but the Swedish Government had unquestionably something much more positive to go upon in what they had said to the Danish Government than mere suppositions as to His Imperial Majesty's intentions. Count Hamilton added that until the spring not a French soldier would move but that if at that time Denmark and Germany were at war he was convinced, from the information he had, that the Emperor Napoleon would then throw his weight into the balance on the side of Denmark, I next enquired of Count Hamilton what induced him to renew at this moment the communication he had read to me. He replied that it was in order to give additional weight to the advice he was instructed to give to the Danish Government to do all in their power to avoid hostilities and to endeavor to come to an arrangement. By reminding the Danish Government that if Germany attacked Sleswig Denmark was certain of support, he thought there was more chance of the Government consenting to withdraw the troops from Holstein. As Sweden was bound to aid Denmark in a certain case although there was no treaty between them his government was, of course, anxious that everything should be done to prevent this case occuring, and would use their influence for this purpose.[120]

[120] Paget to Russell, No. 11, December 16, 1863, confidential, (Record Office, London).

In a report presented to the Danish *Rigsraad* in August, 1864, a committee, of which Hall was a member, declared that the attitude of Sweden had exerted an important influence on Danish policy. The Danish government, it stated, had taken as its point of departure the conviction that the result of the verbal negotiations had been to establish the existence of an agreement of both governments that there was a solidarity in the interests of the Scandinavian kingdoms which would not let Sweden remain an inactive spectator if the quarrel with Germany led to an attack on Schleswig and that Sweden was ready to confirm this solidarity by a treaty of alliance.[121] It was in reliance on the fact that Sweden-Norway shared the belief in the solidarity of the cause of "the North" that plans were made to accept the possibility of conflict with Germany.[122] The report, however, refers directly only to the negotiations for the treaty of alliance and to the situation in November and the first few days of December. There is no hint in it of a second communication of Manderström's note of October 5. There is no reason, on the other hand, to suppose that Hamilton would not carry out his intentions on December 12. Such an action, it can be shown, was not inconsistent with his position at that time nor with the attitude of his chief at Stockholm and it is not improbable that this was what Hall had in mind when, on December 26, he answered a question of one of his colleagues about the Swedish alliance by implying that Sweden still recognized an obligation to defend Schleswig.[123]

The negotiations for a formal alliance of Denmark and Sweden had been begun in July 1863 by King Charles XV, himself. Count Manderström, the minister for foreign affairs, had succeeded in eliminating from the discussion the points on which the King had gone too far but had continued the negotia-

---

[121] *Rigsraadstidende*, Tillaeg B, Overord. Samling 1864., coll. 467 f.

[122] *Ibid.*, col. 470. Cf. Monrad, *Deltagelse i Begivenhederne 1864*, p. 52.

[123] Under the date of Monday, December 28, Krieger notes in his diary: "Fonnesbech afæskede da i Løverdags Hall Erklæring om det svensk-norske Forbund. Hall svarede meget korttilsidst uærligt, idet han udtalte sig, som om Sverrig endnu erkjendte det som sin Pligt at forsvare Slesvig." *Dagbøger*, III, p. 33. Krieger's comment "uærligt" ("not quite honestly") seems to indicate that Hall had not told his colleagues and friends of Hamilton's confidences. For a similar reticence on Hall's part, cf. *ibid.*, p. 28.

tions. The opposition of other ministers, as revealed during the discussions at Ulriksdal in September had shown that there were serious obstacles in the way of the conclusion of the alliance treaty and the Danish government had received formal notice of this in Manderström's dispatch to Count Hamilton of October 5.[124] This dispatch, however, contained the explicit statement which Hamilton was authorized to make to the Danish government:

> If, contrary to expectations and in spite of the representations which have been made, Germany attempts an invasion of Schleswig, we believe that we can affirm with confidence that Denmark will be able to count in full security on the active support of more than one Power, and on our part— whether or not a treaty has been concluded—we do not hesitate to affirm in the most explicit manner, that, in case of aggression by Germany in Schleswig, we shall still be of the same disposition, as in the past and in proportion to our strength and the means at our disposal, to offer to Denmark the aid which she may demand of us.[125]

It was not difficult to allege that the circumstances under which this was written had changed and that the passage cited must be understood in the light of the rest of the dispatch and of the situation when it was presented. It must be kept in mind, however, that the passage cited was communicated to the Danish government in writing and without its context.[126] The Danish government can hardly be criticised severely for accepting it at face value, especially as the negotiations for the alliance were not broken off.

On October 19, Count Hamilton was informed by Manderström

---

[124] Cf. pp. 67 ff. above.

[125] "Si contre toute attente et au mépris des représentations qui lui sont faites, l'Allemagne tentait une invasion dans le Slesvic, nous croyons pouvoir affirmer avec confiance, que le Danemarc pourrait compter en toute sécurité sur un appui actif de plus d'une Puissance, et que pour notre part—qu'un Traité soit intervenu ou non—nous n'hésitons point à affirmer de la manière la plus explicite, que, dans le cas d'une agression de l'Allemagne dans le Slesvic, nous serions toujours dans les mêmes dispositions que jusqu'ici et dans la mesure de nos forces et des moyens, dont nous pouvons disposer, d'offrir au Danemarc le secours qu'il pourrait réclamer de notre part. Cette assurance Vous êtes autorisé, M. le Comte, à la donner au Gouvernement Danois, dans les termes mêmes dont j'ai fait usage dans cette dépêche." Koht, *Die Stellung Norwegens und Schwedens im deutsch-dänischen Konflikt*, p. 272.

[126] For the discussion on this point, cf. Koht, *op. cit.*, pp. 139-144.

that as soon as constitutional forms permitted, he would receive full powers and instructions for the continuance of his discussions with the Danish government. A week later, on October 27, Manderström proposed a revised draft at a meeting of the joint Swedish-Norwegian ministry at Stockholm. This draft, too, met with some opposition, but during the first weeks in November, both the King of Sweden and his minister for foreign affairs seem to have believed that they would succeed in carrying their point.[127] As late as November 16, Manderström told the Danish minister that the death of Frederick VII would make no difference in the attitude of the Swedish government towards the treaty of alliance and Count Hamilton, at Copenhagen, made a similar communication to the Danish government.[128]

Soon after this, as the situation became more serious with the increasing agitation in Germany and the claims of the Prince of Augustenburg to the succession in Schleswig-Holstein, the Swedish government began to change its tone. King Charles, whose personal friendship with Frederick VII had played an important part in the shaping of Swedish policy, did not have the same love for, nor confidence in, Christian IX, whose sympathies were reputed to be for Germany and Russia.[129] Manderström began to emphasize the European rather than the Swedish interest in the support of Denmark under the new set of circumstances. On November 20, he directed a circular dispatch to the Powers to ask what they intended to do about the danger threatening the integrity of the Danish Monarchy. A few days later, the Swedish government asked the *Rigsraad* for three millions of rigsdalers for armament but the motives given for the request were not encouraging to the friends of the alliance. Finally, on

---

[127] Koht, *op. cit.*, pp. 150-154. W. Scheel-Plessen to Hall, Stockholm, November 10, 1863, in *Archives diplomatiques*, XVI, p. 212. Cf. *Les Origines diplomatiques de la guerre de 1870-1871*, IV, p. 76, note 2.

[128] Neergaard, *Under Junigrundloven*, II, p. 945; Dotézac to Drouyn de Lhuys, Copenhagen, November 26, 1863; *Les Origines diplomatiques de la guerre de 1870-71*, p. 76, note 3.

[129] Cf. Fournier to Drouyn de Lhuys, Stockholm, November 18, 1863, *Les Origines diplomatiques de la guerre de 1870-1871*, IV, p. 77; and Dotézac to Drouyn de Lhuys, Copenhagen, December 18, 1863 (Paris Archives).

December 2, in reply to two dispatches from Copenhagen, Manderström practically broke off the negotiations. The danger, he declared in his dispatch to Count Hamilton, was now not of Federal Execution but of a German attempt to deprive Denmark of provinces, the possession of which was assured her by the Treaty of London. The question concerned all the signatory Powers and, in view of the greater support which this offered Denmark, the King of Sweden regarded the signature of the proposed treaty, for the time being, as inexpedient. At the same time, however, the dispatch did not exclude the possibility of concluding a formal treaty under other circumstances in the future and it was accompanied by a commentary on the part of Count Hamilton, "as an individual rather than as a representative" that seems to have given evidence of Manderström's continued support of the Danish point of view.[130]

A few days later, however, in the speech from the throne closing the session of the Swedish *Rigsdag*, King Charles was made to say: "In the Councils of the Powers, I shall ever seek to lay the word of the United Kingdoms in the scales on the side of right. It must not be asked of us, however, that we also place our sword there without regard for the question whether our object can be attained with the means at our disposal."[131]

In well informed circles in Copenhagen, the news spread on December 9 that the negotiations with Sweden had come to an end and that Denmark stood alone. Various adherents to the plan of a Scandinavian union now formed the idea of making a last attempt to bring about the alliance by personal influence on King Charles. To a visitor sent from Copenhagen, who had an audience with him on December 14, His Majesty said that he would act if he had to dismiss the whole ministry, with whom he had been struggling all day. He would defend Schleswig whether an alliance were concluded or not. This news was telegraphed in more cryptic form to the Copenhagen paper *Fædrelandet*, which

[130] Cf. Krieger, *Dagbøger*, III, p. 10; and Hall to Hamilton, October 6, 1864, in Carlquist, *Ur Henning Hamiltons Brefsamling*, II, pp. 181 f. Neither of these sources gives any definite indication of what Hamilton said.

[131] Koht, *Die Stellung Norwegens und Schwedens im deutsch-dänischen Konflikt*, p. 172.

on December 15 published without commentary the concluding sentence: "22,000 are coming and himself."

This news created a sensation in Copenhagen which was, however, somewhat cooled by the attitude of the semi-official Stockholm papers. De Geer and Gripenstedt, the members of the cabinet most influential in all but the actual conduct of foreign affairs, held to the position they had taken at Ulriksdal, that Sweden must not take part in a war on the side of Denmark unless one of the Great Powers, either England or France, set the example. Any other policy, they believed, would result in risks for Sweden which would far outweigh any possible benefits for Denmark.[132] Their point of view prevailed in the official Swedish dispatch of December 2 and in the King's speech from the throne. To some extent, Manderström seems to have shared the point of view of his colleagues.[133] Between their hesitation, however, and the impulsive actions of the King, he found himself in a difficult and embarrassing position.[134] He felt personally compromised by his share in the negotiations which, in his opinion, had involved Sweden in a moral obligation to assist in the defense of Schleswig. "He reminded me," Fournier, the French minister reported of a confidential conversation on December 17,

of his efforts in August last to free the Swedish government from the too compromising engagements that had been contracted without his knowledge.[135] He had succeeded in this and in doing so, prided himself on having done the best possible service to the Crown.

He had replaced the intimate relations between the United Kingdoms and Denmark within the limits which he had always had at heart to fix, that is that Denmark could count on Sweden if ever Germany attempted, in order to secure the success of her demands, an enterprise against non-German territories, i. e.: beyond the boundaries of Holstein and Lauenburg.

The assurance of this aid on the part of Sweden in the case mentioned

[132] Cf. De Geer to Hamilton, December 29, 1863, in Carlquist, *Ur Henning Hamiltons Brefsamling*, II, pp. 133-137; Koht, *Die Stellung Norwegens and Schwedens im deutsch-dänischen Konflikt*, pp. 174-178.

[133] Cf. Fournier to Drouyn de Lhuys, December 2, 1863, in *Les Origines diplomatiques de la guerre de 1870-71*, IV, p. 82, note 1.

[134] Cf. Björnstjerna to Hamilton, Stockholm, December 28, 1863, in Carlquist, *Ur Henning Hamiltons Brefsamling*, II, pp. 129-132.

[135] By the King at Scodsborg. Cf. p. 64 above.

had been given to King Frederick and the government of the United Kingdoms regarded itself as bound although no treaty had been signed at the time of the death of that Prince.

Although, since the death of that Sovereign, the question has taken on larger proportions, M. de Manderström does not admit that Sweden can refuse her coöperation to Denmark when Germany, carried away by ambition and by the popular movement, which the Princes will, perhaps, be unable to control, passes the limits of the territory of the Confederation and shows signs of unwillingness to halt at the Eider.

He regards Sweden as bound in honor, and himself even more than Sweden, because, since he has been at the head of affairs, his views on this point have been clearly known at Copenhagen. There are at stake on the banks of the Eider issues, which in his view, are as much Swedish as Danish, Scandinavian interests.

He told me then, in confidence, that he will not remain in office, if the government does not hold to its former promises and is not ready to fulfil them.[136]

King Charles informed Fournier that if the Germans did not halt at Rendsburg, he would bring fifteen or twenty thousand men to the aid of Denmark. His mind was made up and he would not change it unless he received positive representations from France and England. "If I acted otherwise, it would be all up with the idea of Scandinavian union. I cannot do that and do not want to."[137]

In one respect, however, Manderström's ideas differed from those of the King. The former wished to have the Swedish troops prepared at once and moved to points from which they could conveniently be shipped to Denmark. The King, on the other hand, did not regard such a demonstration as useful so long as the German troops were still in Holstein[138] and showed no signs of going beyond. He hoped that the negotiation could postpone the opening of hostilities until spring and may have regarded the immediate preparation of the auxiliary corps as a provocation which would hasten the action of the Germans.[139]

Manderström tendered his resignation but was persuaded to

[136] Fournier to Drouyn de Lhuys, December 18, 1863, in *Les Origines diplomatiques de la guerre de 1870-71*, IV, p. 84, note 2.

[137] Fournier, *loc. cit.*

[138] The occupation of that duchy was not complete until the end of December.

[139] Cf. Fournier, *loc. cit.*; and Björnstjerna to Hamilton, December 28, 1863, in Carlquist, *Ur Henning Hamiltons Brefsamling*, II, p. 131.

remain in office. He had failed to carry his point but probably did not give up all hope of securing the desired support for Denmark.[140] For even if Manderström's colleagues were unwilling to risk the single-handed intervention of the United Kingdoms in the coming struggle, they were pledged to follow England or France.

It was a common belief in Europe at this time, appearing not only in the press but even in the reports of diplomats who knew more about what the Emperor was saying than did the Danish minister at Paris,[141] that Napoleon planned a war for the spring of 1864, probably against Austria in the interest of Italy. Although Napoleon and Drouyn de Lhuys repeatedly said that they would do nothing against the national movement in Germany, Count Moltke-Hvitfeldt, the Danish minister at Paris, wrote in a report to Hall that he did not intend to prejudge the future and that there was no telling what combinations would develop in the spring. Nigra, the Italian minister at Paris, had told him that if war with Germany should come, "it is quite possible that we will be able to make a diversion in your favor next spring." Italy could not continue much longer to support the weight of her armaments and as long as Austria continued to hold Venetia, there was no possibility of reducing them. "In transmitting to the Emperor the King's reply to the Congress invitation," Nigra continued, "I explained these considerations to him. I even added that His Majesty's proposal...had awakened hopes,— that it would be difficult to dash these, and, in view of the absolute impossibility for Italy to endure longer the existing state of affairs, we would probably be forced in the spring to take the risks of a war."[142]

---

[140] Cf. Björnstjerna, *loc. cit.*; Krieger, *Dagbøger*, III, p. 28; Fournier to Drouyn de Lhuys, No. 43, confidential, December 21, 1863 (Paris Archives).

[141] E. g., Count Goltz. Cf. Bismarck, *Gedanken und Erinnerungen*, II, p. 5.

[142] Moltke-Hvitfeldt to Hall, *lettre confidentielle*, December 5, 1863 (Copenhagen Archives). Cf. Krieger, *Dagbøger*, III, p. 48 and *Fædrelandet* (Copenhagen), January 2, 1864, for similar rumors. Moltke-Hvitfeldt reported on December 29, 1863 that Drouyn de Lhuys "ne pouvant rien nous promettre pour le moment, il me fait entrevoir cependant un avenir moins sombre qui pourrait être la conséquence des écartes du développement révolutionnaire en Allemagne; aussi ce Ministre nous conseille de ménager le plus possible notre trésor, notre flotte et

Even after the interviews of December 20, both Lord Wode-house and Sir Augustus Paget believed that Hall hoped for eventual aid from France.[143]

M. Hall was very guarded in his reply, . . . [the British minister reported] but I certainly derived the impression that General Fleury had not spoken to him in the decided and positive terms which he represented it as his intention to do. M. Hall said that General Fleury's advice had been that Denmark should endeavor to avoid war if possible, and His Excellency [Hall] added that of course neither France nor any other Power would go to war for the interests of Denmark irrespective of their own, but His Excellency's whole tone in speaking as to what might be expected from France, was not one of such complete discouragement as one might have anticipated if General Fleury's language had been as categorical to him as it had been to Lord Wodehouse and M. d'Ewers.[144]

Count Hamilton's language was even more definite. After learning from Lord Wodehouse of General Fleury's declaration to himself and to Hall that France did not intend to support Denmark by arms in the event of war with Germany, Sir Augustus Paget asked his Swedish colleague whether he was aware of this and how he reconciled it with what he had told the Danish government.

Count Hamilton replied that General Fleury had told him that the object which the Emperor had in view was the meeting of a Conference to be followed by a Congress; that while pursuing this object, by which His Majesty trusted that all questions would be peacefully settled, he could not hold out to any Power the prospect of his support in case of war; but in the event of his proposals for a settlement by pacific means being rejected, His Majesty would then consider Himself free to adopt any policy which might suit Him.

A communication in this sense, Count Hamilton informed me, had also been made to the Swedish Government by that of France; and he added that neither this communication nor his conversation with General Fleury, gave him any reason to believe that the dispositions of the Emperor towards this country had undergone any change.[145]

notre armée de façon à pouvoir mettre à profit les chances que le cours du temps pourra faire naître en notre faveur." (Copenhagen Archives).

[143] "I cannot help suspecting that the Danes still count upon support from France in the spring." Wodehouse to Russell, telegram, December 21, 1863, 12:45 P. M. (Record Office, London).

[144] Paget to Russell, No. 319, December 22, 1863, (Record Office, London).

[145] Paget to Russell, No. 317, confidential, December 21, 1863 (Record Office, London).

Was Hamilton's view of French policy based merely on the interpretation of ambiguous statements reported from Paris or was there really a "communication in this sense to the Swedish government from that of France?"[146] It is at present impossible to say. The available correspondence to the French minister at Stockholm throws no light on the problem. Whether or not the information at the disposal of the Swedish government justified the belief that French policy would change in favor of Denmark,[147] that belief existed and undoubtedly influenced the decisions of those who held it. It is only from the vantage point of after years and with the knowledge of what happened after, that we can fully realize how vain were the illusions of 1863.

The ten days that followed the dissolution of the Danish *Rigsraad* were filled with excitement and uncertainty. King Christian, who had opposed the policy of the Ministry in dissolving the *Rigsraad*, began to try to save the situation. On December 23, he decided to demand that the *Rigsraad* be recalled to consider the abolition or suspension of the November Constitution.[148] Negotiations with leaders of the 'Whole State' party to form a new ministry failed and the King had to appeal again to Hall. That night there was a long meeting of the cabinet. For a time, the idea of meeting the King's wishes to the extent of recalling the *Rigsraad* and laying before it a proposal to postpone the going into force of the constitution for one year seemed to have a majority in its favor. But Orla Lehmann was against the proposition from the start and the final decision was that the cabinet would refuse to yield and would tender its resignation. Nevertheless, as time was pressing, ministers agreed to countersign the Letters Patent summoning the *Rigsraad* while the King

---

[146] Unless we assume that the Swedish Government still counted on such assurances as those in the instructions to Fournier of September 23, 1863. Cf. *Les Origines diplomatiques de la guerre de 1870-1871*, IV., pp. 74 f.

[147] Manthey notes in his diary: "23 December. Stang meddeler et Telegram som han har modtaget fra Sibbern, [Norwegian representative at Stockholm] om at Frankrig nu lader til at ville gribe sig an for Danmarks Sag. ..." *Dagbøger*, I, p. 352. Cf. Krieger, *Dagbøger*, III, p. 48, [January 4, 1864], and *Fædrelandet* (Copenhagen), January 2, 1864.

[148] Paget to Russell, No. 316, Confidential, December 21, 1863 (Record Office, London); Neergaard, *Under Junigrundloven*, II, p. 972.

was finding some one willing to take the responsibility for the new policy.

At noon on December 24, Hall notified the King of this decision. But that afternoon, objections were raised by some of the leading National Liberals, and the King was informed that a new ministry would have to countersign the summons.

King Christian was now deeply irritated by the ministers' attitude and especially vexed with Hall. He redoubled his efforts to secure the formation of a new ministry but it was not until December 28 that he had found a leader for it and could accept the resignation of the Hall cabinet. On December 31, the list of ministers was announced: Bishop Monrad, as President of the Council and Finance Minister, was the only outstanding political figure in it.[149]

VIII

The refusal of the Danish ministry to follow the advice of the foreign envoys was of great value to Bismarck. It had been with difficulty that he had obtained King William's assent to regard the Treaty of London as binding on Prussia until the November Constitution should go into force on January 1 and thus consummate the violation of the agreements of 1851-1852.[150] Every rumor from Copenhagen that Danish policy might change, made the King feel that the golden opportunity to free the duchies was escaping.[151] If the Danes, by yielding, had deprived Bismarck of

[149] For details of the cabinet crisis, cf. Neergaard, *Under Junigrundloven*, II, pp. 971-983; Krieger, *Dagbøger*, III, pp. 25-44; C. N. David, "Optegnelser," in *Historisk Tidsskrift*, 1914, pp. 54-65. For Monrad, cf. especially, P. Vedel, "D. G. Monrad," in Bricka, *Dansk Biografisk Lexikon*, XI, pp. 446-457, and Neergaard, *op. cit.*, p. 986.

[150] Cf. *Anhang zu den Gedanken und Erinnerungen von Otto Fürst von Bismarck*, I, Nos. 91, 94 ff, 100, 102.

[151] *Ibid.*, p. 95. In the Berlin Archives is a copy of a telegram from the Russian Legation in Copenhagen to that in Berlin for transmission to St. Petersburg, reporting that the Danish ministry had resigned on December 25 and that the *Rigsraad* was to be reconvened before the end of December. On this King William has scrawled: "Adieu schöne Hoffnung der Traktat loszukommen.—W. 25/12-63."

his plausible justification for action, his hold on his Sovereign might have been shaken if not broken.

Bismarck's position was being attacked from many sides. The attempt of the House of Representatives to influence the government's conduct of foreign policy merely made the King hold more closely to his official adviser but the opinions of the ambassadors to France and England, of Schleinitz, and of the Crown Prince and of other relatives of King William carried more weight.[152] Consideration of domestic policy and the revolutionary direction which the Augustenburg movement seemed to be taking, tended to counteract the anti-Bismarck influences. Yet if Bismarck's calculations had gone wrong in foreign policy, in the past successes of which the King took great pride,[153] it would undoubtedly have been difficult, if not impossible, to hold to the prudent and skillful line of action which was actually followed.

Even after the first of January, Bismarck was driven almost to despair by the King's sympathy for the Augustenburg cause. In spite of Bismarck's opposition, King William went to the Crown Prince's palace on the evening of January 17 to receive a letter from Prince Frederick and talked to Samwer, who had brought it, in a tone quite different from the formal and cold reply drafted by Bismarck and actually sent to Kiel.[154]

It is, of course, obvious that Bismarck would not have idly accepted the check to his plans involved in the withdrawal of the November Constitution, the immediate object of the controversy. If the Danes had yielded and if he had still remained in office, he would undoubtedly have renewed the demand for the literal fulfilment by the Danish government of the agreements of 1851-

---

[152] Cf. Bismarck's letter to Goltz in Bismarck, *Die Gedanken und Erinnerungen*, II, pp. 1-8; *Aus dem Leben Theodor von Bernhardis*, V, pp. 224-227; Max Duncker, *Politischer Briefwechsel aus seinem Nachlass*, Nos. 454 ff; Buchanan to Russell, Nos. 630 and 631, December 22, 1863 (Record Office, London).

[153] *Kaiser Wilhelms I. Briefe an seine Schwester Alexandrine und deren Sohn*, No. 60.

[154] Jansen-Samwer, *Schleswig-Holsteins Befreiung*, pp. 201-205 and appendices Nos. 11, 12, 14, 15; Gebauer, *Herzog Friedrich VIII*, pp. 90 f; *Anhang zu den Gedanken und Erinnerungen von Otto Furst von Bismarck*, I, Nos. 106 f; M. Duncker, *Politischer Briefwechsel aus seinem Nachlass*, No. 459; Roon, *Denkwürdigkeiten*, II, pp. 173 f.

1852.[155] At least, in such a case, however, he would have had to face the embarrassment of modifying his line of action and of keeping the Schleswig-Holstein question open over grievances that, in the eyes of Austria and the other Great Powers, would not justify incisive and positive exploitation. It is difficult to imagine how, if Denmark had not remained so flagrantly in default, Bismarck could have secured the war which he had declared to be necessary for the solution of the Schleswig-Holstein question except by taking all the risks involved in putting Prussia at the head of the national and liberal movement in Germany.

IX

The proceedings in the Diet at Frankfurt on January 14 and the Austro-Prussian ultimatum to Denmark on January 16 made it clear that the Schleswig-Holstein question had been taken out of the hands of the 'third Germany' by the two Great Powers.[156]

The Danish government had been prepared for the ultimatum by a telegram from its Legation in Berlin on January 13. The imperious form of the document and the forty-eight hour time limit aroused much resentment. Even Quaade, the new minister for foreign affairs, who had favored concession to Germany, now came to the conclusion that Austria and Prussia wanted war and that it was useless to try to avert it. The Danish King and ministers were alive to the danger of the situation but the excitement which prevailed in the country and especially in Copenhagen made a *coup d'état* impracticable and the time limit made the abrogation of the constitution by legal means impossible. There was nothing to do but to reject the ultimatum.[157]

Monrad, who was an amateur in diplomacy, made a rather naïve attempt to initiate a direct understanding with the Austrian minister. He wished, he said, to settle the matter by direct conversations with Austria and Prussia, without the parapher-

---

[155] Cf. pp. 144 f. above.

[156] Cf. pp. 103 f. above.

[157] Neergaard, *Under Junigrundloven*, II, pp. 1008 ff.; A. Friis, "Kammerherre Quaades Redegørelse for sin Intrædelse i Ministeriet Monrad" in *Personalhistorisk Tidsskrift*, 7 R., VI, (1921), pp. 51-66.

nalia of foreign mediation or congress, on the basis of the royal proclamation of 1852. He was confident that an agreement would be reached in a few days and he was ready to push such an agreement through the new *Rigsraad*. The discussion with Baron Brenner showed, however, that agreement was unlikely. Promises were no longer enough to satisfy Austria and Prussia and, on the other hand, Monrad indicated that Denmark would fight to the end before accepting the probable Austrian program of Schleswig-Holstein in personal union with Denmark.[158]

On January 21, the announcement was sent to the Courts of London, Paris, St. Petersburg, and Stockholm that the present ministry was ready to call the *Rigsraad* with the least possible delay in order to lay before it a law abolishing the Common Constitution of November 18, 1863. This constitution should be replaced by an organization of the Monarchy answering to the royal proclamation of January 28, 1852,[159] as interpreted by negotiations under the auspices of the foreign powers. If this proposal were accepted, the ministry would hold the elections and make the adoption of the new law by the *Rigsraad* a cabinet question.[160]

Monrad seems to have cherished the illusion that Denmark's situation was improved by this offer,[161] which had been suggested by the British minister at Copenhagen[162] and was supported by British diplomacy, but it made no impression on the German Powers.

The plan of holding a conference on the Danish question, suggested as early as December 15 by Bismarck, had been eagerly taken up by the British government and accepted in principle by Austria, Russia, and Sweden. But even before a formal proposal was made in Lord Russell's circular of December 31, both Napoleon and his minister for foreign affairs, Drouyn de

---

[158] Brenner to Rechberg, No. 5, Copenhagen, January 19, 1864 (Vienna Archives); Paget to Russell, No. 30, Copenhagen, January 19, 1864 (Record Office, London).

[159] Cf. p. 13, note 31, above.

[160] *Denmark and Germany, No. 4, 1864*, No. 813.

[161] Neegaard, *Under Junigrundloven*, II, pp. 1012 ff.

[162] Paget to Russell, No. 16, January 13, 1864 (Record Office, London).

Lhuys, showed their unwillingness to accept such a limited meeting in place of the greater Congress on which the Emperor's heart was set.[163] To be sure, Drouyn de Lhuys had stated that France would be represented at the conference if all the other Powers were, but this conditional acceptance was coupled with a series of objections. As soon as Bismarck realized that the French government did not really desire the conference, he too ceased to show any enthusiasm for it.[164] The acceptance of the conference by the Diet of the German Confederation, which was one of the conditions posed by Drouyn de Lhuys,[165] was not made more probable by a French circular to the minor German states which emphasised the difficulties in the way of the conference and spoke of the London Conference of 1852 as having resulted in only "*une œuvre impuissante.*"[166]

The British cabinet then made the suggestion to the governments of France, Russia, and Sweden that they coöperate in pressing Germany to accept the conference.[167] This was coolly received and a proposal for a representation to the Diet at Frankfurt that the invasion of Schleswig, a non-German land, would be an act of war and that the Diet would incur a heavy responsibility in ordering it, met a similar fate.[168] Gorchakov reserved his answer until he could consult the Emperor Alexander and remarked that it merely perplexed the question to entertain a new project until the previous one had been matured and

---

[163] Cf. Muret, "La Politique française dans l'affaire des Duchés." In support of Muret's view that the idea of the congress played a great rôle in Napoleon's policy at the time, cf. Goltz to Bismarck, December 26, 1863 (Berlin Archives); Cowley to Russell, No. 1199, December 25, 1863 (Record Office, London). Colonel Claremont, British military attaché at Paris reported to Earl Cowley on January 5, 1864, that General Fleury had told him that he, Fleury, had told the Emperor that the only chance of preserving peace in the duchies was by holding a conference to discuss the whole subject, but that he had found the Emperor out of humor and disinclined to listen to any such proposition. "J'ai invité à diner et on m'offre à déjeuner."

[164] *Les Origines diplomatiques de la guerre de 1870-1871*, I, No. 38.

[165] *Ibid.*, No. 23.

[166] *Ibid.*, No. 51.

[167] January 5, 1864, *Denmark and Germany, No. 4, 1864*, No. 615.

[168] January 10, 1864. *Ibid.*, No. 642.

tried.[169] Drouyn de Lhuys did not answer Lord Cowley's written communication of the proposition and, when Cowley called in person the next afternoon, said that he had not yet had time to speak to the Emperor about it.[170]

After the Austro-Prussian ultimatum the British government turned to put pressure on Denmark to revoke the constitution and on Austria and Prussia to give her time to do so. On January 18, Earl Russell addressed a note to all the Powers signatory to the Treaty of London—including Austria and Prussia—asking whether they would "concert and co-operate" with Great Britain to maintain the Treaty of London and especially to uphold the integrity of the Danish Monarchy.[171] On January 23, he urged Austria and Prussia to allow Denmark six weeks from the first of February to withdraw the constitution in a legal manner.[172] On January 26, he proposed that the Powers sign a protocol to the following effect:

> Denmark on her part, would engage to convoke without delay the Rigsraad, and to lay before that Assembly on its meeting, a proposal that it should revoke the Constitution of November 18, so far as that Constitution applied to the Duchy of Schleswig; and Denmark would further engage that the Danish Government should employ their utmost efforts in order to induce the Rigsraad to consent to such a revocation.
>
> Austria and Prussia, on their part, would declare that they accepted the diplomatic engagement so contracted by Denmark, and as a consequence of such acceptance would agree to delay the passage of the Eider by any military force until the result of the measures to be taken by Denmark should be ascertained.[173]

---

[169] Napier to Russell, No. 20, St. Petersburg, January 10, 1864. Gorchakov approved the second proposal but only against the action of the lesser German states and in the interest of Austria and Prussia. Napier to Russell, No. 21, St. Petersburg, January 21, 1864 (Record Office, London).

[170] Cowley to Russell, No. 70, Paris, January 12, 1864 (Record Office, London).

[171] *Denmark and Germany, No. 4, 1864*, No. 741.

[172] *Ibid.*, No. 777.

[173] *Ibid.*, No. 815. Russell's lack of sense of the realities of the situation is illustrated even better by his naïve dispatch of January 5, 1864 to the British ministers at the courts of some of the German states: "In case the vote of the Diet should be given in favor of the claims of the Prince of Augustenburg to the sovereignty of Holstein, the Federal troops ought, in the first place evacuate that Duchy in order to give the Danes an opportunity of resisting the entry of an invading force if they choose to do so. Unless this is done, a fraud will have been committed

As might have been expected, no one of these proposals was accepted by all the Powers and every attempt to bring about collective intervention failed. In London, the press, especially the *Morning Post*, which was supposed to stand in close relation to Palmerston, thundered against Germany and held out prospects of assistance to Denmark. But although Russell's notes to Germany and the language of the British representatives there emphasized the dire consequence to the peace of Europe if the Germans crossed the Eider, the Danish minister at London listened to quite different language. Russell read him a letter from Palmerston in which the latter violently criticized Danish policy: "Denmark mustn't expect that Europe will tolerate breaches of treaties and a system of misgovernment [in Schleswig] comparable to that practiced by Russia in Poland; Denmark is too small and weak for that, and it mustn't imagine that for its sake England will wage war with all of Germany.[174]..."

The British cabinet, however, was seriously considering the question of armed intervention. At a cabinet meeting on January 2, the peace party backed by a letter from the Queen,[175] carried the day and it was decided to seek the coöperation of France and the other Powers "before talking about the use in any event, of force."[176] On January 5, there was talk in London of the Channel Fleet being sent to Copenhagen[177] but the majority in the cabinet, strongly backed by the Queen, was opposed to intervention without the aid of at least one of the Great Powers.[178] No promise of that could be obtained.

The Russian government was anxious to prevent the war, but less for the sake of Denmark than of averting a breach between the German Powers and Great Britain. Gorchakov's chief

in the occupation of Holstein, which has taken place under pretence of a Federal Execution." *Ibid.*, No. 614.

[174] T. Bille to Quaade, London, January 20, 1864, Neergaard, *Under Junigrundloven* II, p. 1019.

[175] *Letters of Queen Victoria*, 2nd series, I, pp. 138-140.

[176] Gladstone to Mrs. Gladstone, January 2, 1864, Morley, *Gladstone*, II, pp. 104 f. Palmerston was ill and could not attend the meeting. Vitzthum von Eckstädt, *St. Petersburg and London*, II, p. 295.

[177] *Les Origines diplomatiques de la guerre de 1870-1871*, I, No. 55.

[178] *Letters of Queen Victoria*, 2nd series, I, p. 153.

interest was to maintain the *entente* of the four Powers against France.[179] When the news of the Austro-Prussian ultimatum to Denmark reached him he declared that he deplored this action, but that Russia would never join in any *démarche* which might wound Austria and Prussia. After all, it was better that Schleswig be occupied by them than by the minor states,[180] and he advised Denmark not to resist the occupation.[181] In view of this attitude it is no wonder that Russian counsels of moderation at Berlin and Vienna led to no results.[182]

Continued efforts of the British government to secure the coöperation of France were equally futile. Drouyn de Lhuys made no effort to conceal his opinion that the Danish question must end in hostilities.[183] ''He regretted,'' he said,

the estrangement which circumstances had produced between the British and the French governments because he saw no probability of their assuming such an attitude together as could alone conjure the dangers which threatened Europe. The Emperor, therefore, had resolved upon acting with the greatest prudence and circumspection in the Danish question. There were many reasons which inclined France towards the cause of Denmark. It was the cause of an honest government and of an honorable people to whom France was attached though rather by the romance of tradition than from any interested motive. It was, moreover, a cause sanctioned by a treaty,

---

[179] Redern to Bismarck, Petersburg, January 8, 1864, (Berlin Archives); Bismarck, *Die gesammelten Werke*, IV, No. 243; Napier to Russell, telegram, January 5, 1864. ''The leading aims of Prince Gorchakov are to combat the notions of democracy and nationality and to control France; he will support Denmark as far as possible consistently with those objects.'' Napier to Russell, No. 53, January 20, 1864 (Record Office, London).

[180] Redern to Bismarck, No. 8, January 16, 1864 (Berlin Archives). Cf. Napier to Russell, No. 55 and 57, January 22, 1864 (Record Office, London).

[181] Neergaard, *Under Junigrundloven*, II, p. 1002.

[182] ''After the Russian chargé d'affaires had communicated to Count Rechberg the wish of his Government...that six weeks should be granted to Denmark... he immediately read to [Rechberg] despatches...to the effect that the Russian Government has full confidence in the intentions of Austria and Prussia with regard to Schleswig, and that they are ready to admit that Austria and Prussia have been irresistibly impelled to adopt their present policy by a laudable desire to prevent the National Party in Germany from taking the lead in this affair, and that they hope success will attend their efforts to stem the torrent of revolution which is seeking to find an outlet in the question of Schleswig-Holstein.'' Bloomfield to Russell, No. 72, January 28, 1864 (Record Office, London).

[183] Cowley to Russell, No. 1194, Paris, December 26, 1863 (Record Office, London).

but a treaty containing no guarantee, in which France had, so to say, but a sixth responsibility.

While, therefore, the sympathies of the French government might be with Denmark, there was nothing which bound them or made it incumbent upon them to interfere by arms in her support. And France would certainly not interfere alone, particularly if, as might be apprehended, Austria and Prussia were to side with the rest of Germany. When he looked around to see who might be the possible allies of France in defense of Denmark, he found none that could be counted upon. Russia, even supposing that under present circumstances an alliance between Russia and France were possible, had enough on her hands at home and was not likely, moreover, to engage in hostilities with Germany. Sweden might be willing to take up arms in defense of Scandinavian interests, but Sweden up to this time had not recovered from the wars of Charles XII and Gustavus III and could be of but little assistance. The question of Poland had shown that Great Britain could not be relied upon when war was in the distance. ......
France did not wish a collision single-handed with Germany but would wait the development of events.[184]

In Cowley's opinion, the influences which combined to produce "this lamentable conduct" of France were:

1. A rankling disappointment at the failure of the projected Congress, and a desire to justify the project in the eyes of the world by the spectacle of a conflict which might have been avoided had the project been accepted.
2. Anger toward Her Majesty's Government for their imputed abandonment of France on the Polish question.
3. The possibility that out of the complications something may turn up advantageous to France.[185]

Sir Henry Bulwer, the British ambassador at Constantinople, who was returning to his post via Paris, was no more successful than Lord Cowley in securing the cordial coöperation of France.[186]

All that the British government had to show for its efforts was an identic note from the Prussian and Austrian ambassadors in London which stated that their governments, by basing upon the agreements of 1851-52, the rights which they were proceeding to enforce upon Denmark, recognized *ipso facto* the principle of the integrity of the Danish Monarchy established by those

[184] Cowley to Russell, No. 23, January 3, 1864; cf. Nos. 89 and 161, January 14 and 25; (Record Office, London).

[185] Cowley to Russell, No. 99, January 15, 1864 (Record Office, London).

[186] La Tour d'Auvergne to Drouyn de Lhuys, No. 152, London, December 13; Nos. 160, December 24, 1863 (Paris Archives); H. Bulwer to Russell, Paris, January 5, 12, 1864 (Record Office, London).

agreements.   In occupying Schleswig, the allied Powers had no intention of departing from that principle.

If, however, in consequence of complications which may be brought about by the persistence of the Danish Government in its refusal to make good the promises of 1851-52 or of the armed resistance of other Powers in the Dano-German conflict, the Imperial [Royal] Government were to find itself compelled to renounce combinations which would no longer offer a result proportionate to the sacrifices which events might impose upon the German Powers, definitive arrangements could not be made without the concurrence of the Powers who signed the Treaty of London.   The British government would then find the Imperial [Royal] government ready to come to an agreement with it as to the final settlement of the Dano-German question.[187]

Although these notes were dated January 31, they were not finally agreed on until February 3 and were presented only on February 4, in time for communication to Parliament.   As hostilities had already commenced at the frontier of Schleswig, they were worth little more than the paper on which they were written[188]

[187] *Denmark and Germany, No. 5, 1864*, Nos. 880, 881.
[188] Cf. Stern, *Geschichte Europas*, IX, pp. 352, 584 ff.

CHAPTER V

THE BEGINNING OF THE WAR.

I

On January 20, two days after the rejection by Denmark of the Austro-Prussian ultimatum, Field Marshal Wrangel, "*der alte 'Abjott Deitschlands'* ",[1] who had commanded the Prussian troops in the War of 1848, took command of the allied forces concentrated on the lower Elbe. On the following day, they entered Holstein and marched towards the Eider, the occupying Saxons and Hanoverians sullenly yielding to them the lines of communication in the eastern part of the peninsula. On January 31, the Danish commander-in-chief, General de Meza, was called upon to evacuate Schleswig, and as he refused to do so, on the following morning, February 1, the Austro-Prussian troops crossed the Eider, the Danish outposts falling back before them.

The Danish defense was based on the famous *Dannevirke*, a line of forts constructed south of the town of Schleswig, with its right flank covered by the marshes of the west coast and its left by the Schlei, a narrow fiord, extending far into the land. It was believed in Copenhagen that this position could be held for a long time. But in winter, because of the freezing of some of the bodies of water in the system of defenses, it lost part of its natural strength. To avoid the cutting off of his army, de Meza decided not to await the decisive attack from his numerically superior and better organized foe, and, on the night of February 5-6, evacuated the position.[2] The larger part of the Danish forces was now concentrated in the entrenched lines on the peninsula of Düppel and in the neighboring island of Alsen, while the cavalry and one infantry division retired into Jutland.

[1] Roon, *Denkwürdigkeiten*, II, p. 191.
[2] Cf. Neergaard, *Under Junigrundloven*, II, pp. 1049-1056.

The allied troops spread over the whole of Schleswig outside of Düppel and Alsen, and on February 18, the Prussian advanced guard pursued a party of Danes over the frontier of Jutland and occupied the town of Kolding in Denmark proper.

II

Soon after the outbreak of hostilities, the Danish government appealed to England, France, and Russia for aid in the defense of Schleswig in conformity with the treaties of guarantee made in the eighteenth century and confirmed in 1848. All three refused: England would act only in coöperation with France and Russia and referred to the declarations of Austria and Prussia that they did not have the intention of destroying the integrity of the Danish Monarchy; France used a similar argument; and Russia, while expressing the intention of doing everything possible to restore peace, admonished Denmark to fulfil her obligations.[3]

An appeal to the Swedish government was equally unsuccessful. King Charles XV, spurred on by enthusiasts for the Scandinavian cause, would probably have been glad to act but he could neither persuade his ministers to intervene without the active support of France or England nor could he find others to take their places. Manderström, in his reply to Copenhagen, declared that he would withdraw nothing of what had previously been said as to the solidarity of interest of the Scandinavian states but also called attention to his more recent official utterances. He emphasized especially the fact that, after the evacuation of the Dannevirke, it was no longer a question of defending Schleswig but of reconquering it. The strength of the United Kingdoms was unquestionably inadequate for that.[4]

At the same time, Manderström turned again to the neutral Great Powers and again received unsatisfactory replies. Russell

---

[3] Koht, *Die Stellung Norwegens und Schwedens im deutsch-dänischen Konflikt*, p. 216; Neergaard, *Under Junigrundloven*, II, pp. 1123 f.

[4] Koht, *op. cit.*, pp. 216 ff. Cf. *Les Origines diplomatiques de la guerre de 1870-1871*, I, p. 253. On February 14, Count Hamilton gave up his post as Swedish minister at Copenhagen.

made it clear that England would not act with Sweden alone. Drouyn de Lhuys was more evasive: France would not intervene now but intended to reserve her freedom of action. Unsuccessful at London and Paris and fearful that Russia might actually intervene against them, the Swedish-Norwegian ministers continued slowly to develop their armed forces but did nothing more effective in support of Denmark.[5]

III

The British government had failed to avert the invasion of Schleswig. In December 1863, Palmerston had written to Russell:

I quite concur in the views you state, in your letter of yesterday, of the matters to which it relates.

Holstein is part of the German Confederation; and, if the Germans determine to commit therein an act of gross injustice and of diplomatic perfidy, we should content ourselves with a strong and indignant protest. But Schleswig is no part of Germany, and its invasion by German troops would be an act of war against Denmark, which would in my clear opinion entitle Denmark to our active military and naval support. But you and I could not announce such a determination without the concurrence of the Cabinet and the consent of the Queen.[6]

Unfortunately for the reputations of the two statesmen concerned, the last condition made it impossible for them to back up the strong language they had so often used. A threatening paragraph, which Palmerston had wished to include in the

---

[5] Koht, *op. cit.*, pp. 210-231. Cf. Hallendorff, *Illusioner och Verklighet* and *Sveriges Historia* XII, pp. 339-346. Apparently, Drouyn de Lhuys had not intended to discourage the Swedish government from acting in support of Denmark and during March and the first half of April, the influence of Fournier, the French minister at Stockholm was for intervention. Cf. *Les Origines diplomatiques de la guerre de 1870-1871*, II, Nos. 248, 263, 295, 308, 359, 377, 410, and especially 448; and Karnicke to Rechberg, March 10, No. 28B, April 8, No. 37 A-B (Vienna Archives). There are traces of secret correspondence between Paris and Stockholm, most of which seems not to have survived. For example, a confidential dispatch from Drouyn de Lhuys to Fournier of April 21, (*Les Origines diplomatiques*, II, No. 448) contains the information that on April 19, Napoleon telegraphed to Charles XV: "Dans l'intérêt de Votre Majesté, je crois qu'il est maintenant trop tard pour faire une manifestation armée en faveur du Danemark."

[6] S. Walpole, *Lord John Russell*, II, p. 388.

Queen's speech which was read at the opening of Parliament on February 4, had to be omitted and the section on the Danish question concluded with the tame and colorless statement that "Her Majesty will continue Her efforts in the interest of peace."[7]

In the debate in the House of Commons, Palmerston attempted to cover up the diplomatic defeat by boasting that "within the last very few hours we have received information from the Austrian and Prussian governments, that they are prepared to declare that they abide by the Treaty of 1852, and will maintain the integrity of the Danish monarchy in accordance with the terms of that treaty."[8] "....They have now declared," he said a little later, "that they mean as soon as possible to send us a formal declaration that they abide by the Treaty of 1852; that they will maintain the integrity of the Danish monarchy; that the invasion of Schleswig, however lamentable it may be and however much to be deplored, is not undertaken for the purpose of dismembering the Danish monarchy; and they are thus committed to evacuate Schleswig whenever the conditions which they attach to the entrance shall have been complied with."[9] In the House of Lords, Earl Russell read the text of the Austro-Prussian note of January 31 and his admissions of uncertainty, together with the conditions set forth in the note, exposed the hollowness of the Prime Minister's interpretation.

The public, especially in London, was watching the actions of Austria and Prussia with suspicion and anger. The younger leaders of the Tory party were eager to assist Denmark and some observers believed that a majority in Parliament could have been obtained for their policy. But neither Derby nor Disraeli, the real leaders of the Opposition, desired war or was ready for office. In the debates, Russell's policy of "meddle and muddle" was sharply criticised but the position of the cabinet was not shaken.[10]

[7] Cierpinski, "Die Politik Englands in der schleswig-holsteinischen Frage," in Z. f. s.-h. G., XLV, p. 111; Letters of Queen Victoria, 2nd series, I, p. 154; Fitzmaurice, Granville, I, pp. 457 f.

[8] Hansard, 3rd series, CLXXII, col. 107.   [9] Ibid., col. 111.

[10] Cierpinski, "Die Politik Englands in der schleswig-holsteinischen Frage," in Z. f. s.-h. G., XLV, pp. 103-115; Letters of Queen Victoria, 2nd series, I, p. 154;

Within the cabinet, however, the differences continued. The eleventh hour offer of the Danish government to convoke the *Rigsraad* and to lay before it a proposal for the repeal of the November Constitution had made a good impression in Downing Street.[11] Hitherto, Earl Russell "had a twinge or feeling" that Germany had much right on her side, and that Denmark was not a little wrong, but the refusal of the German Powers to delay the invasion of Schleswig convinced him that from then on, Germany was utterly in the wrong.[12] For a moment, to be sure, he was so delighted to hear that Bismarck had succeeded in winning the King's consent to the note of January 31 that he admitted to the Austrian ambassador "that in the present circumstances, Bismarck was the best minister that Prussia could have."[13] It was only with reluctance, however, that he acquiesced in the decision of the majority of the cabinet not to assist Denmark by force unless France would join in an alliance for that purpose.[14]

The evacuation of the *Dannevirke* lines, whose strength had been greatly overestimated, came as a great surprise. The first impression in London was that the war was now really over and that Denmark would have to accept the best terms she could get.[15]

Henry Greville, who dined with Palmerston on February 6, found his host in "high feather." "He told me," Greville noted in his diary, "the Danes had evacuated Schleswig, and he

Lang, *Sir Stafford Northcote*, I, pp. 207 ff.; Monypenny and Buckle, *Disraeli*, V, pp. 343 f.; Malmesbury, *Memoirs of an Ex-Minister*, II, p. 310.

[11] T. Bille to Quaade, London, January 26, 1864, received February 2 (Copenhagen Archives).

[12] S. Walpole, *Lord John Russell*, II, p. 389.

[13] In a conversation at the Foreign Office on February 2. "Lord Russell est enchanté que M. de Bismarck l'ait emporté en definitive sur les idées personelles du Roi et finit par me faire l'aveu, assez piquant dans sa bouche, que dans les circonstances actuelles, Bismarck était le meilleur Ministre qu'on peut avoir en Prusse...." Apponyi to Rechberg, February 3, 1864 (Vienna Archives).

[14] S. Walpole, *Lord John Russell*, II, p. 389. Cf. Fitzmaurice, *Granville*, I pp. 458 f; *Letters of Queen Victoria*, 2nd series, I, pp. 156-159; Russell to Napier No. 46, February 10, 1864 (Record Office, London).

[15] Neergaard, *Under Junigrundloven*, II, pp. 1122 f., citing T. Bille's report of February 10.

supposed the fighting was over. He seemed sanguine that the allies would keep their word and restore to the King of Denmark his dominions, whenever he had revoked the Constitution.'' To Greville's objection that Austria and Prussia had not been strong enough in Germany to resist the cry for the invasion of Schleswig, and that it was not impossible that they might feel equally weak when it became a question of their retiring from that duchy, the Prime Minister expressed the opinion that time might do much and that they would see that it would be wiser and safer to do what was right. The conduct of Austria and Prussia had been inexcusable. They had shown great cowardice and should have defied the popular clamor in Germany with a much higher hand.[16]

A few days later, Herr Klindworth, the famous secret agent, reported to Count Apponyi, the Imperial and Royal ambassador, that in years, he had not seen Lord Palmerston in such a state of irritation, especially against Austria. ''Anger, threats, and thirst for vengeance sum up his true feelings towards us. These sentiments were the more violent as he purported to have counted more on our support and now felt himself isolated, impotent, and compromised.'' Palmerston complained bitterly of the Queen, ''who raised difficulties in his way by following a policy of her own in espousing the cause of Prussia and in exercising her influence on the party leaders in Parliament in favor of a policy of peace and non-intervention.'' He spoke even of his failure in the matter of the speech from the throne. According to Klindworth, Palmerston admitted that his perplexities and difficulties were increased by the passive and enigmatic attitude of the Emperor of the French.

[He] now regrets the strained relations with the French cabinet in which the rejection of the Congress has placed him and desires a rapprochement at any price. If he does not receive overtures from Paris within a fortnight, he will himself take the initiative and his aim will be to induce the Emperor Napoleon to adopt joint action in the Danish question by giving him *carte blanche* in the Italian. Lord Palmerston accuses Austria of bad faith in the Danish business; our alliance with Prussia is, according to him, the biggest mistake we could have made; it will lead us to ruin. Our policy is alienating

[16] H. Greville, *Diaries*, 4th series, pp. 175 f.

the sympathies not merely of Germany but of the whole of Europe. We will end by losing Venetia and Galicia; 'so much the better'; we will lose Hungary too, 'so much the worse'— (these were his very words); but England will stand aside. She can attach no importance to an alliance with a State which is in hot water with the half of its peoples. If we had managed to satisfy Hungary, as he has always advised us, our position would be quite different. It is there that we should find our strength and not in the support of the little Kings and Princes of Germany, who, as far as he can see, will play us false at the first opportunity. The so-called Federal Reform of last summer had at bottom no other object than to secure for us the support of Germany in case of an attack on Venetia. That attempt having failed, Austria is now trying to reach the same goal by the alliance with Prussia, and Lord Palmerston has a strong suspicion that a secret understanding in regard to Venetia exists between Vienna and Berlin. What he emphasized especially, however, was his conviction that Prussia, in following her present policy in the Schleswig-Holstein question, is supported secretly by Prince Gortchakoff. .... Alliance with France is still the favorite idea of Prince Gortchakoff and he needs to humor Prussia, who is to form the connecting link for this alliance.[17]

Apponyi, while unwilling to guarantee the accuracy of Klindworth's observations, confirmed the impression of irritation on the part of Palmerston. "The key to the Premier's irritation is his impotence. He senses the fact that the direction of general policy is escaping him and that, in the isolation in which he finds himself, unable to count on any of the Great Powers and not even supported by the Queen and the majority of his colleagues, he can undertake nothing. ...."

As Palmerston knew that Klindworth was an Austrian secret agent[18] and as he had expressed the desire to discuss the general situation with him, it is probable that much of what he said was intended somewhat less to express his own views than to make an impression at Vienna. As he wrote to Earl Russell a few days later, "it was very useful to remind the Austrians privately of the danger they were running at home, in Italy, Hungary, and Gallicia."[19]

In a memorandum to the Prime Minister on February 13, Russell had proposed that the British government suggest to

[17] Apponyi to Rechberg, No. 11. A-F., secret, London, February 10, 1864 (Vienna Archives).

[18] Apponyi to Rechberg, secret, London, May 21, 1862, (Vienna Archives).

[19] Cf. p. 176 below.

France that the two Powers offer their mediation to the combatants and that

if Austria and Prussia refuse mediation, decline to accept the bases proposed,[20] or insist on terms which are, in the opinion of France and England, inconsistent with the integrity and independence of Denmark, Great Britain will at once despatch a strong squadron to Copenhagen, and France will place a strong corps of troops on the frontiers of the Rhine Provinces of Prussia.

For once Palmerston was more prudent than Russell. ''I share fully your indignation,'' he replied.

The conduct of Austria and Prussia is incredibly bad, and one or both of them will suffer for it before these matters are settled. I rather doubt, however, the expediency of taking at the present moment the steps proposed. The French Government would probably decline it, unless tempted by the suggestion that they should place an armed force on the Rhenish frontier in the event of a refusal by Austria and Prussia—which refusal we ought to reckon upon as nearly certain. The objections which might be urged against the measures suggested as the consequences of the refusal of Austria and Prussia may be stated to be: First, that we could not for many weeks to come send a squadron to the Baltic; and that such a step would not have much effect upon the Germans unless it were understood to be a first step towards something more; and I doubt whether the Cabinet or the country are as yet prepared for active interference. The truth is, that to enter into a military conflict with all Germany on continental ground would be a serious undertaking. If Sweden and Denmark were actively coöperating with us, our 20,000 men might do a good deal; but Austria and Prussia could bring 200,000 or 300,000 into the field, and would be joined by the smaller German states.[21] Secondly, though it is very useful to remind the Austrians and the Prussians privately of the danger they are running at home—Austria in Italy, Hungary, and Galicia; Prussia in her Rhenish provinces—yet it might not be advisable nor for our own interest to suggest to France an attack upon the Prussian Rhenish territory. It would serve Prussia right if such an attack were made; and if Prussia remains in the wrong we could not take part with her against France. But the conquest of that territory by France would be an evil for us and would seriously affect the position of

---

[20] ''That the bases of the mediation should be the integrity of the Danish Monarchy and the engagements of 1851-52 as regards the Duchies of Holstein, Lauenburg, and Schleswig.''

[21] On December 26, 1863, Palmerston had written to Russell: ''The Prussians are brave and make good soldiers; but all military men who have seen the Prussian army at its annual reviews of late years have unequivocally declared their opinion that the French would walk over it at will and get without difficulty to Berlin, so old-fashioned is it in organization and formation and manœuvre.'' S. Walpole, *Lord John Russell*, II, p. 388, n. 1.

Holland and Belgium. On the whole, I should say that it would be best for us to wait awhile before taking any strong step in these matters.[22]

On February 11, the Danish minister in London presented to the British government an appeal for support against the German Powers. The request was based on the guarantee of Schleswig to the Crown of Denmark contained in the Treaty of 1720, which had been recognized in 1848 as still binding, and especially on the more recent expressions of opinion by British ministers. It was probably in consequence of this appeal that Palmerston and Russell ordered Sir Alfred Horsfold ''to prepare the scheme for an English army to be landed on the shore of Denmark.''[23] The opinion of the cabinet as expressed in meetings on February 13 and 17, continued to be against single-handed intervention so in a dispatch dated February 19, Sir Augustus Paget at Copenhagen was informed that Her Majesty's government would take no steps towards arresting the progress of the present unhappy contest until after full consideration and communication with France and Russia.[24] Russell added, when communicating this dispatch to the Danish minister in London, the statement that the correspondence which had taken place with Paris and Petersburg gave no reason to believe that either France or Russia were prepared to join Great Britain in giving material aid to Denmark in support of the integrity of the Danish Monarchy.[25]

Reports that the Austrian fleet was coming to the north and rumors that an attack on Copenhagen was intended led to renewed activity of both Palmerston and Russell.[26] On February 20, Palmerston wrote to the Duke of Somerset, First Lord of the

[22] Russell's memorandum in Walpole, *Lord John Russell*, II, pp. 389 f.; Palmerston to Russell, February 13, 1864, Ashley, *Palmerston*, II, pp. 247 f. The extracts of Palmerston's letter in Walpole, *op cit.*, differ in a few minor words from the text quoted. Voelkle, *Die Haltung Englands in der deutsch-dänischen Frage, Herbst 1863-Juli 1864*, attributes the memorandum to Palmerston, the letter to Russell.

[23] J. F. Maurice, *The Balance of Military Power in Europe*, p. 15.

[24] Cf. Sir A. W. Ward in *Cambridge History of British Foreign Policy*, II, pp. 573 f; *Les Origines diplomatiques de la guerre de 1870-71*, I, No. 219.

[25] Russell to Paget, No. 43, confidential, February 19, 1864 (Record Office, London).

[26] *Letters of Queen Victoria*, 2nd series, I, p. 163.

Admiralty, that he quite agreed with Russell that a British squadron ought to go to Copenhagen as soon as the season permitted and that it should have orders to prevent any invasion of, or attack upon Zealand and Copenhagen. "It is not unlikely that Austria and Prussia, reckoning upon our passive attitude, contemplate the occupation of Copenhagen, and think to imitate what the first Napoleon did at Vienna and Berlin, and mean to dictate at the Danish capital their own terms of peace. We should be laughed at if we stood by and allowed this to be done."[27] That same evening, Russell sent a warning inquiry to Vienna: "Is it intended by the Austrian Government to send their men of war to the British Channel? Further, is it intended that they should attack Copenhagen? This matter is very serious, and should be clearly explained."[28]   At the same time Sir Andrew Buchanan at Berlin was informed that the invasion of Jutland was regarded as "a very serious affair."[29]   On the following day February 21, it was decided by the cabinet that the Channel Squadron should be ordered home and this decision was duly communicated to the Queen.[30]   At the same time, Earl Russell announced to the ambassadors of France and Russia, the intention of Great Britain to send a squadron to Copenhagen and expressed the wish that France and Russia join in the demonstration.   Telegrams in this sense were despatched to Cowley at Paris and to Napier at Petersburg.[31]

Russell's communications to France and Russia had been made, however, without the consent of the cabinet or of the Queen.   The only decision respecting the fleet which had been adopted by the cabinet and approved by Her Majesty had been that the fleet should be ordered home in case its presence should be necessary to protect British commerce in the Channel and so

[27] Ashley, *Palmerston*, II, 249.

[28] Telegram 5 P. M. reported in No. 72 to Bloomfield (Record Office, London).

[29] Telegram 5:10 P. M., reported in No. 88 to Buchanan (Record Office, London).

[30] *Letters of Queen Victoria*, 2nd series, I, pp. 160 f.

[31] *Les Origines diplomatiques de la guerre de 1870-1871*, I, Nos. 232, 234; Russell to Cowley, telegrams, February 21, 22, to Napier, February 21 (Record Office, London).

that it would be ready for any contingencies that might arise. Palmerston answered the Queen's objections with some heat but failed to carry the cabinet with him. At a meeting on February 24, the cabinet, with the exception of Lords Palmerston and Westbury,[32] was unanimous in condemning the communication that had been made and protested against any step of the kind being taken which would be looked upon as the first step in drifting into war; and particularly against any measure being adopted without previous consultation. It was decided that Earl Russell was to inform Russia and France that there was no more question of sending the fleet to Copenhagen, "the contingency which alarmed him not having arisen, viz. the attack upon Copenhagen by the Austrian fleet."[33]

IV

During the first part of February, French policy followed the general lines laid down during the preceding months. After the first crossing of the frontier of Jutland, however, it seemed for a moment as if the Imperial government were prepared to follow the suggestion from London and agree on a demonstration in favor of Denmark.

Napoleon and his mouthpiece, Drouyn de Lhuys, had contributed toward blocking a peaceful settlement by their attitude towards the plan of a conference and to the encouragement of Prussia by their secret suggestions to Goltz. Napoleon did not conceal his joy at the outbreak of hostilities. He purported to believe that the development of the Schleswig-Holstein question had made the international position of France more favorable than that of any other Power. He openly congratulated himself that, by his policy, he had convincingly given the lie to the suspicions against him and had given proof to the world of his disinterestedness and love of peace. It was obvious that Napoleon realized the advantages of a situation that would enable him to throw the weight of French power into the balance at a

[32] Lord Chancellor.
[33] *Letters of Queen Victoria*, 2nd series, I, pp. 160-168.

favorable moment. At the same time, he took a certain malicious delight in the embarrassment of the British Government. In conversation with the Austrian ambassador, he discussed the possible eventualities of a war of England against Germany and each time came to the conclusion that England would not be able to do very much. ''It is certain,'' Metternich wrote,''that he desires that the war come to amuse the public, that England intervene in it, and above all that she remain impotent.''[34] Napoleon's pleasure seems to have been alloyed, however, by the fact that England was not intervening by force. ''It is curious,'' Lord Cowley reported to his government,

> to observe...the vexation caused by the seeming determination of Her Majesty's Government not to give material aid to the Danes under present circumstances. If I am correctly informed, (for naturally some reserve is observed towards me) this irritation is evinced in no measured language by the Emperor, by the Government, and in French society in general. That the press is very violent I can myself bear witness. In a word the conduct of Great Britain is condemned in terms not very agreeable to English listeners in society, nor to English readers of the French journals. It would almost seem as if some French plan must have been defeated by the passive attitude of Her Majesty's Government.[35]

On January 31, in a discussion with Goltz of the situation that might develop out of the occupation of Schleswig, Drouyn de Lhuys remarked: ''As you see, we remain calm and conciliatory and without doubt we will use our influence to prevent European complications; but if such arise, well, we will see whether we can do any business with Prussia.''[36] A few days later, at a dinner where the two men were seated together, Drouyn de Lhuys, ''in a half joking manner,'' renewed his confidential suggestions to Goltz.

> He said to me that we should annex Schleswig-Holstein, and some of the other lands nearby. France would gladly be of help to us and would be

---

[34] Metternich to Rechberg, private letter, Paris, February 3, 1864 (Vienna Archives). Cf. Goltz to Bismarck, No. 43, February 1 (Berlin Archives), and Cowley to Russell, No. 217, February 5 (Record Office, London).

[35] Cowley to Russell, No. 217, February 5, 1864 (Record Office, London).

[36] Goltz to Bismarck, No. 43, February 1, 1864 (Berlin Archives). The extract just quoted is published in Oncken, *Die Rheinpolitik Kaiser Napoleons III.*, I, p. 25, n. 1, and in Brandenburg, *Untersuchungen und Aktenstücke*, p. 416, note.

content with compensation which would amount more to an outward satisfaction for the French nation than a real equivalent to such an increase in the power of Prussia. When I called his attention to the fact that we had no such compensation to offer, he remarked that a slight rectification of the frontier would be enough to satisfy France; there was, for example, Landau, which, so far as he knew, should have been left to France in 1814. He then developed the idea that an independent, neutralized state on the model of Belgium should be formed out of the Prussian Rhine Province—a thought which has often been expressed by the Emperor Napoleon. My question whether this state should belong to the German Confederation was answered in the negative.[37]

In his last report dispatched before the dinner conversation with Drouyn de Lhuys, Goltz had suggested that an official exchange of notes with France should no longer be postponed. He had, however, suggested that the agreement be on a limited and general basis: France to agree to oppose English or Russian intervention in favor of Denmark, Prussia to promise general support in the Eastern question, insofar as this would not conflict with Austrian interests, and readiness to coöperate in realizing the Emperor's plans for a Congress.[38] He was opposed, however, to any transaction involving changes in Prussian territory and limited his reply to Drouyn de Lhuys' suggestion of a buffer state on the Rhine to an exposition of the German and Prussian feelings of the population there. He could not, he said, understand how Prussia could be expected to give up such loyal and flourishing provinces in a territorial deal nor what interest France could have in erecting a barrier against Prussia, to whom no desire of annexations at the expense of France could be attributed. It was, however, inexpedient to carry the discussion further at the moment.[39] It was not until February 9, that Goltz reported the conversation to his government.

In the meantime, the rapid progress of the allied armies and especially, the unexpected evacuation of the *Dannevirke*, the news

[37] Goltz to King William, Paris, February 9, 1864, Oncken, *Die Rheinpolitik Kaiser Napoleons III.*, I, p. 29. The conversation took place "vor acht Tagen," i. e. probably February 2 or 3.

[38] Goltz to Bismarck, No. 43, Paris, February 1, 1864 (Berlin Archives).

[39] Goltz to King William, Paris, February 9, 1864, Oncken, *Die Rheinpolitik Kaiser Napoleons III.*, I, pp. 30 f.

of which reached Paris on the evening of February 6, made a great, and in Goltz's opinion, rather displeasing impression.[40]

On the next day, Goltz called on Drouyn de Lhuys in an attempt to find out the views of the French government. "You find me surrounded by flowers and you are covered with laurels"[41] was the greeting of the Minister, who was preparing his house for a fancy dress ball. He continued in a more serious and somewhat less friendly vein, however, in remarking that he still regretted *this* war because the object to be achieved stood in no just relation to the sacrifices and did not justify the amount of blood shed.[42] Goltz replied that the object of the occupation of Schleswig really had been to compel the King of Denmark to fulfill the agreements of 1851-52 and that the allied powers would without doubt have been satisfied with this if Denmark had evacuated the province without resistance. He was not in a position to say whether or not the Prussian government was going to extend its aims because of the resistance but it was a question whether the precious blood which had flowed should be the price for just a constitution which Denmark might again shortly throw to the winds. The preliminary diplomatic skirmishing was leading nowhere until, in the course of the conversation, Drouyn de Lhuys mentioned the Scandinavian union. He expressed the opinion that this combination would inevitably come into close relationship with Prussia and North Germany and would thus enable Prussia to become a respectable sea power, which would be in complete accordance with the tendencies of French policy. This in turn led to a discussion of the possible conditions and aims of a Franco-Prussian alliance.[43] Drouyn de Lhuys, who had received no answer from Berlin to his previous feeler, remarked that Prussia would not, after all, want to found a new minor state in northern Germany but would rather keep Schleswig-Holstein and at the same time round out her territories in other ways. In return, France would be satisfied with a

---

[40] *Ibid.*, pp. 26 f.

[41] Oncken prints "lanciers." A. Luzio suggests that it must have been "lauriers" in the original. *Rivista storica italiana*, 1928, p. 315, note 6.

[42] Cf. Metternich to Rechberg, telegram, February 3, 1864 (Vienna Archives).

[43] Oncken, *op. cit.*, I, pp. 27 f.

rectification of frontier corresponding to the peace settlement of 1814. "The Minister," Goltz wrote,

did not seem to be quite clear in his own mind as to the difference between 1814 and 1815. He spoke of Landau, of an unsightly angle made by the Franco-Prussian frontier, at the same time denying any interest in the low grade coal of Saarbrücken, and finally mentioned the possibility of the incorporation of Dutch Limburg with the Kingdom of Netherlands and the cession of part of Luxemburg to France. In any case, he said, the latter Power would ask for much less than we would acquire.

Goltz, who had not yet reported the earlier conversation, felt called upon to take this opportunity of combating illusions which, in his opinion, should never have been entertained and the continuance of which could only result in the danger of bitter disappointment. "I said to the Minister...," he reported,

that a policy of annexations corresponded neither to the principles of Your Royal Majesty nor to the well-understood interests of Prussia. With reference to Schleswig-Holstein, which, in view of the not indubitable claims of the Prince of Augustenburg, might perhaps come to be regarded as a lordless land, there was perhaps room for differences of opinion. The annexation of other German states, however, would place the governments of those that were left in such definite and irreconcileable opposition to Prussia that it seemed a real question whether the disadavantages would not outweigh the advantages. Prussian policy must aim at strengthening the bonds which linked that Power with the other German states. It must, therefore, aim at uniting the forces of the rest of Germany as much as possible under Prussian leadership. Considering the preponderance of France and the purely defensive character which such a union of the German states would have, I really did not see in what way that Power could be in need of a compensation. Besides, it would be a most flagrant contradiction to its policy of nationalities to want to acquire German land. I regarded it as more easily attainable and wiser, to regulate the relations of Prussia and France on quite another basis. 'Is it,' I asked the Minister, 'of no significance at all to France that Prussia has no cause to further the forming of a coalition [against France] but rather through refusing to join, to make such impossible? We have had, except for the Polish policy of the preceding year, nothing to complain of the Emperor Napoleon's attitude towards Prussia since his accession to the throne. It seems to me very important for France by continuing such a policy to interest us in the maintenance of her position. Many other things can develop out of this without making over the whole map of Europe. We could support the Emperor's idea of a Congress; we do not need to object to its being held in Paris; at it, we could be useful to France in many questions. M. Drouyn de Lhuys admitted that all this would be very valuable, but did not conceal the fact that it was less than the Emperor would wish.[44]

[44] *Ibid.*, pp. 31 f.

Goltz's replies to Drouyn de Lhuys merely repeated the policy which he had recommended during the past two months. He probably knew little of what Bismarck had been saying to Talleyrand and the "illusions" which he was attempting to destroy were just those which Bismarck had been trying to keep alive. The real answer to the French Emperor and minister is found in Bismarck's conversation with Talleyrand at Berlin on February 9, before the report of either of the Paris discussions had been received.

There is no reason to suppose that, even if the King had been less averse to dealing with France than he actually was, Bismarck would have accepted Drouyn de Lhuys' terms or Goltz's suggestions. He continued, however, to give the impression that he differed from the King in the aims of his policy and that he was more susceptible to temptation.

The King and the Crown Prince, Bismarck told Talleyrand, secretly sympathize with the Prince of Augustenburg. "As for me," he continued,

> my ideas on the Danish question have not changed. Of all the policies we could follow, the most inept would be for Prussia to coöperate to establish a new German Grand Duchy, to create a Prince who, in time of peace will vote against us at Frankfurt and in time of war will compromise us if he does not betray us. Believe me, it is not for a nobody[45] like the Prince of Augustenburg that Prussia is spending the blood of its soldiers and the money of its treasury. The incorporation of two such fine provinces with our monarchy is just made to tempt our ambition; but of all sovereigns, the King is perhaps the most disinterested, and besides, he knows that the other Powers will not consent without compensation to an increase of territory for him. There remains then, reconciliation with Denmark: that is what I want and it is in view of that, that I adhere to the principle of the integrity of the Danish Monarchy. ....[46]

The suggestions of Drouyn de Lhuys to Goltz remained unanswered. No wonder, then, that the French Emperor began to doubt whether the policy of temptation was a sound one. Rumors of a guarantee of Austria's non-German possessions had continued to come to Paris. It was suspected that Prussia was

---

[45] *pleutre*.

[46] Talleyrand to Drouyn de Lhuys, No. 25, February 9, 1864, *Les Origines diplomatiques de la guerre de 1870-71*, I, pp. 281 f.

going to concede this to Austria in return for Austrian support in carrying the war beyond the limits originally agreed upon.[47] The first reports of the invasion of Jutland naturally confirmed the belief that an agreement on this basis had already been reached and reports as to the intentions of the Prussian government with regard to the disposition of the duchies probably added to Napoleon's suspicions.[48] He had no objection to the separation of the duchies from Denmark or to their annexation by Prussia but he wanted this to be the result of a Franco-Prussian, not of an Austro-Prussian, understanding.

As late as February 19, Lord Cowley, the British ambassador, believed that France would not intervene in the war, although the Emperor seemed to desire Great Britain to do so. "During a conversation which I had with the Emperor," he reported,

carried on, however, in the presence of too many persons to admit of its leading to any results, His Majesty in speaking with sympathy of the position of Denmark, asked me whether England would not go to her assistance. I replied that under the present circumstances it did not seem to be the intention of Her Majesty's Government to depart from the pacific policy.... If France, a great military nation, hesitated at entering the lists with the whole of Germany, it was not to be expected that Great Britain, whose army was limited, should attempt to cope with such a superior force as Germany could put into the field. Without replying to this remark, the Emperor said that England might render invaluable aid to the Danish cause by sending a fleet to coöperate in the defense of Alsen.[49]

This conversation with the Emperor was followed by one with Drouyn de Lhuys, who appeared no closer to the British point of view than before.

After the events of the last few months, it was hardly possible to suppose that the Duchies would resume their former allegiance to the Danish Crown. The utmost that could be hoped for was a personal union between them. Perhaps a part of Sleswig might be preserved to Denmark, but even that was problematical. He must ask himself, therefore, whether war would be justified to obtain such a result. On the other hand, the creation of another small state in Germany, and the annexation of Denmark to the two other Northern Kingdoms would not interfere with the balance of power in Europe, except indeed to act as a counterpoise to Russia. Although therefore such a

---

[47] Metternich to Rechberg, No. 8 A-B, February 11, 1864 (Vienna Archives).
[48] Cf. Döhler, *Napoleon III. und die deutsch-dänische Frage*, pp. 54-62.
[49] Cowley to Russell, No. 280, February 19, 1864 (Record Office, London).

solution of the Dano-German question, he repeated, could only be prospective, he could see nothing to regret in it, were it to be effected, and he
could not conceive that it would embarrass Her Majesty's Government.[50]

On the afternoon of February 20, Lord Cowley found that the
situation had completely changed.

M. Drouyn de Lhuys proceeded to say that if I had not called upon him'
he should have requested to see me, in order to speak to me respecting the
latest intelligence which he had received from Germany. This represented
M. de Bismarck as making arrangements for the disposal of the Duchies of
Schleswig-Holstein, and as menacing Saxony with military occupation if she
opposed the policy of Prussia. In the disposal of the Duchies.....M. de
Bismarck seemed to consult Russian and Prussian interests alone, for it
was upon some member of the House of Oldenburg,[51] brought up at St.
Petersburg, that the Sovereignty of the Duchies was, according to M. de
Bismarck's notions, to be conferred, an arrangement that would be all but
tantamount to giving them to Prussia herself. A scheme of this nature
would alter the complexion of the Dano-German question, and the success
of it, he did not hesitate to tell me, would not be seen with indifference by
France.

Then again the invasion of Jutland proved that the two Great German
Powers were quite indifferent to the means by which they might accomplish
their ends.[52]

Adverting then to the conversation I had with him a few days ago[53]....
M. Drouyn de Lhuys said that he had been much struck with the observations which I had made to him as to the influence necessarily exercised over
the policy of Her Majesty's Government by the attitude of France—that he
had recounted that conversation to the Emperor, and had asked His Majesty whether he had done right in giving me the assurance *that the solution
of the Dano-German question which His Majesty was most desirous to see
effected was the maintenance of the settlement of 1852*, and that speaking of a
Scandinavian Monarchy, His Majesty had in view, what might possibly,
rather than what would probably occur. The Emperor had permitted
him to give this assurance and had added that the expectant attitude which
His Majesty had taken, had been dictated solely by the feeling of responsibility which would weigh upon him in engaging in a war with Germany,

---

[50] *Ibid*. In a dispatch of February 20, Cowley speaks of these conversations
as having occurred "a few days ago."

[51] On February 15, Prussia signed a treaty with Oldenburg for a naval station
at the mouth of the Jahde. Cf. *Les Origines diplomatiques de la guerre de 1870-
1871*, I, No. 218 and p. 341.

[52] A similar communication was made to Earl Russell by the Prince de La
Tour d'Auvergne at London on February 21 and undoubtedly influenced Russell's
statements about the fleet. Cf. *Les Origines diplomatiques de la guerre de 1870-71*,
I, p. 346.

[53] Cf. p. 185 above;

and by the apprehension of the selfish views which would immediately be attributed to him.

Lord Cowley thought it prudent not to call the minister's attention to the change in language and replied merely that "Her Majesty's Government fully appreciated the difficulties of the Emperor's position, and would, I did not doubt, acknowledge the prudence of his conduct in avoiding hostilities with Germany. I asked myself, however, whether something might not be effected for Denmark by the united efforts of Great Britain, France and Sweden without inflicting the horrors of war upon France and Germany....." Drouyn de Lhuys replied that he would take an early opportunity of speaking to the Emperor on the subject.[54]

That evening, Drouyn de Lhuys telegraphed to Vienna and Berlin to ask whether Austria and Prussia intended to recall to Schleswig the troops which had entered Jutland.[55] At about the same time, Goltz sent to Bismarck a warning telegram that France was preparing to adopt an unfavorable attitude towards Prussia.[56] The Prussian ambassador had noted with alarm that

[54] Cowley to Russell, No. 282; February 20, 1864. Received February 22. This dispatch was received too late to influence the decision to send the British fleet to Copenhagen, which was communicated to the French Ambassador on February 21. But on February 20, at 5:15 P. M., Cowley despatched a telegram to Russell: "... There are symptoms which coincide with the opinion expressed in your private letter of yesterday." Cowley to Russell, No. 281, February 20, (Record Office, London). Russell's letter begins: "I should not be surprized if the wrangling in Germany should induce the Emperor to turn once more to us for an intimate alliance. In that case you cannot say more than that you will at once transmit the suggestion to London." (Record Office, London, G. D. 22: 106.) On February 21, Cowley telegraphed: "The invasion of Jutland and the Prussian threat to occupy Saxony have made a great impression here, and we might profit by the moment, if we think it advisable. Perhaps coöperation in a naval demonstration might be obtained." On the same day, Russell received from the French ambassador, the information contained in Drouyn de Lhuys' dispatch of February 19, *Les Origines diplomatiques de la guerre de 1870-71*, I, No. 223.

[55] February 21, 1864, 8:30 P. M. *Les Origines diplomatiques de la guerre de 1870-71*, I, No. 230. Thimme suggests that Talleyrand acted on his own initiative. He has overlooked the note in *Les Origines diplomatiques* which states that the telegram cited was sent to Talleyrand as well as to Gramont. Bismarck, *Die gesammelten Werke*, IV, p. 335, note 1 to No. 281.

[56] H. Oncken, *Die Rheinpolitik Kaiser Napoleons III.*, I, p. 32, note 1.

the press, which, until a few days before, had maintained an attitude not unfavorable to the policy of Austria and Prussia in the Danish question, had adopted a tone which reminded him of the worst days of the Polish crisis. The change was simultaneous and so unanimous that he could only conclude that it was based on instructions from the government.

The alleged obscurity as to the real object of the war, the occupation of various points in the Duchy of Holstein by Prussian troops, newspaper reports of an inspection of the harbor and vicinity of Kiel in view of the erection of fortifications, the mobilisation of the 8th army corps interpreted as a demonstration against Saxony—all these circumstances were exploited by papers of every shade of opinion to ascribe ambitious intentions to Your Majesty's Government. At the same time, the attitude of the German 'middle' and 'small' states was praised as 'national,' Austria was treated tenderly by the governmental press, the heroic struggle of Denmark against the overwhelming might of two Great Powers was glorified, and, finally, in the radical papers, references were made to the policy of Henry IV, Louis XIII, and Louis XIV, with emphasis on the point that France had always been the protector of the liberty of Germany, which is now again threatened by Austria and Prussia.

Goltz remembered, too, that Drouyn de Lhuys had repeatedly said that the ostensible object of the war stood in no reasonable relation to the expenditure of treasure and blood.[57] He was struck by the way in which, after for some days avoiding conversations with him, both the Emperor and Empress now treated the Austrian ambassador with marked attention and seemed to be trying to sow suspicion between the allies. He had been warned by leaders of the Orleanist and Legitimist parties, notably Thiers and Berryer, of an impending shift in the Imperial policy. The more long drawn out the struggle in Schleswig, the more obstinate the Danish resistance, the more would public opinion in Europe and especially in France take sides with Denmark. Napoleon would take advantage of this to put through his aims. Last, but surely not least, on February 20, the chief of the Paris branch of the House of Rothschild had shown the liveliest apprehension that the war could no longer be localised. He had, he told Goltz, the most alarming news from London: such passion had overpowered the English statesmen that they would

[57] Cf. p. 182 above.

be capable of buying the aid of France for the rescue of Denmark, even at the price of the left bank of the Rhine.[58]

On the morning of the twenty-first, Goltz received official news of the crossing of the frontier of Jutland and of the intention of the allied Powers to remain in occupation of Kolding. At the first opportunity that afternoon, he called on Drouyn de Lhuys to explain the situation to him. The frontier of Jutland had been crossed not by order of the governments but as a result of events in the theater of operations. Military considerations, the protection of the allied forces in Schleswig and the operations against Düppel and Alsen, made it undesirable to give up the position in Kolding and the threat to the rest of Jutland. Denmark obviously regarded herself at war with the German Powers as shown by the capture of German ships and the blockade of the coast. Under these circumstances the operations could hardly be limited to the occupation of Schleswig but must aim at forcing an acceptable peace as soon as possible. Even the extension of operations in Jutland could hardly justify a change in attitude on the part of the neutral Powers.

Drouyn de Lhuys replied that Prussia and Austria had gone on so rapidly that the Imperial government would have to consider whether it could look on passively any longer. He could not, he said, express an opinion on this point without obtaining the commands of the Emperor, with whom he claimed not to have discussed the situation since the evacuation of the *Dannevirke*.[59] He did point out, however, that the attitude at Paris was changing and repeated the argument that this change was resulting from the unequal combat, the advance of the German Powers from one aim to another, and the obscurity of their ultimate aims. "First we had seized Holstein on the pretext of Federal Execution, then although this security should have been enough for Schleswig too, we had occupied that duchy as a 'material guarantee'; we had declared, though in not very clear

[58] Cf., however, p. 176 above.

[59] The British Ambassador reports that a council was held on the morning of February 21. Cf. p. 193 below. Drouyn de Lhuys' statement that he had not discussed the situation with the Emperor since the first week in February seems patently incredible.

terms, that we only wanted to enforce the stipulations of 1851-52; now we advance into Jutland and are going on to 'exterminate' the Danes; for what else can we intend in ruining Denmark financially, taking one province after another from them, and finally getting on to Copenhagen?''

Goltz's reply was a defense of the two German Powers. Thanks to their moderating influence, the Diet, which had wanted to occupy Holstein in favor of the Prince of Augustenburg and in contradiction with the Treaty of London, had voted and carried out Federal Execution in Federal territory. Then, in the interest of maintaining the Treaty of London, the two Great Powers had announced and carried out the occupation of Schleswig as a pledge for the fulfilment of the conditions precedent to that treaty. The two operations were quite distinct in object and in aim. The formal statement which had preceded the march into Schleswig stated that armed resistance on the part of Denmark might lead the two Powers to go beyond the stipulations of 1851-52, but that if, in consequence of this, the integrity of the Danish Monarchy were called in question, an agreement with the co-signataries of the Treaty of London would be reached. The intention of going beyond that limit had not yet been expressed although the first named eventuality had come about through the resistance of Denmark. How far beyond the stipulations of 1851-52, Prussia and Austria would go and what new combinations would be sought, could not be stated in advance without encouraging Denmark to continued resistance and promising what perhaps could not be carried out in the face of public opinion after great sacrifices. Goltz then argued that the smallness of a state should not secure impunity for its actions and pointed his statements from the recent history of France and England. ''No one wants to exterminate the Danes and unfortunately we can't swim to Copenhagen. So long, however, as the Danes neither fulfil their obligations nor completely abandon Schleswig as a pledge, but rather try to destroy German commerce, we would be fully justified in carrying the war into Jutland. That, nevertheless, has not yet come to pass.''

Drouyn de Lhuys replied that so long as it was merely a

question of Holstein, France had been unwilling to interfere in a conflict which was claimed to be a question of German domestic politics. The seizure of Schleswig had given the affair an international character but France had still remained a passive spectator. The invasion of Jutland would compel the French government to take into consideration what its attitude should be towards an act which had created a sensation in London and Stockholm. The British and Swedish cabinets had approached the Imperial government in this matter and it would have to decide what answer to make. ''The two German Powers have declared that they are acting in the interests of Germany; but the Federal Diet, which is certainly German, disapproves of their action. It is, besides, hardly credible that a war like this is undertaken merely to replace 30 or 50 Danish schoolmasters by German.''

Goltz attempted to rebut these arguments, too. ''The last remark of the Minister,'' he wrote,

I answered with the counter question as to whether he really believed that we wished to conquer the duchies. .... I reminded him that in various confidential conversations he had raised the idea of getting the duchies for Prussia but that this had always been decidedly rejected by me as involving too dangerous a policy. These utterances of mine, I had reported confidentially to Your Majesty's Minister President and had never received the slightest indication in reply that my view of the situation was not shared by him. It was hard for me to see how any such suspicions could be held on the part of France.

Drouyn de Lhuys answered that the suspicions were based solely on the obscurity of Prussian policy and the lack of proportion between the object expressed and the means employed. All this was, he repeated, an academic conversation as he did not know the Emperor's intentions.

When Goltz asked what Drouyn de Lhuys would advise the Prussian government to do to avert the threatened complications, the French minister came at once to the real point of the interview.

Drouyn de Lhuys replied that it was difficult to give advice seeing that we had already gone so far. He could only recommend that, if we wanted to limit ourselves to the 'little question,' we should express our intentions as soon as possible and as clearly and moderately as possible. If, on the contrary, we were aiming at a solution of the 'big question,' there were three possible cases: the solution we wanted would be either harmful or indifferent or advantageous to France. In the first case, France would definitely oppose it; in the second, would maintain her present passive attitude; in the third, he would want to know in advance so that he could support it. In any case, France could not look on with indifference, if new combinations in northern Europe were created without her coöperation.

During most of the conversation, the tone and attitude of the French minister reminded Goltz of the Polish crisis; the conclusion, however, was as friendly and confidential as the other discussions of the same subject during the past few months.[60]

On the morning of February 22, however, the attitude of Drouyn de Lhuys was again what it had been during the earlier negotiations. The telegram of the French ambassador in London that Great Britain expected to send the fleet to Copenhagen had been followed late on the night of the 21st by a second which announced that Lord Russell regarded the explanations given by the Austrian and Prussian ambassadors as sufficient at least to suspend the resolutions previously taken.[61] "Under these circumstances," said Drouyn de Lhuys to Cowley, "the proposal which you make to me falls to the ground, and there is no occasion for me to take further notice of it." He had conversed at length with the Emperor on the subject of giving material assistance to Denmark and had found him determined to be very circumspect.[62]

The return to this policy is not surprising. The reasons which Drouyn de Lhuys gave for not taking part in the war were as valid in February as in January. In case of hostilities with Germany, Great Britain could limit herself to naval demonstrations and blockade, France would be exposed to the full weight of a national war.[63] The interesting problem is to explain the temporary change of attitude shown by Drouyn de Lhuys in his conversation with Cowley on February 20.

[60] Goltz to King William, Paris, February 21, 1864, Oncken, *Die Rheinpolitik Kaiser Napoleons III.*, I, No. 14.

[61] *Les Origines diplomatiques de la guerre de 1870-1871*, I, No. 233.

[62] Cowley to Russell, No. 289, February 22, 1864 (Record Office, London).

[63] Cowley to Russell, No. 289, February 22, 1864 (Record Office, London). Cf. Drouyn de Lhuys to La Tour d'Auvergne, February 23, 1864, *Les Origines diplomatiques de la guerre de 1870-1871*, II, No. 245. Cf. V. Duruy, *Notes et Souvenirs*, II, p. 118; Randon, *Mémoires*, II, p. 91.

Lord Cowley believed that the influence of certain ministers who favored the *entente* with England, and the news of the invasion of Jutland, accompanied by reports of the intentions of the Prussian government with regard to the duchies, determined Napoleon to take a more active part than he had yet done in the Dano-German question.[64] "I should inform your Lordship," he wrote to Russell on February 23,

> that sometime back, despairing of inducing M. Drouyn de Lhuys to advocate with the Emperor a more conciliatory policy with Her Majesty's Government, I had endeavored through other Ministers, whom I know to be well inclined to the re-establishment of a better understanding between the two Governments, to effect this desirable end. I believe that the counsels tendered by these Ministers to the Emperor, aided by other adventitious advice, had produced a certain effect when the news of the invasion of Jutland, accompanied by reports of the aim and intention of the Prussian Government with regard to the Danish Duchies, determined His Majesty to take a more active part than he had yet done in the Dano-German question. This determination was conveyed to M. Drouyn de Lhuys after the council on Saturday [February 21], and led to the conversation which I had with His Excellency on Saturday afternoon. M. Drouyn de Lhuys had not been prepared for the change in the Emperor's views, but he acquiesced in them rather than risk his place, and in his desire to please His Majesty possibly exaggerated the Emperor's intentions. But he did not the less disapprove. I have reason to believe that he put himself in communication with Prince Metternich, who naturally, under present circumstances cannot be supposed to favour any understanding between Great Britain and France. Prince Metternich has the Empress's ear and sees her when he pleases. He did see her on Saturday, and if I am correctly informed, again on Monday. Her Majesty's present antipathy to England is no secret. In her, therefore, Prince Metternich and M. Drouyn de Lhuys found a willing ally. Unfortunately the Prince de la Tour d'Auvergne's second telegram of Sunday[65] came to their aid. It was represented to the Emperor that no dependence was to be placed in Her Majesty's Government—that the slightest assurance given by the German Powers was sufficient to modify their policy and that the only safe course for France to pursue was to maintain her expectant attitude. The Emperor yielded to these insinuations.[66]

[64] Under February 19, Viel Castel notes: "Des renseignements positifs permettent d'affirmer que l'Alliance Anglo-Française est un fait accompli. Cette alliance se combine avec le concours de l'Italie et elle a pour formule la défense de l'intégrité du Danemark." *Mémoires*, VI, p. 306.

[65] Cf. note 61 above.

[66] Cowley to Russell, No. 299, February 23, 1864 (Record Office, London). Cf. telegram, February 24, noon: "Rouher told me last night that with patience all would come right—that Metternich had alarmed the Emperor by stating that

Goltz had no doubt but that the entrance of the German troops into Jutland, the feeling of sympathy for the weaker side, and respect for public opinion were pretexts for the sudden unfriendly attitude of the French government. In his opinion the reasons which seemed to determine the Emperor Napoleon to adopt a more active policy in favor of Denmark were the coöperation of Prussia with Austria, the apparent limitation of the object of the war to the constitutional reorganization of the Danish monarchy and the consequent sidetracking of his cherished idea of the Scandinavian union, and irritation at the reserve of the Prussian government in its relations with him.[67]

The assurances from Berlin and Vienna as to the accidental character of the advance into Jutland[68] indicated that the Austro-Prussian agreement was not yet an accomplished fact. Additional information about the mission of General Manteuffel to Vienna tended to confirm this.[69] Napoleon, then, could afford to wait to see what Bismarck would have to say about affairs. It was not yet clear that his hopes were vain.

The ill-humor of the French government lasted only a few days. Count Goltz attributed the return to a passive attitude especially to the fact that England would not accept the conditions necessary to secure Napoleon's coöperation.[70] It is probable, however, that the most significant explanation of the restored good humor of Paris appears in the telegram which Drouyn de Lhuys sent to Talleyrand on February 25.

I have received your private letter of the 23rd. Let Bismarck take the initiative but try to get him to make his overtures more definite. Don't lay too much stress on the evacuation of Kolding; speak of it as a matter of form.[71]

a combined movement on the part of England and France would keep Austria and Prussia together, whereas Austria desired to get out of the scrape." (Record Office, London).

[67] Goltz to King William, February 22, 1864, Oncken, *Die Rheinpolitik Kaiser Napoleons III.*, I, No. 15.

[68] *Les Origines diplomatiques de la guerre de 1870-1871*, I, Nos. 231, 235.

[69] *Ibid.*, II, No. 236.

[70] Goltz to King William, February 24, 1864, Oncken, *op. cit.*, p. 42.

[71] *Les Origines diplomatiques de la guerre de 1870-1871*, II, No. 266.

Talleyrand's private letter of February 23rd is unknown. In a confidential dispatch of that date, he reports a conversation with Bismarck in which the latter gave him the Prussian version of the Kolding incident. In reply to his question whether the occupation of that city was to be taken as the prelude to the invasion of Jutland, Bismarck replied that in his opinion, the extension of the campaign to Jutland was called for by the naval operations of the Danes. "We have seized Schleswig," he said,

as a security for the fulfilment of obligations incurred with respect to the Elbe duchies. Today, our ships are being captured by the Danes at sea and in port; we must seek another pledge if we are not going to remain unarmed against the naval attacks of our opponents. We would, in my opinion, incur well deserved reproach if we accepted such injury without reprisal. That is what I am trying to make the Cabinet of Vienna understand and it is that which General von Manteuffel is instructed to explain. But Austria still refuses to consent to the entry of the allied troops into Jutland. On the other side, Russia, apprehensive of a Scandinavian union, lays stress on an armistice, a conference, and the integrity of the Danish Monarchy. England threatens us and, if Prussia has to meet the opposition of France in addition, she will have to call a halt, for she cannot alienate the four Great Powers. . . . .

In the course of the conversation, Talleyrand brought up again the mission of General von Manteuffel to Vienna and the disadvantages of negotiating at this moment about a campaign in Jutland. "M. de Bismarck," he writes, "has understood it as I do, for he told me without being asked, that he was going to telegraph the King's aide-de-camp not to press the cabinet of Vienna but to leave the decision to it."[72] It may have been in this connection or, less probably, in the discussion of the British proposal for a conference, that Bismarck let drop the hints which Talleyrand thought worthy of a private letter.

After the receipt of Drouyn de Lhuys' telegram of February 25, Talleyrand had a confidential and interesting conversation with Bismarck. "I should have little to report to you today," Talleyrand wrote in a confidential dispatch on February 26, "if M. de Bismarck had not yesterday, in an interview which took on an intimate and confidential character, read me a report addressed to the King by Count von der Goltz. The ambassador

---

[72] *Les Origines diplomatiques de la guerre de 1870-1871,* II, No. 249.

draws in it a rather gloomy picture of the present disposition of
the Imperial government toward Prussia, and it seems that this
report has made as painful an impression on the King as on his
minister, for whom I thought it my duty to attenuate its colors.''
After he had finished reading the document, Bismarck explained
that he knew that Goltz was easily impressed and that he,
Bismarck, did not attach quite as much importance to the
symptoms and facts reported. He could not, however, but be
struck by some of them. Talleyrand responded that it was true
that the representatives of the foreign Powers in Paris often had
to take precautions against misleading information supplied by
hostile or interested sources. The newspapers did indeed reflect
public opinion on this war and did not need to be inspired by the
government. The Emperor, ''with his habitual sagacity,'' had
foreshadowed in his letter to the Prince of Augustenburg this
shift of opinion in favor of Denmark, ''and you know,'' Talleyrand added,

''the extent to which His Majesty attempts to place his conduct and that
of his government in accord with public sentiment.''
    ''It is true,'' Bismarck said, ''but admit that that makes it difficult for
a foreign Power to attach itself intimately to French policy, if that is based
upon prevailing sentiment.''   ''Based?'' I replied, ''No; but certainly influenced by opinion.''
    ''M. Drouyn de Lhuys is then agreed that the situation has changed?''
    ''I must confirm,'' [Talleyrand went on] ''that M. von der Goltz has made
an accurate report of the words of M. Drouyn de Lhuys.   The plain language which our minister used to your ambassador gives clear proof of the
desire to check your advance along a path which is dangerous and compromising our good relations; but my own impression of the situation differs
somewhat from that of Count von der Goltz in his appraisal of the general
situation.   My correspondence bears no trace of the change of sentiment of
which he informs you; on the contrary our confidential relations are looked
on with favor at Paris and I am rather encouraged to proceed with them
than bidden to let them drop.''
    ''If empty rumors or false appearances have deceived Herr von der
Goltz,'' Bismarck replied, ''he does not the less incur heavy responsibility
in echoing them, for, as you will admit, a report such as I have just read to
you is well calculated to make an impression on a government.   Some days
before sending Herr von Manteuffel to Vienna to negotiate on the campaign
in Jutland and on our differences with the Confederation, the King asked
me: 'What is the state of our relations with France?' I replied to him,
'Very good, Sire, for the present, and I hope also for the future.'   I must

confess that after having received the information from our ambassador, I thought that I had been a little rash, and I modified the instructions for General von Manteuffel. For," he added with a smile, "from the moment that you show us *faccia feroce*, it is necessary for us to put ourselves on good terms with Austria."

Talleyrand saw Bismarck again on the 26th but had nothing new to add to the above discussion. He was convinced, he reported, that for the moment, Austria was more than ever the decisive factor in the decisions to be made with regard to both Denmark and the German Confederation. "The Prussian Court, as Your Excellency knows, has consented to join in a conference on the Danish-German question. I doubt that at bottom people here expect it to come to pass; at least, M. de Bismarck said to me yesterday, speaking of the situation and the eventualities he looked for: 'We are still only at the prologue.' "[73]

Without the private correspondence of Talleyrand and Drouyn de Lhuys, which apparently cannot be found, it is risky to draw too definite conclusions about the influence of Bismarck's words on the French government. The evidence that we have, however, suggests that Napoleon, at least, looked with favor on Bismarck and that Bismarck did his best to nourish illusions in Paris by hints of more intimate relations of Prussia with France, by statements of the influence of France on Prusso-Austrian relations, and by suggestions of eventual complications growing out of the existing situation.

A tradition grew up in French diplomatic circles that at this period in February, 1864, France had been ready to intervene in the struggle but that the withdrawal of Great Britain made the Emperor decide not to do so.[74] This seems to be an error. The shift in the attitude of the French government was so sudden and so quickly abandoned that it appears to have been due to a nervous outburst of ill-temper rather than to any real desire to intervene by force. It was calculated perhaps as an incitement to Great Britain to adopt a more active policy,[75] but more

[73] Talleyrand to Drouyn de Lhuys, February 26, 1864, confidential, *Les Origines diplomatiques de la guerre de 1870-1871*, II, No. 273.

[74] Cf. J. Hansen, *Les Coulisses de la diplomatie, 1864-1879*, pp. 10-15.

[75] "....One fact may be taken for granted; namely: the solicitude of the Imperial Government to see Great Britain actively engaged in the struggle which

probably as a warning to Bismarck.[76]   If France entered the war, it would be for reasons more important than the invasion of Jutland.[77]

V

The Russian government showed even less inclination than the French to join Great Britain in a demonstration in the Baltic. Lord Napier, the British ambassador at Petersburg, called on Prince Gorchakov on the morning of February 23 and communicated to him the substance of Earl Russell's telegram of the preceding day that Her Majesty's government judged it desirable to send a squadron to the Baltic and that they would be glad to learn that Russia and France would coöperate for the protection of Copenhagen, a demonstration, for the present, however, merely of a mediatory character.   Gorchakov, who had already heard of this from Baron Brunnow, his ambassador at London, replied that the question would have to be referred for decision to the Emperor.   For his own part, he could only say that he would not be disinclined to join with England in such a step, as it was his earnest desire to continue to act in harmony with that Power, but as the Gulf of Finland was frozen until May, the Russian squadron could not appear in the Baltic before the middle of that month.   To Napier's suggestion that there were Russian vessels of war in the ports of the United States, which might be employed to coöperate with the British ships, Gorchakov

is pursuing in the North....." Cowley to Russell, No. 299, February 23, 1864, most confidential, (Record Office, London).

[76] "M. de Bismarck persiste à considerer l'incident de l'interpellation de la France à l'égard de Kolding comme définitivement vidé.   Selon lui la France se montre satisfaite des explications transmises par le Baron Talleyrand....An und für sich sei aber das Verhältniss zu Frankreich ein gespanntes.   Indem das französische Cabinet die Absicht voranstelle die Situation zu klären, liesse sich dessen Sprache Preussen gegenüber dahin resumiren—wir wollen mit Euch Freunde oder Feinde sein.   Versuche einer directen Verständigung mit Preussen fänden in eindringlicher Weise statt.   Man wolle die Allianz der beiden Mächte spalten....." Karolyi to Rechberg, telegram No. 58, February 29, 1864, 11:44 A. M.   (Vienna Archives).

[77] Cf. Adelsvärd to Manderström, Paris, February 24, 1864, Koht, *Die Stellung Norwegens und Schwedens im deutsch-dänischen Konflikt*, pp. 319 f.

objected that even these vessels could not be recalled and reach the Baltic in less than two months and that, in any case, they were of a class too insignificant to be sent on this service. If Russia appeared before Copenhagen, she must appear with befitting dignity, with vessels of commensurate force and dimensions.

As he had already made the communication to Prince Gorchakov and telegraphed the reply to London, Lord Napier thought it best not to withdraw the overture when he received a telegraphic order not to act on his previous instructions.[78]

On February 24, Napier was informed that there was no case at present for sending the fleet to the Baltic and the question was dropped. Gorchakov, who had persisted in regarding the entry of the Prussian troops into Jutland as a military operation which did not in the least invalidate the political pledges given by the governments of Austria and Prussia in regard to the integrity of the Danish Monarchy, expressed his approval of the change in the plans of the British government. He told Lord Napier that he agreed with the view taken by Russell on this subject. The invasion of Jutland by the Austro-Prussian forces had naturally aroused the apprehension of Her Majesty's government and he would have been very reluctant to separate himself from England in a demonstration of that character. The recent declarations of the Austrian and Prussian cabinets might, however, naturally justify abstention from the action previously contemplated.[79]

Lord Napier reported that although Gorchakov approved of the resolution of the British government not to send its fleet to the Baltic at the moment, he did not regret that they considered the measure and made it known. "The Vice-Chancellor thinks," Napier wrote,

> that the attitude taken by Her Majesty's Government had a good effect at Vienna and Berlin. The decision of the Emperor with reference to the coöperation of the Russian squadron with that of Her Majesty's Govern-

[78] Telegrams, Russell to Napier, February 22, 23, 24, 1864; Napier to Russell, February 23, 5:40 P. M., February 24, 12:20 A. M.; Napier to Russell, No. 24, February 23, 1864 (Record Office, London).

[79] Napier to Russell, Nos. 119, 132, February 20, 25, 1864 (Record Office, London).

ment was not communicated to me. I risk nothing, however, in asserting that the sentiments of the Emperor would have been found to be conformable to those of the Minister on this subject and that the Russian flag would not have been wanting eventually if Her Majesty's Government had persevered in their intention to support their mediation by a naval demonstration.

Her Majesty's Government can best judge whether the presence of the allied fleets before Copenhagen might not in certain contingencies be useful not only as a mark of sympathy and as a means of support to the Danish Monarchy, but also with a view to confirm the authority of the sovereign and the Government in a capital which appeared to be dangerously agitated by democratic and national passions. I find the Russian Government much impressed by the influence exerted in these affairs by the townspeople at Copenhagen, who shape the resolutions of the administration to the prejudice of the country, the voice of which remains unheard or inoperative.[80]

In his memoirs, Lord Redesdale, who was attached to the British Embassy at Petersburg at this time, insists even more vehemently that Russia would have followed the lead which Napier so obviously wished his government to take in support of Denmark.[81] Even disregarding the fact that the Russian fleet on account of ice probably could not have reached Copenhagen before the middle of May,[82] it seems improbable that the Russian government would have intervened with anything but words. Both Gorchakov and the Emperor regarded it as very important to support the conservative policies of Rechberg and Bismarck and to do all in their power not to allow the thread to be broken which attached the cabinets of Berlin and Vienna to the engagements of 1852.[83] The Russian government seems to have regarded it of even greater importance to block any action that might break up the combination of England, Austria, Prussia, and Russia that had formed against Napoleon's Congress scheme.[84] Gorchakov frequently impressed upon the Austrian and Prussian governments the importance of moderation in the Danish

---

[80] Napier to Russell, No. 137, confidential, March 1, 1864 (Record Office, London).

[81] *Memories*, I, p. 238; *Further Memories*, p. 302.

[82] Napier to Russell, No. 156, March 16, 1864 (Record Office, London).

[83] Napier to Russell, No. 106, February 16, 1864 (Record Office, London).

[84] Napier to Russell, No. 166, most confidential, March 18, 1864 (Record Office, London).

question and especially of doing nothing that might force England to take action, but he did not conceal the fact that Russia would not use force.[85] The rumors of secret treaties, a revived Holy Alliance, were without foundation, but the policy of Russia continued favorable to Austria and Prussia.

VI

The news of the occupation of Kolding came as an unwelcome surprise to Bismarck.[86] The convention of January 16 provided for the occupation of Schleswig only. The Austrian government feared that the invasion of the Kingdom of Denmark would be the signal for a general European war and the Emperor Francis Joseph had given the commander of the Austrian troops strict orders not to enter Jutland. Because of this attitude of Austria, Field Marshal Wrangel received on the morning of February 16 telegraphic orders from King William that the allied operations should be limited to the territory of the duchies. This order, however, had not been communicated to the troops ''lest it have a depressing effect on their morale.''[87] The campaign had proceeded so rapidly that the military events had outstripped the diplomatic preparation.

The negotiations for the extension of operations began on February 16. Moltke had recommended the occupation of Jutland and, if necessary, of some of the Danish islands, as the only means of forcing the Danish government to accept terms of peace. To overcome the Austrian hesitation, General Edwin von Manteuffel was sent on a special mission to Vienna. He was successful and on March 6, Bismarck and Karolyi signed the formal agreement, which was communicated to the other powers in a note dated March 7.[88]

[85] Knorring to Rechberg, Vienna, February 22, 1864; Thun to Rechberg, telegram, February 22, 1864 (Vienna Archives). Cf. p. 166 above.

[86] Bismarck, *Die gesammelten Werke*, IV, Nos. 270, 275, 305.

[87] *Der deutsch-dänische Krieg, 1864*, I, pp. 230 f.

[88] *Les Origines diplomatiques de la guerre de 1870-1871*, II, No. 305; Cf. Sybel, *Begründung des deutschen Reiches*, III, pp. 256-267; Friedjung, *Kampf um die Vorherrschaft in Deutschland*, I, pp. 87 f; *Deutsch-dänische Krieg, 1864*, I, pp. 309-312

The terms of the new convention represented a compromise but one that turned more to the advantage of Bismarck than of Austria. The Austrians agreed to support the invasion of Jutland, which the Prussians had wished to make a major operation to enable them to insist on the evacuation of Düppel and of the island of Alsen[89] as conditions of an armistice; the Prussians agreed to press the siege of Düppel.[90] The Austrians agreed that, as the hostilities foreseen in Article V of the convention of January 16 had actually broken out, the negotiations could no longer be on the basis of the agreements of 1851-52; in return, the Prussians agreed that at the prospective conference, Austria and Prussia would propose peace conditions on the basis of a real union of the duchies in personal union with Denmark.

and App. 32; Bismarck, *Die gesammelten Werke*, IV, pp. 314-350; Roon, *Denkwürdigkeiten*, II, pp. 209 f.

[89] The only points of the duchy of Schleswig still occupied by Danish troops.

[90] Protocol of Council of Ministers under the presidency of the Emperor, Vienna, March 2, 1864. During the discussion of the new agreement with Prussia, the Emperor said that "die Invasion Jütlands, vom rein militärischen Standpunkte aus, *nicht* hinlanglich motivirt sei, Allerhöchst-diesselben aber die Zustimmung dazu aus den Grunde nicht verweigern zu sollen erachten, weil es bloss durch das Eingehen auf diese preussische Lieblingsidée möglich ward zu erwirken dass die Einnahme der Düppler Schanzen als Hauptobjekt in der Vordergründ gestellt wurde, während die Preussen bisher noch nicht daran wollten. ...." (Vienna Archives).

CHAPTER VI

THE LONDON CONFERENCE.

I

The war had hardly begun before Earl Russell again took up negotiations for a conference of the Powers to put an end to hostilities. But it was not until the last week in March that the formal invitations could be issued and not until nearly a month later that the conference met.

There were several reasons for the delay. In the first place, it was hoped that an armistice could be arranged before the conference. But the belligerents would not agree on terms and, indeed, it required nearly three weeks of the time of the conference to bring one about. In the second place, the Danish government was, for several weeks, unwilling to accept a conference at all, on account of the excited state of national feeling in Copenhagen.[1] It also tried to set up as a condition for the conference, the basis of the Treaty of London.[2] But as the

---

[1] Paget to Russell, telegram, February 23, 1864 (Record Office, London). "[Quaade said] that, nevertheless the feeling of the country was, and it was shared by most of the Cabinet, that Denmark was now in so bad a position for negotiating that it would be better to trust to the chapter of accidents for the chance of things turning to their advantage. The hope was not so much in the spontaneous action of the different Governments as in the force of public opinion acting on them .... [Monrad] admitted the possibility of some understanding between France and Sweden, but he did not consider that it necessarily followed that it would be unfavorable to this country. France, he said, would attack Germany in the summer in concert with Italy.—Denmark would be the ally of France, and France would not betray her.—He expressed, moreover, the conviction that England and France would ere long be drawn closer together, and nothing would tend more to this end than if the reported alliance between Russia and Prussia (which His Excellency informed me he had seen mentioned in the last newspapers) turned out to be a fact. ...." Paget to Russell, No. 139, March 9, 1864, confidential (Record Office, London).

[2] Paget to Russell, telegram, March 11, 1864 (Record Office, London). "We shall be ready perhaps to go into a conference," M. Monrad added, "without a

German Confederation, which had been invited to participate, was not a party to the Treaty, this created more difficulty and took more time. In the third place, the election of the representative of the Diet and the drawing up of his instructions was a slow process. Bismarck secretly worked to drag this out in order to give the Prussian forces time to capture the lines of Düppel before the opening of the conference.[3] This was accomplished on April 18. The date for the opening had been postponed from April 12 to April 20, but the meeting on that date was a purely formal one. The representative of the Diet had not yet reached London and those of Austria and Prussia declined to attend without him.[4]

II

The military situation, when the Conference met to discuss the fate of the duchies, was in favor of the German Powers. They had defeated the Danes in every major action on land and held all of the mainland of the Danish Monarchy. Of Schleswig, the Danes retained only the island of Alsen and a few other islands of no strategic importance. At the last moment before the armistice, the Danish fleet had driven an Austrian squadron, which had been sent to the North Sea to protect German com-

basis next October or, if Zealand is successfully attacked, before that period, but we cannot do so now." Paget to Russell, No. 157, March 16, 1864 (Record Office, London).

[3] Telegram dated Kolding, March 11, 1864: "Der Kronprinz wünsche sehr ..., dass die Konferenz-Unterhandlungen 14 Tage oder 3 Wochen in die Länge gezogen werden, um Düppel vorher zu nehmen." Draft answer in Bismarck's hand: "Antw: Dem Wünsche Sr. K. H. wird, u. wie ich glaube mit Erfolg, entsprochen werden." Copy of telegram, Flensburg, April 8, 1864: "An welchem Tage tritt der Conferenz zusammen? Friedrich Wilhelm, Kronprinz." "Antwort: Berlin den 8. April 1864. Zusammentritt noch heute unbestimmt. Ich lehne soeben einen von Oesterreich befürwortete englische Antrag auf Eröffnung am 12[t] und sofortige Vertagung bis zur Theilnahme des Bundes ab. Der Bund wird vom 20[t] ab bereit zur Theilnahme sein und wir haben deshalb heut nach Wien vorgeschlagen, den 24ten in Aussicht zu nehmen. Wenn es militärisch nothwendig ist, worüber ich Mittheilung bitte, so halten wir die Eröffnung jedenfalls bis 20[t] auf." (Berlin Archives). Düppel was stormed on April 18.

[4] Details of the negotiations leading up to the Conference in Neergaard, *Under Junigrundloven*, II, pp. 1126-1144.

merce, into the shelter of neutral Helgoland. But this success hardly matched the advantage held on land by the Germans.

The diplomatic situation, too, was unfavorable to Denmark. At the conference, Denmark could count upon the support of Sweden but the value of that depended upon the attitude of the Great Powers, especially Great Britain and France. Baron Brunnow could be depended upon to uphold the Treaty of London in the discussions but Russia had shown again and again that she had no intention of supporting Denmark beyond that point. For really effective support, the Danes were dependent on Great Britain and France. Yet the breach between those two Powers, which for a moment in February had seemed to be healed, had widened again in March and April.[5]

In spite of the increasing coolness of their relations, the British government, on the eve of the conference, again attempted to secure an understanding with France. For this purpose, Lord Clarendon, was sent to Paris to see Napoleon, whose respect and friendship he enjoyed to a higher degree than any of the other British ministers.[6] Napoleon received him with much personal sympathy but showed clearly that his coöperation in favor of Denmark could not be counted on.

"The Emperor seems desirous," Clarendon reported,

that his policy with respect to Denmark should not be misunderstood by us. He said that there was no denying that we had received a *gros souflet* with respect to Poland from Russia, and that to get another from Germany without resenting it was more than he could stand, as he would have fallen into contempt. He could not therefore join us in strong language to the German Powers, *not being prepared to go to war with them.* The question did not touch the dignity or the interests of France, and caused no excitement here. The Corps Législatif faithfully represented public opinion here, which was for peace, now that France had had glory enough to save her from the charge brought against Louis Philippe of being servile to the foreigner. He was determined not to go to war for another reason, viz.

[5] Cf. Ollivier, *L'Empire libéral,* VII, pp. 85, 87 f.; Wellesley, *The Paris Embassy during the Second Empire,* pp. 263 ff.

[6] He had been chief British plenipotentiary at the Congress of Paris. He was in Paris from April 13 to 18, 1864 and had conversations with the Emperor on April 14 and 15. Preliminary soundings and preparations for the mission had been made through Henry Reeve and Achille Fould at Paris. Cf. J. K. Laughton, *Memoirs of the Life and Correspondence of Henry Reeve,* II, pp. 103 f.

that France would look for some compensation on the Rhine, and that would set all Europe against him. The universal belief that he wanted to extend the French frontier in this direction made him doubly cautious. The policy of nationalities was popular in France and congenial to his own feelings. He could not, therefore, be party to replacing the Holsteiners under the rule of Denmark which they detested; and, as his great desire was to see Venetia wrested from Austria and restored to Italy, he could not lay himself open to the charge of pursuing one policy on the Eider and a totally different one on the Po.[7]

It is possible that a frank acceptance of the Emperor's program in Venetia and an agreement not to oppose his satisfying his people by a rectification of their northeastern frontier might have overcome Napoleon's dread of a war with Germany.[8] Just as in February, however, the British statesmen regarded this as a great evil.[9] A lesser evil would be the sacrifice of part of Denmark's desires. For it must be remembered that Austria and Prussia were still ostensibly maintaining the principle of the integrity of the Danish Monarchy and had agreed not to depart from it except in concert with the other Powers.[10] It was still possible that at the conference the essential interests of Great Britain could be protected.

III

The chief reason for the failure of Clarendon's mission in Paris was undoubtedly the fact that Napoleon was waiting for the answer to a new proposal made to Prussia.

[7] Walpole, *Russell*, II, pp. 390 f. Cf. Clarendon to Lady Clarendon April 16, 1864, Maxwell, *Clarendon*, II, p. 291; to Delane, May 2, 1864, Dasent, *John Thadeus Delane*, II, p. 102.

[8] Cf. Döhler, *Napoleon III und die deutsch-dänische Frage*, pp. 59 f. In a report to the Danish Foreign Office dated April 8, 1864, Admiral Steen Bille, who was in Paris on a mission from Christian IX, reports that in answer to his remark that the Danish government had hoped for France's effective support for the land that had been Napoleon I's last ally and as a result of that had lost half its territory, Napoleon III replied that an eventual war with Prussia demanded no little preparation. Bille said that the general opinion in Europe was that France was always prepared for war, to which Napoleon answered that this was a point upon which there existed many illusions. Neergaard, *Under Junigrundloven*, II, p. 1148, note 2. It is a curious coincidence that on that very day, a revolt broke out in Algeria, that required great efforts on the part of the French army to suppress.

[9] Cf. p. 176 above.

[10] Cf. p. 168 above.

As the preliminary negotiations for the conference had approached their conclusion, the French government, which had hitherto been very reserved, came out with a suggestion for the settlement. In a dispatch to the ambassador in London, on March 12, Drouyn de Lhuys indicated the difficulties in the way of upholding the Treaty of London and pointed out that

The cause and distinguishing characteristic of this conflict is clearly the rivalry of the populations that make up the Danish Monarchy. There exists in each of them a national sentiment, the strength of which cannot be doubted. What is more natural, then, in default of a unanimously accepted principle, to take as a basis, the wishes of the population? This way, in conformity with the true interests of the two parties, seems to us most suited for bringing about an equitable arrangement and to offer a guarantee of its stability. In calling for the application of a principle of our public law and in claiming for Denmark as for Germany the benefit of this principle, we believe that we are proposing the justest and easiest solution of this question.[11]

The Danish government was urged to accept this principle in a note of March 27, and it was communicated to the other Great Powers and to the chief states of Germany in a circular of March 29.[12]

Great Britain, Russia, and Austria had serious objections. The British ministers were apparently ready to accept the division of Schleswig between Holstein and Denmark but regarded the French proposal as much too radical. To consult the population, Russell and Palmerston admitted, might be the way to solve the problem of the mixed zone in Schleswig but if the principle were adopted by Great Britain and France before the conference had made its decision, it would certainly be opposed by a majority of the participants. The very suggestion, Russell declared, might prevent, or at least paralyze, the results to be hoped for from the discussion.[13] Gorchakov found the time and place most inopportune for consulting the popular will and emphasized the importance of holding as closely as possible to the

[11] *Les Origines diplomatiques de la guerre de 1870-1871*, II, No. 349.

[12] *Ibid.*, Nos. 378, 383.

[13] *Ibid.*, Nos. 355, 368, 395, 396. The Prince of Wales was especially angered by the suggestion, which threatened the integrity of his father-in-law's dominions.

Treaty of London.[14] The Austrian government rejected the plan most definitely and vigorously of all. Any recognition of the principle of self-determination of peoples was dangerous to the Austrian state.[15] Bismarck, as usual, showed himself more accommodating. He, too, had objections but they were to details, not to the principle, which along with the rights of the Princely Houses, international treaties, and the "political convenience" of the Powers, formed one of the important factors to be taken into account by the conference.[16]

Napoleon can hardly have been so naïve as to suppose that his principle would be accepted as the basis for the conference. The Duke of Saxe-Coburg-Gotha, who had gone to Paris to win the Emperor's support for the Prince of Augustenburg, believed that he had inspired the French dispatch of March 20, but Goltz reported to Bismarck that the details of what Napoleon said to Duke Ernest went in no way beyond what he, Goltz, had known for four months.[17] It is probable that Napoleon wanted to gain the sympathy of the German Liberals and almost certain that he hoped to sow discord between the other Powers.[18] Rumors of the revival of the Holy Alliance, which became frequent at this time, seemed to have been confirmed by the Austrian proclamation of the state of siege in Galicia although Gorchakov denied the

[14] *Ibid.*, No. 400. "The Prince...added, in speaking to the French chargé d'affaires that if ever there was a locality and a time in which it was impracticable to give effect to the popular vote in an impartial manner, that locality was in the Danish Duchies and that time was the present one. In order to obtain an unbiased expression of opinion, it would be requisite to withdraw the Austrian and Prussian forces from Jutland and Schleswig, to expel the Prince of Augustenburg, to permit the Danish functionaries to return to many of the places from which they had been arbitarily removed, to withdraw the civil authorities of the allied governments; was such a project practicable and if not what was the use of the present proposal?" Napier to Russell, No. 193, April 5, 1864 (Record Office, London).

[15] *Les Origines diplomatiques de la guerre de 1870-1871*, II, Nos. 401, 404.

[16] *Ibid.*, No. 408. Bismarck, *Die gesammelten Werke*, IV, Nos. 326, 332.

[17] Ernst II., *Aus meinem Leben*, III, pp. 409-417; Mager, *Herzog Ernst II und die schleswig-holsteinische Frage*, pp. 68-71; Goltz to Bismarck, No. 95, March 20, 1864, Hähnsen, *Ursprung und Geschichte des Artikels V des Prager Friedens*, I, No. 6.

[18] Sybel, *Die Begründung des deutschen Reiches*, III, p. 296, believes that the proposal was intended as a blow against Austria.

existence or the intention of any such treaty. There were also rumors of a treaty for common action against France in the question of the Danubian Principalities and a British 'Blue Book' on the Schleswig-Holstein question had contained a dispatch which quoted Gorchakov as alluding to a question in which England, Austria, Prussia, and Russia were acting in harmony. According to the Russian ambassador in Paris, "the very notion even of a defensive combination of the European Powers opposed to the designs of France is intolerable to the French Sovereign: if such a combination existed, the Emperor would feel bound to shatter it in pieces."[19] Lord Cowley, the British ambassador at Paris, believed that Napoleon hoped to divide Austria and Prussia and to gain the sympathy of the German people as a set-off against the feelings of the rulers and governments.[20]

At any rate, the French dispatch of March 20 was followed by confidential overtures to Russia and to Prussia. Of the former, little can be said. On March 14, Gorchakov asked the French *chargé d'affaires* to call on him and then spoke most confidentially of the Imperial *ukazes* in favor of the Polish peasants as offering the opportunity for a *rapprochement* of France and Russia as they gave French public opinion the desired satisfaction. Drouyn de Lhuys replied on March 25, expressing his pleasure at the views of Prince Gorchakov and his doubt as to whether the measures of the Russian government were adequate to restore peace and order in Poland. "A political alliance," he added,

does not consist of reciprocal assurances of good will and of friendship. It manifests itself by practical agreement of opinion on the questions arising from day to day in the natural course of events. It cannot fail to furnish the two governments frequent opportunities to make common cause. We therefore attached a great value, under the circumstances, to securing the coöperation of Russia, and the Cabinet of St. Petersburg will find us ready to receive in an amicable spirit the communications which it may have to

[19] Napier to Russell, No. 166, most confidential, March 18, 1864 (Record Office, London). Cf. *Les Origines diplomatiques de la guerre de 1870-1871*, II, Nos. 332, 333, 337; Napier to Russell, No. 151, March 15, 1864 (Record Office, London).

[20] Cowley to Russell, No. 458, confidential, April 6, 1864 (Record Office, London).

make to us, as well as on our part to set forth the ideas which we believe in conformity with the interests of the two Powers.[21]

The hint was not taken and the negotiation seems to have come to an end. Gorchakov told the British ambassador of a letter addressed by M. Drouyn de Lhuys to the French *chargé d'affaires* in which overtures were made for a reconciliation between France and Russia. To these proposals he said he had replied as before "that he regrets that the course pursued by the French Emperor in a question vital to Russia has produced an alienation between the two cabinets, that he would be happy to see a greater cordiality restored between them by the return of France to a more friendly and conservative policy."[22]

The negotiations with Prussia were more serious. On the afternoon of April 9, after a meeting of the Council of Ministers in the Tuileries, Drouyn de Lhuys had a long conversation with Count Goltz in which he expressed his desire to reach an understanding with Prussia for common action at the conference. The British plan, to have the principle of the integrity of the Danish Monarchy and the order of succession based on the Treaty of London confirmed by a new convention and then to leave to the belligerents the task of reaching an agreement on the position of the duchies in the monarchy, was not, in the opinion of the French government, adapted to bring about a real settlement.[23] It could hardly be acceptable to the German Powers and France, too, was ready to oppose it for it would leave the affair much as it had been from 1852 to 1863. After all that had happened the Treaty of London could hardly be maintained intact. The personal union of the united duchies with Denmark would not, in the long run, satisfy either side. A much better solution, the French minister suggested, would be the complete separation of Holstein and of southern Schleswig from the Danish Monarchy, taking, perhaps, as the frontier, the projected Baltic-North Sea

---

[21] *Les Origines diplomatiques de la guerre de 1870-1871*, II, Nos. 334, 369.

[22] Napier to Russell, No. 187, secret and confidential, April 5, 1864 (Record Office, London).

[23] The plan seems to have been suggested to the British ministers by Baron Brunnow, the Russian ambassador at London; *Les Origines diplomatiques de la guerre de 1870-1871*, II, No. 409.

Canal which Bismarck had brought to the attention of the French government.[24] On this point, the opinion of the population would have to be taken. The French government would not insist on the form of a plebiscite nor on universal suffrage but would be willing to accept the vote of a regularly elected representative body. If this vote turned out in favor of founding an independent state under the Augustenburg dynasty, France would not oppose this; although she was not bound in any way to the Prince and would regret very much the creation of a new little duchy. If, on the other hand, the vote should turn out to be for union with Prussia, France would be ready to adopt this solution in the conference. She would ask in return for this not the slightest cession of territory but would be satisfied with the compensation which a frank and firm *entente* would offer her in other spheres.

Prussian expansion in this direction would not be unwelcome to France. In connection with the plan of a canal, it might be made acceptable to all parties concerned. The Emperor, who had enthusiastically supported the plans for the Suez and Panama Canals, would be interested in this one too. The territories[25] in question, in receiving such a valuable artery of commerce which would bring increased prosperity and in being united with a powerful state whose model administration would help them develop and increase their rich resources, would be reconciled to the loss of the mixed and, perhaps even, to a part of the pure German districts of Schleswig. Even the Danes, who were prepared for the loss of Holstein, would not be opposed to the cession of such a small part of Schleswig, when they were convinced of the value of the canal, which would bring the two peoples closer to each other, and especially when they realized that the proposed solution would ensure their future peace. Germany would surely prefer to see the territory, to which Lauen_ burg would be added in exchange for the mixed districts of

[24] On March 31, Goltz had been instructed to try to interest Napoleon in the project of a Baltic-North Sea ship canal. Poschinger, *Aktenstücke zur Wirtschaftspolitik des Fürsten Bismarck*, I, pp. 18f.; Bismarck, *Die gesammelten Werke*, IV, No. 326. Cf. *Les Origines diplomatiques de la guerre de 1870-1871*, II, No. 407.

[25] *I.e.*, Schleswig-Holstein.

Schleswig, free from foreign rule and in the hands of a German Great Power, which could use them effectively for the development of German trade and of German sea power. Even the German 'Middle States' must certainly be glad to see the ambitions attributed to Prussia satisfied in this direction. If England could raise itself above petty maritime jealousy, it could have no serious scruples against the combination in question. It would not, it was true, be pleasing to Vienna; perhaps not to Petersburg either, but Russia would not be able to go beyond high-sounding phrases and would therefore accept the situation rather than risk her good relations with Prussia, while France would even renounce the idea of a dynastic union of the three Scandinavian kingdoms. Only in such a far-reaching solution would Prussia find the possibility of coming out of this bloody war with honor and profit and with the prospect of a complete reconciliation with the opposition at home and in Germany.

A proposition of this nature, ''new, startling, and vast,'' supported at the Conference by two such powers as France and Prussia, would be the more irresistible as all the other participants would be either divided or advocating solutions which were antiquated, impracticable, or unacceptable to one or the other side.

After developing his ideas on the subject in full detail, Drouyn de Lhuys assured Goltz that they met with the complete approval of the Emperor. He was not, he said, in a position to make a formal proposition in the name of the Emperor but if the Prussian government agreed with his views, the Emperor would accept them and nothing would remain but to make the agreement formal.[26]

On the evening of April 9, a telegram from Goltz arrived at Berlin. It contained merely the information that there was on the way a letter containing ''a very important offer from France,

---

[26] Goltz to Bismarck, April 9, 1864. *Bismarck und die Nordschleswigsche Frage 1864-1879*, No. 2. Cf. Sybel, *Die Begründung des deutschen Reiches*, III, pp. 300 f. and Brandenburg, *Untersuchungen und Aktenstücke zur Geschichte der Reichsgründung*, pp. 417 ff.

which may have decisive influence on the instructions for the London Conference.''[27] On the evening of April 11, Goltz telegraphed again to ask for a preliminary expression of opinion by telegraph as Lord Clarendon was expected in Paris the next day.[28] The letter with the details of the French offer did not, however, arrive at the Foreign Office in Berlin until sometime after noon on April 12.[29]

The French proposal again placed Bismarck in a delicate position. If he rejected it, Napoleon might decide to act with Great Britain; if he accepted it, he would break his agreement to settle the future of the duchies in concert with Austria.[30] But, as usual, he managed to keep the advantage of operating with both Powers.

By April 14, when Clarendon had his first audience with Napoleon, the Emperor had received from Talleyrand a favorable impression of Bismarck's reception of his overtures, and, Drouyn de Lhuys promised Goltz, he would adopt a reserved attitude towards Great Britain while awaiting the definite answer from Prussia.[31] In his conversation with Talleyrand, Bismarck had at once agreed that the British plan of action at the conference as outlined by Drouyn de Lhuys, would be quite unacceptable. He was willing to enter on an exchange of views to establish a different policy and expressed his gratitude for the suggestions of the French government which he would discuss with the King that very day.[32]

[27] No. 118, April 9, 1864; 7:25 P. M., received 8:49 P. M., Hähnsen, *Ursprung und Geschichte des Artikels V des Prager Friedens*, I, No. 20.

[28] No. 122, April 11, 1864; 10 P. M., received 11:15 P. M. (Berlin Archives). Goltz was mistaken in the date of Lord Clarendon's arrival.

[29] Draft telegram to Goltz, No. 140, April 12, 1864; 11:40 A.M. (Berlin Archives).   [30] Cf p. 103 above.

[31] ''Lord Clarendon arrivé hier au soir sera reçu aujourd'hui par l'empereur, Drouyn de Lhuys m'a promis de se tenir vis-à-vis de la Grand Bretagne, en attendant réponse du Gouvernement à ses propositions, autant que possible sur la réserve. La circulaire de Votre Excellence du 7 Avril lui parait ne rien préjuger. L'Empereur m'a confirmé qu'il approuve les propositions de son Ministre et désirait s'entendre avec nous avant d'entrer en conférence. Talleyrand a télégraphié première impression de son ouverture.'' Telegram, Goltz to Bismarck, No. 124, Paris, April 14, 1864, 11:10 A. M., received 1:20 P. M. (Berlin Archives).

[32] Telegram, Talleyrand to Drouyn de Lhuys, April 13, 1864; 3 P. M., *Les*

King William was much disturbed by the French offer. He did not understand what Napoleon wanted in return and feared that acceptance would mean that Austria, Germany, England, and Russia would be united against Prussia who would stand alone except for the "arch enemy and her enigmatic ruler."[33] Bismarck succeeded, however, in overcoming enough of the King's objections so that on April 17,[34] he could telegraph to Goltz that His Majesty had agreed in principle to the French suggestions but desired a more favorable boundary for the German element in Schleswig and certain modifications in procedure.[35] These were developed more fully in a dispatch of the same date. Goltz was instructed to try to secure a more favorable boundary for the German element in Schleswig than would be given by the line of the canal. But these efforts were not in any way to be regarded as a rejection of the French plan. It was important to keep France from an *entente* with Great Britain as it was not to be expected that Russia, Sweden, and Denmark would accept conditions more favorable than those agreed upon between France and Great Britain. The latter would hardly be more favorable than those now suggested by France so, if the worst came to the worst, a line from Schleswig to Husum could be accepted.

But it was desirable that the procedure suggested by Drouyn de Lhuys be modified. It was clear that a plebiscite in the duchies, or in Schleswig alone, would be in favor of their complete separation from Denmark and their union under the Prince of Augustenburg. To secure the acceptance there of the idea of the division of Schleswig, it must be shown that the complete cession of that duchy cannot be attained at the conference.

Origines diplomatiques de la guerre de 1870-1871, II, No. 427. Talleyrand was informed of the objections to the British plan in a despatch of April 11, *Ibid.*, No. 418. Drouyn de Lhuys' private letter containing the more secret details of the negotiation has not been found. *Ibid.*, p. 259, note 4.

[33] William to Bismarck, April 16, 1864, *Anhang zu den Gedanken und Erinnerungen von Otto Fürst von Bismarck*, I, No. 117.

[34] He felt sure enough of the result to inform Talleyrand on April 16.

[35] Bismarck, *Die gesammelten Werke*, IV, p. 383, note 4. Cf. telegram, Talleyrand to Drouyn de Lhuys, April 16, 1864, *Les Origines diplomatiques de la guerre de 1870-1871*, II, No. 433.

For this reason, therefore, it is recommended that the program agreed on between here and Vienna for the mere personal union of the Duchies with the Crown of Denmark be proposed to the conference. I believe that this has no prospect of success, and that finally the cession of Holstein and part of Schleswig will be preferred even by Denmark; especially after we have agreed with Austria to demand in addition to the personal union the entry of Schleswig into the German Confederation, the establishment of Rendsburg as a federal fortress, the canal, and the repayment of the cost of the war. If this falls through at the conference, it offers, in the first place, proof that even in this form the integrity of Schleswig cannot be maintained; in the second place, we gain time during the negotiations to exert influence on the sentiments of the population; in the third place, we have already gone too far in our negotiations with Austria decently to free ourselves from the proposal of the personal union in any other way than through its rejection by the conference. The latter will be the more easy if, to the opposition of Denmark and her associates, is added that of France. Then it will be necessary to negotiate for new combinations; all those which offer less to Germany than the personal union are unacceptable for us, and so far, Austria too has shown herself ready to reject them. It will then be inevitable that dynastic separation be discussed, and we will then, quite apart from the question of the dynasty, have to try to secure the most favorable possible boundary for Germany, and in an extreme case, have to be satisfied with the line of the Schlei. . . . .

If we are agreed as to the extent of the cession to be demanded, there remains the decision on the question as to which dynasty the new state is to be given. The way in which the political situation has developed up to this time seems to point to the Hereditary Prince of Augustenburg as the foremost candidate. I leave out of account the legal point of view according to which for lack of a rule of primogeniture neither he nor any other member of the House of Oldenburg has a claim to the whole of Holstein or Schleswig. From the political point of view, however, the Augustenburg possibility, in the present situation, is not in opposition to our interests, although it is not of such great value for us that we would risk an unequal European war for its sake. The menace of the latter, however, is materially lessened now that France is willing to abandon in our favor its previous attitude of reserve; and besides, the most recent development of our relations in Germany and with the Pretender himself permits a more favorable opinion of his candidacy.[36] Nevertheless, it is still only natural for the Prussian government to give its preference to the direct acquisition of the duchies by Prussia if an acceptable prospect is offered. I believe that it may be possible to win the vote of the population for this if we gain time, but in my opinion it will be probable only if first the programs of personal union and Augustenburg candidacy fail.

As an acceptable program for Prussia, Bismarck indicated the following three possibilities:

[36] Cf. pp. 221-225 below.

1. the personal union with the totality of the three duchies joined into a single state with the above mentioned conditions;
2. the independence of the German parts of the Duchies under a separate dynasty, either Augustenburg or Oldenburg;
3. the acquisition by Prussia of the territory severed from Denmark.

The Augustenburg solution, he added, would require a more complete separation of the German element than if the duchies were to go to Prussia.

Public opinion will be bitterly opposed to the sacrifice of any German population; but if the settlement satisfies the particular interests of Prussia, that section of German public opinion which is of weight for us, that is, the Prussian, will be reconciled, and we shall have to endure the hostility of the rest. This calculation would not, however, apply to the installation of another dynasty in the mutilated remains of the duchies.

We have no illusions that we can realize any part of this program without the sincere and complete coöperation of France and we wish ardently, therefore, that Your Excellency's exertions may succeed in bringing about a definite understanding about this coöperation. Especially in accordance with the King's wish, item No. 3, is never to be brought forward through our own initiative but we must wait for its suggestion from the duchies or from France.

In conclusion let me add that I regard a postponement of the definitive solution, while we remain in military occupation of the Duchies and of Jutland, as in conformity with our interests and as furthering the chances for a favorable final result.[37]

With this in mind, I suggest that your Excellency find out whether the French government is thinking, in case the conference come to no solution, of renewing the proposal of a congress in order to deal with the Danish question in connection with others; but I request Your Excellency to touch on this theme only for your own and our information.[38]

Although Drouyn de Lhuys continued to raise objections on many points,[39] Napoleon himself, in an audience to Goltz on April 22, accepted the program outlined. He had gained nothing definite from these negotiations, not even an assurance of the "services" which Drouyn de Lhuys had indicated as sufficient compensation for France. But, as before, he was satisfied with thoughts of the future. The program which France and Prussia

[37] Cf. Talleyrand to Drouyn de Lhuys, April 16, 1864, *Les Origines diplomatiques de la guerre de 1870-1871*, II, No. 434.

[38] Bismarck, *Die gesammelten Werke*, IV, No. 334.

[39] Hähnsen, *Ursprung und Geschichte des Artikels V des Prager Friedens*, I, Nos. 35, 40, 41, 43, 44, 52.

planned to pursue at the conference was hardly likely to meet the approval of Austria,[40] and out of it—who could tell?— might come the opportunity to follow one and the same policy on the Eider and on the Po.

Bismarck, on the other hand, gained time. As long as negotiations were pending, and as long as Napoleon hoped for results from his support of the Prussian program, an Anglo-French *entente* was unlikely. Moreover, and this was important in the eyes of King William, he had been able to adhere to the letter of the program agreed upon with Austria. Yet the understanding with France made it more than ever improbable that the plan of personal union would be accepted by the conference. After that, he, too, had hopes, and, in addition, plans. If necessary, he could accept the candidacy of the Prince of Augustenburg with suitable conditions binding him to Prussia. Finally, there was his preferred goal, annexation of the duchies to Prussia. The understanding with France gave him a better chance of blocking combinations which he disliked and of engineering those which would help him on his way.

IV

The Austro-Prussian Convention of March 6 had laid down the general lines for the political as well as the military coöperation of the two allies. It had been agreed that, as hostilities had actually broken out, Austria and Prussia could no longer negotiate on the basis of the agreements of 1851-52 with Denmark but would propose, at the prospective conference, the real union of the duchies of Schleswig and Holstein, in personal union with the Crown of Denmark.[41] Later in March, however, when Rechberg wished to begin formal discussions of the details of the peace conditions and for common action at the conference, Bismarck seemed in no hurry to commit himself and was unwilling to say whether the first formulation should come from Vienna or Berlin.[42]

[40] *Ibid.*, Nos. 41, 49. [41] Cf. p. 202 above.

[42] Karolyi to Rechberg, No. 37 A-G., Berlin, March 26, 1864 (Vienna Archives).

Bismarck did outline, however, what purported to be his personal views of the position the two Powers ought to adopt. The *status quo ante bellum* was, of course, no longer possible as a basis for discussion. So that the negotiations would end with satisfactory results, Austria and Prussia must begin by presenting their maximum demands. Schleswig-Holstein, in no more than personal union with the Crown of Denmark, must be protected by guarantees on a European basis against the recurrence of Danish oppression. The most effective guarantee would be the incorporation of Schleswig in the German Confederation. Whether or not the predominately Danish North Schleswig should be excepted from the rest of the duchy and incorporated in the kingdom, would form an important element in the negotiations. An increase of territory for the German Confederation, the first since its creation, would be accepted by German public opinion with great satisfaction. It would, in part at least, reconcile the policy of the two Powers with the German national point of view and would help the position of the two governments at home. Such a result of the war would be justified by the significant losses already suffered by Austria and Prussia and they must use all their efforts to secure it. Among the details of the settlement, Bismarck mentioned the establishment of Rendsburg as a federal fortress and the demand for a war indemnity from Denmark.

Bismarck then went on to discuss the plans for the Baltic-North Sea Canal. He recommended it as an undertaking which would not only be of great importance for the course of the world's commerce but would also bring great honor to the two Powers under whose auspices it was brought into existence. Karolyi, however, thought that Prussian capital and Prussian trade would get the lion's share of advantage.

Even more specifically Prussian, in Karolyi's opinion, was Bismarck's discussion of the further eventualities of the negotiations. In case the personal union should be impossible because of Danish opposition, and the separation of Holstein and southern Schleswig prove to be the most likely solution and the one favored by Denmark, this must not be opposed by the German

Powers. They could not be "more Danish than Denmark." It would then be necessary for them to see to it that the new German state did not fall to the Prince of Augustenburg. That would be looked on as a triumph of the "democratic" party and of the *Nationalverein* and would be in glaring contradiction to the whole attitude of Austria and Prussia. Bismarck preferred the Duke of Oldenburg who had certain hereditary claims and would be a better choice than the Prince of Augustenburg.[43]

The discussion then lapsed until Freiherr von Biegeleben, the second Austrian plenipotentiary to the conference, arrived in Berlin on the evening of April 16.[44] In two long conversations with Bismarck, at the first of which Karolyi too was present, he attempted to hold Bismarck to the Austrian point of view. "I attempted, as definitely as possible," he reported to Rechberg,

to give the Prussian minister the impression that, at Vienna, the whole German-Danish imbroglio was looked upon as of relatively secondary importance and that the agreement between Austria and Prussia, if it was to correspond to the higher demands of the world situation, must gain another and more significant content than a common attitude toward Denmark. Hints as to the decisive services which the alliance of the two German Powers is called upon to render to the cause of stability[45] could not but meet with the approval of Herr von Bismarck.

From the latter's replies, Biegeleben gained the impression that up to a certain point, Prussia would, after all, go with Austria.

Bismarck's attitude was not, however, entirely satisfactory. The way in which he spoke of the possible grouping of the European Powers made it clear that he was not especially preoccupied with the coincidence of the dangers threatening the legitimate governments and that he was moved primarily by speculation on special advantages for Prussia. It was not yet his intention to advise the King to accept definite obligations but rather to use the *rapprochement* with France, which he represented as a mere flirtation, to keep open the possibility of securing as glorious a peace as possible. Biegeleben tried to

[43] *Ibid.*

[44] Bismarck, *Die gesammelten Werke*, IV, p. 387; *Les Origines diplomatiques de la guerre de 1870-1871*, II, p. 266.

[45] "der Sache der Ordnung."

argue that France would sacrifice its old protégé, Denmark, only for French but not for Prussian interests and that England must not be offended lest they play into the hands of France. "He admitted," Biegeleben wrote, "that the two western powers must be kept apart, but seemed to regard it as a quite proper division of rôles if England was kept in a good humor by Austria, and France by Prussia, which I ventured to declare to be a somewhat doubtful game."

It would be difficult, Biegeleben concluded, to persuade the Prussians to give up conditions for which they could count on the connivance of France. Bismarck did not, however, intend to accept a plebiscite and, for the benefit of his visitor, modified a dispatch to Vienna, the draft of which had laid "undue weight on the vote of the Estates."

What Bismarck especially emphasized was his need of strengthening his position with reference to the King by securing an honorable peace, for the latter was not uninfluenced by the prevailing sentiment in Germany and in the army, which did not want to seem to have fought in vain. "He [Bismarck] sees in this also the means of bringing about from coöperation against Denmark, a firmer alliance of Austria and Prussia, for Austria, by helping Prussia to secure such a peace, would win for itself, not, to be sure, a province, but the Prussian army."[46]

In a letter to Bernstorff, Bismarck summed up his understanding of the results of the discussion.

In the preliminary draft of instructions for the plenipotentiaries which was drawn up at Vienna and communicated to us were the following three points: joint Assembly of Estates for the two duchies; the establishment of Rendsburg as a Federal fortress; and a common Schleswig-Holstein citizenship. In addition, there was made the reservation of a legal decision as to the succession in the duchy of Holstein.

I was able to accept these three points as well as the reservation of the legal decision. Further discussion brought about an agreement that the plenipotentiaries of the two powers were to hold to the following points of view:

1. autonomy of the united duchies on the analogy of Norway;
2. a common and united representative body for the duchies;

[46] Biegeleben to Rechberg, April 19, 1864, enclosed in Karolyi to Rechberg, No. 42, April 20, 1864 (Vienna Archives).

3. the establishment of Rendsburg as a Federal fortress;
4. construction of a ship canal connecting the North and Baltic seas;
5. establishment of a German naval base on the Baltic coast;
6. admission of Schleswig to the German Confederation;
7. guarantee of the constitution of the duchies by the Confederation.

While these are the essential conditions for the future of the duchies, it will be necessary to maintain for the conclusion of peace:

8. repayment of the costs of the war;
9. the return of the ships captured by the Danes and compensation for losses suffered; and
10. occupation of the duchies by the allied or by German troops until the new arrangement is carried out.

The relation of the Schleswig-Holstein army to the Danish was a point of special difficulty. On our part, we must insist on complete separation with two ministries of war. But as Herr von Biegeleben was not empowered to yield the objections of the Cabinet of Vienna on this point, we agreed to leave it for further consideration and agreement.[47]

Bismarck had given up nothing that was essential to his program. He had avoided committing himself to the narrow Austrian one and had secured the inclusion of the main conditions that he had wanted.[48] The more numerous and serious were the conditions attached to the personal union, the less chance there was of its being accepted by the Danes. The way would then be open for the steps called for by the understanding with France and this might lead to the acquisition of the duchies by Prussia. From his conversations with Biegeleben, Bismarck had gained the impression that Austria would consent to this rather than see the duchies go to the Prince of Augustenburg.[49]

V

Bismarck had been violently opposed to the recognition of Prince Frederick of Augustenburg as Duke of Schleswig-Holstein. In his instructions of April 17 to Goltz, however, he wrote that the way in which the political situation had developed up to

[47] Bismarck to Bernstorff, Berlin, April 21, 1864, Bismarck, *Die gesammelten Werke*, IV, No. 341. Cf. Biegeleben to Rechberg, telegram, No. 80, Berlin, April 20, 1864, 7:30 A. M. (Vienna Archives).

[48] Cf. p. 215 above.

[49] Bismarck, *Die gesammelten Werke*, IV, No. 343, p. 397.

this time seemed to point to the Prince as the foremost candidate.

From the political point of view, the Augustenburg possibility, in the present situation, is not in opposition to our interests, although it is not of such great value for us that we would risk an unequal European war for its sake. The menace of the latter, however, is materially lessened now that France is willing to abandon in our favor her previous attitude of reserve; and besides, the most recent development of our relations in Germany and with the Pretender himself permit a more favorable opinion of his candidacy.[50]

In spite of King William's curt letter of January 18,[51] the Prince and his advisers had continued their efforts to secure the support of Prussia for his candidacy by undermining Bismarck's influence with the King. All their attempts failed.[52] William refused to give any promises or even to recognize the Augustenburg claims. To a deputation of professors from the University of Kiel who came to Berlin to ask for the recognition of Frederick as Duke, the King replied that the dynastic question was still a subject of negotiation.

Bismarck, in his discussion with the leaders of the deputation, pointed out in detail his objections to the Prince. He spoke of the claims of the Russian Tsar as head of the House of Gottorp and hinted that these claims would probably be transferred to the Grand Duke of Oldenburg.[53] It might turn out that the latter could be established in the duchies and Prince Frederick in Oldenburg. He criticized Prince Frederick's 'democratic' connections with Gotha and others of the minor states and with the *Nationalverein* and expressed his disapproval of the Prince's choice of advisers from the ranks of the liberals. But when one of the professors emphasized the importance to Prussia of freeing the duchies, which would lean for support on the great North German Power and which would be ready to make important concessions to Prussia, in military and naval affairs, for example, Bismarck became more sympathetic. He replied that he had as

---

[50] Cf. p. 215 above.   [51] Cf. p. 160 above.

[52] Cf. Max Duncker, *Politischer Briefwechsel aus seinem Nachlass*, Nos. 460, 463, 454.

[53] See genealogical table, Appendix XI below.

yet heard nothing of such concessions "as during his visit to Berlin, the Hereditary Prince had been very reserved." He was, he said, glad that now, apparently, real advantages would be offered to Prussia.[54]

To others, however, Bismarck continued to speak harshly of Prince Frederick and his advisers. They had thrown themselves into the arms of "Coburg-Germany" and would always be on the side of the opponents of Prussia. If they seemed to be offering sureties of friendship, they could always evade them with the help of the Confederate Diet. The establishment of the Duke under Prussian protection would endanger the hard-won coöperation with Austria and would provoke the intervention of the foreign Powers. His policy, he said, was to keep Schleswig-Holstein under military occupation as long as possible; "*interim aliquid fit*": a European war might develop and, in such a case, territorial increase for Prussia might be possible. Otherwise, the personal union of the united duchies with Denmark might be endured until circumstances were more favorable for a definitive solution of the question.[55]

The latent difference in the views of King William and of Bismarck was, of course well known to the court at Kiel. The Prince was urged by his advisers to offer definite concessions to Prussia in the hope of reaching an agreement with the king which would be a safeguard against the minister's ambitious projects.[56] On February 19, then, the Prince of Augustenburg wrote a confidential letter to his friend, the Crown Prince of Prussia, and enclosed a list of the concessions he was prepared to make. On account of the delicacy of the negotiation and in fear that Bismarck might use the letters to his detriment with Austria and the minor states, he asked the Crown Prince not to show the

[54] Gebauer, *Herzog Friedrich VIII*, pp. 92 f; Jansen-Samwer, *Schleswig-Holsteins Befreiung*, pp. 252, 321, 704 f.

[55] Gebauer, *Herzog Friedrich VIII*, p. 93; Jansen-Samwer, *Schleswig-Holsteins Befreiung*, p. 287.

[56] Gebauer, *Herzog Friedrich VIII*, p. 94. Droysen, in a letter to Samwer on February 3, had suggested the offer of Rendsburg as a Federal fortress with Prussian garrison, Kiel harbor as a Prussian naval base, a military convention like that of Coburg with Prussia, and Prussian military control of a Baltic-North Sea canal.

memorandum to the king but to present the concessions as his own ideas. A second letter, to be shown to King William, mentioned concessions only in general terms. Prince Frederick William answered in friendly terms and gladly carried out his friend's request. King William acknowledged receipt of the communication in a letter to his son but again declined to reply to Prince Frederick.[57]

On March 16 and 17, another Augustenburg agent, von Ahlefeldt-Olpenitz, who had been a university friend of Bismarck, was received by the Prussian minister. The latter was still anything but encouraging. Prussia, he said, could not bleed itself white to rescue the duchies and to make Prince Frederick sovereign. For a just cause like that of the duchies, Prussia would always have a few thousand men and a few millions of thalers to spare but it could not be made a matter of life and death. She would, therefore, hold with Austria to the program of personal union. Bismarck admitted that it was conceivable that the Prince might yet be invested with the duchies but blamed him for going to Kiel against King William's advice instead of entering the campaign with the Prussian army. He disapproved especially the Prince's recognition of the Schleswig-Holstein Constitution of 1848. It was impossible he argued, to negotiate with the Prince because that constitution provided for responsible ministers. Concessions from the Prince had little value for this same reason. Bismarck declared that he could promise nothing and that the Prince would receive no official or even written answer.[58]

A letter congratulating King William on his birthday had no more success in bringing a political reply but on the eve of the London Conference, Prnce Frederick made still another attempt to win Prussian support. On April 13, Prince Löwenstein, a former member of the Prussian diplomatic service, placed before King William a definite statement of the propositions which had been outlined in the confidential letter of February 19 to the

---

[57] *Ibid.* The letters are printed in Jansen-Samwer, *Schleswig-Holsteins Befreiung*, pp. 705-708.

[58] Jansen-Samwer, *Schleswig-Holsteins Befreiung*, pp. 324 f.

Crown Prince. The King declined to commit himself to Löwen-stein but he wrote to the Crown Prince on April 16, that he did not wish thus to rebuff Prince Frederick and was ready to listen to his proposals "when he makes them in writing and direct to me."[59] At the same time, Bismarck inserted in his dispatch to Goltz, the passage that the most recent development of Prussia's relations with the Pretender permitted a more favorable opinion of his candidacy.[60]

Although King William refused to grant Prince Frederick a personal interview, the latter hastened to send a detailed statement of the obligations he would undertake if he became duke with the support of Prussia. He offered a naval station in one of the harbors of the duchies for the Prussian fleet; the establishment of Rendsburg as a Federal fortress with a Prussian garrison; naval and military conventions with Prussia, which would provide for the organization and training of the armed forces of the duchies on lines similar to those of the Prussian; the accession of the duchies to the Prussian *Zollverein*; and the construction of a canal capable of accommodating the largest warships.[61] These conditions were, as Bismarck had pointed out before, subject to ratification by the Assembly of the Estates of the duchies, but if they were obtained, they would give Prussia almost as much advantage as direct annexation. In any case, the Prince was now committed to Prussia while Prussia was not bound to him.

VI

The first full meeting of the Conference took place on April 25. Earl Russell, who was as a matter of course chosen to preside, was anything but a brilliant diplomat. He was ably assisted, however, by the second British representative, Lord Clarendon, who had entered the cabinet at the beginning of

[59] *Ibid.*, pp. 325 f.; *Anhang zu den Gedanken und Erinnerungen von Otto Fürst von Bismarck*, I, No. 116.

[60] Cf. p. 215 above.

[61] Jansen-Samwer, *Schleswig-Holsteins Befreiung*, pp. 326 ff., 717 ff.

April for this purpose.[62] France was represented by her ambassador in London, Prince de la Tour d'Auvergne, but because of the difference between the official attitude of the French government and the personal policy of Napoleon, and especially as he was not fully initiated into the latter, he took up a reserved attitude during the proceedings. Russia and Sweden, too, accredited only their regular diplomatic representatives in London. Baron Brunnow, the Russian ambassador, was an experienced diplomat. He had been one of the negotiators of the Treaty of London and was notoriously sympathetic to Denmark. In spite of the close relations between his Court and that of Prussia, he was, at the Conference, the staunchest defender of that treaty. Count Wachtmeister, the Swedish minister, naturally played a minor rôle. In general, he supported the Danish case and was a useful adviser to the Danish delegation.[63]

Austria was represented by Count Apponyi, her ambassador in London, and by the more able and influential Biegeleben, counsellor on German affairs in the foreign office, and noted for his opposition to Prussia. That Power was represented by Count Bernstorff, Bismarck's predecessor as minister for foreign affairs and now ambassador in London, seconded by Herr von Balan, late Prussian minister at Copenhagen. Bernstorff, a Lauenburger by birth, was hostile to Denmark and leaned toward the Augustenburg cause, so that Bismarck did not give him his full confidence. But in general, the Prussian delegation worked efficiently and in harmony with the views of the government. Between Austria and Prussia, with their opposing interests on the Danish question, the plenipotentiary of the German Confederation occupied a delicate position. Count Beust, the Saxon minister president, who had been elected to this post of honor—

[62] Among other things, Russell could not understand or speak French well enough to take a leading part in the discussions.

"I have a pressing letter from Johnny asking me to assist him at the Conference. That will be an awfully long business and a most unsatisfactory one, I am sure, as we shall be the only people there not bent upon defeating the object for which it professes to meet. Of course, I could not decline." Clarendon to Lady Clarendon, April 5, 1864. Maxwell, *Clarendon*, II, p. 290.

[63] Neergaard, *Under Junigrundloven*, II, p. 1206.

the first and the last representative of the Diet at an international conference—acted with Austria and Prussia when they were agreed, and when they were not, went with the one which demanded most. As the German Confederation was not a party to the Treaty of London, he was of value to Bismarck's schemes of getting it completely set aside. Beust's greatest service to the German cause during the Conference was in blocking the reëntry of plans that had originally been rejected by the Danes, but which were less favorable to Germany than those discussed later.

Denmark was represented by Quaade, Torben Bille and A. F. Krieger. The former had been minister to Prussia and then foreign minister in the Monrad cabinet. He had had more diplomatic experience than his colleagues and had a much cooler and sounder view of the realities of the international situation. But his position at the Conference was weakened by the fact that the ministers in Copenhagen did not give him their full confidence. The political support which Quaade lacked, was, however, enjoyed to the full by A. F. Krieger. He was the real representative of the Danish National Liberals and represented accurately their bold and fantastic views.[64] Torben Bille, the third plenipotentiary was a less important figure. He was minister in London, an experienced but impressionable diplomat.

VII

The first task of the Conference was to end the actual fighting. It was not until the session of May 9 that it was possible to bring about an agreement on the terms of an armistice for four weeks, dating from May 12. One of the chief points of difficulty was that the Danes wished to continue their blockade of the German ports, while Austria and Prussia, as victors in the fighting on land, refused to accept this.

At the fourth session, on May 12, the Conference began to consider the real problem before it. It had been called without the establishment of a basis for its deliberation, "to find the

[64] Neergaard, *Under Junigrundloven*, II, pp. 1209-1212. Krieger's diary and dispatches confirm this view.

means of restoring to the north of Europe the blessings of peace.''
There was one basis common to all except one of the participants:
the Treaty of London. It was soon apparent, however, that the
integrity of the Danish Monarchy could not be maintained. For
all practical purposes the Treaty of London ended its unhappy
career at the meeting of May 12, when Count Bernstorff, in the
name of Austria and Prussia read a vague declaration to the
effect that the German Powers regarded themselves as freed
from any restriction ''resulting from engagements which may
have existed before the war between their Governments and
Denmark,'' and that they regarded the basis on which fresh
combinations were to be formed as one of the principal objects
of the negotiations.[65]

But as had been agreed upon by Austria and Prussia before the
Conference,[66] the two Powers would regard as a satisfactory
solution the personal union of Schleswig-Holstein with the Kingdom of Denmark. Their demand, however, which was presented
by Bernstorff at the next session, on May 17, was also very
vaguely worded.

In the last sitting, the German Plenipotentiaries pointed out that the
principal object of the deliberations of the Conference was to find the basis
of new combinations which should be of a nature to ensure a solid and
durable pacification. They think it is right to explain today what they
understand by a solid and durable pacification. It is a pacification which
would ensure to the Duchies absolute guarantees against the recurrence of
any foreign oppression, and which, by thus excluding for the future any
subject of dispute, of revolution, and of war, would guarantee to Germany
that security in the North which she requires in order not to fall again
periodically into the state of affairs which brought on the present war.
These guarantees can only be found in the complete political independence
of the Duchies, and their close connection by means of common institutions.

---

[65] Protocol of the session of May 12, 1864. In a despatch to Bernstorff, dated
May 15, 1864, Bismarck declared that Prussia was no longer bound by the Treaty
of London, but in accordance with the identic notes of January 31, 1864, would
discuss the other possible combinations with the signatory Powers. *Das Staatsarchiv*, VII, No. 1660. Bismarck had often insisted that the fact that the treaty
was signed by Denmark on the one side and the other Powers, on the other, and
that the ratifications had been exchanged with Denmark alone, justified Prussia in
regarding herself as bound only to Denmark by the Treaty.

[66] See pp. 202 and 220 f. above.

All that this statement expressed clearly was the revival of the Schleswig-Holstein doctrine of the close connection of the duchies as independent states, which Austria and Prussia had waived in the negotiations of 1851.[67] Personal union under the Crown of Denmark was not mentioned.[68] In the discussion that followed, the German plenipotentiaries upheld the right of the Diet to determine the legitimate successor to the throne of Holstein. Personal union, however, was not excluded, but in spite of Biegeleben's exhortation to refer the matter to Copenhagen, the Danish delegation declared that the proposal would be entirely inacceptable even on the supposition that the rights of the king of Denmark to the duchies were admitted.[69]

The personal union was dead and Beust nailed up the coffin. When Clarendon and Brunnow continued to urge the Danes to send the protocols to Copenhagen and to await new instructions, Beust declared that he had not joined in the proposal made by the representatives of Austria and Prussia; and that, although not directed to do so by his instructions, he could not help affirming officiously that the majority of the Diet would not consent to an arrangement which, even under an eventual or conditional form, would restore the union between the duchies and Denmark.[70]

In Denmark, politicians of practically every shade of opinion were opposed to a personal union of that nature.[71] But the absolute rejection of the idea was a tactical blunder; for it excluded later consideration of the plan of a personal union, based on the division of Schleswig by nationalities.[72]

The Conference had now reached the point foreseen in the

[67] See p. 13 above.

[68] Even Rechberg had opposed the direct mention of the personal union on account of its unpopularity in Germany. Werther to Bismarck, April 29, 1864, Sybel, *Die Begründung des deutschen Reiches*, III, p. 317.

[69] Protocol of the session of May 17, 1864.

[70] Protocol of the session of May 17, 1864. Beust's report to the Diet, May 18, 1864, in Beust, *Aus drei Vierteljahrhunderten*, I, pp. 382 f.

[71] It meant the abandonment of the Schleswig Danes to a German majority and the loss to the Kingdom of any control over or benefit from the revenues and armed forces of the Duchies.

[72] Neergaard, *Under Junigrundloven*, II, pp. 1188-1199, 1239 ff.

April negotiations between France and Prussia. So far all had gone as Bismarck desired.[73] The Powers had made no serious objection to the tacit abandonment of the Treaty of London and the Danes had done him the service of rejecting the personal union.

VIII

The way was now open for the further development of Bismarck's program and he prepared to begin negotiations with Rechberg for the next steps to be taken at the Conference. Soon after the detailed report of the session of May 17 had been received at Berlin, Bismarck drew up two dispatches to Werther at Vienna and they were approved by King William.[74]

The first dealt with the demands to be made on Denmark. Now that the personal union had been so categorically rejected, there was no use in discussing the conditions to be attached to it; they were not likely to make the scheme more attractive to the Danes. The two German Powers, however, could not accept a solution which gave the duchies a less favorable position than a mere personal union with the Kingdom. So, as King Christian IX was unwilling to rule the duchies as independent states, his rule was out of the question. Austria and Prussia must, therefore, demand the complete separation of the duchies from Denmark. If, for reasons of European politics, it was not desirable to weaken Denmark too much, the northern part of Schleswig might be returned to that kingdom in exchange for Lauenburg. If the

---

[73] Bismarck to Bernstorff, telegram, No. 230, May 15, 1864, and Sybel, *op. cit.*, III 316. Hähnsen, *Ursprung und Geschichte des Artikels V des Prager Friedens*, I, No. 67. "Drouyn de Lhuys satisfait de séance du 17. C'est là le point où il voulait arriver et que déclaration austro-prussienne a rendu possible. Le Prince de Latour d'Auvergne ne sait pas dernier mot: il sait seulement que la France désapprouve union personnelle et vise à séparer des nationalités...." Goltz to Bismarck, telegram, No. 167, May 19, 1864, Hähnsen, *op. cit.*, I, No. 74.

[74] Nos. 380, 381, *vertraulich*, May 21, 1864. Bismarck, *Die gesammelten Werke*, IV, Nos. 373, 374; Sybel, *Die Begründung des deutschen Reiches*, III, 323-326. Sybel's quotation differs from the phraseology of the original only in one or two unimportant points. He does not, however, indicate that there were *two* dispatches from Berlin.

personal union plan had succeeded, the division of Schleswig would have been unacceptable, but with the complete separation, the objections would lose their force. For tactical reasons, however, the demand at the Conference must be for the whole of the two duchies.

The second dispatch dealt with the question of the future ruler of the duchies. Bismarck declared that he did not wish to see this taken up at the Conference yet, but that he was not unwilling to discuss it with Rechberg. Three possibilities were mentioned. The Augustenburg claim was without doubt the one that could, under existing circumstances, most easily be realized. It was not incontestable legally, but it was generally recognized in Germany and no opposition to it need be feared from the duchies. Any approach to universal suffrage could, therefore, be avoided.

But, although the Augustenburg candidacy seemed the most practicable, Bismarck was not at all desirous of excluding other combinations if the cabinet of Vienna desired to consider them. The Grand Duke of Oldenburg had claims which, out of consideration for the Prince of Augustenburg, he had not yet brought forward. And, above all, in Prussia itself the idea was growing, that the best solution of the question was the annexation of the duchies to Prussia. "Even in the duchies themselves, this idea is said to be not without response, for the enthusiasm for Duke Frederick represents only the momentary expression of aversion to Denmark."

Yet though this sentiment in Prussia had great weight with the government which would not reject such a solution if it developed from the course of events, it was anything but their desire to conjure up European complications or to endanger the agreement with Austria by efforts in this direction. "The King would never strive for the realization of such an idea which has recently been brought to his attention, though without our initiative, by addresses from many of his subjects, *except in complete agreement with his imperial ally.*"

The Austrians, too, had been considering the situation created by the Danish rejection of the personal union and, with the news from London that the neutral Powers were preparing to abandon the integrity of the Danish Monarchy, had decided on a complete change of policy.[75] For Austria, the personal union of the duchies with Denmark would have been the most acceptable solution.[76] It would have safeguarded the London Treaty and so have avoided the difficulties which she feared from the non-German Powers. It would have avoided any application of the principle of nationality, and it would have averted the danger of Prussian aggrandisement in the duchies.

For some time, the Vienna cabinet had been suspicious of Prussia's intentions,[77] and by the middle of May was thoroughly alarmed at the growth of the annexation sentiment in Prussia, which had followed the capture of Düppel.[78] To the Austrian chargé d'affaires, Bismarck had spoken of conditions under which Prussia might be allowed territorial gains in the duchies in return for concessions to Austria in other fields. "It would be," he said, "the inauguration of a policy of mutual compensation."[79]

The suggestion fell on deaf ears and to checkmate the Prussian ambitions, Austria took up the cause of Augustenburg. In his interview with the Prussian minister, Baron Werther, on May 23, Rechberg expressed his agreement with Bismarck's dispatch of the 21st, in so far as it concerned the conditions for the separation of the duchies from Denmark. But he wished to take up the dynastic question at the Conference at the same time and

[75] Cf. J. Fröbel, Ein Lebenslauf, II, pp. 305-309.

[76] Instructions to the plenipotentiaries in London for the session of May 28, 1864. Revertera, "Rechberg und Bismarck 1863 bis 1864" in Deutsche Revue, December, 1903, pp. 265 ff. Cf. Apponyi's remarks to Quaade, Neergaard, Under Junigrundloven, II, p. 1207 and Gramont to Drouyn de Lhuys, May 20, 1864, Les Origines diplomatiques de la guerre de 1870-1871, III, No. 556.

[77] Revertera, "Rechberg und Bismarck 1863 bis 1864 "in Deutsche Revue, November, 1903, p. 135.

[78] "[Rechberg] then said that he had been very useful these last few days at Berlin in assisting M. de Bismarck to keep the King from following a course that would have been full of danger to Prussia and to Europe; there was a powerful party, he said at Court and in the Army which was pushing at nothing less than the annexation of the Duchies to the Prussian Crown. The King had been taken with the idea, but M. de Bismarck had valiantly opposed this popular project, and he hoped with a good prospect of success. ...." Bloomfield to Russell, No. 302, May 12, 1864, confidential, (Record Office, London).

[79] Chotek to Rechberg, May 15, 1864. Appendix VI, pp. 323 f.

made it clear to Werther that the Prince of Augustenburg was the candidate favored by Austria.[80] The Austrian program was developed in greater detail in a series of dispatches sent to Berlin on May 24 but drafted before Werther had presented Bismarck's views. The Austrian government definitely rejected "any territorial changes which would result in a disturbance of the existing equilibrium among the Great Powers" and suggested that, "in conformity with the wishes of the duchies and of Germany," the two Powers supply by their rights as victors, whatever legality the pretensions of the Prince of Augustenburg might lack. The exchange of North Schleswig for Lauenburg would be accepted by Austria but only after the dynastic question had been settled. It should appear as a transaction between two sovereigns, not as a concession to the French principle of nationality.[81]

IX

Because of King William's sympathy for the Augustenburg claims, Bismarck had long faced the possibility of having to reckon seriously with them. But he seems not to have expected such a complete change in the Austrian attitude.[82] Biegeleben, when passing through Berlin in April on his way to London, had left him with the impression that Austria would more readily accept the annexation of the duchies to Prussia than the Augustenburg candidacy.[83] As late as May 19, in conversation with Max Duncker, the *confidant* of the Crown Prince of Prussia, Bismarck

[80] Telegram, Werther to Bismarck, May 23, 1864, quoted in telegram, Bismarck to Bernstorff, May 24, 1864. Bismarck, *Die gesammelten Werke*, IV, No. 378.

[81] Rechberg to Karolyi, May 24, 1864. Nos. 1 and 2 were written before, a postscript to No. 2 and all of No. 3 were written after the communication of Bismarck's dispatches. The phrasing of the section on the claims of the Prince of Augustenburg was taken from Biegeleben to Rechberg, private, London, May 19, 1864. For the Austrian correspondence on the change of policy, see appendix VII, pp. 332-348 below.

[82] Talleyrand to Drouyn de Lhuys, May 25, 1864, *Les Origines diplomatiques de la guerre de 1870-1871*, III, No. 575.

[83] Bismarck, *Die gesammelten Werke*, IV, No. 343.

stated that Austria would rather see the duchies in Prussian hands than in those of Prince Frederick.[84]

The Austrian action compelled Bismarck to adopt the Prince of Augustenburg as the Prussian candidate for the throne of the duchies but it was not at all certain that he would be accepted by the Conference. The Tsar of Russia was bitterly opposed to the Augustenburgs and Bismarck knew that the claims of the House of Gottorp had been brought out of the archives for the benefit of the Grand Duke of Oldenburg.[85] The fact that the Austro-Prussian proposal included the cession of all of Schleswig and Holstein was sure to meet opposition from other Powers at the Conference. Bismarck knew that the neutrals were going to propose the division of Schleswig.[86] The important thing was to get the duchies, or as much of them as possible, away from Denmark.[87] The Augustenburger might still be side-tracked or, at the worst, turned to the advantage of Prussia.

Bismarck attempted first of all to persuade Rechberg to demand merely the complete separation of the duchies from Denmark and to leave the question of succession to the throne for later discussion.[88] This failed[89] and on May 28, Count Apponyi, in the name of Austria and Prussia, read the following carefully worded statement:

[84] Haym, *Das Leben Max Dunckers*, p. 343.

[85] Sybel, *Die Begründung des deutschen Reiches*, III, p. 338. The initiative may have been Bismarck's. "Im engsten Vertrauen sagte mir Fürst Gortschakoff heute, dass er jetzt damit beschäftigt sei, das Warschauer Protocoll [of 1851, *Das Staatsarchiv*, VI, No. 1000] einer Umarbeitung zu unterziehen, indem der Preussische Hof es für seine Pflicht halte, seine eigne, sowie auch die Ansprüche des Oldenburgischen Hauses auf die Herzogthümer aus dem Schatten an das Licht zu ziehen." Redern to Bismarck, St. Petersburg, January 8, 1864 (Berlin Archives). "The Russian chargé d'affaires has mentioned to me confidentially that he had just called on Count Rechberg with a view to remind the Austrian Minister that in the event of the Treaty of London being set aside and the integrity of the Danish Monarchy ceasing to be essential as an European arrangement, the rights of Russia would have to be considered. ...." Bloomfield to Russell, No. 336, May 27, 1864 (Record Office, London).

[86] Cf. Ringhoffer, *Im Kampfe für Preussens Ehre*, p. 565.

[87] Cf. Philippson, *Kaiser Friedrich III*, pp. 145, 459.

[88] Bismarck, *Die gesammelten Werke*, IV, Nos. 380, 387.

[89] *Ibid.*, Nos. 381, 383, 384. Cf. *Anhang zu den Gedanken und Erinnerungen von Otto Fürst von Bismarck*, I, No. 120.

Since the demands of Austria and Prussia presented in the last sitting of the Conference have been declared inadmissable by the Danish Plenipotentiaries even supposing that a decision of the Diet were to admit the rights of Succession of His Majesty the King of Denmark in the Duchies, the Plenipotentiaries of the German Powers have received orders to demand, in concert with the Plenipotentiary of the German Confederation, the complete separation of the Duchies of Schleswig and Holstein from the Kingdom of Denmark, and their union in a single State under the Sovereignty of the Hereditary Prince of Schleswig-Holstein-Sonderburg-Augustenburg, who can not only bring forward, in the eyes of Germany, the greatest right to the Succession in the said Duchies, and whose recognition by the Germanic Diet is consequently assured, but who also possesses the undoubted suffrages of an immense majority of the population of those countries.[90]

At the same time, as usual when carrying on negotiations with Austria, Bismarck's next care was to safeguard his relations with France. Copies of the two dispatches to Werther were sent to Goltz at Paris and on May 24, Bismarck telegraphed that they had been communicated to Rechberg. "Should you perceive that they are being used by the Austrian cabinet to arouse French suspicion with regard to the emphasis which is therein laid on our relations to Austria, you will call attention to the urgent necessity in which we found ourselves of bringing over Austria to our point of view of the Conference situation without entering upon treaty obligation."[91] He also discussed the problem in detail with the French ambassador at Berlin and made it clear that Prussia was still in agreement with the French policy of the division of Schleswig by nationalities.[92]

Drouyn de Lhuys tended to make difficulties. "He saw in the proposal of the Duke of Augustenburg," telegraphed Goltz on May 29, "a concession to Austria and a drawing away from France, was disposed to give Denmark the whole of the so-called mixed district and to permit the vote only on the question of the sovereign,[93] but finally recognized the elements of an accomoda-

---

[90] Protocol of the session of May 28.

[91] Bismarck to Goltz, draft telegram, No. 209. May 24, 1864 (Berlin Archives).

[92] Talleyrand to Drouyn de Lhuys, May 24, 1864, *Les Origines diplomatiques de la guerre de 1870-1871*, III, No. 575. Cf. Bismarck, *Die gesammelten Werke*, IV, No. 384.

[93] "Sehr gütig" was Bismarck's comment on this.

tion. ...."[94] The Emperor as usual showed himself more accommodating than his minister.[95]

Bernstorff in London was notified that a passage in a telegram of May 26 to the effect that it was not necessary to consult the population, had been included by oversight from the Austrian draft and, out of regard for France, was not to be upheld by Prussia. He was warned to beware of Austrian attempts to wreck the partition scheme in the hope of bringing the Conference back to the basis of personal union.[96] If the opposition to the Austro-Prussian proposal should be directed especially against the person of the candidate named, he was instructed not to emphasize the dynastic question but to do all in his power to put through the principle of complete separation of the duchies from Denmark.[97]

Bismarck then moved to get in touch with the Prince of Augustenburg.

Already on May 19, Bismarck had invited Max Duncker, the confidential political adviser of the Prussian Crown Prince, to an interview at the Foreign Office and had given him a frank *exposé* of the situation. Prussian policy, he pointed out, had entered a very important phase and, as the interests of the Royal House and of the state were in question, he wanted the Crown Prince to be informed of the most secret details.

"I have succeeded," Duncker reports Bismarck as saying,

in what seemed to most people impossible, in bringing Austria to declare itself no longer bound by the Treaty of London.[98] The independence of the duchies with the material guarantees which we demanded for them has been rejected in the conference by the Danes. The dynastic question thus comes into the foreground. I have nothing against the Augustenburger.[99] It is of no decisive importance to Prussia to possess 200 to 300 square miles[100] more

---

[94] Goltz to Bismarck, telegram No. 180, May 29, 1864, Hähnsen, *Ursprung und Geschichte des Artikels V des Prager Friedens*, I, No. 101.

[95] Goltz to Bismarck, telegram No. 185, May 31, 1864 (Berlin Archives).

[96] Bismarck, *Die gesammelten Werke*, IV, No. 383 and n. 1, p. 443.

[97] *Ibid.*, No. 385.

[98] Cf. Protocols of the sessions of May 12 and 17.

[99] On Bismarck's attitude toward the Prince, see pp. 221 f. and A. O. Meyer, "Die Zielsetzung in Bismarcks schleswig-holsteinischer Politik von 1858 bis 1864." In *Z. f. s-h. G.*, LIII, *passim*.

[100] One sq. mi., German = approximately 24½ sq. mi., English.

territory with half a million subjects if the advantages which dominion over this territory offers can be won for Prussia in other ways. It is chiefly a question of the navy. .... We need, in addition, the canal, which we have already demanded in London. A military convention is desirable, but not a matter of the first importance.

Besides such a position in the duchies, we need guarantees of a conservative system of government. Under no circumstances is it to be expected that Austria would decide to recognize the Duke without these. And without them, we too, would have no security that any concessions promised would or could be executed. The Duke has proclaimed the Constitution of 1848. It contains, along with a broad democratic basis, full ministerial responsibility. If the Estates, elected in accordance with this constitution do not ratify the Duke's promises, we are out our treaty. Even if the Duke, faced by an obstinate majority should wish to change his ministry, he would, thanks to the law of ministerial responsibility, find no one who would undertake to force through the treaty. ....

It is contrary to the honor of the Prussian government to take Schleswig-Holstein away from Denmark only to give the government of the duchies into the hands of men who have incited and encouraged the opposition in Prussia against the government. If the Duke continues to surround himself with these councillors, we shall have to look forward to the fact that we shall have established a second Gotha on the Elbe, that the Duchies will be ruled on similar principles, that officials whom we have dismissed will be appointed to office there, that our opposition press will be supported and the Liberals, in the future, be advised and guided from Gotha and from Kiel.

To Duncker's defense of Prince Frederick, Bismarck retorted that from the beginning, the Prince had taken up a false position. He, Bismarck, had not cut off all hope of support when the Prince had visited him on November 17, but merely pointed out the difficulties which stood in the way.[101] Nevertheless, the Prince had thrown himself first into the arms of the 'democrats,' then into those of the 'Middle States,' and then, only when neither the one nor the other had produced results, had he attempted a rapprochement with Prussia. It was only later that the Prince had offered concessions. He had opened negotiations through an intermediary and then let them drop. "Prussia," said Bismarck,

could not go with the first 'democratic' wave that came along. If we had done that, things would have gone as they did in 1848. We should soon have been isolated and have had all the Powers against us, with the aid of only the 'middle' and minor states of Germany, which at the beginning

[101] Cf. p. 81 above.

couldn't be estimated at more than 40,000 men.   Then, as in 1850, we should have been forced to end a great effort by a great defeat.

Bismarck then came to his immediate object.   The initiative for an understanding should come from the Prince of Augustenburg. As the Crown Prince was his friend, it would be a good idea for him to give Prince Frederick an indication of the "conservative guarantees" that would be an indispensable condition of the recognition of his claims.   "Speaking frankly," continued Bismarck,

we could carry out the annexation if we wanted it.   Austria would rather see the duchies in our hands than in those of Duke Frederick.[102] Bavaria and Württemberg look with such aversion at the establishment of a center of democracy on the Elbe that they would prefer even the aggrandisement of our territory.   France admits the annexation in the hope of embroiling us with England and Austria.   As far as England is concerned, that hope might be realized, unless the English, as I expect, yield to the *fait accompli*; with respect to Austria, not.   I do not act in the Danish question without the agreement of Austria; on that rests our security against France.   Russia is again seeking an arrangement with France in the Eastern Question.   It has, perhaps, scruples about our annexation but will not act against us. .... We *can* annex; we *will* not provided that the Duke gives us guarantees for a conservative regime.[103]

To Duncker and the Crown Prince, as supporters of the Augustenburg claims, Bismarck, no doubt exaggerated somewhat the strength of the Prussian position.   When he realized that Austria had shifted its policy,[104] he no longer waited for the Prince to take the initiative.   "Bismarck himself said to me yesterday," wrote the Crown Prince to his friend on May 25,

that now England and Austria are for you (France has been inclined that way for some time) and that therefore the moment has come to negotiate with you directly.   It is a question, first of all (i. e. for Bismarck) to know whether you would place yourself on the 'conservative basis' and would be disposed to give such assurances or guarantees.

This last point refers especially to the constitution of 1848, which, as you know, is detested here and which you took as your point of departure after the death of Frederick VII.

I tell you this in the greatest haste .... because Bismarck added that it

[102] Cf. n. 49 p. 221 above.
[103] Haym, *Das Leben Max Dunckers,* pp. 339-344.
[104] Cf. p. 233 above.

would be desirable that you either come here to Berlin or that you meet me somewhere else to reach an agreement on this point.[105]

On June 1, Prince Frederick arrived in Berlin and was received cordially by the Crown Prince and the King. The monarch, who was delighted with the turn events had taken,[106] had called on the Prince's mother the day before and said that her son was now certain to obtain the duchies and that he wished to be the first to bring her the good news.[107]

But the King had reckoned without Bismarck. In the famous three-hour discussion on the evening of June 1, Prince Frederick failed to win the Prussian minister to his cause. The next morning Bismarck telegraphed his instructions to Bernstorff at London:

> After thorough discussion with Hereditary Prince of Augustenburg, it seems to me required in special Prussian interests to further his candidacy no more than has already been done, and, as soon as objections to it are expressed, to declare that the dynastic part of our proposal is not the first consideration.[108]

The accounts of the conference left by the two participants differ both as to the general character and as to many details of the discussion.[109] Bismarck's, which seems obviously to have been intended to prejudice the King against Prince Frederick, represents the latter as adopting a cool and reserved attitude toward Prussia[110] and as making objections to many details of the concessions demanded.[111] The Prince's version, which is less condensed, undoubtedly reproduces the spirit of the conversation more

[105] Crown Prince Frederick William to Duke Frederick, Potsdam, May 25, 1864, Jansen-Samwer, *Schleswig-Holsteins Befreiung*, pp. 722-723.

[106] Karolyi to Rechberg, Berlin, June 1, 1864, No. 55 A-E, Appendix VI, p. 324 below.

[107] Gebauer, *Herzog Friedrich VIII*, p. 108.

[108] Bismarck, *Die gesammelten Werke*, IV, No. 391. Cf. Bismarck to Goltz, *ibid.*, No. 392.

[109] Cf. A. Wahl, "Die Unterredung Bismarcks mit dem Herzog Friedrich von Augustenburg am 1 Juni, 1864," *Historische Zeitschrift*, XCV, pp. 58-70.

[110] E. g.: "Er sagte, die Herzogtümer hätten Preussen nicht gerufen; ohne uns würde der Bund die Befreiung der Herzogtümer mit mehr Leichtigkeit unter weniger lästigen Bedingungen bewirkt haben." Bismarck, *Die gesammelten Werke*, IV, p. 450.

[111] *Ibid.*, No. 394.

accurately.[112] According to this, Bismarck began with a frank discussion of the international situation, of the Prince's advisers, of the claims of the Grand Duke Oldenburg, and of the Schleswig-Holstein Constitution of 1848; all of which, Bismarck's summary omits. Then came the examination of the concessions. Here, too, the accounts differ in details but they are in essential agreement that Prince Frederick regarded the consent of the Estates as necessary to an agreement with Prussia and that he was unwilling to accept Bismarck's suggestion of any written agreement, for the time being, beyond the letter of April 29 to King William.[113]

Opinions differ as to whether Bismarck was sincere in his negotiations with the Prince and as to whether the latter, by more clever tactics, could have reached a binding agreement with the Prussian minister.[114] In his memoirs, Bismarck indicates that the Prince "by refusing the so-called February conditions, missed the favorable moment."[115] But it seems clear that the fate of the Prince depended not upon himself but upon factors over which he had no control: Austria, King William, and the course of events. Whenever Bismarck judged that he would have to accept Prince Frederick as Duke of Schleswig-Holstein, he would do so; whenever Bismarck judged that he could dispense with him, he would.[116]

X

The Austro-Prussian demand for the cession of the whole of the duchies of Schleswig and Holstein had been followed by a British proposal for the division of Schleswig. The frontier was to run no farther north than the mouth of the Schlei and the line of the *Dannevirke*. No fortresses or military ports were to be established in the ceded territory; there was to be no further

---

[112] Text in Jansen-Samwer, *Schleswig-Holsteins Befreiung*, pp. 731-736.

[113] Jansen-Samwer, *Schleswig-Holsteins Befreiung*, pp. 731-736. Cf. *ibid.*, pp. 337-343, footnotes; 736-741; and Gebauer, *Herzog Friedrich VIII*, pp. 108-112.

[114] Gebauer, *op. cit.*, pp. 109 f.

[115] Bismarck, *Gedanken und Erinnerungen*, II, p. 25.

[116] Karolyi to Rechberg, No. 55. A-E., June 1, 1864. Appendix VI, pp. 324-327.

interference by Germany in the affairs of Denmark; the destiny of Holstein, Lauenburg, and the ceded portion of Schleswig was not to be settled without their consent.[117] This was accepted in principle by all and the rest of the Conference turned on the question of where the frontier should be drawn.[118]

The Schlei-Dannevirke line was suggested with regard to military rather than national considerations.[119] In spite of the experience of the opening days of the war, it had maintained a considerable reputation as a defensive position. But a division on that line was too far south for the German Powers. They claimed, and justly, that it left purely German districts to Denmark and in their turn, suggested the equally unjust line of Apenrade-Hoyer. Between these two lines, compromise proved impossible. In an effort to bring one about, Bernstorff suggested that his government might be willing to accept a line from Flensburg to Hoyer, leaving Flensburg to the Germans.[120] But the Danes held firm to the Schlei-Dannevirke and the Conference broke up without a decision.

Two other schemes to save the Conference had failed in the same way. Bernstorff proposed that the people of the disputed district be consulted as to their nationality,[121] and the British delegation proposed that the selection of a compromise line be

[117] Protocol of the session of May 28, 1864.

[118] The dynastic question played a secondary part. The most important incident in regard to it was the announcement made by Baron Brunnow at the session of June 2, that the Tsar of Russia had ceded all his rights and claims in Holstein to the Grand Duke of Oldenburg. According to Oncken, *Grand Duke Peter of Oldenburg*, p. 69, the Tsar had promised this already in 1860, in case the Treaty of London should be abrogated. According to statements, reported by the British and French diplomatic representatives at St. Petersburg, the cession was made in 1862. Napier to Russell, No. 282, May 30, 1864, confidential (Record Office, London); *Les Origines diplomatiques de la guerre de 1870-1871*, III, No. 600. Gorchakov assured Lord Napier that the announcement at the Conference was not based on previous agreement with Prussia. But see above, p. 234.

[119] Russell to Cowley, No. 500, June 11, 1864 (Record Office, London).

[120] Session of June 2, 1864. This had been authorized by Bismarck's telegram of May 27, 1864. See above, p. 236, note 96.

[121] This plan was strenuously opposed by Austria in the confidential negotiations between the two German Powers in June. It was presented at the session of June 18 by direct order of Bismarck to Bernstorff. Telegram No. 351, June 17, 1864, Bismarck, *Die gesammelten Werke*, IV, No. 409.

left to the mediation of a neutral sovereign. The former proposition, which Austria supported in terms that were equivalent to a rejection, was refused by the Danes and even more emphatically by Russia. The second was accepted by Prussia and Austria on condition that the mediator should be a sovereign not represented at the Conference, and that his decision should not be a binding arbitral award. The Danes flatly rejected it and demanded either the Schlei-Dannevirke line or the maintenance of the Treaty of London.

Again, as in December, the Danes had done Bismarck's work for him. They had rejected the compromises; Prussia had offered to be reasonable. It is, of course, true that the Prussian delegates had kept plenty of loopholes for eventual escape from their offers, but the Danes had never left them the initiative of rejecting a compromise.

The Danes had agreed to accept a division of Schleswig at the Schlei-Dannevirke line. From the national point of view, that would include in Denmark all the Danish-speaking populations and also the district of Angeln, which had been completely Germanized only in the nineteenth century. From the historical point of view, it was almost as satisfactory. The Eider had been the historical frontier of Denmark, but the *Dannevirke* had been its defensive one. This frontier was the Danish ultimatum.

The mediation proposal was rejected because it was feared that the frontier might be drawn north of Flensburg. The frontier which was established after the plebiscite of 1920 might well have been obtained in 1864, perhaps even more.[122] But "aside from the fact that the Schleswigers themselves were opposed to a division of the duchy, a Schleswig north of Flensburg did not in those days seem of especial value; not dynastic to the Royal House, not historical or cultural to the 'Whole-State' party, not legitimate or economic to the Eider-Danes, and not even national to the advocates of partition.'"[123]

[122] In the elections of February 12, 1867, for the North German Reichstag, Flensburg gave 1836 votes for the Danish candidate as against 1648 for the two German candidates. Mackeprang, *Nordslesvig*, 1864-1909, p. 35.

[123] M. Rubin, in *Historisk Tidsskrift*, (Copenhagen), 8 R., V, p. 123.

The National Liberals, who still controlled Danish policy, and especially Krieger, their representative at the Conference, had never really liked the negotiations. They felt that they were being dragged from concession to concession and that it would be better to keep up the fight. Untaught by the experience of the first stages of the war, they overestimated the strength of Denmark's military position and they still hoped for foreign aid.[124]

[124] During the Conference, the Danish plenipotentiaries were in close touch with some of the minor leaders of the Opposition. They were frequently advised to break up the Conference as the Tories intended to avoid a serious attack on the Government's Danish policy as long as the Conference was in session. Bille to Monrad, No. 58, June 7, 1864 (Copenhagen Archives). Cf. Krieger, *Dagbøger*, III, pp. 140 f, 155, 156 f, 159 f, 163, 167.

CHAPTER VII

THE END OF THE SCHLESWIG-HOLSTEIN QUESTION.

I

With the break-up of the Conference, the Danes hoped that public opinion and Parliament would force the British cabinet either to support them or to give place to a cabinet that would.[1] As the war had progressed, public opinion, press, and Parliament had continued loud in favor of Denmark. The appearance of the Austrian fleet in the Channel on its way to the North Sea at the end of April had increased the excitement and Palmerston had warned Apponyi that if it approached the entrance to the Baltic, it would be followed by a superior British squadron.[2] The news

[1] "D'après ce qu'un membre du parti Tory m'a dit hier, il paraît certain que l'opposition parlementaire s'est décidée à s'abstenir d'attaquer sérieusement le Gouvernement sur la politique à notre égard pendant la durée de la Conférence. Mais mon interlocuteur m'a assuré que si la Conférence venait à se dissoudre sans avoir obtenu aucun résultat et cela parceque l'Allemagne n'aurait pas voulu suivre notre exemple en acceptant purement et simplement la proposition anglaise du 28 Mai,—que l'opposition parlementaire serait alors bien décidée à faire une démarche au Parlement dont le but serait d'amener le Gouvernement soit à prêter au Danemark un secours efficace pour le maintien de son indépendance, soit à céder la place au parti Tory qui alors entreprendait de nous secourir. Mon interlocuteur crut que la forme que prendrait cette démarche serait celle d'une addresse à la Reine, priant Sa Majesté à prendre les mesures nécessaires pour maintenir l'indépendance et l'intégrité du Danemark. Il était d'avis que le Gouvernement du Roi dût tenir fermement à la proposition anglaise du 28 Mai, au moins pour ce qui concerne la frontière, et il était convaincu que le pays et le Parlement ne toléraient jamais que le Ministère abandonnât cette frontière proposée par lui-même pour une autre plus désadvantageuse au Danemark. .... Je crois devoir ajouter que le sentiment d'indignation contre l'Allemagne s'étend et s'accroit ici de jour en jour et qu'il manque, selon moi, très peu à l'heure qu'il est que l'opinion publique ne se prononce ouvertement pour une prise d'armes en notre faveur, si la Conférence ne dût pas nous procurer une paix honorable et satisfaisante." Bille to Monrad, No. 58, London, June 7, 1864 (Copenhagen Archives).

[2] Ashley, *Palmerston*, II, pp. 249-253; Apponyi to Rechberg, No. 42-C, May 3, 1864 (Vienna Archives).

of the Danish victory of Helgoland had been acclaimed enthusiastically in London. During the Conference, the indignation against Germany and especially Prussia reached dangerous heights. If he were to believe some organs of the English press and the reports of his own agents in London, Bismarck said to Buchanan on June 17, he would consider it probable that England and Prussia would be at war in a fortnight; he believed, in fact, this eventuality to be almost inevitable.[3] To Bernstorff, at about the same time, Clarendon said: "We are drifting into war just as we did ten years ago. I can't, of course, declare this officially, but I assure you as a friend, that as surely as we are at this moment here in Buckingham Palace—England will take part in the war if it begins again."[4]

Before coming to a final decision, the cabinet tried to win the support of Napoleon in securing the Schlei-Dannevirke frontier for Denmark. Early in June, Lord Cowley had reconnoitered the terrain in Paris and reported that it was unsatisfactory. Drouyn de Lhuys had seemed well disposed but the Emperor had refused. The line of frontier proposed by the British plenipotentiaries would leave to Denmark a considerable portion of territory inhabited solely by Germans, and "His Majesty, with the opinions which he had always entertained and expressed in respect to nationalities could not press this arrangement to extremities [*à outrance*]."[5] A telegram on June 6, from Manderström to the Swedish minister in Paris, stirred the French cabinet out of its reserve. It directed him to inform Drouyn de Lhuys that Russia was proposing that Denmark enter the Germanic Confederation with all its territories.[6] Drouyn de Lhuys telegraphed to London that France was prepared to join her forces

[3] Buchanan to Russell, No. 522, June 18, 1864, Confidential (Record Office, London).

[4] Bernstorff to King William, June 17, 1864, Ringhoffer, *Im Kampfe für Preussens Ehre*, p. 572. Cf. Clarendon's letter to Cowley in Wellesley, *The Paris Embassy during the Second Empire*, p. 267.

[5] Cowley to Russell, telegram, June 4, 1864, 6:30 P. M.; No. 659B, June 5, 1864, most confidential (Record Office, London).

[6] Manderström to Adelsvärd, telegram, June 5, 1864, *Les Origines diplomatiques de la guerre de 1870-1871*, III, No. 610. Cf. *ibid.*, No. 621; Neergaard, *Under Junigrundloven*, II, pp. 1311-1314.

to those of Great Britain and Sweden to prevent the accomplishment of such a project.[7] But the crisis died away almost as quickly as it had arisen. Gorchakov formally denied that Russia had proposed the plan;[8] Monrad declared that neither he nor his colleagues would accept it;[9] Bismarck assured Talleyrand that French opposition to it would have the entire sympathy of Prussia.[10]

Although for the first time France had made a direct advance to England, Russell seems to have received it coolly. He evidently suspected that what irritated the French was not so much the hard fate of Denmark as the fact that the incorporation of that monarchy in the Confederation would make a Scandinavian union impossible. The incorporation of Denmark with the Germanic Confederation, he said to the French ambassador, would be no less distasteful to Her Majesty's government than it would be to France. What the British government desired was to see Denmark maintain her independent position and neither form part of Germany nor of a Scandinavian kingdom. But the best mode of preventing the absorption of Denmark into the Confederation was, in his opinion, that France and Great Britain should join in preventing by force, if necessary, any attempt to deprive Denmark of the position of an independent Power. As both were now desirous of upholding Denmark as an independent monarchy, they might very well unite their efforts to prevent the projects of the German Powers for confining Denmark to such narrow limits as would render it impossible for her any longer to maintain herself without associating herself with the German Confederation or with a new Scandinavian union. For if Denmark should find herself entirely without the support of the

[7] Drouyn de Lhuys to La Tour d'Auvergne, telegram, June 6, 1864, 4:30 P. M., *Les Origines diplomatiques de la guerre de 1870-1871*, III, No. 612.

[8] Massignac to Drouyn de Lhuys, June 7, 1864, *ibid.*, No. 622.

[9] "Il n'y a pas de proposition russe; ce sont des idées émises, dans sa correspondance, par le Ministre de Danemark à Petersburg, attendu ces jours-ci. Le Président du Conseil me déclare qu'en aucun cas ni lui ni ses Collègues n'y prêteraient les mains." Dotézac to Drouyn de Lhuys, telegram, June 9, 1864, *ibid.*, No. 637.

[10] Talleyrand to Drouyn de Lhuys, June 8, 1864, *ibid.*, No. 627.

Great Powers in maintaining her independent position, she might consider it to be for her interest to join the German Confederation, and in that case it would be impossible for England to join in resisting such a step by force of arms. It was obvious to him, however, that the most effectual mode of preventing such a measure was to secure to Denmark such independence as would take from her any temptation to do so; and in order to attain this object, the coöperation of France and England seemed to afford the surest means.[11]

Although Napoleon was willing to use threats and perhaps even force to prevent a settlement of the Danish question which would have made the Scandinavian union impossible and have served as a precedent for the inclusion of Venetia in the Confederation,[12] he was not willing to do so for the sake of preserving a few square miles of territory and a few tens of thousands of inhabitants to the Danish Monarchy. In the present state of feeling in Germany, such action would mean war. A naval demonstration in which shots were fired would mean for France war by land as well as by sea. England could limit her operations, France could not; and a war on her frontiers against all of Germany would be a most serious enterprise. "In such an eventuality," Drouyn de Lhuys asks in his dispatch to La Tour d'Auvergne, "would England be prepared to give us her unlimited support? The government of His Majesty, in demanding the support of the legislative bodies would have to explain to them the advantages for which the blood of France was to be spilt. Will the British cabinet put us in a position to answer that question?"[13]

Whether these questions were intended to be more than rhetorical, it is impossible to say.[14] To the Danish minister in

[11] Russell to Cowley, No. 491, June 8, 1864 (Record Office, London); La Tour d'Auvergne to Drouyn de Lhuys, June 8, 1864, *Les Origines diplomatiques de la guerre de 1870-1871*, III, No. 631.

[12] Döhler, *Napoleon III, und die deutsch-dänische Frage*, p. 97.

[13] Drouyn de Lhuys to La Tour d'Auvergne, June 10, 1864. *Les Origines diplomatiques de la guerre de 1870-1871*, III, No. 640.

[14] "Morny had a long conversation with the Emperor this afternoon. He endeavored to persuade His Majesty to coöperate with Her Majesty's Government on the Danish question. The Emperor refused, declaring he would not risk a war for the sake of Denmark. His Majesty is convinced that England must give

Paris, Drouyn de Lhuys admitted that "there was a shade of difference of opinion between himself and the Emperor as to what should be the attitude of France at the present moment in the Danish question."[15] The correspondence of both Cowley and Goltz shows that in general Drouyn de Lhuys was more willing to take a firm stand against the German Powers than was the Emperor. At this very time, however, Drouyn de Lhuys again brought up in conversation with Goltz the idea of incorporating the German duchies with Prussia. "He would much rather see Holstein, Lauenburg, and a moderate part of Schleswig in the hands of Prussia, which would know how to make use of them and whose government would be a blessing to them, than in the hands of a petty duke. To be sure, besides himself, only the Emperor Napoleon shared this view, which, if it became known in political circles in Paris, would create the greatest dissatisfaction. Nevertheless, they were both determined to carry it out if Prussia were ready."[16]

Was Napoleon asking for bids? Whatever the answer to that may be, Drouyn de Lhuys' question cooled the ardor of the British.[17] It was never answered and on June 25, the British cabinet "divided and came to a tolerable, not the best, conclusion."[18] On June 27, Russell in the House of Lords and

material assistance to Denmark, and this is evidently what he desires. Should this assistance extend to the Adriatic, the Emperor would profit by it to obtain the liberation of Venetia. The Emperor gave the same assurance to Morny which he had given to others, that nothing but aggression on the part of England would induce him to quarrel with her." Cowley to Russell, telegram, June 25, 1864, 12:15 A. M., private (Record Office, London). Cf. Rouher's statements to Cowley, in Walpole, *Russell*, II, pp. 394 f.; Drouyn de Lhuys' to Cowley, in Wellesley, *The Paris Embassy during the Second Empire*, pp. 268 f.

[15] Cowley to Russell, No. 685, June 11, 1864, most confidential (Record Office, London).

[16] Goltz to Bismarck, No. 196, June 9, 1864, *sehr vertraulich*. Goltz replied by referring to the April negotiations and the program then agreed upon. Hähnsen *Ursprung und Geschichte des Artikels V des Prager Friedens*, I, No. 154.

[17] Walpole, *Russell*, II, pp. 394f. "Lord Russell writes to the Queen that it will be very difficult to avoid giving assistance to Denmark; yet he admits that without France our aid will be inefficient. He hesitates with reason at the price asked by France for her co-operation...." C. Grey to Granville, Windsor Castle, June 23, 1864, Fitzmaurice, *Granville*, I, p. 473.

[18] Morley, *Gladstone*, II, p. 118.

Palmerston in the House of Commons announced the decision of the government to let events take their course. Only if Copenhagen itself were menaced, would they think it necessary to come to a fresh decision.[19] A vote of censure was proposed in both houses. In the Lords, the government was defeated by nine votes; in the Commons, it was saved by eighteen.[20]

"We have done better than could be expected in both Houses," wrote Russell to Cowley, "and I trust the Foreign Ministers will now see that they had better keep on good terms with us and not expect the Tories to walk into my room. .... I am very glad that we have not given in to the temptation of a war between France and Germany. The French, if they get an inch, will certainly take an ell.'"[21]

II

The armistice, which had been renewed for two weeks from June 12, expired on the day after the last session of the Conference. During that time, old Marshall Wrangel had been superseded in command of the allied armies by Prince Frederick Charles of Prussia. The Prussians wanted to adopt the plan of operations drawn up by Moltke for a simultaneous landing on the islands of Alsen and Fünen. But although King William and Bismarck, who were with Francis Joseph and Rechberg at Carlsbad, urged this, the Austrians would agree only to the occupation of Jutland north of the Liim fiord and the attack on Alsen.[22]

[19] Hansard, 3rd series, CLXXVI, coll. 323, 351.

[20] Walpole, *History of Twenty-five Years*, I, pp. 449-453. It is open to doubt whether, if the Tories had overthrown the government, they would have aided Denmark. See above p. 172, note 10. Also Laughton, *Henry Reeve*, II, pp. 106 f. Malmesbury, *Memoirs of an Ex-Minister*, II, p. 319.

[21] Russell to Cowley, July 9, 1864, Walpole, *Russell*, II, p. 396.

[22] Rechberg believed that the attack on Fünen would be an unnecessary provocation to Great Britain. He feared that that Power was likely to enter the war and that Palmerston would stir up revolutionary movements in the Austrian dominions. Von Sybel, *Die Begründung des deutschen Reiches*, III, p. 354. Clarendon had said to Bernstorff shortly before the end of the Conference: " ....You can do what you will on the mainland, but not on sea. You won't reach Copenhagen, nor the Sound, nor even Alsen." Ringhoffer, *Im Kampfe für Preussens Ehre*, p. 572.

On June 29, the Prussians succeeded in crossing to Alsen and the Danish troops were withdrawn by sea. The capture of Alsen really broke the resistance of the Danes. They had counted on being able to keep the Germans out of the islands, but they now realized that the fleet could not prevent the Prussians from crossing a narrow channel under the protection of their superior artillery. A landing in Fünen was seen to be possible, and faith in the inaccessibility of Zealand was shaken. On July 8, the Monrad ministry, which had long ceased to command the King's confidence, resigned and on July 12, the new ministry which had been formed under Bluhme, proposed an armistice. It began on July 20 and before the end of the month, the peace negotiations were opened at Vienna. The most important provision of the treaty of peace, signed on October 30, was that King Christian IX ceded to Austria and Prussia his rights to the three duchies of Schleswig, Holstein and Lauenburg.[23]

III

With the Treaty of Vienna, the problem of the relations of the duchies to Denmark was solved. One aspect of the Schleswig-Holstein question, that of the succession to the throne of the duchies, continued for two more years until the guns of Königgrätz ended it forever. In 1852, assembled Europe had solemnly pronounced the integrity of the Danish Monarchy to be a necessary element of the balance of power; in 1864, not a hand had been raised to defend it. The old Danish Monarchy had come to an end. It was mourned by few in any of its parts. The King of Denmark and the conservative 'Whole State' elements, in Denmark and in the duchies, regretted its passing[24]

---

[23] A preliminary treaty had been signed on August 1. A few changes were made in the northern frontier of Schleswig to compensate Denmark for the Jutish enclaves in Schleswig.

[24] Neergaard, *Under Junigrundloven,* p. 1299. "...Est-ce irrévocablement fait de l'intégrité de l'antique et noble Monarchie? Ce que des siècles avaient réuni, des dispositions qu'on appellera un jour passagères, vont-elles le scinder à tout jamais?" O. Plessen to Monrad, No. 26, St. Petersburg, June 1, 1864 (Copenhagen Archives).

but the great majority of the people had long lost their interest in the monarchy as a whole. The Germans in the duchies were happy to be free from Denmark and the people of the kingdom were glad to be rid of the Germans.

For Denmark, a new question had arisen. The Danes had hoped to be able to save most of Schleswig, but when all had been lost, attention was turned to North Schleswig. The Danish point of view had been political and historical; it became purely national. A few politicians continued to think in the old way and to hope for a new settlement on the former basis. P. Vedel, permanent under-secretary for foreign affairs, who was in close touch with the politicians who had made the final decision, wrote to Count Hamilton that he hoped that the last word had not been said in a peace that took away all of Schleswig. "I hear many complaining now," he continued,

> that we did not in London accept the Apenrade-Hoyer line. I find it good that we did not and though I did not approve of all that we did, or rather, did not do, at London, I shall always be ready to defend our Government and our negotiators for a policy that offered great chances and which, with a little luck could have led to a really acceptable result. As conditions now are, I regard it as best to strive for favorable financial terms but not to give the least bit for a useless fragment of North Schleswig, which, besides, would give the peace the appearance of finally having paid some regard to the principle of nationality. Much rather a peace that is recognized by everyone to rest upon no principle at all, for there will be then much more prospect of an opportunity, that will not have to be waited for too long, for revising it on a real basis that will be either political-historical or national. Rather let the Germans incorporate the whole of the Danish nationality in North Schleswig...with Germany than a fragment that will perhaps lack the strength to offer energetic resistance to Germanization. ...I hope, then, for a third act in the drama. ....[25]

The third act came, but not until over fifty years later, and it brought back to Denmark no more, and probably less than might have been obtained in 1864.

The policy of the Danes had been faulty. That they underestimated the real danger of their situation is explicable when we look back at the events of 1848 and at the attitude taken by the

[25] Vedel to Hamilton, August 1, 1864, Carlquist, *Ur Henning Hamiltons Brefsamling*, II, pp. 168f

Powers since that time.   Their misunderstanding of Bismarck's
policy was shared by the statesmen of greater states than
Denmark.   They misjudged the possibilities of the international
situation, especially the intentions of Napoleon III, but so did
most of Europe.   At the end, it was only by a very narrow margin
that the British Parliament adopted the policy of non-intervention.   By more clever tactics, however, the Danish government
could have greatly improved its position.   Instead of putting Bismarck into difficulties by showing greater moderation and willingness to compromise than did Prussia, the Danes twice, in December
1863, and in June 1864, played into his hands.   If they had
yielded on the question of the constitution in December, it would
have been much more difficult for Bismarck to have secured a
satisfactory pretext for war; and if they had accepted mediation
in June, it would have been much more difficult for him to obtain
all of Schleswig or even the maximum that he really wanted.
"We lacked," wrote Monrad in later years, "a political
genius."[26]   Even without a political genius, the Danish government might have realized that a small Power must not run the
risks involved in playing high politics.   "Why is it," the Danish
minister asked Gorchakov, "that I find that you do not apply
in your own policy [in the Polish question] the same principles
that you advise us to follow?"   The Russian vice-chancellor
replied: "I have always talked to you as a sincere friend of
Denmark.   You are not seventy millions as we are."[27]

Sweden learned this lesson at a smaller cost.   Like Denmark,
she had expected the 'Western Powers' to intervene against the
Germans and was prepared to support them.   The expectation
of Swedish support had been an important factor in the decisions of the Danish ministers during 1863.   But there were two
points of view struggling for mastery in the Swedish government and her policy was ambiguous and unsteady.   The King.
the Crown Prince, and possibly the minister for foreign affairs,
looked forward to the creation of the Scandinavian union.   Most
of the ministers, however, favored non-intervention in foreign

[26] Monrad, *Deltagelse i Begivenhederne, 1864*, p. 22.
[27] O. Plessen to Hall, No. 38, August 5, 1863 (Copenhagen Archives).

politics and the concentration of Sweden's efforts and resources on political and economic reform at home. Insufficient encouragement from the 'Western Powers' and the dread that Russia would support Austria and Prussia if Sweden joined Denmark combined with the sentiments of the majority of the people to give the victory to the policy of non-intervention. During the war, the King of Sweden intrigued with the ultra-Scandinavian elements at Copenhagen and held his fleet ready for action, but the government followed a policy of caution and reserve.[28]

British policy had aimed first at securing a peaceful settlement of the Schleswig-Holstein question, then at maintaining the integrity of the Danish Monarchy, and in the end, at securing the division of Schleswig on a line favorable to Denmark. It failed at every point. The material defeat was not so great as the moral. It was half a century before a German fleet based on Kiel was a menace to England but the loss of British prestige was immediate and complete. The British government had given good advice at Copenhagen, but the outspoken support of Parliament and Press made the Danes believe that the warnings of Earl Russell were not to be taken seriously. Worse still, in giving this impression, were the threatening notes to the German states and the rash bluster of Palmerston. The bull dog was barking loudly; but he seemed no longer capable of biting. "England had recoiled with vigor," was the comment of Drouyn de Lhuys.[29] Gorchakov told Lord Napier that he "did not take even into contemplation the contingency of armed intervention from any quarter whatever."[30] And Bismarck told Sir Andrew Buchanan that he didn't care whether England joined in the war or not.[31] It was not until the Congress of Berlin that the words of a British statesman again had weight in the councils of Europe. Palmerston and Russell made the fatal blunder of

---

[28] Many points in Swedish policy are still obscure. This is especially true of her relations with France.

[29] Mülinen to Rechberg, No. 26B., July 4, 1864; Appendix V, p. 308 below.

[30] Napier to Russell, No. 267, May 24, 1864, secret and confidential; Appendix VIII below.

[31] Buchanan to Russell, No. 522, June 18, 1864, confidential, (Record Office, London).

adopting a policy that they were not willing to carry through to the limit. Even when they were suggesting intervention to France and Russia they shrank from accepting the consequences of such action. When it was all over, they breathed a sigh of relief that their proposals had not been taken up.[32]

Russia had followed a consistent policy and was not dissatisfied with the result. The integrity of the Danish Monarchy had been given up and the Germans had the port of Kiel. But interests which Russia regarded as of much greater importance had been safeguarded. Austria and Prussia had successfully resisted the "Revolution" in Germany; Napoleon III had found no ally for his supposed warlike plans; the Scandinavian union had been avoided; and the *entente* of the three 'Eastern Powers' had been strengthened.[33]

At the end of the Danish War, the situation had not yet shaped itself in accordance with Napoleon's wishes. The war had come, but not the profit that he had hoped from it. The duchies had been taken away from Denmark, but Schleswig had not been divided on national lines and the Scandinavian union was as distant as ever. More important from his point of view was the fact that Austria and Prussia were still allied and the complications that Bismarck had indicated to him had not yet come to pass. The war had remained localized and he had not had a chance to throw the weight of France into the scales and thus dictate the terms of a general settlement. But there was no more reason for him to give up hope for the success of his policy than there had been in January or in February. The agreement of Austria and Prussia on the Augustenburg candidacy had been momentary. The final disposition of the booty had not been arranged and the two German Powers were as far from an agreement as ever.

In view of the later course of Franco-Prussian relations, the policy of Napoleon III in the Schleswig-Holstein question is generally regarded as the origin of the downfall of the Second

---

[32] See above, pp. 246, 249, and Ashley, *Palmerston*, II, pp. 255-258.

[33] Cf. Dalwigk's account of his conversation with Alexander II in June 1864, Vogt, *Die hessische Politik*, pp. 210 f.

Empire. De la Gorce, for example, believes that the crossing of the frontier of Jutland by Prussian troops was the moment indicated for a decisive intervention.[34] That seems to me an unjustified criticism. Napoleon was quite justified in not risking war with all of Germany at that time. His fatal mistake was made not in 1863 or 1864, but after Königgrätz in 1866. That was the culmination of his policy in the Schleswig-Holstein question. It had brought him to a position where France could dominate events. That he did not take advantage of it was the fault of his character, not of his policy.

For Austria, it has been said that the death of Frederick VII came three months too late.[35] If the crisis in the succession question had come at the time of the *Frankfürter Fürstentag*, while Austria was still the 'Liberal' leader in Germany and while she was still associated with France and Great Britain in the Polish question, it might have marked the end, not the beginning of Bismarck's career. But in November, Austria was caught at a moment of practical isolation, in the course of a re-orientation of policy. A great man at Vienna might, even in November, have carried through an anti-Prussian policy by putting Austria boldly at the head of the national movement in Germany. But it would have required a man with strength of character, breadth of vision and disregard for scruples,—in a word, a Bismarck, not a Rechberg. The latter, however, adopted the policy of co-öperation with Prussia against the liberal and national elements in Germany. The course of events brought the Austrians deeper and deeper into a situation that could bring them no profit. But once engaged, Austrian prestige and the declared intention of Prussia to go ahead even without her, kept the alliance intact.[36] If Rechberg had been able to maintain his policy of coöperation with Bismarck, the result might not have been so fatal to Austria. That Austrian hegemony in Germany was doomed seems certain, but that dualism was impossible cannot be proved. In his

[34] De la Gorce, *Histoire du second Empire*, IV, p. 518.
[35] Lenz, *Geschichte Bismarcks*, pp. 219 f.
[36] Cf. Chotek to Rechberg, No. 59 A-B, Berlin, June 14, 1864 (Vienna Archives.)

Reflections and Reminiscences,[37] Bismarck assures us that he would at this time have been satisfied with equality with Austria. As long as he was Prussian minister, there could have been little question of equality of control—1863 and 1864 showed that,—but the dualistic plans which Bismarck had so often described might have been realized. Rechberg's position, however, was shaken as the spring of 1864 progressed. The anti-Prussian elements regained their influence and Austria refused to admit the possibility of mere equality with Prussia. In May, 1864, Bismarck's suggestion of a policy of "mutual compensation" was disregarded and by adopting the Augustenburg candidacy, Austria swung back to the policy she had abandoned in October and November 1863. The result was 1866.

Bismarck had the most reason to be satisfied with the position of his country at the close of the Danish War. The first stage of his policy in the Schleswig-Holstein question had been carried to a successful conclusion. The duchies had been taken away from Denmark and the question of their final disposition was still open. His position cannot be better summarized than as it was in 1865 to Beust.

Bismarck...boasted with the candor peculiar to him of how from the beginning he had conducted the Schleswig affair in accordance with Prussian interests. He had posed conditions to the Danes which he knew they could not possibly have accepted. At the same time, he had by indirect means encouraged them to active resistance. Through his secret agents, he had put before them the certain prospect of English assistance, while he had assured himself in advance that France did not want to go to war and therefore that England too would keep her sword in the scabbard. At the London Conference, he had (*verba ipsissima*) hitched the Duke of Augustenburg as an ox before the plough to bring it ahead. As soon as the plough was in motion, he had again unhitched the ox. His own aim is the annexation of the duchies; the difficulty is to bring the King to do it. About Austria and the cleverness of its policy, Bismarck merely smiled.[38]

IV

The problem of the disposition of the duchies, after they had been taken from Denmark, involved the solution of the German

---

[37] *Gedanken und Erinnerungen*, I, Ch. XVII.

[38] Dalwigk to Gagern (quoting Beust), September 20, 1865, Vogt, *Die hessische Politik*, pp. 212 f. See Appendix X, below.

question. Bismarck had left Frankfurt in 1859, convinced that Prussia's position in the Confederation was a sickness that sooner or later would have to be healed *ferro et igni* if, at the proper time, no other cure could be found.[39] During the first year of his ministry, it appeared that the struggle for the hegemony in Germany was inevitable. Austria seemed determined to persist in the objectionable policy of mobilizing the minor states against Prussia and of pushing through the Austrian schemes for the reform of the Confederation with complete disregard for Prussia. That, Bismarck was equally determined to prevent. "You are accustomed," he remarked, in September 1863, to the Russian minister at Berlin, "to a Prussia that lives quietly between Berlin and Sans Souci and goes, if necessary, to Olmütz. The time for that is absolutely past."[40] But when, in November, Austria turned away from the minor states and sought to coöperate with Prussia, Bismarck accepted the change with satisfaction.[41] He had not said that *ferro et igni* was the only way of settling the German question and he seems to have been quite willing to accept for Prussia a position of equality with Austria in the Confederation.[42] If Austria would sincerely abandon her policy of using the majority of the Diet against Prussia and, especially, admit Prussian hegemony in north Germany, the two Powers could, so far as Bismarck was concerned, live in reasonable harmony.

From November 1863 to October 1864, such a situation existed. Indeed, Bismarck used the alliance with Austria almost as much against the other states of Germany as against Denmark and the Great Powers.[43] The way in which, in January, Austria and Prussia took into their own hands the management of the

[39] A. O. Meyer, *Bismarcks Kampf mit Oesterreich 1851-1859*, pp. 481 f.

[40] Oubril's report No. 297, September 15, 1863, from notes taken in the Russian archives in 1917 by Dr. R. H. Lord. Cf. Lord, "Bismarck and Russia in 1863" in *American Historical Review*, XXIX, pp. 47 f.

[41] Bismarck, *Gedanken und Erinnerungen*, II, pp. 3, 5.

[42] Von Ruville, "Bismarck und die grossdeutsche Gedanke" in *Forschungen zur Brandenburg-Preussische Geschichte*, XVI, and Thimme's introductions to vols. IV and V of Bismarck, *Die gesammelten Werke*.

[43] Cf. E. Marcks, *Otto von Bismarck, ein Lebensbild*, pp. 77 ff.

Schleswig-Holstein question showed the palpable weakness of the 'third Germany.' During the next few months, Bismarck drove the lesson home. In February, Marshal Wrangel was allowed to bully the Federal troops in Holstein and Austria supported Prussia in rebuffing the protests of the Diet. In July, after friction had developed between Hanoverian and Prussian troops at Rendsburg, the Prussians took over the city. An armed collision was barely avoided.[44]

Rechberg continued to support Bismarck in dealing with the Diet and with the claims of the Prince of Augustenburg. In settling the future of the duchies, the two ministers were less successful. At Schönbrunn, on August 22, 1864, Emperor Francis Joseph, King William, Rechberg, and Bismarck, met to discuss their common problem. Bismarck urged the Austrians to allow the Prussians to annex Schleswig-Holstein without territorial compensation for Austria. The latter Power, he argued, had no interest in the duchies but a very real one in her relations with Prussia. For a time, he felt that he was making an impression, but when King William, in reply to a direct question, declared that he had no right to the territory and therefore could not lay claim to it, Bismarck's arguments were to no avail.[45] Bismarck, in his *Reflections and Reminiscences*, points out this conference as the real end of the possibility of dualism in Germany. As a matter of fact, however, the two ministers agreed that they would continue to coöperate in German affairs and the monarchs approved the decision.

Rechberg fell from power, however, on October 27, after the Prussian ministry, in spite of Bismarck's pleading, refused to meet his moderate wishes in the *Zollverein* negotiations. Schmerling had gradually undermined his rival's position and the anti-Prussian forces at Vienna were gradually gaining the upper hand. Rechberg's successor at the Ballhausplatz was Count

---

[44] Cf. A. Stern, *Geschichte Europas*, IX, pp. 361 f, 386 f.

[45] Bismarck, *Gedanken und Erinnerungen*, I, pp. 344 ff.; Pahncke, *Die Parallelerzählungen Bismarcks zu seinen Gedanken und Erinnerungen*, pp. 102-105. Cf. the interesting letter of Jan. 9, 1867, from Rechberg to his brother, in F. Engel-Jánosi, *Graf Rechberg*, pp. 147-150.

Mensdorff-Pouilly, a high-born, well-intentioned soldier.   The real control of Austria's German policy was in the hands of Biegeleben.   Yet the breach was not immediate.   The allies worked together in formally ending the Federal Execution and in forcing the evacuation of Holstein by the Saxon and Hanoverian troops.   As late as February 20, 1865, Bismarck wrote to Goltz that the value of the Austrian alliance for Prussia had not yet been used up.

The question of the duchies had, however, become the touch-stone of the alliance.[45a] If Austria accepted the Prussian demands, it would be an earnest of her good will in the German question; if she did not, war would sooner or later be inevitable.   For the time being, the Austrian government was not unwilling to let Prussia have the duchies in exchange for the cession of a bit of Prussian territory, the County of Glatz, to Austria.   Neither Bismarck nor King William would consider such a deal and on February 22, 1865, Bismarck finally transmitted to Vienna, the conditions under which Prussia would agree to the establishment of a State of Schleswig-Holstein.   He demanded a permanent and indissoluble, offensive and defensive alliance between the new state and Prussia; the amalgamation of the army and navy with those of Prussia, to whose king the soldiers and sailors would take the oath of military obedience; actual cession to Prussia of the land needed for coast defense works and naval bases; complete control of the projected Baltic-North Sea canal and of the postal and telegraph systems; and the accession of Schleswig-Holstein to the Prussian customs union.[46] If these conditions had been accepted, annexation would have been superfluous.[47]

The Prussian King was gradually becoming more susceptible to suggestions of Prussian annexation.   His visit to the battlefield of Düppel in 1864 had aroused in him the desire to possess the

---

[45a] This was written before I had seen F. Frahm's use of the same figure in "Die Bismarcksche Lösung der schleswig-holsteinischen Frage", *Z. f. s-h. G.*, LIX, (1930), p. 428.

[46] Bismarck, *Die gesammelten Werke*, V, No. 62.

[47] Bismarck admitted to the Crown Prince of Prussia that the conditions had been drafted with the intention of making them unacceptable to the Prince of Augustenburg.   Haym, *Das Leben Max Dunckers*, p. 363.

land consecrated by the blood of his soldiers. Bismarck's careful manipulation was steadily undermining the Augustenburg influences at the Prussian court and the last serious scruples disappeared in the summer of 1865 when the majority report of the crown jurists declared that in November 1863, Christian of Glücksburg had been the rightful heir to the duchies.

The friction between Austria and Prussia increased rapidly. On May 29, 1865, a Prussian Crown Council formally discussed the question of war with Austria. The situation was grave but Bismarck felt that the possibilities for peaceful agreement were not yet exhausted. He recommended that the two conditions which had met with most opposition at Vienna, the amalgamation of the Schleswig-Holstein army with the Prussian, and the oath of obedience to the King of Prussia, be dropped and that a serious attempt be made to induce Austria to accept Prussia's minimum demands.[48] The agitation in the duchies in favor of the Prince of Augustenburg was, however, irritating not only the Prussian ministers but also King William. At the end of July, at another Crown Council meeting, it was decided to send what was practically an ultimatum to Vienna. Until "order" was restored in the duchies, Prussia would cease negotiations. When the agitation was checked, Prussia would discuss the candidacy of the Grand Duke of Oldenburg. If Austria was unwilling to act against the Augustenburg demonstrations, the Prussian commander-in-chief in the duchies would be ordered to do so alone.[49] But once more, the breach was averted. By the Gastein Convention of August 14, the Austrian Emperor sold his rights over Lauenburg to the King of Prussia and the administration of Holstein was awarded to Austria, that of Schleswig to Prussia.[50]

The Gastein Convention was a provisional measure. It brought the important question, that of the future sovereignty of Schleswig-Holstein, no nearer to solution. The fall of Schmerling, which had occurred on June 27, led to no real improvement in the situation, although for a time, Austria stood with Prussia

---

[48] Bismarck, *Die gesammelten Werke*, V, pp. 189 f.
[49] Von Sybel, *Die Begründung des deutschen Reiches*, IV, p. 153.
[50] Christian IX's right to succeed in Lauenburg had not been questioned.

in defending the convention against the indignation of the rest of Germany. Each of the allies was suspicious that the other was seeking support from France and Italy. In the administration of Holstein, the Austrians were less strict than the Prussians in Schleswig in suppressing popular and press demonstrations in favor of the Prince of Augustenburg and Bismarck's notes of protest were coolly received. In November, Bismarck tried to persuade the Austrian government to let Prussia have the duchies for a money payment. At last, on February 28, 1866, the Prussian government formally reached the conclusion that Austria was determined not to meet Prussia's wishes and that war must settle the questions at issue. The King was advised to begin military and diplomatic preparations for the impending struggle.

Much more than the possession of Schleswig-Holstein was now at stake. On April 8, the Prusso-Italian alliance was signed; on April 9, the Prussian representative in the Diet at Frankfurt raised the German question. Step by step, Bismarck wore out the scanty patience of the Austrian government. Early in June, Austria called upon the Diet to deliberate on the succession to the duchies. In reply, Bismarck published Article V of the Convention of January 16, 1864, by which it had been arranged that the two Powers would settle the future of the duchies only in mutual agreement, and charged Austria with violating the Gastein Convention. General von Manteuffel was ordered to enter Holstein and resume the exercise there of Prussia's rights to co-sovereignty. On June 12, Austria severed diplomatic relations with Prussia. On June 14, the Prussian representative at Frankfurt declared that his government regarded the Confederation as ended by the action of Austria and her satellites. On July 3, the Prussians won the decisive victory at Königgrätz in Bohemia.

By Article V of the Treaty of Prague of August 23, 1866, The Emperor of Austria ceded to the King of Prussia, all rights over the duchies of Schleswig and Holstein acquired under the treaty of Vienna of October 30, 1864, ''with the condition that the populations of the northern districts of Schleswig, if they give evidence in a free vote of their desire to be united with Denmark, shall be ceded to Denmark.'' Schleswig and Holstein were incorporated into the Prussian state in 1867 but the condition, which had been inserted as a concession to Napoleon III, was not fulfilled. Prussia and Denmark were unable to reach an agreement on the conditions for the vote and cession. In 1878, a treaty between Germany and Austria-Hungary abrogated the clause.[51]

The Danes in North Schleswig continued to protest against the annexation and to demand the execution of "Article V." They resisted all efforts of the Prussian administration to break up their national unity and succeeded in holding their own until the Treaty of Versailles in 1919 granted their demand for a plebiscite. In 1920, that part of Schleswig north of a line drawn south of Tønder and north of Flensburg, gave a majority of three to one in favor of union with Denmark. The small Danish minority in Flensburg still feels bitterly the separation from the north but with few exceptions, Danes and Germans are at last reasonably satisfied with the result.

[51] Cf. Platzhoff, *Bismarck und die nordschleswigsche Frage 1864-1879*, Hähnsen, *Ursprung und Geschichte des Artikels V des prager Friedens*, and Aage Friis, *Den Danske Regering og Nordslesvigs Genforening med Danmark*.

APPENDIX I

The "Ritterschaft"

The *Ritterschaft* (Dan. *Ridderskab*) included the principal noble landowners of the duchies. Kr. Erslev, in the article "Ridderskab" in Salmonsens *Konversationslexikon*, points out that the term is sometimes used for the nobles as an estate but sometimes, for a special group in the fighting class. In Germany, a distinction was made between *Reichsritter* and the *Ritter* of the imperial vassals; in Denmark, between the *Ridderskab* and the *Riddermændsmændene*. When Schleswig and Holstein were joined to Denmark in the 15th century, the *Ritterschaft* had many important privileges and very great influence in the diets. When the divisions of the duchies between the various princely lines began, the *Ritterschaft* continued to form a unit under the common rule of the princes. Gradually, the princes stopped calling the diets and when the King of Denmark brought all of Schleswig under his own rule in the 18th century, he confirmed the privileges of the *Ritter* of each duchy separately. He continued, however, to recognize the *nexus socialis*, giving the *Ritterschaft* certain rights common to both duchies. In 1778, the *Ritter* of the two duchies were permitted to choose a 'permanent deputation' to look after their interests. By the beginning of the nineteenth century, the *Ritterschaft* had, in practice, lost its political rights and even its exemption from direct taxation.

The importance of the *Ritterschaft* in the early history of the Schleswig-Holstein movement is due in part to the fact that it had a corporate organization, common to the two duchies, represented by the 'permanent deputation.' In part, its importance was due to the fact that this corporate group included practically all the landed magnates. Their estates, mostly in the southeast and east sections, covered about one-fourth of the surface of the duchies. Even after the emancipation of the serfs, the landowners were long the most important leaders in what was essentially an agrarian community. They had prestige, wealth, culture, and contacts with both Denmark and Germany.

The traditional account of the origins of the Schleswig-Holstein movement begins with the attempt of the *Ritterschaft*, guided by Dahlmann, who was employed as secretary of the 'permanent deputation,' to recover its political position by demanding the fulfilment of Article XIII of the German Federal Act of 1815. This provided that ''in allen Bundestaaten wird eine landständische Verfassung Statt finden.'' It was hoped that the constitution established under this article would include Schleswig because of the connection of the *Ritter* of the two duchies. O. Brandt has attempted to show that the origin of the movement is to be found earlier in the century, in the general struggle of the *Ritterschaft* against the centralising monarchy. He finds that principal stimulus, and even the beginnings of a national feeling, in the group that gathered at Emkendorf about Fritz Reventlow and his brilliant wife, Julia. The controversy that has developed over this is important for the study of German nationalism but is irrelevant to the main purpose of this monograph.

On the *Ritterschaft* and its position in the Schleswig-Holstein question, cf. Kr. E[rslev], article ''Ridderskab'' in Salmonsens *Konversationslexikon*, xx (1926), p. 153; Springer, *Friedrich Christoph Dahlmann*; Brock, *Vorgeschichte der schleswig-holsteinischen Erhebung von 1848*, pp. 9 ff., 16 f., 27; P. von Hedeman-Heespen, *Die Herzogthümer Schleswig-Holstein und die Neuzeit;* and especially, O. Brandt, *Geistesleben und Politik in Schleswig-Holstein um die Wende des 18. Jahrhunderts*, the same writer's rebuttal of the criticism of his work, Brandt, ''Zur Vorgeschichte der schleswig-holsteinische Erhebung,'' in *Archiv für Politik und Geschichte*, 1926, pp. 470-521; and Hagenah, ''1863. Die nationale Bewegung in Schleswig-Holstein,'' in *Z. f. s-h. G.*, LVI.

APPENDIX II

I

The "Agreements of 1851-1852"

Treaty of London, May 8, 1852. (*Nouveau Recueil Général de Traités*, XVII, pt. 2, pp. 313-317.)

Au nom de la Très Sainte et Indivisible Trinité.

Sa Majesté l'Empereur d'Autriche, Roi de Hongrie et de Bohême, Le Prince Président de la République Française, Sa Majesté la Reine du Royaume-Uni de la Grande-Bretagne et d'Irlande, Sa Majesté le Roi de Prusse, Sa Majesté l'Empereur de toutes les Russies, et Sa Majesté le Roi de Suède et de Norvège,

Considérant que le maintien de l'intégrité de la Monarchie Danoise, lié aux intérêts généraux de l'équilibre Européen, est d'une haute importance pour la conservation de la paix, et qu'une combinaison, qui appellerait à succéder à la totalité des Etats actuellement réunis sous le sceptre de Sa Majesté le Roi de Danemark la descendance mâle, à l'exclusion des femmes, serait le meilleur moyen d'assurer l'intégrité de cette monarchie, ont résolu, à l'invitation de Sa Majesté Danoise, de conclure un Traité, afin de donner aux arrangements relatifs à cet ordre de succession un gage additionel de stabilité par un acte de reconnaissance Européenne.

En conséquence, les Hautes Parties Contractantes ont nommé pour leurs Plénipotentiaires savoir:

[Names of the plenipotentiaries.]

Lesquels, après s'être communiqué leurs pleins-pouvoirs respectifs, trouvés en bonne et due forme, sont convenus des Articles suivants:

Art. 1. Après avoir pris en sérieuse considération les intérêts de Sa Monarchie, Sa Majesté le Roi de Danemark, de l'assentiment de Son Altesse Royale le Prince Héréditaire et de Ses plus

proches Cognats, appelés à la succession par la Loi Royale de
Danemark, ainsi que de concert avec Sa Majesté l'Empereur de
toutes les Russies, Chef de la Branche aînée de la Maison de
Holstein-Gottorp, ayant déclaré vouloir régler l'ordre de suc-
cession dans Ses Etats, de manière à ce qu'à défaut de descendance
mâle en ligne directe du Roi Frédérik III de Danemark Sa
Couronne soit transmise à Son Altesse le Prince Christian de
Slesvig-Holstein-Sonderbourg-Glücksbourg, et aux descendants
issus du mariage de ce Prince avec Son Altesse la Princesse Louise
de Slesvig-Holstein-Sonderbourg-Glücksbourg, née Princesse de
Hesse, par ordre de primogéniture, de mâle en mâle; les Hautes
Parties Contractantes, appréciant la sagesse des vues qui ont
déterminé l'adoption évenuelle de cette combinaison, s'engagent
d'un commun accord, dans le cas où l'eventualité prévue viendrait
à se réaliser, à reconnaître à Son Altesse le Prince Christian de
Slesvig-Holstein-Sonderbourg-Glücksbourg, et aux descendants
mâles, issus en ligne directe de son mariage avec la dite Princesse,
le droit de succéder à la totalité des Etats actuellement réunis
sous le sceptre de Sa Majesté le Roi de Danemark.

Art. 2. Les Hautes Parties Contractantes, reconnaissant
comme permanent le principe de l'intégrité de la Monarchie
Danoise, s'engagent à prendre en considération les ouvertures
ultérieures que Sa Majesté le Roi de Danemark jugerait à propos
de Leur adresser, si, ce qu'à Dieu ne plaise, l'extinction de la
descendance mâle, en ligne directe, de Son Altesse le Prince
Christian de Slesvig-Holstein-Sonderbourg-Glücksbourg, issue de
Son Mariage avec la Princesse Louise de Slesvig-Holstein-Sonderbourg-Glücksbourg, née Princesse de Hesse, devenait imminente.

Art. 3. Il est expressément entendu que les droits et les obligations réciproques de Sa Majesté le Roi de Danemark et de la
Confédération Germanique, concernant les Duchés de Holstein
et de Lauenbourg, droits et obligations établis par l'Acte Fédéral
de 1815 et par le droit Fédéral existant, ne seront altérés par le
présent Traité.

Art. 4. Les Hautes Parties Contractantes se réservent de
porter le présent Traité à la connaissance des autres Puissances,
en les invitant à y accéder.

Art. 5. Le présent Traité sera ratifié, etc.

Fait à Londres, le huit Mai, l'an de grâce mil huit cent cin-quante-deux.

(L. S.) Bille.[1]

(L. S.) Kubeck.
(L. S.) A. Walewski
(L. S.) Malmesbury
(L. S.) Bunsen.
(L. S.) Brunnow.
(L. S.) Rehausen.[2]

II.

THE "AGREEMENTS OF 1851-1852." (*Nouveau Recueil Général de Traités*, XV, pp. 366-407).

1. EXTRACT FROM ANNEX II TO A DISPATCH FROM THE DANISH MINISTER FOR FOREIGN AFFAIRS (BLUHME) TO THE DANISH LEGATIONS AT VIENNA AND BERLIN, DECEMBER 6, 1851.

1. Wenn Seine Majestät, aus Rücksichten auf den Rath und Wünsch Seiner hohen Alliirten, beschliessen, nicht nur das Herzogthum Holstein, sondern auch das Herzogthum Schleswig bis weiter als absoluter König unter Mitwirkung berathender Provinzialstände zu regieren, so geschieht dies, was das Herzogthum Schleswig betrifft, übrigens lediglich aus freier Machtvollkommenheit, auch keinesweges in der Absicht, auf die Wiedereinführung der Provinzial-Stände-Institution im Königreich Dänemark, mit Beseitigung des für letzteres angenommenen und in Wirksamkeit bestehenden Grundgesetzes, hinzuarbeiten, sondern mit dem Ziel vor Augen, auf gesetz- und verfassungsmässigem Wege, d. h. durch die berathenden Provinzialstände jedes der gedachten Herzogthümer für sich, und was das Königreich betrifft durch Beschlüsse des Reichstags, sowie in Betreff Lauenburgs, unter Mitwirkung von Ritter- und Landschaft, eine organische und gleichartige verfassungsmässige Verbindung sämmtlicher Landestheile zu einer gesammten Monarchie herbeizuführen.

[1] Denmark.
[2] Austria, France, Great Britain, Prussia, Russia, Sweden and Norway.

2. Sowie der König einestheils bereits zugesagt hat, auch ferner erklärt, dass weder eine Incorporation des Herzogthums Schleswig ins Königreich stattfinden, noch irgend dieselbe bezweckende Schritte vorgenommen werden sollen, so können Seine Majestät anderntheils Nichts genehmigen, wodurch eine Zusammenschmelzung Holsteins und Schleswigs, oder überall irgend eine andere oder nähere Verbindung dieser Herzogthümer unter einander als zwischen einem jeden derselben und dem Königreich Dänemark, gleich eintreten oder in Zukunft herbeigeführt werden würde. ....

3. Dieser Grundsatz, wodurch der sogenannte ''Schleswigholsteinismus'' vom Könige definitiv verworfen wird, tritt keineswegs dem Fortbestehen solcher Bande hinderlich entgegen, welche sich zwischen Grenzländern auf Grund ähnlicher Territorialbeschaffenheit und analoger Nahrungsverhältnisse der Bewohner ganz einfach aus der Sache ergeben, weil sie die Bedingung des socialen und commerciellen Verkehrs in sich tragen. Diese werden S. M. der König selbstverständlich durch eine gleichartige Gesetzgebung für die gedachten Herzogthümer, wie für die übrigen Theile der Monarchie, nach Möglichkeit zu fördern und zu beleben suchen. Ebensowenig kann jener Grundsatz dem Fortbestehen solcher Bande hinderlich sein, die entweder in den für beide Landestheile gemeinsam gewordenen Instituten nicht staatsrechtlicher Natur begründet sind (der Eidercanal, das Taubstummen Institut, die Irrenanstalt in Schleswig, die Strafanstalten in Glückstadt, die Benutzung und Erhaltung der Kieler Universität) oder auf privatrechtlich gemeinsamen Verhältnissen gewisser Klassen beruhen (ein nicht politischer *nexus socialis* der schleswigschen und der holsteinischen Ritterschaft).

2. EXTRACT OF A DISPATCH FROM PRINCE SCHWARZENBERG
     TO THE AUSTRIAN LEGATION AT COPENHAGEN, DECEMBER
     26, 1851.

Aus unseren früheren Mittheilungen sind Ew. etc. vollständig mit den Gesichtspunkten bekannt, aus welchen wir diese Eröffnungen des Dänischen Hofes im Allgemeinen betrachten. Hoch-

dieselben werden daher darauf vorbereitet sein, dass wir, um
den Ausgang dieser Angelegenheit zu beschleunigen, bereitwillig
über die uns nunmehr kundgegebenen Absichten S. M. des
Königs uns aussprechen werden, dass wir dies unsererseits aber
nur in der Unterstellung thun können, eine von ihrem Urheber
als verpflichtend betrachtete, daher in der Ausführung gesicherte
Erklärung vor Augen zu haben.

. . . .

Die beifolgende Aufzeichnung, welche Punkt für Punkt der
Anlage II der Dänischen Depesche folgt, erläutert die Be-
weggründe unserer Zustimmung, sowie die Erwartungen, welche
wir von einer entsprechenden Ausführung hegen.

Das Dänische Cabinet wolle daraus insbesondere sich überzeugen, dass wir weit entfernt sind, für alle Zukunft die un-
veränderte Beibehaltung der provinzialständischen Verfassung
der Herzogthümer ausbedingen zu wollen. Wir erkennen
vielmehr die volle Geltung des Bestrebens, die bestehenden
politischen Einrichtungen aller Theile der Monarchie durch
entsprechende Aenderungen oder Ergänzungen in den künftigen,
nach conservativen Grundsätzen herzustellenden Organismus
des Gesammtstaats einzufügen. So wie wir aber bereits wiederholt veranlasst waren, uns gegen die früher von vornherein
erklärte Absicht der Dänischen Regierung auszusprechen, die
Provinzialstände nur zum Zwecke ihre definitiven Beseitigung
wieder einzuberufen, und die Verfassung der Monarchie aus-
schliesslich dem im Königreich Dänemark geltenden Grundgesetze
anzupassen, so muss uns auch jetzt daran gelegen sein, der
möglichen Deutung entschieden vorzubeugen, als liege eben diese
Absicht auch in dem Sinne des uns gegenwärtig mitgetheilten
Programms.

Die Erhaltung selbständiger Verfassungs- und Verwaltungs-
einrichtungen in den verschiedenen Landestheilen, unbeschadet
der im Mittelpunkte vereinigten Leitung ihrer gemeinsamen
Angelegenheiten, erachten wir für eine unerlässliche Bedingung
der befestigung der innern Ruhe der Monarchie.

Wenn die Dänische Regierung an die Bedenken erinnert,

welche sich gegen eine, sei es auch nur vorübergehende Wieder-
belebung schleswigscher Provinzialstände, aus den Erfahrungen
der letzten 10 Jahre für sie ergeben, und wenn sie den Zweifel
äussert, ob von dem Versuche, durch ein solches Organ zu einer
gemeinschaftlichen Verfassung für die Monarchie zu gelangen,
ein gedeihlicher Erfolg erwartet werden könne, so wollen wir
zwar das unverkennbare Gewicht ihrer desfälligen Bemerkungen
nicht bestreiten, aber auch nicht unerwähnt lassen, dass es
hauptsächlich die Unsicherheit der Erbfolge war, durch welche
die mit der Integrität der Monarchie unvereinbare Richtung der
ständischen Thätigkeit hervorgerufen und genährt wurde.
Unter den jetzigen Umständen, nachdem der Grundsatz der
gemeinsamen Erbfolge gegen jeden Versuch der Anfechtung
bereits hinlänglich gesichert erscheint, dürfte die Hoffnung nicht
unbegründet sein, es werde künftig ein erspriessliches Zusammenwirken der Regierung mit den Provinzialständen nicht vergeblich
angestrebt werden, wenn von beiden Seiten die gegebenen
Grundlagen, einestheils des bleibenden Verbandes der Monarchie,
anderntheils der gleichen Berechtigung aller Bestandtheile
derselben, aufrichtig angenommen und in ihren nothwendigen
Folgen anerkannt werden.

Wenigstens glauben wir, dass die Schwierigkeiten, mit welchen
ein mit Repräsentativständen und vielfach getheilter ministerieller
Verantwortlichkeit überhäufter Organisationsplan, wie der uns
früher durch den Grafen Sponneck vorgelegte, die Regierung des
dänischen Gesammtstaats unvermeidlich umgeben müsste, nicht
von geringerer Art, ja vielleicht weit schwerer zu überwinden sein
würden, als diejenigen, welche von der Wiederherstellung der
provinzialständischen Institutionen der Herzogthümer besorgt
werden könnten

. . . .

Würde nun die Dänische Regierung sich bewogen finden,
diejenige Auffassung ihres Programmes, die wir in dem gegenwärtigen Erlasse und in der Anlage desselben niedergelegt haben,
würde sie uns zugleich der wirklichen Ausführung der Absichten
die uns bis jetzt officiell nur als eine mögliche Eventualität zur

Kenntniss gebracht hat, in der bindenen Form einer auf Befehl
S. M. des Königs abgegebenen Erklärung versichern, und darnach
auch ihre Handlungen einrichten, soweit dazu schon jetzt Veranlassung gegeben ist, so könnten wir auf einen baldigen versöh-
nenden Ausgang der seitherigen Irrungen zwischen den verschiedenen Theilen der Dänischen Monarchie, wie zwischen dieser
und dem Deutschen Bunde zuversichtlich vertrauen; wir würden
das Mandat, kraft dessen wir in Gemeinschaft mit Preussen den
Deutschen Bund in dieser Angelegenheit vertreten, unter gleich-
zeitiger Räumung Holsteins und Wiederherstellung der vollen
Landesherrlichen Gewalt in diesem Herzogthum zurücklegen, in
der Bundesversammlung für die getroffene Vereinbarung einste-
hen, und zugleich die neue innere Begründung des Verbandes
der unter Einem Herrscher vereinigten Lande für weit genug
vorgeschritten erachten, um uns an der völkerrechtlich Verbürgung der Integrität der gemeinsamen Erbfolge zu betheiligen.

ANLAGE.

1. Der Kaiserlich Oesterreichische Hof vernimmt mit Befriedigung den Entschluss S. M. des Königs von Dänemark,
nicht nur im Herzogthum Holstein, sondern auch im Herzogthum
Schleswig die zu Recht bestehenden provinzialständischen
Institutionen wieder in Wirksamkeit treten zu lassen, und wenn
S. M. zugleich die Absicht kundgeben, auf gesetz- und verfassungsmässigem Wege, also nach Berathung mit den Provinzialständen der gedachten Herzogthümer, und was das Königreich
Dänemark angeht, durch Verhandlungen mit dem Reichstage,
sowie in Betreff Lauenburgs unter Mitwirkung der Ritter- und
Landschaft, eine organische und gleichartige verfassungsmässige
Verbindung sämmtlicher Landestheile zu einer gesammten
Monarchie herbeizuführen, so vermag der Kaiserliche Hof
diese Willensmeinung des Königs nur als auf die Erfüllung einer
unabweislichen Aufgabe gerichtet anzuerkennen.

Die gegenwärtige Provinzialverfassung Holsteins, auf welche
der Art. 56 der Wiener Schlussakte Anwendung findet, wird der
Verwirklichung dieser Königlichen Absicht um so weniger

hindernd im Wege stehen können, als schon in den Gesetzen, welche die provinzialständischen Institutionen in Holstein begründet haben, der Fall der Abänderung derselben, nach vorgängiger Berathung mit den Ständen, vorgesehen ist.

So aufrichtig aber S. M. der Kaiser die Ruhe und Wohlfahrt des Dänischen Reichs durch eine seinen Bedürfnissen angemessene definitive Organisation bald möglichst befestigt zu sehen wünschen, ebenso zuversichtlich überlassen Allerhöchstdieselben Sich der Hoffnung, dass die Dänische Regierung bei ihren auf diesen wichtigen Schritt gerichteten Bestrebungen nicht etwa den Institutionen, welche dem eigentlichen Königreiche Dänemark während der letzten Jahre verliehen wurden, eine ausschliessliche Bevorzugung zuwenden, sondern dass sie dabei die bleibenden Verhältnisse der gesammten Monarchie und den Zweck der inneren Kräftigung ihres Verbandes zu einem Ganzen als die einzig sichere Richtschnur vor Augen haben werde. Einmal hierüber beruhigt, werden S. M. nicht säumen, an der Sicherung jenes Verbandes durch völkerrechtliche Verbürgung einer gemeinsamen Erbfolge in alle Theile der Monarchie mit anderen befreundeten Mächten sich zu bethätigen.

2. In der Erklärung S. M. des Königs von Dänemark, dass weder eine Incorporation des Herzogthums Schleswig in das Königreich stattfinden, noch irgend dieselbe bezweckende Schritte vorgenommen werden sollen, erblickt der Kaiserl. Hof mit Genugthuung eine neue Bestätigung jener Zusage, welche bereits von dem Hochseligen Könige Christian VIII. Seinen Unterthanen gegebenen, dann von des jetzt regierenden Königs Majestät alsbald nach dem Friedensvertrage vom 2ten Juli 1850 in dem Manifeste vom 14ten d. M. erneuert, auch in Gemässheit des 4ten Art. des erwähnten Friedensvertrags dem Deutschen Bunde als eine zur Pacification des Landes gefasste Entschliessung des Königs zur Kenntniss gebracht wurde. ....

3. Mit dem Punkt 3 der Dänischen Anlage erklärt die Kaiserliche Regierung sich einverstanden.

4. ....

5. Bekanntlich hat die Kaiserl. Regierung sich wiederholt darauf berufen, dass durch den Friedensvertrag vom 2ten Juli

1850, indem derselbe beiden Theilen alle Rechte vorbehält, die ihnen vor dem Kriege zustanden, zunächst auf die Wiederherstellung des status quo ante in den streitigen Verhältnissen hingewiesen werde. Ihre Billigung ist daher der Königl. Dänischen Regierung gesichert, wenn diese ihrerseits erklärt, dass sie bis zur definitiven Organisation der Monarchie die praktische Leitung der Staatsgeschäfte, unter den von ihr bezeichneten Einschränkungen, auf welche die obige Erklärung unter 1 und 2 Bezug hat—auf den status quo ante nach Möglichkeit zurückzuführen gedenke; S. M. der Kaiser sprechen in dieser Hinsicht insbesondere die vertrauensvolle Erwartung aus, dass der König, gleichwie in der Frage der künftigen Organisation der Monarchie, so auch in der einstweiligen Leitung der Staatsgeschäfte, die den verschiedenen Landestheilen gebührende Stellung als Glieder eines Ganzen, in welchem kein Theil dem anderen untergeordnet ist, durch entsprechende Einrichtungen mit gleichmässiger Sorgfalt zu wahren wissen werde. ....

3. EXTRACT FROM A DISPATCH FROM THE DANISH MINISTER FOR FOREIGN AFFAIRS (BLUHME) TO THE DANISH LEGATIONS AT VIENNA AND BERLIN, JANUARY 29, 1852.

Unter diesen Umständen kann es mir nur zur besonderen Befriedigung gereichen, in Folge der mir Allerhöchstenorts ertheilten Ermächtigung die Erklärung hiedurch abzugeben:
"das der König, unser allergnädigster Herr, die in dem Erlasse des Kaiserlich-Königlichen Cabinetts vom 26sten December v. J. und in der Anlage desselben niedergelegte Auffassung der den Höfen von Wien und Berlin (Berlin und Wien) kundgegebenen Allerhöchsten Absichten—wie im Allgemeinen, so auch namentlich was die Nicht-Incorporation Schleswigs in das Königreich betrifft,—als mit der Seinigen übereinstimmend anerkennt."

APPENDIX III

VARIOUS DOCUMENTS FROM THE BRITISH ARCHIVES.

I.

MAGENIS TO PALMERSTON, No. 169, VIENNA, SEPTEMBER 9, 1851. (F. O. Supplement 125. *Denmark. Schleswig-Holstein Question.*)

[The first, second, and last paragraphs of this dispatch were published in *Correspondence respecting the Affairs of Denmark: 1850-53*, presented to Parliament, 1864.]

[Extract.] With regard to the latter question [the withdrawal of Austrian troops from Holstein], I learn from an undoubted source, that Prince Schwarzenberg was very favourably disposed towards it, but that the receipt while at Ischl of the news from Copenhagen that the Ultra Danish party represented by Count Sponneck, Mr. Madvig, etc. in the Cabinet at Copenhagen were likely to prevail over the more moderate counsels of M. de Reedtz and Count de Moltke, has very seriously modified His Highness' views.

Prince Schwarzenberg's language to me this morning in a conversation which I had with him on the subject of the two Danish communications confirms the above statement. His Highness repeated the desire of this Government to withdraw their troops from Holstein: enumerated as he has frequently done before, the services which Austria had rendered to the King of Denmark, their disinterested conduct, and the opposite course which Austria had pursued to the other German Powers, since the commencement of the struggle of which the Duchies have been the scene. He then added, that if the Federal troops were at once withdrawn, they had no guarantee that the state of things which had existed in 1846 might not be reestablished, and that if the States of Holstein addressed new complaints on that head to the Diet of Frankfort, the whole dispute would again be brought before that Body. His Highness said they had no reason to be dissatisfied with what the Danish Government promised with respect to the future Government of Holstein, but he expressed himself strongly with respect to what they were doing in Schleswig; he maintained that the object was to incorporate the latter Duchy with Denmark: and He added in very emphatic terms that he had never expressed his concurrence in the proposals made here by Count Sponneck for the pacification of the Duchies, proposals to which, as He says, Count Sponneck very erroneously states the two German Powers had given their assent. . . . .

His Highness said they too only desired a solid and lasting arrangement, but that such could not be attained by the course pursued at present by the Danish Government; they were anxious to maintain the integrity of the Danish Monarchy; what was doing in Schleswig would sever the link which bound Holstein; and He added that if Austria once withdrew her troops, happen what might, She would not send them back. This is not improbably a threat that Denmark would be left in that case to the tender mercies of the German Powers less disinterested than Austria.

2.

BUCHANAN TO CLARENDON, NO. 123, CONFIDENTIAL, COPEN-HAGEN, MARCH 3, 1857. (F. O. Supplement 137. *Denmark. Schleswig-Holstein Question.*)

M. de Scheele called upon me last night, and after observing that he wished to speak with me in strict confidence, said he had received on the previous day a Despatch from the Danish Minister at Paris, with the contents of which he was anxious to make me acquainted, and for which I would probably be as little prepared as he had been himself.

M. Dirckinck Holmfeld stated that the Scandinavian opinions expressed at the "Palais Royal" had not escaped his attention since his arrival at Paris, but that he had not attached much importance to them. A conversation, he said, had however lately taken place between the Emperor and a gentleman who had repeated it to him, to which he considered it necessary to call the serious notice of his Government. His Imperial Majesty, on the occasion of the late illness of the King of Denmark is represented to have observed to Baron Dirckinck's informant, that the possible death of His Majesty would bring on a crisis in the affairs of Denmark and the partition of the Danish Monarchy, and that as France owed nothing to Denmark and was intimately allied with Sweden, she would of course give her support to an arrangement by which the northern Provinces of the former would be added to the Swedish Monarchy, while the German Provinces of Denmark might be erected into a small State under the Sovereignty of the son of the Prince of Noer.

Baron Dirckinck's informant represented himself to have replied that in the event of its being proposed to make any new arrangement with regard to the States at present constituting the Danish Monarchy, the Duke of Augustenburg's pretensions to the Sovereignty of the Duchies would probably be supported by some Governments, while others might either insist upon the maintenance of the Protocol of London, or if a partition of the Monarchy should take place, endeavour to secure Prince Christian of Denmark's accession to the Sovereignty of the Duchies; and the Emperor is said to have rejoined that the young Prince of Noer would at all events have his cordial support, and that with respect to the difficulties which had been suggested to him—"on passera outre."

M. de Scheele said that Baron Dirckinck did not name his informant, but had assured His Excellency he might rely with implicit confidence on the conversation having actually occurred, of which I have had the honour to report the substance to Your Lordship. .... (Rec'd March 9.)

BUCHANAN TO CLARENDON, No. 124, CONFIDENTIAL, COPEN-HAGEN, MARCH 3, 1857. (*Ibid.*)

[Reports a long conversation with Scheele on the views of the King of Sweden with respect to the Danish succession. Among other things, Scheele said that he had learned that Manderström at Paris, who was supposed to be acting in accordance with the King's private instructions, was on terms of intimacy with the young Prince of Noer.]

3.

Draft, Clarendon to Buchanan, No. 65. Foreign Office, March 11, 1857. (*Ibid.*)

[H. M. G. are trying to prevent question coming before Diet where Denmark's legitimate interests may be adversely affected by German sympathies. But also told Count Reventlow Criminil that they hope the Danish Government would consider whether the redress of real grievances would not be the most effectual mode of preventing the interference of Germany in the internal affairs of Denmark.]

4.

Malet to Clarendon, No. 22, confidential, Frankfurt, March 26, 1857. (*Ibid.*)

. . . . Knowing very well that M. de Bismarck's opinions on the general question are very decided, and altogether in favour of the claims of the Duchies, I have only sought to learn from him what were the views of his Cabinet on this moot point, and find that they consider it as a purely German question. . . . . (Rec'd March 30.)

Cowley to Clarendon, No. 560, confidential, Paris, April 10, 1857. (*Ibid.*)

M. de Bismarck Schönhausen the Prussian Minister to the German Diet, has been for some days at Paris. I believe that it is his intention to proceed at the end of next week to London. He has seen Count Walewski and has expressed a wish to have an audience of the Emperor. Count Walewski is of the opinion that M. de Bismarck is on a confidential mission from his government.

I was well acquainted with M. de Bismarck formerly at Frankfurt, and although I often disagreed with his policy, I always found him fair and frank in the expression of his opinions, and as he has no doubt, great weight with his Government, it may not be uninteresting to Your Lordship to be made acquainted with the substance of a conversation I had with him yesterday.

He said that he had profited by the adjournment of the Diet to pass a few days in Paris—He gave me to understand that he had no political mission, but that he should not be sorry to learn how the Danish Question was viewed abroad. It was supposed, he continued, that Prussia was desirous of detaching Holstein and Lauenburg from the Sovereignty of the King of Denmark. There could not be a greater mistake. The present state of the north of Europe was the best for Prussia. Were Holstein to be separated from Denmark and placed for instance under the Sovereignty of the Duke of Augustenburg, it would not be for the benefit of Prussia. Not only the maritime Powers but the States of Germany would be jealous of the influence of Prussia in the new Sovereignty, and Prussia would be far more likely to find therein an enemy than a friend. Besides which Denmark stripped of the Duchies could not stand alone—She must look to Great Britain or to Russia for protection, neither of which eventualities could be contemplated with indifference by Prussia. The true interests of Prussia therefore led her to desire that things should remain as they are, and it is the object which both Austria and Prussia had in view. He did not see why this should not be. There had been a moment when Holstein was sincerely attached to its relations with Denmark. It depended in his opinion upon the King-Grand Duke whether these sentiments should return or not. But they never could return so long as the Danish Government continued to aim at incorporating Holstein [sic] politically with Denmark.

With regard to bringing the question before the Diet, M. de Bismarck said, that if Denmark was prudent, it might be avoided for the present. If the King of Denmark promised Austria and Prussia to convoke the States of Holstein, Austria and Prussia would express themselves satisfied. Some months would elapse before those States could be convoked, the Diet would have separated for its vacations and time would thus be gained. But the very convocation of the Holstein States, M. de Bismarck continued, must force the matter before the Diet, because those States would immediately petition the Diet, and neither Austria nor Prussia could prevent the entertainment of the petition by the Germanic Confederation. On his part however he thought the apprehensions entertained of what might be the proceedings of the Diet, to be greatly exaggerated. The opposition made to the jurisdiction of the Diet in this question gave the smaller states force in agitating it. Let the question come before them and they would be satisfied. Some way of settlement would be found which neither Austria nor Prussia alone would, in order not to jeopardise their influence in Germany, venture to propose.

I observed that M. de Bismarck was no doubt aware that both in Paris and London the Cabinets were of opinion that the question of the Duchies was not one which concerned Germany alone, but that it was of general European interest. M. de Bismarck replied that it was of course impossible to prevent the interference of any country in any question, when that country might think that its interests would be benefitted by interference. Nobody could prevent this question being brought before the Diet, and certainly nobody could prevent the interference of Europe therein, if Europe chose to interfere. I said that there was no intention on the part of either the British or French governments to deny the interest which Germany must take in the affairs of Holstein but that if in pursuit of that interest, a war between Germany and Denmark was threatened, it would be the duty of Europe to see whether by her interference so great a misfortune might not be prevented.

M. de Bismarck's language throughout this conversation was most moderate and conciliatory, which is of no small importance, considering the influence he must have with the Diet, and that which, as I said before, he is known to exercise over his own

Government. He said however that if the question was to be settled amicably some concessions must be made by Denmark to the Duchies, and he hinted that the advice of the great Powers should be given in this direction.

I was anxious to learn M. de Bismarck's opinion upon the question of Scandinavian Unity and I gave him an opportunity in the course of the conversation to let me hear it if it so pleased him. He said supposing it to be practicable, it was not the interest of Prussia to encourage it. If indeed a Scandinavia, a great naval Power, could be formed in close alliance with Germany, the question would become materially altered, but it would be idle to suppose that Great Britain or Russia would not be the Powers on which such a Scandinavia must depend for support, and, without offence, he need hardly add an unity to produce such results could not be desired by Germany and Prussia. (Rec'd Apr. 12.)

MALET TO CLARENDON, NO. 44, CONFIDENTIAL, FRANKFURT, JUNE 24, 1857. (F. O. Supplement 139. *Denmark. Schleswig-Holstein Question.*)

[Reports conversation with Bismarck on the Danish question. Among other things Bismarck said: "I said the other day to Count Rechberg, that we were like two cowards marching on a battery, each anxiously watching a sign of hesitation in the other, to justify his own turning back."]

5.

ORME TO CLARENDON, NO. 86, COPENHAGEN, JULY 7, 1857. (F. O. Supplement 140. *Denmark. Schleswig-Holstein Question.*)

....[Hall] said that...as far as he and his colleagues were concerned they were ready to sacrifice much in the interests of peace, that their wish certainly was (instrumental as they had been in passing the present constitution and popular as the idea had also been with the great body of the nation) to give it a fair chance of working, and such was still their wish and intention, but if it should notwithstanding be found by the negotiations about to be entered upon with the States, and from inadmissible demands put forward by the latter, that these projects proved abortive, they would then be ready to recommend the loosening of the bonds, which now connect the Duchies of Holstein and Lauenburg with the Monarchy, make its relations to the latter purely Federal, and so break up the present corporate constitution. But, add the Ministers, on one condition, that the Duchy of Schleswig whole and entire be guaranteed to Denmark. Your Lordship will observe by this language that the Ministry are prepared to commit themselves openly to Eider Danism. It has long been known...that the principles of most of the present Ministers have been either avowedly or overtly [*sic*] Eider Danish. .... (Rec'd July 12.)

6.

BUCHANAN TO CLARENDON, No. 208, CONFIDENTIAL, COPEN-HAGEN, AUGUST 25, 1857. (F. O. Supplement 141. *Denmark. Schleswig-Holstein Question.*)

I have the Honor to inform Your Lordship that Count Bismarck at an interview which I have had with him held the same language on the subject of the Duchies which he appears to have done to Mr. Hall, as reported in my despatch No. 267 of this date. He said Prussia was most anxious to see the question arranged, and at all events to have the responsibilities attached to it laid on other shoulders, as it was necessary for her to prevent its continuing to be used by the Austrian Press for the purpose of undermining her popularity with the people of Germany. He said that the Diet would afford the only means of satisfying Germany that German rights would be in future protected from Danish oppression; whereas at present if merely a drunken German was rudely treated by a Danish functionary, the circumstance gave rise to the most exaggerated complaints on the part of numerous enthusiastic defenders of German nationality.

A reference to the Diet had, however, he said more to recommend it with a view to the interests of Denmark as many facilities for a satisfactory arrangement would be afforded through the intervention of the Confederation and in a manner which could have nothing offensive to the dignity of Denmark. Count Oriolla, who was present, observed that every friend of the Danish Monarchy ought to see the matter in this light, as it was evident that the Government could not settle the question without pressure from without, and that to force them in a friendly manner to an arrangement would be a real service to the Country. I asked whether the motive power which he considered necessary was not already in action, and to what other cause the present session of the Holstein States could be attributed. An arrangement, however, come to at Itzehoe, I said, would still have the appearance, even if forced on Denmark, of having been voluntarily entered into, whereas any modification of the Constitution resulting from a decree of the Confederation would increase tenfold the national antipathies of the King's Danish and German subjects, paralyze the efforts of those members of the "Rigsraad" who might otherwise be expected to use their influence in favor of an arrangement and strengthen the cause of Eider Danes and Scandinavian Apostles. . . . . (Rec'd Aug. 30.)

7.

VARIOUS REPORTS FROM BUCHANAN TO RUSSELL, BERLIN, NOVEMBER 1863 TO FEBRUARY 1864, RECORD OFFICE, LONDON, F. O. *Prussia.*

BUCHANAN TO RUSSELL, NO. 525, MOST CONFIDENTIAL, NOVEMBER 21, 1863. (Rec'd November 23.)

M. de Bismarck said to me this morning that he would inform me confidentially that the position of the Holstein Question was daily and hourly becoming more serious, and that he found the King last night disposed to favour the pretensions of the Prince of Augustenburg.

His Excellency said that it was only after a very animated discussion which lasted two hours and a half, and during which he threatened his own resignation that he succeeded in convincing His Majesty that He must abide for the present by the provisions of the Treaty of 1852.

M. de Bismarck then went on to say that the Queen of Prussia and the Duke of Saxe Cobourg, acting with a Holsteiner, who is in the service of His Royal Highness, had been the principal promoters of the present movement in Germany, and that Baron Schleinitz, in consequence of instructions from the Queen, had a long interview yesterday with the King, in which he had satisfied His Majesty that the Treaty of 1852 was merely an arrangement between Denmark and Prussia, and that therefore if Denmark had not fulfilled her engagements, which had induced the late King to sign that Treaty, His Majesty would now be perfectly justified in considering it to be no longer binding upon him.

It appears that M. de Schleinitz had called His Majesty's attention to the Third Article, where it is stated that "the rights and obligations of the Duchies established by the Federal Act of 1815 and by the *existing federal law* shall not be altered by this Treaty"—and it was therefore maintained by M. de Schleinitz not only that the federal law gave the Diet a right to decide in all cases of contested successions; but that the arrangements with Denmark being anterior to the signature of the Treaty were also federal law at that time. The King of Denmark had therefore, it was contended, abrogated the Treaty as far as Prussia was concerned by assenting to the new Constitution for Denmark and Sleswig.

M. de Bismarck said the King was satisfied that this was a correct view of the Question, and all that he could obtain from His Majesty was that his decision should be postponed until the First of January—as the mere assent of the King of Denmark was not sufficient to produce the alleged breach of the engagements of Denmark, and that the new Constitution must have entered into force before the King could avail himself of it in the manner suggested by M. de Schleinitz.

M. de Bismarck then said that he had sent for Baron Schleinitz this morning and had had a long and angry discussion with him in which he observed that if the Baron wished to direct the foreign policy of Prussia, the door of the Foreign Office was open to him. I am sorry to say however that M. de Bismarck had apparently been induced to believe that M. de Schleinitz's view of the question could be justified if the King of Denmark does not withdraw his assent to the new Constitution before the 1st. of January next, or place the new law in a provisional State until a definitive arrangement be come to with Germany. I therefore said to His Excellency that I was not competent to form an opinion as to how far the Right of the Diet to decide questions of disputed succession could invalidate the formal recognition by Prussia as a European Power of the Rights of the King of Denmark to the Sovereignty of Holstein, but that I believed he was under a grave error if he expected that other powers would consider the international engagements of the King of Denmark with Germany to be identic with the Federal Law existing in 1852, and whatever motive the King of Prussia might have for refusing to fulfill the engagements he contracted under the Treaty, they could not be found in the laws of the German Confederation if the King of Denmark granted to the Duchy of Holstein all the privileges and rights, which the Confederation could claim for it as a German State.

With respect to the claims of the Prince of Augustenburg, M. de Bismarck said three or four days ago to the French Ambassador that he had given His Highness to understand that he should endeavour to commute them for a pecuniary indemnity, but he hinted to-day that he might perhaps limit them to the Duchy of Holstein.

In the course of a very long conversation in which I recalled to His Excellency the nature of our past understanding on the question, I acknowledged that until the last few days I had no reason to doubt that he would have done everything in his power to bring about an amicable arrangement between Denmark and Germany, he said that his position in the question had now become extremely difficult. That the King, his colleagues, his supporters in the Chambers, the opposition, his own agents and the public were all more or less favorable to the claims of the Prince of Augustenburg, and he now stood almost alone in advocating the maintenance of the Treaty.—As he understood however that Austria was favorable to a mediation he hoped that something might yet be done to prevent war, which he did not disguise from himself was a possible contingency.

He is evidently very sensitive lest it should appear to Germany that he has asked for the mediation of Her Majesty's Government and wished to establish today that I had always spoken of it as offered to him.

It is difficult to judge what he means to do under present circumstances and whether he has really adopted the opinions of Baron Schleinitz, or whether he merely intends to use them as a means of extorting concessions from the King of Denmark.

BUCHANAN TO RUSSELL, NO. 532, CONFIDENTIAL, BERLIN, NOVEMBER 23, 1863.

With reference to my despatch No. 531 of this date reporting a conversation which I had with Monsieur de Bismarck yesterday on the question of the Holstein succession, I may mention that I met His Excellency afterwards at dinner, when he observed it was difficult to foresee what might be the result if the Diet should refuse its sanction to the engagements which Austria and Prussia have entered into as European Powers, by the Treaty of London, but its refusal to do so might possibly bring about a disruption of the Confederation, an eventuality which His Excellency said he could look forward to with indifference, as he doubted whether Prussia would not be in a better position afterwards and whether Denmark might not prove a more useful friend to her than her present Confederates.

BUCHANAN TO RUSSELL, NO. 546, BERLIN, NOVEMBER 28, 1863.

[Extract; omitted from document as printed on p. 289 of papers presented to Parliament.]

...on my asking what would happen, if the Diet refused to limit their action to an execution, he [Bismarck] said in that case, Austria and Prussia as parties to the Treaty of London would occupy the Duchy and then inform the Diet of their having done so. I objected that such an occupation, if it took place without the consent of the King of Denmark, would be war: to which His Excellency replied that if the two Powers saw a chance of the King's granting his consent, which he ought to do for his own interest, they might ask for it, or if they could obtain the consent of the Diet to their acting in its name, they would then as parties to the Treaty of London, prevent the occupation having an appearance of being hostile to that Treaty.

BUCHANAN TO RUSSELL, NO. 551, CONFIDENTIAL, BERLIN, NOVEMBER 28, 1863.

With reference to my Despatch No. 550 of this date on the subject of the refusal of Her Majesty's Government to attend the Congress which the Emperor of the French has proposed to convoke at Paris, M. de Bismarck has been, I think, rather taken by surprise by the prompt action of Her Majesty's Government in this question. He seemed to regret that it had not been kept open a little longer—being apparently under some apprehension, lest the entire failure of his scheme may render the Emperor Napoleon inclined to take a more decided part in the Holstein question.

I said to His Excellency in answer to his observations on this subject, that if he entertained such an apprehension, he would do well not to give Denmark cause for war by the proceedings of Germany in Holstein, as the question of the Duchies might, through the presence of federal troops in Holstein, very easily assume a character which would give the Emperor of the French a reason for offering armed assistance to King Christian; and I had already informed His Excellency that under certain circumstances Her Majesty's Government might be obliged to interfere in it. I said that I could not therefore understand that when all the Courts of Germany are, I believe, fully aware of the expediency of entertaining cordial and friendly relations with Great Britain, they seemed disposed to incur the risk of a war, in which the sympathies of the people of England and the Treaty engagements of Her Majesty's Government will be entirely opposed to them.

BUCHANAN TO RUSSELL, NO. 560, BERLIN, DECEMBER 4, 1863.

[Reports sending of telegram in cypher:] Private and confidential. Bismarck is anxious for immediate arrival of special Envoy to Copenhagen, as it is essential in order to counteract the daily influences to which the King is exposed that a representation from Her Majesty's Government should be made without delay to His Majesty with more authority than usual, as to the propriety of Prussia observing the Treaty of London. ....

BUCHANAN TO RUSSELL, NO. 566, CONFIDENTIAL, BERLIN, DECEMBER 5, 1863.

....It would be necessary also he [Bismarck] said, that while Austria and Prussia take measures in Germany to prevent the policy of the Confederation from being directed by the Governments of the smaller States acting under the dictation of Democratic Societies, that the Danish Government should emancipate itself from the controul of the mob at Copenhagen:—and if these two conditions are effected, His Excellency observed, a satisfactory solution of the Danish question may yet be looked for.

BUCHANAN TO RUSSELL, NO. 577, BERLIN, DECEMBER 7, 1863.

[Reports sending telegram in cypher:] I was sent for to-night by M. de Bismarck who had received a telegram from Vienna, from which he fears that Austria may propose to change the basis of execution to occupy Holstein as a pledge for justice to Sleswig.

He has replied that if the basis of October 1 is injured by the revocation of the Letters Patent there are grounds for execution in the Federal decree of 1858 and others and that it would be offensive to the Diet to give the Federal intervention the character of an occupation after forcing them to vote for an execution. He says that if the King should suspect Austria of drawing towards the Schleswig-Holstein party or of proposing a door for foreign intervention such a suspicion might entirely change His Majesty's present policy. I replied that Her Majesty's Government considered an execution preferable to an occupation but I did not know whether they would consider either justifiable under present circumstances. ....

BUCHANAN TO RUSSELL, NO. 579, BERLIN, DECEMBER 8, 1863.

[Reports sending telegram in cypher:] The Austrian Minister after a conference with Bismarck this morning was to telegraph to Vienna to urge necessity of maintaining Federal basis of execution. Bismarck insinuates that the King would willingly follow Austria if she were inclined to go beyond that basis.....

BUCHANAN TO RUSSELL, NO. 590, CONFIDENTIAL, BERLIN, DECEMBER 12, 1863.

....M. de Bismarck stated a fortnight ago that the King was only prevented by a threat of His Excellency's resignation from repudiating the Treaty of London—and if we examine the terms on which His Majesty was induced to acknowledge for the present the obligations, there are perhaps grounds for believing that His Excellency does not expect them to be eventually fulfilled,—and that the Treaty was as effectually, though perhaps more decently repudiated by the condition on which His Excellency has made its fulfilment to depend,—if that condition is to be maintained to the letter,—as if the King had at once followed the example of those Sovereigns who have already joined the Crusade against the European arrangement of 1852 to which they had formally adhered.

M. de Bismarck is too well acquainted with the state of public feeling in Denmark, with the obstinacy, national pride and courage of the Danes, and with the Constitutional and other difficulties which stand in the way of an immediate revocation of the fundamental law lately adopted by the Danish Rigsraad, to believe that Lord Wodehouse will easily succeed in inducing King Christian the IX to adopt such a measure before the 1st of January next.—And on the other hand, if he really expects the concession to be made—, why—if the two Great German Powers are acting with good faith to Denmark, has not the Execution in Holstein been deferred for ten days in the hope that it may be unnecessary—? M. de Bismarck must be well aware that the entrance of federal troops into Holstein will in all probability be followed by attempts on the part of the adherents of the Prince of Augustenburg and of the disciples of the National Verein to excite the people to demonstrations in favor of the separation of the Duchies of Holstein and Sleswig from Denmark, and to increase the excitement now prevailing on the subject throughout Germany. His Excellency says that the execution will prevent more serious evils, for if the Danish Government were to expel by force an invasion of the Duchy by free corps, it might be impossible to resist the feeling of animosity against Denmark which would ensue, but it may be asked whether the propagandists of Sleswig-Holsteinism who will follow the Federal army, and with whose proceedings it will be difficult to interfere, are not likely to prove as dangerous to the maintenance of peace, as the free corps, of which the formation and equipment might be easily prevented if the Governments of Germany would honestly use the means at their disposal for doing so.

M. de Bismarck is therefore too sagacious a statesman not to look upon war as a very possible consequence of the occupation of Holstein by the troops of the Confederation. He has however I believe no sympathy with the pretensions of the Prince of Augustenburg, and he has taken several opportunities to state that the King's leanings toward the cause of His Highness are not approved by his ministers. The King on the other hand desires to avail himself of the opportunity which this question has offered for giving the character of an accomplished fact to the new organization of the army and of settling in favor of Germany a political question of long standing by a grand military demonstration, while he is not unwilling, in the event of resistance on the part of Denmark, to accept the alternative of a war in which Prussian troops will take a principal part, and which it is hoped will transfer the Duchies of Holstein and Sleswig with their valuable harbours from the Sovereignty of a Danish to that of a German Prince.

But if the Duchies are to be wrested from Denmark for whom are they to be conquered? M. de Bismarck may perhaps have answered this question to himself, for if the occupation of Holstein leads to war it will not necessarily follow that the war should be carried on in support of the pretensions of the Prince of Augustenburg, whose claims to the Sovereignty in the event of those of the King of Denmark being put aside would be still open to question. May not the war therefore assume a character, by which Prussia as the principal belligerent may lay claim to the territories which she will have conquered? M. de Bismarck's policy has been inclusively Prussian. He had no sympathy with the Sleswig-Holstein party and did not believe the interests of Prussia would be advanced by the Danish question being kept open until the Prince of Augustenburg's pretensions might be brought forward, and he did not wish after the federal decree of October that an execution should take place which would bring Austrian troops into the North of Germany. He therefore adopted a line of his own, by which he hoped through the mediation of Great Britain to effect an arrangement of the Danish question on a basis, which would improve the relations of Prussia with Denmark and perhaps lead to that country becoming hereafter a useful ally of Prussia.

The death of the King of Denmark disconcerted these arrangements—and His Excellency having become alarmed lest he should appear to have been pursuing an anti-German policy, lost no time in protesting at Copenhagen against the adoption of the new Constitution—and when he found the King of Prussia disposed to be carried away by the National cry in favor of the

Prince of Augustenburg he availed himself of the adoption of the new Constitution, as at once offering the means of gaining time to prevent the King from committing himself without due reflection to the cause of the House of Augustenburg, and as a pretext for repudiating the Treaty with some decency, if it should be found convenient to do so.

It was no part of M. de Bismarck's policy to decline receiving an Envoy from the King of Denmark, on the contrary he wished the rights and Sovereignty of the King and those of the Duke of Holstein to be kept entirely distinct—and if the Envoy who was sent to notify the King Christian's accession was not received at Berlin there were reasons for delay, and among them perhaps the intention of requiring money from the Chambers, who have warmly espoused the cause of the Prince of Augustenburg:— for His Excellency said—it would be difficult for the King to explain publicly that in receiving an envoy from the King of Denmark, he had not acknowledged the Sovereign, under the Treaty of London, of the Danish Monarchy—and that he had not left the question of the succession to the Duchies open to discussion.

I do not mean by these observations to imply that M. de Bismarck does not believe that the most honourable would also be the wisest policy for his Sovereign to pursue,—and that he will not continue to advise the King to respect the Treaty, if Denmark makes the concessions which are required of her: but I find that he is now promoting a federal execution in Holstein on grounds, which six weeks ago he would have acknowledged to be inadequate for the justification of such a measure, because he feels with Austria that the occupation of the Duchy by Federal troops may be a means of preventing revolutionary movements in Germany. It is only to be expected therefore that the course of events will be hereafter more or less guided by the exigencies of the Governments and of the peoples of the smaller States of Germany, and if a large force is to be moved into Holstein in deference to a popular cry, it is not likely to be moved out again, until those parties who have raised the cry, have been entirely satisfied.

There are also various eventualities which may result from the abnormal state of things which the federal execution is about to create, and whatever they may be, I shall be surprized if M. de Bismarck does not endeavour to obtain more solid advantages for Prussia in return for the losses and sacrifices which the country will have to suffer in the event of war, than the honour of having placed a Prince of Augustenburg upon the Ducal throne of a Sleswig-Holstein State.   (Received December 14, 1863.)

BUCHANAN TO RUSSELL, NO. 26, BERLIN, JANUARY 7, 1864.

[Reports sending telegram in cypher:] When asked to specify the whole demands which Prussia will make on Denmark, M. Bismarck said, things are not ripe for the King to adopt a decision. He cannot therefore speak officially on the subject; but what he personally thinks necessary will be the formation of two independent states under one dynasty, one of which will consist of Sleswig, Holstein and Lauenburg. He said the division of Sleswig would cause a useless difficulty, if the integrity of the Danish Monarchy is to be maintained, but the complete security of the German population against Danish rule is the only absolute condition he will make. He wishes the settlement to leave Denmark disposed to cultivate friendly relations with Prussia. He is still disposed to prevent invasion of Sleswig, if the new Constitution is abrogated;—but he said, there is no time to lose for the military arrangements cannot be delayed.

BUCHANAN TO RUSSELL, NO. 34, CONFIDENTIAL, BERLIN, JANUARY 9, 1864. (Rec'd Jan. 11.)

The Bavarian Minister is said to have expressed some surprise to M. de Bismarck a few days ago, that he had not repudiated the Treaty of London after the 1st inst., as he had declared that Prussia would be entitled to do so if the Sleswig-Danish Constitution were not repealed before that date. I am told that His

Excellency answered that he had not only said that Prussia would have a right on the 1st of January to decline maintaining the Treaty if Denmark had not repealed before that date a law which is at variance with her engagements to Germany, but he also considered that Prussia had now acquired that right. It did not follow however, he added, that she was obliged to avail herself of it.

BUCHANAN TO RUSSELL, NO. 99, CONFIDENTIAL, BERLIN, JANUARY 26, 1864.

During my conversation with M. de Bismarck this morning on the proposal which I had been instructed to make to him, that a delay of six weeks should be granted to Denmark, in order to give time for the repeal of the Constitution of 1863, His Excellency said he was sorry to find that this proposal had been made to Prussia by Her Majesty's Government after previous concert with France. I replied that the proposal came from Denmark and had been submitted to Great Britain, France, Russia and Sweden, and it was only to be expected that Her Majesty's Government would have communicated with all these Governments, as to the support which should be given to it. His Excellency said he could understand this—but as Prussia's present policy was guided by a wish to act in concert with Great Britain, Russia and Austria, he earnestly trusted that Her Majesty's Government would not give a signal for the commencement of a steeple-chase to Paris.—And he insinuated that seductive temptations held out to Prussian ambition had been hitherto virtuously rejected; but that they may meet with more consideration, if the past self-denial of the Government is not fairly appreciated.

I asked what were the nature of the temptations he alluded to, and who was the tempter. He replied, he supposed I could understand him without further explanation. (Rec'd Jan. 28.)

BUCHANAN TO RUSSELL, NO. 161, STRICTLY CONFIDENTIAL, BERLIN, FEBRUARY 8, 1864.[1]

....M. de Talleyrand having seen M. de Bismarck as he proposed to do, called upon me to-day. .... His Excellency [Bismarck] then added there were three courses which the Prussian Government might follow:—1st., they might support the pretensions of the Prince; 2nd., they might annex the Duchies to Prussia; 3rd., they might maintain the integrity of the Danish Monarchy. He said the first course would be contrary to the interest of Prussia, as it would be establishing a Government in Holstein which would during peace intrigue against her and oppose her in the Frankfort Diet, and during war might give its support to her enemies. The second again was impossible for, if there were no other objections to it, the French Government did not like to see neighboring States increase their territory and resources without obtaining some equivalent. The third course was therefore, in His Excellency's opinion the wisest and the most likely to advance the interests of Prussia, and to ensure her hereafter the goodwill of the Scandinavian Powers, with whom it was his wish to cultivate the most friendly relations— and with whom Prussia could establish a cordial understanding if the question of the Duchies could be settled on a just and permanent basis.

M. de Bismarck also hinted to M. de Talleyrand that, if the King would not support the Government in the policy which he considered ought to be pursued, he would not remain in office and, on M. de Talleyrand replying that in that case he would probably return to his former post in Paris; His Excellency said "no—if I leave—it will be to retire from public life, at all events for a time."

I have reported thus fully M. de Talleyrand's account of his conversation with M. de Bismarck as His Excellency's language to the French Ambassador was generally consistent with that which His Excellency has held to myself. ....

[1] Cf. Talleyrand's report of February 9, *Les Origines diplomatiques de la guerre de 1870-1871*, I, No. 186.

APPENDIX IV

FRANCE AND PRUSSIA.

1. GOLTZ TO KING WILLIAM [EXTRACT], COMPIÈGNE, NOVEMBER 23, 1863.

"... J'avais désiré," m'a-t-il[1] dit, m'entendre avec vous sur quelque chose de plus grand. Je n'ai rien à vous demander, mais vous ne vous dissimulerez pas que vous ne pouvez pas rester dans votre situation actuelle. La Prusse est entourée d'une foule de petits Etats qui gênent son action sans ajouter à sa force. J'avais esperé que la réunion des Souverains nous donnerait l'occasion d'établir, entre nous, une entente sous ce rapport aussi bien que sur les autres grandes questions."

J'ai répondu que, sans doute, la configuration donnée à la Prusse par le Congrès de Vienne ne répondait pas aux circonstances actuelle et qu'elle était même la cause principale de nos difficultés intérieures, que la position de la Prusse entourée de trois grandes Empires avait besoin d'être renforcée et placée dans une situation qui lierait irrevocablement à son système politique les petits Etats limitrophes; mais qu'il ne dépendait pas exclusivement de la volonté de Votre Majesté d'amener un pareil revirement; qu'en outre, les sentiments de loyauté dont Votre Majesté est animée envers Ses Confédérés l'engageraient à employer plutôt la persuasion que la force et à espérer que les Princes allemands eux-mêmes finiraient par comprendre leurs véritables intérêts; que, de l'autre côté, ce serait déjà un grand résultat, si la Prusse et la France constataient par leurs votes dans le Congrès que leurs vues dans la plus grande partie des questions européennes sont identiques et que cette identité emenerait insensiblement une entente qui pourrait plus tard conduire à de plus grands résultats. C'était, ai-je ajouté,

---

[1] Napoleon III,

justement cette conviction qui me faisait espérer que la proposition de l'Empereur constituerait à rétablir les rapports naturels entre les deux pays, rapports qui avaient été faussés par l'affaire de Pologne. L'Empereur a abondé dans ce sens; Il m'a assuré qu'il partageait cet espoir et que ces considérations avaient une grande part dans Sa résolution. . . . .

2. GOLTZ TO BISMARCK, No. 327, PARIS, DECEMBER 1, 1863.

Der Kaiser Napoleon hat gestern den russischen Botschafter in den Tuilerien empfangen. Die Unterredung hat anderthalb Stunden gedauert. Baron Budberg ist im hohen Grade unbefriedigt von derselben. Niemals, so sagte er mir, hat er den Kaiser in einer so bedenklichen Richtung, so geneigt gefunden, sich in eine abenteuerliche Politik zu stürzen.

Er hat aus den Aeusserungen des Kaisers den Eindrück, dass die Kongress-Idee definitiv aufgegeben ist. Seinen ohne Zweifel bitteren Gefühlen gegen England hat der Kaiser dem russischen Botschafter gegenüber keinen Ausdruck verliehen. Von schwebenden Fragen hat Seine Majestät nur die italienische Frage besprochen. Der Versuch des B^n Budbergs, eine Aeusserung über die Deutsch-Danische Differenz herbeizuführen blieb fruchtlos, indem der Kaiser wiederholte Anregungen dieses Gegenstandes unerwiedert liess. . . . [As to Goltz, spoke of new alliance system.] . . .

Die polnische Frage scheint der Kaiser keineswegs aufgegeben zu haben, vielmehr hält es Baron Budberg nicht für unmöglich, dass Frankreich einen isolirten Schritt thue. Der Kaiser hat es dem Russischen Interessen für entsprechend erklärt, Polen die Unabhängigkeit zu geben. Als Entschädigung hat er Ost-Galizien oder die Donaufürstenthumer angeboten. Er hat dabei bemerkt, dass ja die Ausführung auch nur eines einzigen der seiner Zeit vorgeschlagenen sechs Puncte genügt wurde, um die russische Herrschaft in Polen unmöglich zu machen. B^n Budberg hat dem Kaiser versichert, dass sein Souverain auf Vorschläge der bezeichneten Art nimmermehr eingehen würde. Russland sei mit dem Pariser Frieden ganz zufrieden, welcher fremde Flotten vom schwarzen Meere ausschliesse; es habe auch nicht das geringste Interesse seine polnische Unterthanen gegen wallachische auszutauschen. Er hat es bedauert, dass der Kaiser Napoleon gerade in der polnische Frage Concessionen verlange, indem gerade in dieser, Russland keine Concessionen machen könne. Diesselbe sei keine französische, sondern eine innere russische Frage. Sie lasse eine Erörterung mit fremden Mächten nur in einem gewissen Masse, nämlich nur innerhalb der verschiedenen Interpretationen der Wiener Verträge zu. ''Aber diese Verträge bestehen ja nicht mehr'' warf der Kaiser ein— ''Soll ich dies so verstehen, erwiederte der russische Botschafter, dass wir berechtigt wären, Polen zu inkorperiren?'' —Der Kaiser hat diese Frage unbeantwortet gelassen. .... Baron Budberg hat aus dieser Unterredung die Ueberzeugung mitgenommen, dass der Kaiser Napoleon im nächsten Frühjahr Krieg beginnen wurde. Für zunächst bedroht hält er Oesterreich.

3. TALLEYRAND TO DROUYN DE LHUYS, *Particulière*, BERLIN, DECEMBER 17, 1863.

Permettez-moi de prendre aujourd'hui la forme plus intime d'une lettre particulière pour vous rapporter quelques paroles que m'a dites avant-hier M. de Bismarck au sujet de notre proposition de congrès restreint. Je venais de lui faire connaître le terrain que vous avez si habilement choisi dans la question Dano-Allemande et de constater avec lui l'analogie des principes qui nous guidaient avec ceux invoqués par les deux grandes Puissances Allemandes, lorsqu'il me dit:

''J'ai toujours pensé que la question Danoise devait se resoudre en congrès et qu'il convenait en dernière analyse de demander à une assemblée solennelle la sanction des arrangements futurs que la guerre ou la diplomatie imposeront de part et d'autre. Aussi je cherche à utiliser la similitude de nos vues dans cette question en faveur de l'idée d'un congrès restreint mise en avant par votre Gouvernement. Je comprends que l'Empereur Napoléon, ayant proposé la réunion d'un congrès général, ne peut abandonner une si large conception sur le simple refus de l'Angle-

terre. Il faut donc, autant que possible lui donner satisfaction
dans le forme au moins si ce n'est dans le fond.— Je me suis
adressé a St. Petersbourg pour me renseigner sur les intentions
du Cabinet Russe et savoir si le moment était opportun de le
disposer à se prêter à votre désir. Je crois qu'il convient à la
Prusse, dans l'état actuel de la question, plutôt de s'entremettre
pour obtenir des adhésions à votre proposition, que d'y donner
de prime abord un consentement dont la valeur serait beaucoup
diminuée s'il était isolé. Il me semble que c'est la un rôle que
vous ne pourrez désapprouver. Mais savez-vous quelle est
toujours la vraie pierre d'achoppement entre nous? C'est la
question Polonaise. Si elle n'avait pas été posé, vous me trouver-
iez dans de tout autres dispositions. C'est une question qui crée
entre la Russie, l'Autriche et nous une solidarité à laquelle aucune
des trois Puissances ne peut se soustraire. Ainsi, dans un congrès,
je ne pourrais bénéficier de mon indifférence sur les affaires
Italiennes, parce qu'il me faudrait ménager l'Autriche, si je veux
qu'à son tour, elle appuie la défense de nos intérêts Polonais.
Ne pourrait-on pas sur ce chapitre-là, nous donner de sérieuses
garanties, ne pensez-vous pas qu'il serait possible, par exemple,
de soustraire cette question au congrès?''

J'ai répondu à M. de Bismarck que, quant à celà, il n'y fallait
pas penser: qu'un congrès, qui, de toutes les questions qu'il
aurait à traiter, écarterait bénévolement la plus importante,
succomberait sous le ridicule de son impuissance. Je ne com-
prenais pas, d'ailleurs, ses appréhensions. L'Empereur Napoléon, en appelant au Congrès l'Empereur Alexandre, ne pouvait
avoir en vue de faire sur la Pologne des propositions inacceptables
et de nature à amener une rupture dès le début des négociations.
Si rien d'incompatible avec l'honneur national Russe ne devait
être demandé, je ne voyais pas le danger que couraient les titres
de possession Prussienne sur le Grand-Duché de Posen.

''Ces provinces ont pour nous une telle importance,'' a repris
M. de Bismarck, ''que si, par exemple, de grandes calamités
venaient à nous frapper et qu'il nous fallût opter entre la cession
du Grand Duché et celle de la rive gauche du Rhin, je conseillerais
plutôt d'abandonner notre frontière de l'Ouest que de modifier

nos limites du côté du Nord-Est. Tâchons de gagner la Russie à votre project: nous nous addresserons ensuite à l'Autriche. Les difficultés de ce côté seront peut-être insurmontables, mais si l'on parvient à les écarter, il sera bien difficile a l'Angleterre de ne pas suivre le courant.''

[Decypher] Je me garderai, mon cher Ministre, de me porter garant de tout ce que m'a dit le Bon de Bismarck, et de vous assurer qu'il ne veut pas nous leurrer par de bonnes paroles ou de feintes manœuvres. En fait de sincère, je ne réponds que de l'exactitude de mon récit. Cependant je puis ajouter que le Président du Conseil a été moins atteint que personne de l'embarras et du malaise dans lesquels notre proposition de Congrès restreint a jeté le monde politique de Berlin. A en juger par ses paroles, il s'appliquera à tirer profit de la situation et il n'a pas renoncé a l'espérance de former le trait d'union entre Paris et St. Pétersbourg. [End of decypher.]

J'ai vu hier le Comte Karolyi, qui se montre peu satisfait de Lord Wodehouse. Il se plaint de sa particularité et le traite de bavard et de vaniteux personnage. Pour que mon collègue d'Autriche, dont la réserve habituelle est extrême, tienne un semblable langage, il faut qu'il y ait eut entre lui et Lord Wodehouse de sérieux froissements, de date plus ou moins récente.

APPENDIX V

METTERNICH TO RECHBERG, NO. 54 A-F, PARIS, NOVEMBER
27, 1863.

Nous touchons au moment difficile que j'avais prévu et plus
vite même que je ne l'avais pensé.

Les espérances plus ou moins fondées qui m'entouraient à
Compiègne m'avaient fait subir une certaine influence et lorsqu'on s'y est déclaré satisfait des réponses de la Prusse et de la
Russie et que l'on m'assura qu'en principe l'Europe avait accepté
le Congrès je crus m'être trop avancé en prévoyant un nouvel
échec.

De retour à Paris je m'aperçois que les circonstances se sont
singulièrement modifiées et mes conversations avec mes collègues
m'ont laissé l'impression la plus satisfaisante à notre point de vue.
Que la Prusse fasse quelques insinuations plus ou moins sincères,
qu'elle se mette en frais de courtoisie, que la Russie emploie un
langage dont la phraséologie flatte l'oreille de l'Empereur—
toujours est-il que ni l'une ni l'autre n'acceptent le congrès
comme on l'eut désiré ici—c'est à dire sans réserve et en se
plaçant sous la haute protection de l'Empereur.

Le refus définitif, annoncé de Londres a porté un coup sensible
aux dernières illusions que l'on se faisait à Compiègne; la
déception a été cruelle et l'humeur s'en ressentit immédiatement.

Le matin même de mon départ l'Empereur me prit à part et
me dit: "Savez vous que l'Angleterre refuse et qu'elle s'appuie
sur vous de son refus?"

Je répondis à Sa Majesté que je n'avais pas encore appris le
refus de l'Angleterre que je m'attendais, il est vrai, à de graves
difficultés de sa part mais que la seconde partie de la nouvelle
qu'il me donnait avait lieu de m'étonner.

"Oui" me dit l'Empereur "on nous donne à entendre à Londres que l'Autriche a fortement encouragé le Cabinet anglais à prendre l'initiative du refus."

Je me suis permis d'assurer l'Empereur que je doutais fort de la véracité de cette nouvelle et j'ai ajouté: "nous avons toujours eu, et je l'ai souvent répété à Votre Majesté, les plus grandes objections contre la réunion d'un Congrès, mais nous *sommes assez grands et raisonnables* pour refuser nous-mêmes ce que nous croyons contraire à nos intérêts."

J'ai profité de la tournure que prenait la conversation pour revenir sur cette argumentation, que l'Empereur nous ayant réveillé en sursaut le 5. Novembre pour nous proposer ce que nous regardons comme une mauvaise affaire, nous ne pouvions faire autrement que de nous enquérir auprès des autres pour savoir si nous ne faisions pas un mauvais rêve et si tout le monde était d'accord pour nous forcer à nous asseoir autour du tapis vert. Nous nous aperçûmes qu'à Londres comme à Berlin on partageait notre sentiment de stupeur et d'aversion ce qui ne nous empêcha pas d'examiner la question mûrement et sans parti pris. "Nous avons rendu justice "ai-je ajouté" à la tendance pacifique dont Votre Majesté a donné un témoignage mais nous avons demandé certaines explications préalables comme tout le monde."

J'assurai Sa Majesté que jusqu'à nouvel ordre je croyais que tel resterait notre point de vue et que nous ne nous étions pas donné la peine de mettre l'Angleterre en avant.

L'Empereur avait l'air fort chagriné de la nouvelle qu'il venait de recevoir. L'émotion était grande à Compiègne. Les caractères se montrèrent alors sous leur vrai jour. L'Empereur était triste mais resta fort calme—Il prit congé de moi avec les témoignages d'amitié auxquels j'étais accoutumé mais auxquels je fus doublement sensible dans ce moment difficile pour Lui. L'Impératrice au contraire ne mit aucun ménagement dans ses reproches. Elle me dit: "Je vous félicite, vous avez gagné les deux premières manches, nous verrons qui gagnera la troisième. Zürich et Villafranca que j'avais toujours sur la conscience sont devenus aujourd'hui des fardèurs légèrs vis-à-vis de votre conduite dans l'affaire de Pologne et dans celle qui nous préoccupe actuelle-ment.''

J'assurai Sa Majesté que, selon moi la surprise du 5 Novembre devrait constituer un nouveau poids sur Sa conscience et que si Elle se tenait pour quitte, il s'en fallait de beaucoup pour que de mon côté je Lui donnasse mon absolution.''

Je pris place en chemin de fer avec M. Drouyn de Lhuys et après avoir eu occasion avant mon départ de me ressentir du double effet du caractère des Maîtres j'eus pendant une heure et demie le temps d'étudier celui du *Ministre-diplomate.*

M. Drouyn de Lhuys fit exactement le contraire de ce qu'avait tenté l'Impératrice au lieu de procéder par intimidation il essaya de me convaincre que si nous le voulions encore, nous pourrions arriver à une nouvelle entente intime avec la France.

Le Ministre commença par me dire que le refus anglais n'était et ne pouvait être définitif, que nous avions eu tort de nous méfier de la pensée de l'Empereur—que nous aurions dû nous expliquer franchement avec Lui sur les questions qui nous paraissent si désagréables—que Notre Auguste Maître aurait pu par une seconde lettre très confidentielle poser à l'Empereur certaines conditions *sine qua non* de son acceptation et que certainement l'Empereur, touché de cette marque de franchise, Se fût entendu avec Lui.

Mon étonnement était profond en face de ces ouvertures. Je demandais à M. de Drouyn Lhuys si l'Empereur lui avait parlé dans ce sens, ce à quoi il me répondit évasivement.

Le Ministre m'insinua que vu l'influence qu'il me prêtait à Vienne je devrais m'exprimer dans ce sens et qu'il en serait temps encore peut-être.

Je lui répondis ce que j'avais déjà dit à l'Empereur à propos de la désagréable surprise du 5 Novembre. Je l'assurai que pour ne pas user mon influence conciliante j'étais décidé à renoncer pour quelque temps à mon emploi extra-officiel. Le jour viendra, lui dis-je, où je pourrai peut-être rendre quelques services, mais dans les circonstances actuelles je ne veux plus me mêler de politique personnelle et pour le moment je donne ma démission d'employé, d'agent personnel des deux Empereurs. Je le priai de faire faire à Vienne les ouvertures qu'il voudrait et par qui il voudrait mais quant à moi je ne ferais plus d'insinuations qui m'ont si mal réussies, je craindrais qu'un nouveau coup de surprise ne vint renverser derrière mon dos l'échaffaudage que je cherchais a reconstruire.

Il résulte pour moi de l'état présent des choses que l'on continuera à nous ménager—que l'on viendra peut-être frapper encore à notre porte lorsque les petites insinuations à Berlin ou à St. Pétersbourg auront échouées—et c'est ici que je prie Votre Excellence de vouloir bien s'attendre à ce que si la lutte en Pologne n'est pas terminée jusqu'au printemps ce sera certainement sur cette question que l'Empereur Napoléon cherchera de nouveau à se rapprocher de nous.

Je n'ai pas voulu parler encore à Mr. Drouyn de Lhuys des mesures plus sévères que nous serons dans le cas de prendre en Gallicie; la dépêche du 25 de ce mois par laquelle Votre Excellence me transmet des détails intéressants sur les trames dont cette province commence à devenir le théâtre m'étant parvenue par la poste, je pense que le Gouvernement français ne l'aura pas laissé passer inaperçue. Si je mettais personnellement par trop d'insistance à ce sujet j'aurais l'air de vouloir faire ressortir un changement d'attitude de notre part dans la question polonaise qui, par une certaine corrélation avec la ligne de conduite que nous comptons maintenir en face de l'idée du Congrès, aurait pu donner lieu a des suppositions inutiles dans ce moment-ci.

Metternich to Rechberg, No. 59 B, Paris, December, 14, 1863.

Il ne faut pas se dissimuler que notre refus définitif a fortement impressioné l'Empereur. Une assez longue conversation que j'ai eu le 11 ct. avec Sa Majesté m'a convaincu d'une chose— c'est que si M. Drouyn de Lhuys se flatte encore de maintenir le faible fil qui nous rattache, l'Empereur le considère comme rompu. Je n'ai jamais vu l'Empereur si découragé et se donner si peu de peine à ne pas le montrer. Tout le monde à Compiègne en est frappé. Nos amis comme nos ennemis le trouvent impénétrable.

Lord Cowley se plaint même de Son manque de courtoisie. Nigra et Lavalette appuyés par Morny et un peu par Fould ont tenté une campagne contre Drouyn de Lhuys et en faveur d'une politique accentuée dans l'intérêt d'Italie—mais l'Empereur a rembarré tout le monde. Pasolini est parti pour Londres sans avoir rien obtenu, Cowley me l'affirme.

A en juger par ce que l'Empereur m'a dit—ce que L'aigrit le plus c'est l'idée que nous reprenons *la politique de la Sainte Alliance* et que l'Angleterre nous aide et nous encouragerait même *dans les velléités de coalition.* . . . . Il est certain que le moment est venu où l'Empereur pourra Se décider d'un jour à l'autre à faire un coup de tête. Que peut-Il faire aujourd'hui? Je ne vois qu'une guerre possible avec le concours de la révolution, c'est une nouvelle guerre d'Italie. Sur le Rhin comme en Orient, l'Empereur aurait trop de monde contre lui. [Metternich does not think that Napoleon would be supported strongly by France in such an adventure but he may open the floodgates to the Revolution in Italy.]

METTERNICH TO RECHBERG, NO. 59 E, PARIS, DECEMBER 14, 1863.

. . . . En traitant avec moi la question danoise, l'Empereur reste invariablement fixé sur l'argument suivant: "Je ne puis combattre en Allemagne le sentiment national, sans être inconséquent et d'un autre côté je ne puis me ranger contre le Danemark auquel je suis lié par un traité et par d'anciennes sympathies réciproques."

Sa Majesté fera peu pour la solution de cette question qu'Il veut laisser mûrir.

"Si cependant," m'a dit l'Empereur, "on venait *à mettre en question l'existence même du Danemark, l'opinion publique en France me forcerait à le protéger."* . . . .

METTERNICH TO RECHBERG, PRIVATE, PARIS, DECEMBER 20, 1863.

[Bismarck spoke to Talleyrand of the idea of a conference on the Danish question; Drouyn de Lhuys told Metternich in strict confidence. Drouyn de Lhuys sounding Metternich as to possibility of *entente* with Austria. Napoleon, in speaking of *ententes* and alliances ''aurait dit: 'jusqu'à présent je n'ai eu *que des maîtresses*—je cherche *une femme!*' '' Drouyn de Lhuys tried to show that this ought to be Austria. Among other things, he asked why Austria did not say to France: '' 'Si Vous me garantissez qu'il ne sera question ni de la Vénétie ni de la Gallicie—je vous aide à faire aboutir le congrès—si non, je Vous préviens que je travaillerai contre Vos project des pieds et des mains.' Le Ministre me donnait à entendre qu'on eut accepté.'']

METTERNICH TO RECHBERG, NO. 1 B, PARIS, JANUARY 7, 1864.

.... La question des duchés ne préoccupe l'Empereur et Son Ministre que fort indirectement—on dirait même qu'elle n'est venue que pour offrir ici une chance de se montrer désagréable à l'Angleterre, pédant dans les affaires, et d'afficher le plus grand dédain pour tout ce qui ne rapproche pas de la grande idée du Congrès général. [The Emperor now sees that he was wrong to come forward alone on November 5, but events are coming to his aid to give him] un semblant de raison et Le consoler de Son échec. [When all seemed lost, Drouyn de Lhuys had the idea of a special conference at Paris to mask the defeat.] Mais la proposition de la Prusse venant offrir les conférences des signataires du protocole de Londres comme une compensation de son refus de participer au Congrès restreint, parait avoir blessé l'Empereur qui S'en explique franchement envers moi. Je me suis hâté de profiter de la leçon. .... On est bien aise de jouer un tour à l'Angleterre d'autant plus que dans l'affaire des Duchés on ne me semble nullement désirer une prompte solution. On attendra pour se prononcer que les affaires se soient encore plus embrouillées....

METTERNICH TO RECHBERG, TELEGRAM, PARIS, JANUARY 9, 1864. NO. 2. *Chiffre.*

Comte Walewski m'assure tenir de source authentique que Général Fleury aurait rapporté de Berlin proposition de la Prusse de servir d'intermédiaire pour ramener l'ancienne intimité avec la Russie et insinuer de servir les intérêts de l'Empereur en Italie s'il consent à laisser la Prusse s'annexer Kiel et les Duchés et de donner le Danemarc à la Suède. L'Empereur aurait refusé de s'engager mais laisserait faire la Prusse pour se donner un droit de compensation.

Lord Cowley m'en a aussi parlé comme d'une affaire à laquelle poussent le Comte Morny et Mr. Fould.

Die Russenfreundlichen Paragraphen der von Herrn von Morny verfassten Adresse des corps legislatif und die Haltung der Blätter in der dänischen Frage wären allerdings bedeutsame Symptome.

METTERNICH TO RECHBERG, PRIVATE, PARIS, JANUARY 13, 1864.

[As telegram No. 2 of Jan. 9]. .... Il aurait même insinué que si les circonstances permettraient à la Prusse d'annexer ces provinces avec le port de Kiel, on chercherait à indemniser la France du côté du *Palatinat.* ....

METTERNICH TO RECHBERG, NO. 5, PARIS, JANUARY 19, 1864.

[Metternich explained at length to Drouyn de Lhuys the difference in policy of the two Great German Powers.] .... Deux idées dominent la politique française dans ce moment-ci:

On désirerait voir se précipiter les complications, la guerre s'allumer et on voudrait assister à une lutte intérieure en Allemagne.

On est résolu à éviter tout ce qui pourrait faire sortir l'Angleterre des embarras de sa situation. ....

[In case war breaks out, Napoleon will probably not delay to put himself on the side of those who give the most chance of a moral or material increase in power or of arriving at the realization of the idea of the congress. Great rejoicing at the successive checks of England.]

De tout ce qui précede il resulte:

1. Que le Gouvernement français se complait dans son rôle de spectateur désintéressé;

2. Qu'il attendra patiemment l'occasion de s'avancer pour sauvegarder en temps opportun ses intérêts;

3. Que tous les essais de négociations tentés soit par Lord Cowley soit par mes collègues de Prusse, de Danemarc ou par moi ont été et resteront encore infructueux pour quelque temps.

METTERNICH TO RECHBERG, PRIVATE, PARIS, JANUARY 19, 1864.

[Conversation with the Empress. She conceals even less than Napoleon the desire to see affairs get more complicated. Fleury really did try to start negotiations with Bismarck. The Austro-Prussian *entente* "a marqué un temps d'arrêt."]

METTERNICH TO RECHBERG, PRIVATE, PARIS, JANUARY 28, 1864.

[In spite of Drouyn de Lhuys's counsels of moderation, Metternich still affirms that things are not moving fast enough to satisfy the French Government. Drouyn de Lhuys summed up all the reasons that make it almost impossible to reach a pacific solution of the question.]

METTERNICH TO RECHBERG, TELEGRAM NO. 9, PARIS, FEBRUARY 3, 1864, 5:40 P. M. RECEIVED 7:40 P. M.

Chiffre. Le Ministre des affaires étrangères trouve toujours que le Holstein gage suffisant, regrette effusion de sang qui était inévitable mais ne s'associe à aucune action hostile de l'Angleterre. Er hofft, dass der Krieg schnell zu Ende damit die öffentliche Meinung sich nicht zu Gunsten des schwächeren Dänemark anfange. L'Empereur m'assura qu'Il ne se départira pas de sa réserve tant que les complications ne prendront plus grandes proportions. Si l'Angleterre fait la guerre on la regardera la faire, *si non* prolongation de la lutte dangereuse en ce qu'elle pourrait entraîner la France en faveur du Danemarc.

METTERNICH TO RECHBERG, TELEGRAM NO. 18, PARIS, FEB-
RUARY 23, 1864. 8:55 P. M.

Chiffre. Der Kaiser hat mir soeben gesagt, dass weiteres Vorgehen in Jütland diplomatische Intervention und Demonstrationen Seitens Englands und Frankreichs zum Folge hätte, qu'il vaudrait mieux éviter. Il dit que nous devrions aussi prendre garde du côté de Lugano et du Tessin et peser sur la Suisse pour l'enquête, parce que le parti d'action veut forcer le Gouvernement piémontais à la guerre en fomentant l'insurrection dans le midi du Tyrol sur les confines de la Vénétie. Il m'a fait curieuses révélations sur mission de M. Pasolini dont il a refusé proposition d'échanger la Vénétie contre les Principautés.

MULINEN TO RECHBERG, NO. 26 B, PARIS, JULY 4, 1864.

[Among other things, Drouyn de Lhuys said: "Quant à moi, j'aimerais mieux voir la Prusse prendre pour elle une partie des deux Duchés que l'Allemagne s'annexer la totalité de ces pays sous le sceptre d'un Prince quelconque." He prefers Augustenburg to Oldenburg. After a few pleasantries about England, "qu'il taxe *d'avoir reculé avec vigueur*," Drouyn de Lhuys said: "On me dit qu'il a été question à Vienne d'un projet de faire entrer tout le Danemark dans la Confédération Germanique. Nous ne pourrions jamais admettre un tel fait et du moment où l'on voudrait changer l'état de chose constitutif de la Confédération, la France se verrait dans la nécessité de réagir contre ces velléités par tous les moyens en son pouvoir, *sans en excepter un seul.*"]

APPENDIX VI

KAROLYI TO RECHBERG, *Vertraulich*, BERLIN, NOVEMBER 30, 1863.

Die Stellung des Herrn von Bismarck in Vertretung des in der deutsch-dänischen Angelegenheit gemeinschaftlich von den beiden deutschen Grossmächten eingenommenen Standpunktes wird ununterbrochen von vielen Seiten und mächtigen Einflüssen angegriffen.

In dem gestrigen Ministerrathe wurde der Herr Ministerpräsident von mehreren seiner Collegen, welche zu einer offenen Theilnahme für die deutschen Herzogthümer hinneigen und daher in letzter Analyse die Lostrennung derselben von Dänemark und deren selbständigkeit vor Augen haben, direct interpellirt sich darüber auszusprechen welches politische Ziel er in dieser Frage verfolge. Herr von Bismarck antwortete unumwunden, dass sein Ziel die Erhaltung der durch den Londoner Vertrag festgestellten Integrität der dänischen Monarchie sei, unter selbstverständlicher Wahrung und Durchführung der durch die Bundesbeschlüsse bezeichneten Rechte Deutschlands. Er wolle durch die Gründung eines selbständigen Schleswig-Holstein kein zweites maritimes Polen schaffen, welches unaufhaltsam auf Wiedereroberung desselben angewiesen wäre, und die deutschen und preussischen Interessen stets beunruhigen und gefährden würde.

Abgesehen von der durch den Londoner Vertrag auferlegten Verpflichtung und der Gefährlichkeit für Preussen, in seinen Beziehungen zu den Grossmächten, sich derselben zu entziehen, wird Herr von Bismarck in der Festigkeit mit welcher er bisher in unstreitig anerkennungswerthen Weise sich auf den Boden des Londoner Vertrages stellt und den Augustenburgischen Ansprüchen entgegentritt, auch durch die Betrachtung wesentlich unterstützt, dass die nationale Bewegung zu Gunsten der Herzogthümer immer mehr eine revolutionäre Gestaltung anzunehmen droht und gewiss das preussische Gebiet auch nicht verschonen würde. Bei dem schon so schroffen, aber bis jetzt auf das parlamentarische Feld der Discussion und auf die Presse beschränkt gebliebenen Gegensatz zwischen der Regierung und der grossen Majorität des Landes, wäre die Entfesselung materieller revolutionärer Elemente ein neuer gefährlicher Zuwachs fur die Stellung des Ministeriums Bismarck. Seiner eigenthümlichen, kühnen Geistesrichtung folgend, äussert er sich wohl dahin dass er gerade diese Bewegung auf der Strasse abwarte, um die materielle Revolution erfassen und niederschlagen zu können; doch darf dieser Wünsch nicht buchstäblich gedeutet werden, und es ist wohl anzunehmen dass er, um einer solchen Eventualität zu steuern, es für nothwendig erachtet, in dieser wichtigen Conjunctur so sehr als thunlich Farbe zu bekennen. . . . .

KAROLYI TO RECHBERG, NO. 125, A-D *Vertraulich*, BERLIN, DECEMBER 19, 1863.

Den Empfang der hohen Expedition vom 15. d. durch den k. k. Cabinets Courier Weingraber beehre ich mich ergebenst zu bestätigen.

Die letzten Verhandlungen in der Kammer über die schleswig-holsteinische Angelegenheit haben die Zeit des Herrn Ministerpräsidenten so sehr in Anspruch genommen, das ich dieser Tage jedesmal blos wenige Augenblicke im Ministerzimmer des Abgeordnetenhauses mit ihm sprechen konnte, und daher heute noch nicht in der Lage bin über die Erfüllung der durch die Erlässe vom 15. mir gewordenen hohen Aufträge ergebenst Bericht zu erstatten.

Indem ich mir dies für die nächste Zeit durch Abfertigung des genannten Couriers vorbehalte, gestatte ich mir jetzt einer vertraulichen Mittheilung Erwähnung zu tun welche ich der Gefälligkeit des Herrn von Bismarck verdanke.

Nach einem kürzlich eingegangenen Bericht des preussischen

Botschafters in Paris müsse man sich seitens Frankreichs im nächsten Frühjahr auf ein kriegerisches Vorgehen gefasst machen. Die Eindrücke des Grafen Goltz über die Absichten des Kaisers Napoleon sind sehr düster. Veranlassung und Ziel, Allianzen und Gegner welche Er in's Auge fassen würde, könnten vorerst keiner bestimmten Berechnung unterzogen werden, doch hat Sich der Kaiser auch hierüber Grafen Goltz gegenüber anscheinend ohne Rückhalt ausgesprochen.

Seine Majestät hegt die Ansicht, dass bis zum Frühjahr die nationale Bewegung Galizien erfassen, dass daselbst Unruhen ausbrechen würden welche, sich auf Ungarn ausstreckend, den revolutionär-nationalen Tendenzen in Europa mächtigen Vorschub leisten würden. Italien konnte hiebei nicht ruhig verbleiben. Kaiser Napoleon entwarf ein Bild, worin die revolutionär-nationale Idee in den Vordergrund gestellt wurde, und Seinen Hang, Sich eventuell dieser Richtung zu bemächtigen um eine kriegerische Action Frankreichs einzuleiten, liess Er hiebei ziemlich klar durchblicken. Der von Ihm angedeutete Ausgangspunkt stellt Oesterreich in erster Linie als Zielscheibe jener unruhigen, den Frieden bedrohenden französischen Politik hin.

Dieselben Eindrücke, meldet Graf Goltz, theile auch der russische Botschafter.

KAROLYI TO RECHBERG, NO. 6 N., BERLIN, JANUARY 14, 1864.

Ich bin noch in der Lage, durch diese Couriersgelegenheit über eine weitere Besprechung welche ich mit dem Herrn Minister Präsidenten in den Abendstunden hatte, Euerer Excellenz ergebenst Bericht zu erstatten.

Ich muss vorausschicken, dass meine letzteren Unterredungen mit Herrn von Bismarck mir die Ueberzeugung gewähren, dass er die Billigkeit unserer Forderungen in Bezug auf das Princip der gegenseitigen Solidarität, welche eine jedwede einseitige, ohne Zustimmung der anderen Macht erfolgte Schwenkung ausschliesst vollkommen zugiebt und mit aufrichtigster Entschiedenheit beim König vertritt. Seine Majestät aber, nach dem zu urteilen was mir der Minister von seinem heute nachmittags dem König erstatteten Vortrag anvertraute, sträubt Sich noch immer darauf einzugehen. Der König stellt mit Hartnäckigkeit das Argument voran, dass, wenn Er Sich nicht die Freiheit zu der Lossagung vom Londoner Vertrag sichert, Preussen in die Lage kommen könnte, einen viel Geld und Menschen kostenden Krieg gegen Dänemark, aber für die Integrität der dänischen Krone, daher in dieser Hinsicht vielmehr für Dänemark führen zu mussen. Herr v. Bismarck bekämpft diese Anschauung, indem er es als selbstverständlich annimmt, dass unter allen Eventualitäten günstigere Abmachungen als jene von 1851-2 auszubedingen sein werden, und stellt hiebei dem König gegenüber die Personal-Union der deutschen Herzogthümer als das diesfalle anzustrebende Ideal auf, welches den preussischen Interessen eben so sehr, wenn nicht noch mehr entspricht als eine Augustenburgische Dynastie. Dann weist er auf die vorhandene Aussicht hin, dass bei einem Krieg mit Dänemark, welcher nicht gegen die Integrität der dänischen Monarchie gerichtet ist, England factisch neutral bleiben würde, während ein Krieg unter Lossagung des Vertrags, daher die Zerstückelung Dänemarks bezweckend, die active Feindschaft Englands ohne Fehl zur Folge haben würde. Er bemüht sich, dem König begreiflich zu machen, dass man unmöglich von Oesterreich erwarten könne, sich mit Preussen in eine Allianz zur Führung eines gemeinschaftlichen Krieges einzulassen, ohne die Sicherheit zu haben, dass es nicht, durch eine plötzliche Schwenkung Preussens, im Stiche gelassen würde, und dass daher die Stipulation eines gegenseitigen Einverständnisses für die weiteren politischen Phasen, ebensosehr wie selbe von Preussen beansprucht werde müsse, an Oesterreich zuzugestehen sei.

Diese bei Seiner Majestät zu Tage tretende Unbehaglichkeit rücksichtlich der fraglichen bindenden Vereinbarung, zumal wenn ich selbe mit Seiner bisherigen inneren Gemüthsrichtung zusammenhalte, kann ich nicht anders erklären, als dass jetzt, da der Augenblick herangetreten ist zur kriegerischen Action zu schreiten, die Lossagung vom Londoner Vertrage sich immer klarer und bestimmter als das Ziel der Preussischen Politik vor Seinen Augen entfaltet. Diesem Ziele steuert Seine Majestät unbedingt

zu. Und er mag daruber Zweifel hegen, ob Oesterreich an der
Integrität Dänemarks nicht festhalten und die Erreichung dieses
preussischen Zieles nicht vereiteln werde.

Ich will hier nicht eingehend erörtern, ob hiebei blos rein
deutsche Nationalaspirationen oder auch spezifisch preussische
Vergrösserungsgelüste im Spiele sind. So viel darf ich aber jetzt
aussprechen, dass Gedanken, welche letzterer Eventualität
zugewendet sind, gewiss seitens mancher politischen Persönlichkeit Berlins in die Berechnung der Zukunft hereingezogen werden.
Mit offenem Freimuthe hat Herr von Bismarck selbst heute mir
gegenüber diese Möglichkeit ganz leicht angeregt. Er hat selbe,
bei diesem Anlass, mit Entschiedenheit als unklug zurückgewiesen, denn, wolle Preussen eine Annexionspolitik befolgen, so wäre
die Mediatisirung der innerhalb der Mainlinie liegenden deutschen
Länder ein bei Weitem nicht so gefährliches und den preussischen
Interessen ungleich mehr zusagendes Unternehmen, als eine
Eroberung der Herzogthümer. Wenn nichtsdestoweniger solche
Betrachtungen sich im Laufe der Ereignisse ernstlich geltend
machen würden, setzte der Minister hinzu, so könne Preussen
füglich auf die Waffengemeinschaft Oesterreichs zu einem
derartigen Zwecke blos durch Gewährung von entsprechenden
Gegenleistungen rechnen, und dieselben liegen für Oesterreich in
Italien. Herr von Bismarck erwähnte dies nur leicht hin, aber
Beachtung verdient dieser Gesichtspunkt schon jetzt, und er
scheint um so mehr zu der Vorsicht zu rathen, die Bedingung des
gegenseitigen Einverständnisses fur die ferneren politischen
Momente aufrecht zu erhalten.

Mit der veränderten Fassung des in Rede stehenden Passus der
Punctation konnte Sich Seine Majestät nicht befreunden, obwohl
er selbe keineswegs ablehnte. Sie enthalte im Wesentlichen
dasselbe. Auf die Stipulirung einer gegenseitigen Frist für eine
eventuelle Lossagung vom Vertrage kam Herr von Bismarck mir
gegenüber nicht zurück.

Der König wünscht ohne Zweifel, Sich die Allianz mit Oesterreich zu sichern doch möchte er am liebsten selbe im Interesse
der Lossagung vom Londoner Vertrage angewendet sehen. Von
Herrn von Bismarck in Seinen Argumentationen in die Enge

getrieben, erklärte Seine Majestät, dass Ihm dann nichts übrig
bleibe, als Seiner Majestät dem Kaiser, unserem allergnädigsten
Herrn, zu schreiben, um Allerhöchstdemselben Seine Gedanken
und Absichten kund zu geben. Herr von Bismarck konnte mir
nicht sagen, ob Seine Majestät wirklich ein solches Vorhaben
ausführen würde, doch erwähnte er mir diesen Ausspruch seines
königlichen Herrn als Beweis dafür, dass er das Gelingen einer
Einigung mit Oesterreich vor Augen habe. Es wird sich eben
um die Verständigung über die hiezu erforderlichen Bedingungen
handeln. Seine Majestät verwies schliesslich den Minister
Präsidenten auf ein morgen abzuhaltendes Cabinets Conseil
welches Ihm einen definitiven Vortrag über den Punctations
Entwurf zu erstatten habe. Herr von Bismarck sieht darin ein
gutes Omen; der einstimmigen Annahme, seitens seiner Collegen,
der Punctation mit den heute einberichteten Modificationen sei
er sicher, und von einer solchen officiellen Einwirkung des
Ministerrathes auf die Entschlüsse Seiner Majestät glaube er ein
gutes Resultat erwarten zu dürfen.

KAROLYI TO RECHBERG, No. 11 B., BERLIN, JANUARY 24,
1864.

Ich habe seinerzeit nicht ermangelt, sowohl den hohen Erlass
vom 14, d., reservirt, welcher sich auf angeblich zwischen Herrn
von Bismarck und dem General Fleury Stattgehabte Gespräche
bezieht, als das betreffende Schreiben aus Paris zur Kenntnis des
Herrn Ministerpräsidenten zu bringen und habe ihn um eine
offene Erklärung der darin enthaltenen Angaben gebeten.

Derselbe nahm nicht den geringsten Anstand, folgender
Aufklarungen mir in dieser Hinsicht zu ertheilen.

Bei den näheren persönlichen Beziehungen welche zwischen
ihn und General Fleury bestünden, hätten die verschiedenen
Besuche des Letzteren ganz natürlich auf eine in ungebundener
Form gehaltene Besprechung der Politik im Allgemeinen geführt.
Allianz-projecte zwischen Frankreich und Russland waren allerdings hierbei berührt worden, die Initiative in dieser Richtung
wäre aber vom General selbst ausgegangen, welcher, wie Herr

von Bismarck mir bemerkte, durch seinen persönlichen **Wunsch,**
den St. Petersburger Botschaftersposten zu erhalten, hierbei
hauptsächlich geleitet zu sein schien. Weit entfernt nun, zum
Behufe einer Annäherung Frankreichs an Russland, eine Vermitt-
lersrolle angeboten zu haben, hätte Herr von Bismarck vielmehr
eine solche abgelehnt und darauf hingedeutet, dass, so lange die
polnische Frage irgendwie noch auf dem Tapete sich befände, das
erregte Nationalgefühl in Russland einen jeden Versuch zu einer
Schwenkung nach Frankreich hin vereiteln würde. Preussen
müsse auf seinen, in der polnischen Frage eingenommenen
Standpunkte noch viel bestimmter beharren; eine polnische
Lösung derselben, während sie für Russland wohl ein Verlust,
aber doch auszuhalten wäre, würde für Preussen ein Todesstoss
sein; Frankreich werde Letzteres daher diesfalle stets ''intrait-
able'' finden.

Die Angelegenheit der Herzogthümer wäre ferner seinerseits
keineswegs in einem Sinne besprochen worden, welcher die
Absicht des preussischen Cabinets durchblicken liesse, sich
eventuell in einen Länderschacher einzulassen. Das Wort
''Palatinat'' wäre gar nicht augsesprochen worden. Er habe
auf die Eventualität der Annectirung Kiels an Preussen, wie eine
solche Tendenz von vielen Seiten Preussen zugemuthet werde,
gerade in einem Lichte hingedeutet, welches einen ähnlichen
Besitz für Preussen als werthlos darstellt. Er habe die geographische Configuration Kiels hervorgehoben, welche den Kieler
Hafen wohl für einen Handelsplatz aber nicht zur Vertheidigung
geeignet mache. Der höchste Punkt an jener Küste, von welchen
sich eine Abdachung des Terraine bis zum Meere hinstrecke, sei
von selben zu entfernt um den Hafen schützen zu können. Der
durch den Besitz von Kiel erwachsende Gewinn in Beziehung des
Handels würde durch die Unmöglichkeit diesen Punkt gegen
feindliche Angriffe zu halten, zu Nichte gemacht, und bei dieser
Sachlage empfinde Preussen keine Verlockung zu einer Ver-
grösserung nach jener Seite hin.

Gesprächsweise und mehr fragend, um seinem Mitredner auf
den Puls zu fühlen, habe Herr von Bismarck wohl auf die, seit
Jahren der Regierung des Kaisers Napoleon untergestellten

Gelüste, sich wenigstens durch Gewinnung von Saarbrücken ein grosses Kohlenlager zu verschaffen, Bezug genommen. Der gleichen Absichten, sowie jedwede andere Rheingelüste stellte aber General Fleury entschieden in Abrede; Frankreich denke nicht daran sich zu vergrössern und sei durchaus uneigennützig bei allen Fragen die jetzt Europa bewegen.

Endlich, die scandinavische Union anbelangend, so habe er (H. v. Bismarck) wohl zugegeben, dass Preussen an und für sich keinen Grund habe, derselben feindlich entgegenzutreten, doch bei der gegen diesselbe gerichteten Politik sowohl Englands als auch Russlands erschiene es überhaupt rätlich, dieses Ziel nicht zu verfolgen; die letzterwähnte Opposition benehme demselben jedwede Aussicht des Gelingens, und Preussen denke nicht daran, sich wegen dieser Frage gegen die genannten beiden Mächte zu stellen.

Aus diesen Erklärungen des Herrn von Bismarck darf ich sonach entnehmen, dass die in dem Pariser Schreiben erwähnten Punkte in den fraglichen Unterredungen wohl besprochen aber von Herrn von Bismarck in keiner für unsere Interessen Verfänglichen oder das Zusammengehen der beiden Mächte störenden Weise beleuchtet worden sind. Unter den gegenwärtigen Verhältnissen lag es ihm gewiss fern, seinen Ausserungen einen Anstrich zu geben welcher den Wunsch nach einer einseitigen Schwenkung nach Frankreich hin zu insinuiren geeignet wäre. Der Herr Minister verwahrte sich gegen diese letztere Richtung um so entschiedener, als er auf die Gesinnungen des Königs hinwies welche eine ähnliche Politik niemals zulassen würden. Er nahm keinen Anstand, die dahin zielende Tendenz des fraglichen Pariser Schreibens als mit dem Stempel der Erdichtung behaftet, mir gegenüber zu bezeichnen.

KAROLYI TO RECHBERG, NO. 37 A-G, BERLIN, MARCH 26, 1864.

Hinsichtlich der letzten im englischen Conferenzvorschlag eingetretenen Wendung hatte der englische Botschafter, welcher zu den dänischen Interessen so sehr hinneigt, in seinen mündlichen Besprechungen mit dem Herrn Ministerpräsidenten vorerst noch versucht, die dänischerseits bisher aufgestellte Basis zu vertreten und ihr wenigstens als dänischen Ausgangspunkt der Verhandlung eine gewisse Anerkennung beim Berliner Cabinet zu verschaffen. Nachdem Herr von Bismarck rundweg ablehnte darauf einzugehen und das Verlangen stellte, um den englischen Standpunkt der Einladung zu den Conferenzen mit einiger Klarheit beurtheilen zu können, eine schriftliche Mittheilung hierüber zu erhalten, entschloss sich Sir Andrew Buchanan, ein Schreiben an den Herrn Minister Präsidenten zu richten in welchem er sich darauf beschränkte, die ursprüngliche, an das diesseitige Cabinet mittelst offizieller Note vom 23ten Februar gerichtete Einladung anzurufen und die darauf erfolgte zustimmende Erklärung Preussens als eine Annahme des von England gestellten Conferenzvorschlages zu constatieren. Eine neue Annahme erachtet der Minister nicht für nothwendig, da die frühere auch jetzt noch gültig sei.

Als Herr von Bismarck mich vorgestern hievon in Kenntnis setzte, schien er noch keineswegs überzeugt zu sein, dass Dänemark in ähnliche freie Conferenzen so leicht einwilligen würde, und dieselben Zweifel schien er auch rücksichtlich des deutschen Bundes zu hegen. Wie es die Aufgabe Englands sei, auf Dänemark in diesem Sinne einzuwirken, so fiele es den beiden deutschen Grossmächten anheim, den Bund zur Beschickung der Conferenz zu bestimmen.

In Gemässheit Euerer Excellenz Telegrammes v. 22ten d. unterliess ich es nicht, Hr. v. Bismarck gegenüber hervorzuheben, dass es nun an der Zeit sei, zwischen den Cabinetten von Wien und Berlin die Friedensbedingungen in nähere Erwägung zu ziehen und ein gemeinschaftliches Programm aufzustellen. Ich frug den Hr. Minister, ob er selbst die Initiative zu einer schriftlichen Auseinandersetzung diesfalls ergreifen wolle, oder eine eingehende Ausführung hierüber vom kaiserlichen Cabinet erwarte. Er schien in dieser Hinsicht noch zu keiner bestimmten Ansicht gelangt zu sein und war daher nicht in der Lage diese Frage zu beantworten.

Hr. v. Bismarck zählte sodann in allgemeinen Zügen die Friedensbedingungen auf, welche nach seiner Ansicht von den beiden Mächten zu vertreten wären.

Das alte Verhältnis, der status quo ante bellum, müsse selbstverständlich als ein definitiv überwundener Standpunkt betrachtet werden. Wie es im Interesse einer jeden Verhandlung liege, so würde es sich anempfehlen, sogleich mit dem höchsten ziele aufzutreten, damit das im Laufe der Negotiation abgeminderte Resultat noch immer als eine genügende Lösung von Oesterreich und Preussen angesehen werden könne. Denn dass dieselben vom ihrem Standpunkte aus zu Concessionen würden veranlasst werden, dürfe wohl vorauzusetzen sein. Dieses Ziel sei die Personal-Union der Herzogthümer mit Dänemark und die Real-Union, d. h. die Zusammengehörigkeit Holsteins mit Schleswig. Dieses Verhältnis, welches die Herzogthümer blos durch das dynastische Band mit der dänischen Krone verbindet, müsse zudem durch gründliche, auf europäischer Anerkennung beruhende Garantien sicher gestellt werden, damit die in Rede stehenden deutschen Länder auf die Dauer von dänischer Bedrückung befreit würden. Unter solchen Garantien stehe in erster Linie die Einverleibung Schleswigs in den deutschen Bund, welche Massregel allein im Stande sei die Rückkehr der dänischen Vergewaltigungen zu verhindern. Die Frage, ob das ganze Herzogthum dem deutschen Bunde anzuschliessen sei, oder ob der nördliche, überwiegend dänische Theil allenfalls an Dänemark zur Incorporirung in das Königreich überlassen werden müsse, würde einen wichtigen Gegenstand der Verhandlung bilden. Ein ähnlicher Zuwachs des deutschen Bundes, der erste seit dessen Bestehen, würde von der öffentlichen Meinung in Deutschland mit grosser Befriedigung aufgenommen werden, die Politik der beiden Mächte mit dem deutsch-nationalen Standpunkt zum Theil versöhnen, und der Stellung der beiden Regierungen in ihren eigenen Ländern sehr förderlich sein. Ein solches Resultat schiene zumal durch die doch bedeutenden Opfer welche der Krieg bereits Oesterreich und Preussen auferlegt, vollkommen gerechtfertigt und es müssten sonach deren Anstrengungen dahin gerichtet sein.

Die Errichtung von Rendsburg als Bundesfestung führte Hr.

v. Bismarck auch als einen aufzustellenden Punkt des Friedensprogrammes an, sowie das Verlangen einer entsprechenden Kriegsentschädigung.

Ferner erwähnte der Herr Minister eines Planes welcher die öffentliche Aufmerksamkeit schon seit längerer Zeit, besonders vom Handelspolitischen Standpunkte aus, auf sich gezogen hätte, und welcher bei diesem Anlasse von den beiden Mächten vorzubringen wäre. Dieser Plan bestände in der Verbindung der Nordsee mit der Ostsee durch einen Kanal. Zwei Linien seien angeregt worden. Die eine wäre eine Diagonale und ginge von Eckernförde über Rendsburg mit Benützung vieler Seen und der Eider, und es würde der Kanal in den Ausfluss der Elbe münden. Das andere Project bestände in einer geraden Linie von der Neustädter Bucht bei Lübeck, gleichfalls nach den Elbemündungen. Letztere Linie wäre die kürzere, während die erste wegen der zahlreichen inneren Wasserstrassen geringere materielle Schwierigkeiten darböte. Der Handel nach dem letztgennanten Meere (der Ostsee) würde durch eine ähnliche namhafte Verkürzung der Seestrasse einen ungeheuren Aufschwung nehmen und dieser Transit den Herzogthümern grosse Vortheile zuführen. Ein solches Unternehmen, ein Seitenstück des Suezkanals, besässe an sich schon für den allgemeinen Welthandel eine bedeutende Verlockung, und würde den beiden Mächten, unter deren Aegide er ins Leben gerufen worden wäre, zur Ehre gereichen.

Es liegt auf der Hand, dass, welch immer vom allgemeinen Standpunkte des Handels der Nutzen eines solchen, wohl durch eine Actiengellschaft anzulegenden Verbindungskanals auch sein mag, die Interessen des Ostseehandels, daher in erster Linie die preussischen Handelsinteressen, die grössten Vortheile davon ziehen würden, welcher Umstand dieser ganzen, von Herrn von Bismarck mit Vorliebe vertretenen Idee eine spezifisch preussische Färbung aufpräge.

Eine ähnliche preussische Färbung glaubte ich auch in einer andern Ausführung des Herrn Ministers hinsichtlich des Friedensprogrammes zu entdecken. Für den Fall, meinte er, dass die Personal-Union durch den Widerstand der Dänen sich nicht als

durchführbar erweisen und die Lostrennung der Herzogthümer
für Schleswig wohl auf den deutschen Theil beschränkt, als die
mit den meisten Chancen ausgestattete und von Dänemark selbst
vorgezogene Lösung sich herausstellen sollte, so würde erstens ein
solches Resultat von den beiden deutschen Mächten nicht bean-
ständet werden dürfen, da es nicht deren Aufgabe sein könne,
dänischer als Dänemark zu sein. Es wäre dann dafür zu sorgen,
dass dieser neu geschaffene deutsche Staat nicht den Augusten-
burgern zufiele, da die Erhebung des Erbprinzen zum deutschen
souveränen Fürsten als ein Triumph der demokratischen Partei
und des Nationalvereins ausgelegt werden würde und mit der
ganzen Haltung der beiden Mächte in Widerspruch stünde. Herr
von Bismarck zöge in dieser Eventualität den Herzog von Oldenburg als den zukünftigen Herzog von Schleswig-Holstein vor;
derselbe besitze auch Erbansprüche auf diese Länder und würde
in jeder Hinsicht eine geeignetere Wahl als der Erbprinz von
Augustenburg sein.

Diese Ansicht dürfte vielleicht auf der Hoffnung beruhen, dass
eine ähnliche Combination nicht ohne irgendwelchen Länderer-
werb oder sonstige positive Vortheile zu Gunsten Preussens
ablaufen würde. Der Länderschacher welcher in dieser Richtung
als ein förmliches Project bereits in den Zeitungen besprochen
worden, verdient allerdings in der Form wie derselbe in die Welt
geschleudert worden, keine Beachtung, doch mag er als Fühler,
um die öffentliche Meinung auf ähnliche Gedanken zu bringen,
von irgend einer massgebenden Seite in Preussen ins Leben
gerufen worden sein. Herr von Bismarck hat öfters den Herzog
von Oldenburg in dieser Hinsicht vorangestellt. Er dürfte wohl
hierbei mehr seine persönliche Ansicht, als die Seiner Majestät
des Königs ausgedrückt haben, Allerhöchstwelcher, wenn es
überhaupt je zur Lostrennung der Herzogthümer kommen sollte,
Seine Sympathien für das Haus Augustenburg wohl nicht so
leicht fallen lassen würde.

TELEGRAM FROM BIEGELEBEN, BERLIN, APRIL 20, 1864, 7:30–8:50 P M.

Das Resultat meiner Besprechungen mit Herrn von Bismarck ist im Wesentlichen übereinstimmend mit den Instructionspunkten für die kais. Bevollmächtigen. Ich glaubte in Aussicht stellen zu können, dass Oesterreich bereit sein werde, auch die Aufnahme Schleswigs in den deutschen Bund, eine Flottenstation an dem zu gründenden Schiffahrtskanal und die Garantie der schleswig-holsteinischen Verfassung durch den Bund gemeinschaftlich mit Preussen zu beantragen, wogegen ich bevorwortete, die Consequenzen der Personalunion in Bezug auf Heer und Flotte nicht zu scharf zu ziehen, die Dinge nicht zu einer Theilung Schleswigs nach Nationalitäten zu treiben und eine Befragung der Stände jedenfalls nur nach Massgabe ihrer gesetzlichen Competenz zuzulassen. In diesen drei Punkten, in welchen sich die im Grunde weitergehenden Intentionen Preussens aussprechen, ging Herr von Bismarck nicht principiell von seiner Anschauung ab, erkannte jedoch als nöthig an, Meinungsverschiedenheiten wenigstens nicht in den Vordergrund treten zu lassen. Heute früh reise ich nach London ab.

BIEGELEBEN TO RECHBERG, BERLIN, APRIL 19, 1864.

In zwei langen Unterredungen mit Herrn v. Bismarck, deren erste in Anwesenheit des Grafen Karolyi stattfand, die zweite sich mehr auf das Detail der Friedensunterhandlungen bezog, trachtete ich dem preussischen Minister so bestimmt als möglich den Eindruck zu geben, dass in Wien die ganze deutsch-dänische Verwicklung sich nur als eine Episode von verhältnismässig untergeordneter Wichtigkeit darstelle, und dass die Einigung zwischen Oesterreich und Preussen, um den höheren Anforderungen der Weltlage zu entsprechen, noch einen anderen und bedeutungsvolleren Inhalt gewinnen müsse, als das gemeinsame Auftreten gegenüber Dänemark.

Anspielungen auf die entscheidenden Dienste, welche das Bündnis der beiden deutschen Mächte der Sache der Ordnung zu leisten berufen ist, konnten bei Herrn v. Bismarck näturlich nicht ohne Anklang bleiben. Auch kann ich nichts anderes sagen, als dass aus seinen Aeusserungen wenigstens in gewissen Grade die Voraussicht, dass Preussen sich allerdings an Oesterreich werde halten müssen, hervorleuchtete. Aus der ganzen Art und Weise, wie er die verschiedenen möglichen Allianzgruppirungen durchmusterte, ging jedoch deutlich genug hervor, dass er von der Gemeinsamkeit der den legitimen Regierungen drohenden Gefahren nicht eben sehr präoccupirt ist, und dass er sich wesentlich von der Speculation auf specielle Vortheile für Preussen bestimmen lässt. Dem Könige den Rath zu geben, sich auf bestimmte Verpflichtungen einzulassen, liegt daher auch— wenigstens bis jetzt—durchaus noch nicht in seinem Sinne, er will sich vielmehr die Anlehnung an Frankreich, die er als ein blosses Cajoliren hinstellt, offen halten um einen möglichst gloriosen Frieden zu erhalten. Um so mehr glaubte ich darauf hinweisen zu müssen, dass Frankreich sicher nicht im preussischen sondern nur im eigenen französischen Interesse seinen alten Schützling Dänemark aufopfern würde, und dass man England nicht vor den Kopf stossen dürfe, wenn man nicht der französischen Politik in die Hände arbeiten wolle. Er gab zu, dass man die beiden Westmächte auseinander halten müsse, schien es aber als eine ganz zweckmässige Rollenvertheilung anzusehen, wenn England durch Oesterreich bei guter Laune erhalten würde, und Frankreich durch Preussen, was ich mir für eine einigermassen bedenkliche Parthie zu erklären erlaubte.

Von Bedingungen, für welche man auf die Connivenz Frankreichs zählen kann, trennt man sich daher hier nur schwer, doch verwarf Herr v. Bismarck, wie nicht anders möglich, entschieden die Volksabstimmung, und modificirte sogar auf meine Gegenbemerkung nicht unbedeutend die neueste Depesche nach Wien wegen der Ständebefragung, die im ursprünglichen Concept, welches er uns verlas, noch viel weiter ging, und ein ganz ungebührliches Gewicht auf das Votum der Stände legen wollte.

Was der Herr Minister übrigens am entschiedensten betonte, war das Bedürfnis für ihn, bei dem Könige, auf den die in

Deutschland vorherrschende Stimmung wirkte,und bei der Armee, die nicht resultatlos gefochten haben wolle, seine Stellung durch einen rühmlichen Frieden zu befestigen. Hierin sehe er auch das Mittel, aus der Cooperation gegen Dänemark eine festere Allianz zwischen Oesterreich und Preussen hervorgehen zu lassen, denn Oesterreich werde, wenn es Preussen zu einem solchen Frieden behülflich sei, zwar für sich keine Provinz, aber dafür die preussische Armee gewinnen.

Erwähnen muss ich noch, dass Herr v. Bismarck mich fragte, ob ich in Wien nichts von der Absicht gehört habe, die gegenseitigen Gesandtschaftsposten zu Botschafterposten zu erheben, wozu die politische Situation jetzt so wollkommen angethan sei. Ich antwortete, hierüber nicht unterrichtet zu sein, glaube jedoch Eurer Excellenz von dieser Interpellation, die immerhin zu den günstigen Symptomen gehören dürfte, Anzeige erstatten zu müssen.

Den Stand der Zollfrage habe ich mit den Herrn Philipsborn und Delbrueck besprochen, diese Herrn suchten mich zu überzeugen, dass Preussen uns nicht weiter entgegenkommen könne, als in Prag geschehen sei, was ich jedoch in keiner Weise gelten liess. Ihr letztes Wort haben sie, meine ich, noch nicht gesprochen, wenn uns nicht die Mittelstaaten geradezu im Stiche lassen.

CHOTEK TO RECHBERG, BERLIN, MAY 15, 1864.

Nachdrücklich und mit einem gewissen Wohlbehagen scheint der Ministerpräsident sich allerdings in den letzten Tagen, mit den von allen demokratischen und liberalen Parteifärbungen in Preussen und Deutschland zurückgewiesenen Gedanken einer Vereinigung der Herzogthümer mit Preussen beschäftigt zu haben. Diese contrastierende Würdigung jener Idee ist sehr begreiflich, wenn man erwägt, dass eine glückliche Durchführung derselben, Hr. v. Bismarck für eine Reihe von Jahren, wenigstens solange König Wilhelm regiert, gewiss die politische Herrschaft in Preussen sichern würde.

Ich werde in dem Anfangserwähnten Eindrucke bestärkt durch

einige vertrauliche Andeutungen die er bei seinem letzten gestrigen Gespräche mir gethan.

"Wie ich Ihnen schon sagte, äusserte Hr. v. Bismarck, stehen wir noch auf unserm vereinbarten Programm, und können uns kaum denken, ein so theuer zu bezahlendes Objekt requiriren zu wollen und einer Politik zu befolgen, die nebstdem die Gefahren mit sich führen würde, die Sie mir gestern ganz richtig auseinandersetzten."

"Aber denkbar wäre es doch, dass wenn für Preussen Territorial Erwerbungen an der Schlay [sic] und Eider ohne zu viele Nachtheile zu haben waren, es auch für Oesterreich Bedingungen geben dürfte, unter denen Sie uns diess wohl gönnen könnten."

"Diese Bedingungen, deren Abmachung das gegenwärtige intime Allianz Verhältnis erleichtern würde, wären z. B. wenn wir Ihnen Alle gewünschten Conzessionen machten in Bundes Militär und Commando Angelegenheiten, in der organischen Bundes Reform Frage gemeinsam und durch Preussische Zugeständnisse verständigt mit Ihnen die Lösung herbeiführten, ja eine Garantie des österreichischen Gesammt Besitzstandes zugestehen würden etc. etc."

"Diess wäre die Inaugurirung einer *gegenseitigen Compensations Politik*, die aber wohlgemerkt, soll sie nicht den grossen conservativen Interessen Europa's und den Existenzbedingungen Deutschlands den grössten Schaden thun, *nur zwischen uns Beiden* aber *nie* zwischen einem von uns und einer andern ausserdeutschen Macht stattfinden dürfte."

Diese leicht hin gesprochenen aber gewissermassen mir ins Ohr gesagten, von mir aber mit dem reservirtesten jedenfalls aber nicht billigenden Schweigen aufgenommenen Aussprüche, glaubte ich in der gegenwärtigen vertraulichen Form ehrfurchtsvoll wiedergeben zu sollen, und bitte Euer Excellenz den Ausdruck meiner tiefsten Ehrfurcht genehmigen zu wolle.

KAROLYI TO RECHBERG, NO. 55 A-E, BERLIN, JUNE 1, 1864.

Die hohe Expedition vom 24ten vg. M. Nr. 1 bis 3,[1] betreffend die zu Gunsten der Lostrennung der Herzogthümer von Dane-

[1] Cf. pp. 342-348.

mark und des Augustenburgischen Erbanspruches von den alliirten deutschen Grossmächten beschlossene Wendung, hat sich, wie Euere Excellenz bereits andeuteten, mit den hierseitigen bezüglichen Ausführungen gekreuzt, und haben sich die gegenseitig dargelegten Standpunkte und Vorschläge vollkommen begegnet.

Ein Anlass zu einer sachlich detaillirten Auseinandersetzung jener Entgegnungen zu welchen die hohen Mittheilungen vom 24ten Mai seitens der hiesigen Regierung Gelegenheit geboten haben, scheint mir sonach beinahe gänzlich zu entfallen.

Es erübrigt mir also nur der besonders bei dem Könige bestehenden aufrichtigen und tiefgefühlten Befriedigung zu erwähnen welche die nunmehr vorliegende Lösung im Innern Seiner Majestät hervorgebracht hat. Man kann ein Gleiches von Herrn v. Bismarck nicht in so entschiedener Weise sagen, ebenso wie eine bedeutende, nicht blos in den höheren Classen Preussens zu findende Partei mit der nunmehr an den Tag getretenen Combination sehr unzufrieden ist. Der Herr Ministerpräsident hat mir diese seine intimen Gedanken auch gar nicht verhehlt und zugegeben, das *er* unter den drei Lösungen—Personalunion, Annexion an Preusen und Augustenburgische Herrschaft für die Herzogthümer—entschieden der zweiten den Vorzug gegeben hätte, allerdings nur vorausgesetzt die Gestattung seitens Oesterreichs und nicht allzugrosse Gefahrdrohung von ausserdeutscher Seite her.

Anders geartet sind die Gesinnungen des Königs; das Glück und Wohlbehagen welches Seine Majestät empfindet, stammt daher, dass Seiner ehrlichen Uneigennützigkeit und Seinen redlichen conservativen Empfindungen die Annexions Idee widerstrebte, und Er in Seinem feurig gefassten Entschlusse, dass das preussische Schwert im Vereine mit Oesterreich den deutschen Interessen einen grossen, greifbaren Gewinn erkämpft haben müsse, durch die Verwirklichung des Gedankens der Personalunion eine Befriedigung zu finden nicht vermochte.

Zudem war Seine Majestät immer insgeheim von der Gerechtigkeit des Augustenburgischen Erbanspruches überzeugt und in diesem Sinne von der auf Ihn nicht ohne Einfluss bleibenden

Hohen weiblichen Umgebung bearbeitet, ein Umstand, dem wir ja während der letzten fünf Monate so viele Mühen und Kämpfe verdankten. Also "ein wahrer Stein vom Herzen" soll, nach Herrn. v. Bismarcks vertraulicher Andeutung, die fragliche Lösung fur seinen königlichen Herrn sein.

Dazu kommt noch, das die wirklich hervorragenden Verdienste welche sich der Kronprinz während der letzten kriegerischen Ereignisse erworben hat, den erlauchten Sohn dem weichen Herzen des königlichen Vaters wieder doppelt theuer gemacht haben, und dies erhöhte den Wunsch die Anlässe des gegenseitigen Zwiespaltes auf ihr geringstes Mass gebracht zu sehen. Bei dem Umstande nun, als der Kronprinz die Augustenburgischen Ansprüche besonders warm verfocht und auch *dies* einer der Zwistigkeitsgründe in der königlichen Familie war, ist es leicht begreiflich, wie lieb es dem Könige sein muss, gerade Angesichts der erhöhten Wertschätzung welche Er dem Erben Seiner Krone dermalen schenkt, diese Veranlassung zu Meinungsverschiedenheiten in Schoosse Seines Hauses entfernt zu sehen.

Die Ausführungen der hohen Depesche Nr. 2 betreffen den Vorschlag eines Austausches des Herzogthums Lauenburg gegen einen entsprechenden Theil von Schleswig, worin ein ganz angemessenes Auskunftsmittel geboten wäre, um dem Wunsche der Anhänger des Nationalitätsprincips factisch entgegenzukommen, ohne sich dieses selbst und die möglicher weise daraus zu ziehenden Folgerungen anzueignen,—und wodurch auch die fragliche Transaction den Character einer Auseinandersetzung zwischen dem König von Dänemark und dem neuen Herzog von Schleswig-Holstein erhielte statt für eine ebenso schwierige als bedenkliche Scheidung nach nationalen Gegensätzen zu gelten. Mein gestriges Telegram, auf die diesseitigen letzten Eröffnungen Bezug nehmend, enthielt die hervorragenderen Andeutungen über die diesfalls von Hn. v. Bismarck empfohlene Verhaltungsweise.

Im principiellen Standpunkte stimmt er ganz mit den vom kaiserlichen Cabinet aufgestellten Grundsätzen überein. Den Vorschlag welchen mein gestriges Telegram bespricht, stellt Hr. v. Bismarck hauptsächlich als Negotiationsmittel hin, um eine für Deutschland günstigere Demarcationslinie zu erlangen. Er machte hierbei darauf aufmerksam, wie es der *französische* Vorschlag wäre, dass über die Frage, *wer* der Souverän der bezüglichen Länder zu sein hätte, eine Volksabstimmung stattfände; dies sei nicht *seine* Ansicht; die Fragestellung wäre nur: *zu* Dänemark oder *los von* Dänemark. Uberdies würde es seiner Ansicht nach vielleicht gar nicht zur wirklichen Ausführung der Abstimmung kommen, sondern die darin liegende Drohung die erwünschte Wirkung äussern. Doch auch die Inscenesetzung des fraglichen Negotiationsmittels, indem es den Character einer blossen Informirung der Conferenz nicht zu überschreiten hätte, würde in letzter Analysis mit unserem grundsätzlichen Standpunkte, d. h. dem des territorialen Austausches zwischen der Krone Dänemark und Schleswig-Holstein, in formaler Hinsicht in Einklang zu bringen sein. Wenn eine derartige Votirung in den Herzogthümern stattfände, so brauchte man ja nicht die ausgedehnte Agitation einer Allgemeinen Abstimmung durch diese Länder gehen zu lassen, sondern man könnte sich beschränken vom *rein* deutschen und dänischen Theile die Abstimmung vorauszusetzen und nur in den gemischten Districten durch die Municipien das Votum vornehmen zu lassen.

Wie dem aber sei, diese durch die Verhältnisse im deutschen Interesse so sehr verlangte Negotiationsmodalität wird nur dann, nach Hn. v. Bismarck's Ansicht von dem gewünschten Erfolge begleitet sein, wenn Oesterreich auch hierbei mit Preussen Hand in Hand geht oder wenigstens einem ähnlichen Vorgehen Preusens nicht entgegentrete. Wie schon früher gesagt, würde hierdurch noch keineswegs die Annahme des Abstimmungsprincips für eine dynastische Fragestellung implicirt und jedenfalls auch noch immer die Möglichkeit offen gelassen werden auf den in der hohen Depesche Nr. 2 vom 24. v. M. entwickelten Gesichtspunkt zurückzukommen.

Hinsichtlich des hohen Erlasses Nr. 3 vom selben Tage, betreffend die Modalitäten des Benehmens der beiden Grossmächte dem Erbprinzen von Augustenburg genenuber, enthält mein heutiges Telegramm bereits das Wesentliche was ich in Erledigung dieser hohen Weisung Euerer Excellenz zu melden hätte.

KAROLYI TO RECHBERG, NO. 56 A-D, BERLIN, JUNE 4, 1864.

Herr von Bismarck hat mir vertraulich von einer Unterredung Kenntnis gegeben, die er dieser Tage mit dem Erbprinzen von Augustenburg gehabt hat.

Dieselbe hat auf den Herrn Ministerpräsidenten keine gunstigen Eindruck gemacht und seitens des Herzogs das Gepräge eines eher prätentiösen und hochfahrenden Auftretens, jedenfalls aber nicht den Character irgend welcher rücksichtsvollen Erkenntlichkeit für die beiden deutschen Grossmächte an sich getragen.

Herr von Bismarck hat versucht, Seine Hoheit zuerst von der Nothwendigkeit zu überzeugen, Sein Regiment in den Herzogthümern auf conservativen staatsrechtlichen Grundlagen zu beginnen, daher von der 1848er Verfassung revolutionären Ursprungs zurückzutreten.

Weit entfernt dieser Zumuthung beizupflichten, hat der Erbprinz dem königl. Hn. Minister zu bedenken gegeben wie es Ihm unter den obwaltenden Verhältnissen nicht thunlich erscheinen könne, auf einer anderen als einer streng verfassungsmässigen Basis vor Seine Länder zu treten, eine Basis, aus der, da ihr die Rechtscontinuität innewohnen müsse, das 1848er Gesetz nicht von vornherein ausgemerzt werden könne. Später könnten vielleicht auf streng constitutionellem Wege verfassungsmässige Verabschiedungen, Ausscheidungen einzelner Bestimmungen dieser Verfassung bewerkstelligt werden; Er fände es aber weder dem Rechte noch der Klugheit entsprechend, dem Herzogthümern gleich vom ersten Anfang an mit einer Octroyirung entgegenzutreten.

Als der Herr Ministerpräsident hierauf trachtete, dem Erbprinzen begreiflich zu machen, wie wünschenswerth es wäre, aus Seiner Umgebung Männer zu entfernen, die, wie er Seiner Hoheit wohl gern zugebe, privatim völlig ehrenhaft, aber vom Standpunkte ihrer politischen Wirksamkeit schädliche und gefährliche Elemente in sich schlössen und ähnliche Tendenzen verfolgten, so stellte dies der Herzog in Abrede und schien durchaus nicht geneigt irgendwelche Concessionen in dieser Hinsicht in Aussicht zu stellen.

Das Gespräch gelangte hierauf zu einem der wichtigsten Punkte, nämlich zu der von Hn. v. Bismarck angeregten Frage der Zahlung der Kriegsentschädigung.

Obwohl der Ministerpräsident nicht ermangelte dem Herzoge auseinanderzusetzen, wie bei den Dänemark zugemutheten bedeutenden territorialen Opfern das Alleintragen dieser ganzen Last seitens des kopenhagner Hofes auch von Seite der Neutralen unter keiner Bedingung zu erlangen sein würde, obwohl er ferner daran erinnerte, wie es unerhört sei, dass einen Lande welches entweder durch Revolution oder Krieg eine von demselben so heiss gewünschte selbstständige Existenz erlange nicht die Uebernahme einer bedeutenden Staatsschuldenlast zugemuthet werde, gelang es ihm nicht eine zustimmende Erwiederung seitens des Prinzen hervorzurufen. Einen weiteren leisen Hinweise des Hn. v. Bismarck, wie es doch wohl blos den beiden Grossmächten habe gelingen können thatsächlich und militärisch Dänemark in so rascher Weise aus den Herzogthümern zu entfernen, begegnete der Herzog vielmehr mit der höchst befremdenden Aeusserung: ''Ja aber weder ich noch meine Herzogthümer haben die Herrn Oesterreichs und Preussens zu diesem Kriege gerufen, also kann man uns auch nicht zumuthen diesen beiden Mächten die Entschädigung der ihnen hiedurch verursachten Kosten zu zahlen.''

Der Erbprinz fuhr weiter fort, auch nur jeden Gedanken als könne Er Seinen Ländern eine derartige Schuldübernahme zumuthen zurückzuweisen, indem Er bemerkte, das eine solche Schuld von den Herzogthümern übernommen werden könnte, *wenn* Er die *ganzen* Herzogthümer bis zur Königsau erhielte, aber ''verstümmelt'' wie sie ihn nach den letzten Londoner Nachrichten zufallen würden könne der Anspruch auf jene Leistung nicht zugestanden werden.

Als endlich Hr. v. Bismarck, als letzten und für Preussen wichtigsten Punkt, auf die Unerlässlichkeit des Schiffahrtscanals und der damit in Verbindung stehenden Befestigungswerke zu reden kam, widersprach ihm zwar der Herzog nicht und gab auch das allgemein Wünschenswerthe einer derartigen Position zu, aber that durchaus nicht dergleichen, als ob es Ihm daran gelegen zu sein schiene, diesen Tendenzen welche die militärische und namentlich die maritime Stellung Preussens so wesentlich zu verstärken bestimmt sind, hülfreiche Hand zu leisten. Und, was nach Hr. v. Bismarck für die dermalige Geistesrichtung des Erbprinzen bezeichnend ist so schien derselbe diese letztere Frage benützen zu wollen um Zwietracht zwischen Oesterreich und Preussen zu säen, indem Er es als fraglich darstellte, ob Oesterreich zu den diesfallsigen Plänen Preussens wohl seine Zustimmung ertheilen würde.

Der Erbprinz schloss die vorgedachte Unterredung zwar mit der Aeusserung, das Er die ernstliche Beantwortung dieser Punkte in Dolzig überlegen und mit seinem Vater berathen werde; auch trägt das Gespräch selbstverständlich durchaus keinen massgebenden Character an sich. Aber als Abglanz der dermaligen Stimmung des nunmehr nach Schlesien abgereisten Fürsten dürfte dasselbe doch von bezeichnendem Interesse sein.

KAROLYI TO RECHBERG, NO. 56 B, BERLIN, JUNE 4, 1864.

Anknüpfend an meinen vorhergehenden gehorsamsten Bericht glaube ich Eure Excellenz darauf aufmerksam machen zu sollen, dass nach den Aeusserungen des Herrn v. Bismarck das Berliner Cabinet die militärischen, maritimen und commerciellen Vortheile welche der Schiffsfahrtcanal, die Flottenstation und die damit dazusammenhängende Küstenvertheidigungswerke P r e u s s e n gewähren dürften in erster Linie und principiell als genügender Ersatz für das aufgegebene Annexionsproject, und in zweiter Linie sowie eventuelle als hinreichende Abschlagszahlung für die Kriegsentschädigung betrachten wurde. Die Frage, ob eine eigene grosse Bundesfestung (eventuell Rendsburg) oder bloss maritime Strandwerke an den beiden Eingangen des Canals anzulegen seien, wäre eine technische Opportunitäts- und Geldfrage. Die Andeutungen des H. v. Bismarck lassen sonach darauf schliessen, dass Preussen sich mit dem erlangten Resultate, sowie es vorstehend dargelegte erscheint nur unter der Bedingung definitiv befriedigt erklären würde, wenn wir ihm das alleinige Garnisonsrecht in allen in den Herzogthümer gelegenen, wie

immer gearteten fortificatorischen Vertheidigungspositionen ein-
geräumt würde. Preussen wäre, was Oesterreich betrifft, hier-
gegen bereit, anstandlos einzuräumen dass nicht bloss Rastadt
(wie H. v. Bismarck dies bereits kürzlich dem Grafen Chotek
angedeutete) sondern auch Ulm zu "volligen und alleinigen
österreichischen Festungen" gemacht würden.

CHOTEK TO RECHBERG, *Vertraulich*, BERLIN, JUNE 10, 1864.

No. 58 C. ..... Was das Verhältnis zu Frankreich betrifft
so läugne er gar nicht dass in den letzten Monaten vielfacher
intimer Meinungsaustausch zwischen hier und dem dortigen
Cabinet stattgefunden habe, dass Frankreich, für den Fall als
Preussen für die Volksabstimmung *zur Wahl des Herrschers der
Herzogthümer* seine Zustimmung geben würde, für die preussische
Annexion sich zu erklären bereit sei;— *so* hatte aber das Berliner
Cabinet den Volksbefragungsgedanken nie aufgefasst, hätte die
lockenden Anerbietungen zurückgewiesen, wäre aber nichtsdestoweniger in fortwährenden confidentiellen Verkehr mit Paris
geblieben.

Die königliche Regierung hätte diese Handlungsweise um so
eher eingehalten Ursach gehabt, als sie aus der bisher geflogenen
Correspondenz wohl zu bemerken Gelegenheit hatte, wie der
practische Sinn des Tuilerien Cabinets stets nur eine für Deutschland um ein Stück Land ungünstigere Demarcationslinie von
vornherein festgesetzt hätte, als dann hinterher durch eine etwa
doch erfolgte Abstimmung als gerechtfertigt erscheinen wäre.

APPENDIX VII

DOCUMENTS FROM THE AUSTRIAN ARCHIVES ILLUSTRATING THE
CHANGE OF POLICY IN THE SECOND HALF OF MAY 1864.

APPONYI TO RECHBERG, LONDON, MAY 13, 1864, *Privatbrief.*

Je ne saurais appuyer avec assez d'insistance sur la prière que
nous Vous adressons dans notre rapport officiel, de nous munir
par le télégraphe d'instructions plus précises pour la séance de
Mardi prochain. C'est dans cette séance que seront discutées
les questions de principe et que nous verrons s'il nous est possible
de continuer à marcher avec la Prusse, comme nous avons taché
de le faire jusqu'à présent. Le plan de campagne imaginé par
le Cte. Bernstorff—surtout à l'instigation du B^{on}. de Beust—celui
de se renfermer dans une attitude passive, de ne point formuler
de propositions et de laisser venir les autres—ne peut être
soutenu à la longue. Nous ne saurions céder ni aux Neutres, ni
aux Danois le droit de dicter les conditions de la paix. L'initiative que nous avons prise dans la guerre et notre position de
vainqueurs nous imposent l'obligation de déclarer nettement nos
intentions. Je l'avais prédit dès le début à nos collègues allemands, et ce n'est que pour faire preuve de bonne volonté, pour
ne pas nous séparer d'eux, conformément à nos instructions, que
nous avons consenti à partager le rôle équivoque et embarrassant
qu'ils ont joué dans la séance d'hier, où pressé de toutes parts sur
la solution à proposer, le Cte Bernstorff n'a répondu que par des
négations à l'égard du traité de Londres et par des récriminations
sur la mauvaise foi des Danois et a fait table rase de toute
obligation et de tout traité antérieur à la guerre. Ce système
pouvait suffire à remplir une séance, mais il ne peut évidemment
être continué; il a eu en outre le grave inconvénient de trahir une
situation embarrassée, l'absence d'un plan concerté entre les
Alliés, et des arrière-pensées qu'on n'ose pas encore avouer.

Il devient chaque jour plus évident que les P. P. prussiens cherchent à éluder le programme de l'union personnelle combiné entre Vienne et Berlin et qui forme la base de nos instructions tandis que dans celles de nos collègues de Prusse ce programme n'est envisagé que comme une des solutions *possible* et pour ainsi dire, comme un pis-aller. L'arrière-pensée d'un protectorat prussien sous le P^{ce} d'Augustenburg ou d'une annexion pure et simple des Duchés, telle qu'elle est formulée dans la manifeste du parti Ultra-Conservateur prussien, devient de plus en plus transparente et se trouve naturellement encouragée par M. de Beust qui ne cesse de déclarer qu'il se verrait obligé de protester solennellement contre toute solution basée sur le traité de Londres et n'assurant pas l'entière séparation des Duchés avec le Danemarc.

Dans cet état de choses le moment me semble venu pour nous de *prendre couleur*. Si nous n'avons pas l'intention d'aller jusqu'au bout avec les Prussiens, il faudrait pouvoir leur dire quelle sera l'extrême limite jusqu'à laquelle nous pourrons marcher ensemble. Mr. de Bernstorff nous insinue toujours que le langage qu'il est chargé de tenir est concerté avec le Cabinet Imp^1 sans que nous puissions jamais lui prouver le contraire. Des instructions précises que nous pourrions invoquer seraient certainement de nature à ramener notre collègue à une attitude plus correcte et plus conforme à ce qui a été convenu entre les deux Cours. Jusqu'à présent, nous ne nous sommes pas cru autorisés à aller au delà de l'union personnelle, et sur ce terrain je pense que les Puissances neutres et même le Danemarc accepteraient la discussion. Cette limite une fois franchie, je crains que nous ne tombions dans l'inconnu et les aventures et je crois qu'il ne faudrait en tout cas risquer cette chance que si le Danemarc refusait obstinément l'Union personnelle. Dans ce cas, la recherche de nouvelles combinaisons, en dehors du principe de l'intégrité, serait justifiée de notre part, et on ne pourrait nous accuser de ne pas avoir fait notre possible pour faire honneur a notre signature au bas du traité de 1852.

Le plus urgent pour les P. P. Autrichiens, c'est de recevoir le mot d'ordre pour la séance de Mardi et de savoir si—dans le cas où nous ne réussirions pas à décider le Cte Bernstorff à formuler avec nous le programme de l'union personnelle—nous devons le présenter pour notre propre compte, ou bien nous associer à un programme basé sur d'autres combinaisons. Je prie Votre Excellence de considérer que notre responsabilité est grande et le moment très urgent, car il agira peut-être de choisir entre le maintien des principes qui nous ont guidé jusqu'à présent dans cette question, et une séparation possible avec la Prusse qui— personne n'en doute ici—poursuit des plans qu'il ne peut être de notre intérêt de soutenir. Comme nos intentions sont loyales et désintéressées et que nous pouvons les avouer hautement, je ne vois pas pourquoi nous nous mettrions dans la fausse position de ceux qui ne peuvent probablement pas en dire autant.

J'ai laissé jusqu'à présent la parole au Comte Bernstorff, quoique ce soit aux P. P. autrichiens que Lord Russell s'adresse toujours en premier. Mais j'ignore qu'il convient à Votre Excellence que nous continuions ce rôle secondaire et passif qui nous fait parfois endosser des paroles que nous n'aurions osé dire de notre propre crû. Cette position pourrait devenir très embarrassante et c'est pourquoi j'ose insister sur vos ordres, nous traçant plus clairement notre conduite.—Vous aurez vu, mon cher Comte, comment on a travesti ici le combat naval du 10 de ce mois en une ''Great Danish naval victory!'' La vérité commence à se faire jour et la relation contenue dans le ''Times'' d'aujourd'hui forme une exception aussi rare qu'honorable à l'esprit partial et hostile qu'anime la presse anglaise.

Je ne saurais terminer cette lettre sans Vous dire à quel point M. de Biegeleben, par son caractère calme et conciliant et par ses connaissances approfondis a su se concilier l'estime et la confiance de tous les membres de la conférence. Il a acquis parmi eux une véritable autorité et de nombreuses sympathies.

APPONYI AND BIEGELEBEN TO RECHBERG, LONDON, MAY 19, 1864. *Reservirt.*

No. 50 C. Eine streng vertrauliche Unterredung, welche Herr von Biegeleben kurz vor der Sitzung vom 17 d. mit Lord Claren-

don hatte, trug nicht wenig dazu bei, uns in der in dem vorhergehenden gehorsamen Berichte dargelegten Auffassung der Sachlage
zu bestärken.

Dass es nicht möglich sei, die Herzogthümer unter irgendwelchen Bedingungen durch einer in London abzuschliessenden
Vertrage ohne Weiteres dem König Christian IX. zu übergeben,
stand zu augenscheinlich fest, als dass wir nicht hätten wünschen
müssen, über die intentionen der englischen Regierung angesichts
dieser offenbaren Unmöglichkeit ins Klare zu kommen. Gab es
überhaupt noch ein Mittel die Trennung der Herzogthümer von
Dänemark vorzubeugen, so bestand dieses Mittel in dem Vorbehalt eines Rechtsverfahrens oder eines Schieds-Spruches in der
Successionsfrage, und es war uns daran gelegen zu erfahren, in
wie ferne wir für einer solchen zwar dilatorisch wirkenden aber
immerhin die Möglichkeit einer conservativen Lösung in sich
schliessenden Vorbehalt, auf das Verständniss und die Billigung
der englischen Staatsmänner zählen könnten.

Herr von Biegeleben sagte daher dem Grafen Clarendon, dass
wenn die deutschen Mächte in der heutigen Sitzung den Gedanken der Personal-Union nicht anders als mit dem Vorbehalte der
Erledigung des Rechtspunktes zulassen würden, dies von Seite
Oesterreichs in der aufrichtigen Absicht geschehe, die Wiederan-
knüpfung des zerrissenen Bandes zwischen Dänemark und den
Herzogthümern möglich zu erhalten und den Einfluss Frankreichs
und der von dieser Macht vertretenen gefährlichen Prinzipien
von der Lösung der Frage fern zu halten. Jenes Vorbehalt habe
zwar den Nachtheil den endlichen Abschluss hinauszuschieben,
aber er verhindere eben dadurch für jetzt einen Ausgang den für
England so wenig wie für Oesterreich angenehm sein könne, und
es sei keineswegs ausgemacht, dass nicht ein wesentlicher Um-
schlag in der ganzen Lage der Angelegenheit hervorgebracht
würde, wenn die verschiedenen Prätendenten auf die Länder der
dänischen Monarchie in dem Fall gesetzt würden, in einem
regelmässigen Verfahren ihre Titel vorzulegen.

Lord Clarendon äusserte hierauf in den lebhaftesten Aus-
drücken sein Bedauern über den ganzen Gang dieser Sache, und
suchte darzuthun, dass Oesterreich, welches er nur mit Schmerz

von Preussen gewissermassen hingezogen erblicke, entweder mit
Dänemark oder mit der deutschen Bewegung gehen und es nicht
zu der jetzigen Verwickelung hätte kömmen können lassen sollen.
Es war leicht dies zu widerlegen und die Schuld auf England
zurückzuwälzen. In dem Wunsch, den monarchischen Grundsätzen keine neue Niederlage und den Nationalitäts-Tendenzen
keine neuen Triumpf zu bereiten, stimmte Lord Clarendon
vollständig ein, und berief sich darauf, dass er in Paris den Kaiser
Napoleon bewogen habe, dass allgemeine Stimmrecht als Mittel
der Lösung wenigstens nicht in die erste Linie zu stellen. Dann
aber fuhr er fort ungefähr wie folgt:

"Es sei einmal Thatsache, dass die Bevölkerung der Herzogthümer nicht anders als mit Zwang wieder unter einem dänischen
Landesherrn gestellt werden könne. Wer solle diesen Zwang
anwenden? *England wolle nur dieser Sache willen keinen Krieg
führen,* und wer seine Macht nicht anwenden wolle, der habe im
Grund keine Macht. Anderseits würde es für die britische
Regierung und Nation bei der Stimmung, welche gegen Preussen
herrsche, geradezu schmachvoll sein, wenn das ende der Verwicklung in eine Annexion der Herzogthümer an Preussen bestünde.
Ganz England würde lieber das linke Rheinufer, wenn nur
Belgien unangetastet bliebe, an Napoleon fallen sehen, als
Schleswig-Holstein an Preussen. Die Personal-Union endlich,
sei keine richtige Lösung. Er und seine Collegen hätten daher zu
keinem anderen Resultate gelangen können, als dass man sich
des Anspruches der Familie Augustenburg bedienen müsse, um
aus Holstein und einen Theil von Schleswig einen eigenen Staat
zu bilden, und dem Rest von Dänemark die Möglichkeit einer
unangefochtenen National-Existenz zu erhalten."

Dieses waren die mit voller Bestimmtheit ausgesprochenen
Ansichten des englischen Ministers, und wenn auch Lord Claren-
don die Wichtigkeit der möglichen Folgen vollkommen zugab,
und versprach, dass er sich überlegen wolle, ob die englische
Regierung sich auf die Idee einer Suspension der dynastischen
Frage einlassen könne, so geschah diess doch in sehr zweifelnder
und auf ein negatives Resultat vorbereitender Weise, und der
Verlauf der gleich nachher stattgehabten Conferenz-Sitzung war

nicht geeignet, ihn in den bereits früher gewonnenen Anschauungen zu erschüttern.

APPONYI TO RECHBERG, LONDON, MAY 19, 1864. *Privatbrief.*

Quoique nos rapports officiels exposeront à Votre Excellence la situation actuelle, telle qu'elle résulte de la séance d'avant-hier et des circonstances qui l'ont précedée et accompagnée, je me permettrai cependant, quitte à tomber dans des redites, d'accompagner ces rapports de quelques reflexions d'appréciations personnelles pour laquelle je réclame toute Votre indulgence.

Notre position à la Conférence devient de jour en jour plus difficile; nous sommes entièrement isolés. Personne ne veut de notre programme de l'union personnelle. Les Danois le rejettent comme inadmissable, les Duchés comme insuffisant; les Neutres le considèrent comme une solution incomplète et impracticable; Beust, en pleine séance, le déclare inacceptable pour l'Allemagne et la Prusse ne cache pas ses répugnances et fait son possible pour s'y soustraire. Lord Clarendon lui-même s'attendait à ce que le programme d'une séparation complète serait formulé par les Plenipotentiaires allemands. Je pense que cette combinaison, si on laissait au Danemarc le Nord du Schleswig, serait plus avantageuse à ce Royaume, que celle, que nous proposons. Les Plenipotentiaires danois semblent partager cette opinion.

C'est là, en effet, la solution qui a le plus de chances d'être acceptée; la Notre, je regrette de le dire, n'en a aucune. La dernière séance et la conversation que M. de Biegeleben a eue peu d'heures auparavant avec Lord Clarendon, ne me laisse aucune illusion à cet égard.

Il est sûr que si nous ne donnons au Roi Chrétien que *titre nominale* d'une Souveraineté, qu'il n'exercerait plus en réalité puisque les Duchés jouiraient d'une entière indépendance, et si en outre nous faisons dépendre ce simple titre d'un verdict futur et très problématique et renvoyons ainsi aux Calends grecques la solution définitive de la question dynastique,—nous faisons à ce Souverain un bien mince cadeau et l'on ne saurait s'étonner s'il hésite à l'accepter et s'il préfère perdre les provinces qui ne lui appartiendraient plus que de nom, plutôt que de laisser son droit en suspens et son territoire occupé par l'ennemi pendant un temps indéterminé.   Même le Baron de Brunnow, dans sa déclaration écrite et soigneusement rédigée d'avance, n'a plus prononcé le mot *d'intégrité*, qui avait été jusqu'ici son cheval de bataille.   Quant à la France, on sait qu'elle préférerait, et pour cause, une solution radicale.   Si donc l'Angleterre, la Russie et la France semblent disposées à abandonner le terrain du traité de Londres, si la Prusse déchire ce traité et si la Confédération le renie, pourquoi resterions nous seuls à le maintenir, même envers le Danemarc qui repousse nos propositions conciliantes et leur préfère la cession d'une partie de son territoire?

Je crains que dans ces circonstances un changement de front ne soit devenu pour nous une nécessité inévitable.   Plus nous le retarderons et plus nous augmenterons les chances de la Prusse, car ses velléités d'annexion et ses intrigues dans les Duchés ne sont plus un secret pour personne.   Je crois même que la crainte de ce danger est pour beaucoup dans le notable modification qui s'est opérée dans l'attitude des Puissances neutres.   Ce qu'elles demandent, et ce qui doit être aussi notre but, c'est une pacification solide et durable, et elles ne trouvent ni l'une ni l'autre dans l'union personnelle, telle que nous l'entendons, et surtout dans les réserves de droit que nous faisons et qui condamneraient d'avance l'oeuvre de la Conférence à une stérilité complète. Comment, quand et par qui cette question de droit serait-elle décidée; trouverait-on en Allemagne une autorité, un tribunal, un Aréopage quelconque qui oserait trancher cette question en faveur du Roi de Danemarc; n'est-elle pas jugée d'avance par l'arrêt passionée et irréfléchée peut-être mais unanime de toute la nation; — est-il politique et sage de nous épuiser en efforts impuissants en faveur d'une combinaison que tout le monde abandonne, que les Duchés et l'Allemagne entière repoussent et de laisser à nos rivaux seuls tous les avantages d'un triomphe et d'une popularité que nous avions pour but de partager et de contrôler en nous embarquant avec eux dans cette malencontreuse affaire? Je laisse à la sagesse du Gouvernement Impérial de résoudre ces problêmes qui me paraissent mériter de fixer sa plus sérieuse attention. Tant que j'ai pu croire notre solution possible, tant que sa modération même me semblait devoir lui assurer de l'appui et des défenseurs, je l'ai soutenue à outrance, au risque même de me brouiller avec nos soi-disants amis; mais je crois maintenant que notre partie est perdue et qu'il faut la recommencer avec de nouvelles cartes. Il s'agira de nous mettre le moins possible en désaccord avec nos principes et nos antécédents, mais il faudra bien, bon gré mal gré en sacrifier quelque chose. Il deviendra peut-être impossible de convoquer les Etats des Duchés et de les consulter; mais on pourra éviter par là le suffrage populaire sous une forme trop démocratique. D'ailleurs la théorie de l'Union personnelle était pour nous, dans son application a la Hongrie, une doctrine presqu'aussi dangereuse, et celle-là du moins se trouverait écartée.

Il y a un fait sur lequel je ne saurais assez insister, c'est l'accord parfait et de plus en plus intime dans lequel travaillent les Plénipotentiaires prussiens avec M. de Beust. Tout en différant peut-être dans leurs arrière-pensées, ils s'entr'aident pour arriver au même but, la séparation des Duchés d'avec le Danemarc. On ne saurait contester le succès de leurs efforts. Ils sont parvenus à déblayer le terrain, à décourager l'Angleterre et la Russie et à gagner la France. Quoique le Prince de la Tour d'Auvergne défende encore pour la forme le Traité de Londres *parcequ'il* le croit devenu impossible, il agit sous main avec Beust que les Prussiens mettent en avant. On m'assure que Beust, profitant des loisirs que lui laisse l'ajournement de la Conférence au 28., part demain pour Paris et qu'il verra l'Empereur. Son activité et son savoir-faire rendent ce voyage important dans les circonstances actuelles et le Prince Metternich fera bien de surveiller ses intrigues.

Je ne me dissimule pas que le payement des frais de guerre— que nous ne pourrions plus réclamer du Danemarc s'il était condamné à perdre le Holstein et une partie de Schleswig,—est un argument puissant à nos yeux, comme pouvant nous faire hésiter à renoncer à l'union personnelle. Mais le Baron de Beust nous a déjà fait entendre que si la séparation complète venait d'être prononcée, les Duchés et l'Allemagne toute entière seraient trop heureux de se charger de la liquidation de ces réclamations, y compris celles qui remontent à l'année 1852. Je crois presque pouvoir affirmer que pour le moment du moins la paix sera maintenue. On m'assure que si les Duchés étaient constitués en Etat indépendant faisant partie de la Confédération Germanique, la France n'y mettrait aucun obstacle et qu'elle ne demandrait des compensations que s'il s'agissait d'une annexion à la Prusse. Dans ce cas même une rectification de frontières ou un échange de territoire s'opérait probablement d'un commun accord et d'une manière pacifique, sans opposition sérieuse de la part de l'Angleterre, car plus l'Empereur Napoléon sera exigeant vis-à-vis de la Cour de Berlin sous le rapport des compensations, plus l'Angleterre y applaudira, tant est grande la haine de ce pays contre la Prusse et sa politique. Quant à défendre l'intégrité du Danemarc, l'Angleterre n'y songe plus, voyant bien qu'elle resterait seule a tenter cette entreprise. Le Parlement pourra s'émouvoir, le Cabinet pourra être menacé ou même renversé, mais les successeurs de Lord Palmerston ne seront guère plus disposés que lui à faire la guerre pour un intérêt aussi indirect et éloigné. L'attitude récente des Plénipotentiaires anglais donne la mesure de ce que le Cabinet de Copenhague peut attendre de l'appui efficace de la Grande Bretagne. Reste la Russie qui se bornera à des réserves stériles de ses droits de succession.

Je me permettrai de terminer par deux considérations qui me paraissent militer en faveur d'une prompte modification de notre attitude. La première c'est que les retards profiteront aux intrigues et à la propagande de la Prusse et *que si* pour le présent on peut encore compter sur ce que les Etats des Duchés se prononceront contre une annexion prussienne, on ne pourra peut-être plus en être aussi assuré dans quelques mois. La seconde, c'est que les Etats du Midi de l'Allemagne dont nous avons le plus besoin dans la question douanière, sont précisément ceux qui se sont prononcés de la manière la plus absolue dans celle des Duchés. En leur donnant satisfaction sous ce dernier rapport, nous raffermirions leur sympathie et leur concours dans la question commerciale.

Quelque soient les ordres que Votre Excellence jugera à propos de nous transmettre, je La prie de nous les faire parvenir en temps utile pour les exécuter dans la Conférence du 28. et pour y préparer nos collègues.

BIEGELEBEN TO RECHBERG, LONDON, MAY 19, 1864. *Privatbrief.*

So lange als irgend möglich und mit aller Kraft der Ueberzeugung habe ich hier unseren seitherigen Standpunkt vertheidigt; aber die Dänen selbst lassen ihre Monarchie im Stich, die Neutralen unterstutzen uns nicht, die Preussen bestellen sich die Vorschläge, die sie sich nicht unmittelbar in Wien anzubringen getrauen, bei den Engländern und Franzosen, und Bon Beust hat so ungünstig als möglich gewirkt. Ich kann nicht läugnen, dass mir die letzte Conferenzsitzung als der Wendepunkt erscheint, über welchen hinaus wir unsere seitherige Richtung nicht weiter verfolgen können.

Möglich ist allerdings, dass Dänemark den Krieg wieder anfängt, oder dass die Unterhandlungen sich an der Schwierigkeit, eine Gränze in Schleswig zu finden, zerschlagen. Wenn aber keiner dieser beiden nicht sehr wahrscheinlichen Fälle eintritt, so steht jetzt unvermeidlich die Phase der Verhandlung bevor, wo es daraufkommt, über Holstein und einen Theil von Schleswig zu disponiren.

Sollen wir in dieser Voraussetzung unsere Opposition gegen den Augustenburgischen Prätendenten fortsetzen auf die Gefahr hin, dass wenn wir den Preussen behülflich wären, diesen Anspruch zu beseitigen, zuletzt nichts Andres als die Annexion an Preussen übrigbliebe? Diese Frage wäre wohl nur dann zu bejahen, wenn uns eine Compensation, und zwar in Deutschland geboten werden könnte, wozu nirgends eine Aussicht vorhanden ist. Ich muss mir also jetzt wohl als möglich denken, dass man sich überzeugen müsste, der Augustenburgischen Dynastie nicht mehr entgehen zu können. Für diesen Fall sei es mir erlaubt, die Meinung auszudrücken, dass diese Wendung mit einem gewissen Glanz und nicht in einer Art, als ob Oesterreich nur willenlos hingerissen worden wäre, zu vollziehen und dadurch die Stim-

mung für uns zurückgewinnen wäre. Eine ostensible Depesche
nach Berlin, worin gesagt würde, dass Oesterreich gerechter
Bedenken getragen habe, von einem feierlichen europäischen
Vertrage zurückzutreten, dass auch die das Erbrecht der Linie
Augustenburg der Kais. Regierung nicht zweifellos erwiesen sei;
—dass aber jetzt, nachdem Dänemark selbst jede die Fortdauer
des Verbandes mit den Herzogthümern ermöglichende Lösung
zurückgewiesen habe, der Augenblick gekommen sei, wo die
deutschen Mächte denWünschen der Herzogthümer und Deutschlands gemäss, durch das Recht des Siegers ergänzen sollte,
was etwa den Ansprüche des Prinzen von Augustenburg fehlen
müsste, eine solche Depesche rechtzeitig erlassen würde die
Annexion an Preussen unmöglich machen, in Deutschland gut
wirken und doch auch die conservativen Principien noch einigermassen wahren.

Erscheint Eurer Excellenz dieser Vorschlag unrichtig oder gar
indiscret, so bitte ich ihn mir aus dem Grunde zugut zu halten,
weil ich damit nur gleichsam mechanisch meiner Gewohnheit
folge, Eurer Excellenz Referent zu sein.

RECHBERG TO KAROLYI, MAY 24, 1864. DRAFT, NO. 1.

Unsere neuesten Nachrichten aus London lassen keinem
Zweifel mehr darüber Raum, dass die Verhandlungen der Conferenz an einem entscheidenden Wendepunkt angelangt sind.

Von Anbeginn des dänischen Streites bestrebt stets im engsten
Einvernehmen mit Preussen zu wirken, haben wir, als die Haltung
des Bundestags die beiden Mächte nöthigte, die Sache in ihre
eigene Hand zu nehmen, uns sofort zur Pflicht gemacht, mit dem
Berliner Cabinet diejenigen Grundsätze zu vereinbaren, welche
sowohl unser gemeinsames Vorgehen bedingen als den Zweck
unseres Handelns feststellen sollten. Mit Rücksicht auf den
europäischen Character, den die dänische Frage durch den Tod
Friedrich VII. angenommen hatte, konnte natürlich nur der
Londoner Vertrag vom 8. Mai 1852, zu welchem Oesterreich und
Preussen in Gemeinschaft mit den anderen europäischen Mächten
mitgewirkt hatten, den Ausgangspunkt bilden, welcher der

Verständigung zwischen den beiden deutschen Höfen zum Grunde gelegt wurde. Wir haben diese Basis während des Krieges wie nicht minder bei den seitherigen Verhandlungen der Conferenz mit jener Gewissenhaftigkeit festgehalten, welche uns jederzeit hinsichtlich der Beobachtung eingegangener Verträge zur Richtschnur dient. Wir haben um so mehr gerechtes Bedenken zu tragen, von einem feierlichen europäischen Vertrage zurückzutreten, als das von fast allen unseren deutschen Bundesgenossen anerkannte Erbrecht des Augustenburg'schen Hauses uns nicht zweifellos erschien.

Nachdem man aber nunmehr, wie aus den Berichten unserer Bevollmächtigten in London hervorgeht, demnächst darauf gefasst sein muss, dass Dänemark selbst jede die Fortdauer des Verbandes mit den Herzogthümern ermöglichende Lösung zurückweise, so scheint uns jetzt der Augenblick gekommen, wo die deutschen Mächte, den Wünschen der Herzogthümer und Deutschlands gemäss, durch das Recht des Siegers ergänzen sollten, was etwa den Ansprüchen des Herzogs von Augustenburg fehlen möchte.

Die königl. preussische Regierung kennt die Grundsätze, welche uns leiten, zu gut, als dass wir zu betheuern nöthig hatten, dass wir einen Standpunkt, der auf der Heilighaltung der Verträge beruht, nicht aufgeben würden, wenn ihn nicht die hierbei zunächst betheiligte Macht, wie sich neuerlich herausstellt, selbst zu verlassen bereit wäre. Es bleibt uns hiernach nichts anderes zu thun übrig, als unter den verschiedenen Combinationen, welche im Falle einer Lostrennung der Herzogthümer von Dänemark sich darbieten, derjenigen uns anzuschliessen, welche, indem sie die Wünsche und Ansprüche Deutschlands erfüllt, zugleich am wenigsten geeignet scheint, eine Unterbrechung des europäischen Friedens zu veranlassen, dessen ungetrübte Erhaltung wir unter unseren Interessen obenan stellen.

Indem sonach die Nothwendigkeit an uns herantritt, uns zu einem Schritte zu entschliessen, der einen neuen Abschnitt in unserer Politik bezeichnet, müssen wir vor allem wünschen, dabei in vollem Einverständnis mit Preussen zu handeln, von der Ueberzeugung ausgehend, dass der Erfolg, der unser treues

Zusammenwirken im Felde lohnte, unter gleicher Voraussetzung uns auch auf dem Gebiete der Verhandlungen nicht entgehen könne. Ich beeile mich daher, um das kgl. Cabinet in genaue Kenntnis von unserer gegenwärtigen Auffassung zu setzen, Ew. hierneben eine Abschrift der neuen Instructionen zu übermitteln, welche ich auf Befehl S. M. des Kaisers u. a. H. an unsere Bevollmächtigten in London eventuell zu richten im Begriffe stehe.

Wir sind überzeugt, dass die kgl. preussische Regierung nicht weniger als wir die ernsten Gefahren würdigt und darum zu vermeiden strebt, die jede Territorialveränderung herbeiführen müsste, welche eine Umgestaltung des bestehenden Gleichgewichtes der Grossmächte zur Folge hätte. Aus diesem Grunde müssten wir uns aufs Entschiedenste gegen eine Lösung aussprechen, die uns ohne allen Zweifel in die bedrohlichsten Verwicklungen stürzen würde, ohne uns dafür irgend einen anderweitigen zureichenden Ersatz zu sichern.

Wir waren schon öfters in der Lage, die kgl. preussische Regierung auf die Bedenken aufmerksam zu machen, die jedes Zugeständnis an das Nationalitätsprinzip, wie es von französischer Seite vorangestellt wird, oder die damit zusammenhängende Entscheidung der Frage mittelst einer allgemeinen Volksabstimmung in seinen weiteren Folgen erregen muss. Eine Befürwortung der Augustenburg'schen Souveränität scheint uns hingegen auch darum sich zu empfehlen, weil bei der diesfalls sattsam verlautbarten Meinung der Herzogthümer eine weitere Befragung der dortigen Bevölkerung als gänzlich überflüssig sich herausstellt und die Thätigkeit der Stände, deren Einberufung nach vollendetem Werke zu London wir für nothwendig erachten, sich von selbst auf einen einstimmigen Huldigungsact beschränken dürfte.

Wir schmeicheln uns mit der zuversichtlichen Erwartung dass das königl. preussische Cabinet, dem ohne Zweifel gleichartige Berichte über die Sachlage in London zugekommen sind, zu ähnlichen Schlüssen gelangt ist, wie wir sie im Vorhergehenden kurz zu entwickeln versuchten. Indem wir wie immer das grösste Gewicht darauf legen, über den wünschenswerten Einklang beruhigt zu werden, der sich durch den Gang der Verhältnisse in der beiderseitigen Auffassung gebildet hat, hoffen wir, dass derselbe demnächst in dem übereinstimmenden Auftreten der betreffenden Bevollmächtigten in London seinen Ausdruck finden wird.

Ich ersuche Ew. den gegenwärtigen Erlass nebst Beilage dem königl. Hr. Minister-Präsidenten vertraulich mitzutheilen und mir über dessen diesfällige Aeusserungen ungesäumt Bericht zu erstatten.

N. B. Mit Depesche vom 24 Mai 1864 Nr. 2 nach *London* mitgetheilt und mit jener vom 24 Mai 1864 Nr. 1 nach *Paris* und mit jener vom 25. und 26. Mai 1864 dem Baron *Kübeck* und nach München und mit *Circulare* vom 28. Mai 1864 den übrigen k. Gesandtschaften sowie dem Gf. Revertera.

RECHBERG TO KAROLYI, MAY 24, 1864. DRAFT NO. 2.

Indem Ew. aus meinem vorhergehenden Erlasse im allgemeinen die wichtigsten Entschlüsse entnehmen werden, bei denen wir durch den Gang der Londoner Verhandlungen angelangt sind, bietet mir Ihr Bericht Nr. 51 A. vom 20. d. M. einen willkommen-en Anlass dar, auf einige damit zusammenhängende Punkte näher einzugehen.

Da wir Werth darauf legen nach aufgeben des Londoner Vertrags von 1852 durch Befürwortung der Ansprüche des Prin-zen von Augustenburg wieder einen Rechtsboden zu gewinnen, welcher eine Entscheidung nach blossen Nationalitätsprincipien zu vermeiden geeignet wäre,so halten wir es auch für zweckmässig, dass die Anerkennung des ebenerwähnten Erbrechtes im Princip auf das gesammte Gebiet der Herzogthümer Schleswig und Holstein ausgedehnt werden sollte. Nachdem wir aber darauf-gefasst sein müssen von anderer Seite nachdrücklich die Forde-rung geltend gemacht zu sehen, dass die dem dänischen Stamme angehörigen Bewohner des nördlichen Schleswig unmöglich unter deutscher Oberhoheit bleiben und dem Bunde einverleibt werden könnten, so scheint uns in dem in Ihrem gedachten Berichte erwähnten Vorschlag eines Austausches des Herzogthumes Lauenburg gegen einen entsprechenden Theil von Schleswig ein ganz angemessenes Auskunftsmittel geboten, um dem Wunsche der Anhänger des Nationalitätsprincips factisch entgegen zu kommen, ohne sich dieses selbst und die möglicher Weise daraus zu ziehenden Folgerungen anzueignen. Es wird daher unter dieser Voraussetzung genügen eine geographische Linie zu ermitteln, welche eine billige Compensation der beiden Objecte bezweckt, jedoch müsste unseres Erachtens einem solchen Ausgleiche die Anerkennung der Augustenburg'schen Souveränität vorhergehen, weil dann die fragliche Transaction den Character einer Auseinandersetzung zwischen dem Könige von Dänemark und dem neuen Herzog von Schleswig-Holstein erhielte, statt für eine ebenso schwierige als bedenkliche Scheidung nach nationalen Gegensätzen zu gelten.

Sollte von der Conferenz eine Lostrennung der Herzogthümer von Dänemark und die Errichtung eines selbständigen Schleswig-Holstein als Glied des deutschen Bundes beschlossen werden, so dürfte nach unserem Dafürhalten auch die Nothwendigkeit hinwegfallen die Gründung einer Bundesfestung auf dortigem Gebiete unter die Bedingungen des Friedens mit Dänemark ausdrücklich aufzunehmen. Es würde sich dieser Punkt dann besser dafür eignen in die Modalitäten einbegriffen zu werden unter welchen der Bund sich dem neuen Souverän gegenüber zu dessen Aufnahme unter die Bundesglieder bereit erklärt.

Ein Gegenstand der für uns von grösster Wichtigkeit ist, betrifft die Oesterreich gebührende Geldentschädigung, welche sich bekanntlich theils auf die vorlängst beim Bunde angemeldeten Kosten der Execution in Holstein vom J. 1851-1852 theils auf die in dem jetzigen Kriege erwachsenen Ausgaben bezieht.

Wenn die Conferenz Dänemark dazu nöthigen sollte, in eine Abtretung der Herzogthümer einzuwilligen, so ist vorauszusehen, dass die kriegführenden deutschen Mächte nicht werden durchsetzen können, der so bedeutend geschmälerten dänischen Monarchie auch noch diese Last aufzubürden. Es scheint uns auch aufrichtig gestanden nicht mehr als billig, dass die Lasten der Befreiung von demjenigen Theile getragen werden, dem sie zu Gute kommen und sind wir daher der Ansicht, dass der entsprechende Ersatz unserer militärischen Auslagen von dem neuen schleswig-holsteinischen Staate zu übernehmen wäre.

Hinsichtlich einer mehr als einmonatlichen Verlängerung der bestehenden Waffenruhe treten wir den betreffenden Ansichten der kgl. preuss. Regierung vollkommen bei und werden unsere Bevollmächtigten in London anweisen, sich diesfalls der von ihren preuss. Collegen zu stellenden Forderung in der nächsten Sitzung anzuschliessen.

Ew. wollen den gegenwärtigen Erlass vertraulich zur Kenntnis des Herrn Ministerpräsidenten bringen, der daraus entnehmen wird, wie sehr unsere eigenen Anschauungen mit den seinigen in den Ihnen gegenüber berührten Punkten übereinstimmen. Es würde uns besondere Befriedigung gewähren, wenn auch die übrigen vorgehends entwickelten Bemerkungen wie wir hoffen dürfen, die Zustimmung Herrn von Bismarck's finden werden worüber wir Ihrer baldigen Berichterstattung entgegensehen.

N. B. Mit Depesche vom 24. Mai 1864 Nr. 2 nach London mitgetheilt und mit jener vom 24. Mai Mr. 1 nach *Paris*.

RECHBERG TO KAROLYI, MAY 24, 1864. *Post-Script ad Nr. 2.*

Ich war gestern eben auf dem Punkte die beiden vorhergehenden Erlässe über die Londoner Conferenzen an Ew. abgehen zu lassen, als mir Frh. von Werther eine Depesche seiner Regierung vom 21. d. M. mittheilte, die denselben Gegenstand behandelt. Es gereichte mir zur ganz besonderen Befriedigung aus deren Inhalte entnehmen zu können, dass die beiden Cabinete, auf gleichartige Wahrnehmungen gestützt, sich völlig in der Beurtheilung der jetzigen Sachlage begegnen und dass somit die Erwartung, die ich am Schlusse meines Erlasses Nr. 1 mir auszusprechen erlaubte, so schnell und vollständig erfüllt worden ist. Der Uebereinstimmung der beiden Höfe nunmehr gewiss, werde ich noch heute die neuen Instructionen an unsere Bevollmächtigten in London befördern.

RECHBERG TO KAROLYI, MAY 24, 1864. DRAFT, NO. 3.

Freih. von Werther hatte die Güte mir einen vertraulichen
Erlass des Königl. Hr. Minister-Präsidenten vom 21. d. M.
vorzulesen, welcher die eventuelle Anerkennung der Erbansprüche
des Prinzen von Augustenburg bespricht.

Wir theilen vollkommen die diesfalls entwickelten Ansichten
des Berliner Cabinetes und würden es namentlich für sehr
wichtig halten, ungesäumt dahin zu wirken, dass der Prinz
alsbald aus der Athmosphäre heraustrete, in der er sich leider
bisher bewegte und die, wie Hr. v. Bismarck treffend bemerkt,
weder den Zwecken, welche die beiden Mächte bei Errichtung
des neuen schleswig-holstein'schen Staates im Auge haben, noch
auch den wahren Bedürfnissen und Stimmungen der Herzogthümer selbst entspricht.　Es erschiene uns aus diesem Grunde
als wünschenswerth, wenn die kgl. Regierung sich bewogen
fände ohne Aufsehen und Verzug eine geeignete Vertrauensperson
an den Prinzen abzusenden, welche denselben in dem oben
erwähnten Sinne aufklären und ihn zu einer mit seinen wohlver-
standenen Interessen mehr im Einklang stehenden Haltung
verpflichten könnte.

Ew. wollen gefälligst dem H. v. Bismarck den gegenwärtigen
Erlass vertraulich mittheilen . . . .

APPENDIX VIII

EXTRACTS FROM THE PRUSSIAN, AUSTRIAN, AND BRITISH AR-
CHIVES ILLUSTRATING RUSSIAN POLICY.

EXTRACT OF REPORT FROM THE PRUSSIAN MINISTER, COUNT
REDERN, ST. PETERSBURG, FEBRUARY 3, 1864.

No. 13. .... "C'est donc la guerre générale que Vous
voulez," rief der Fürst [Gorchakov]. "Certes" sagte er, "personne ne peut Vous empêcher de déclarer la guerre au Danemarc,
mais personne ne saurait empêcher la France, l'Angleterre et la
Suède de venir au secours du Danemarc. La Russie ne fera
jamais rien contre la Prusse mais vous aurez les trois autres sur
les bras et vous aurez ramené l'entente entre la France et l'Angleterre."

Ich bemerkte dem Fürsten nochmals, dass Preussen so wie auch
Oesterreich sehr weit davon entfernt seien, Dänemark den Krieg
erklären zu wollen. Dänemark erkläre uns vielmehr den Krieg,
wenn es sich uns in Schleswig feindlich gegenüber halte. Ich
bezweifle indess sehr, setzte ich hinzu, dass England den Dänen
in diesem Falle zu Hülfe eilen werde; ebenso wenig könne ich
glauben, dass Frankreich gemeinschaftlich mit England gegen
uns vorgehen wolle. Ich halte mich vielmehr zu der Annahme
berechtigt, dass der Kaiser Louis Napoleon, den Unwillen
Englands mit Schadenfreude betrachten, und in Stillen darüber
frohlocken würde, dass England in der obschwebenden Frage auf
dem Rücken der Dänen einige Schläge davontrage.

"Mais ce n'est pas pour les beaux yeux des Danois que
l'Europe est reconnue de son intégrité, c'est dans un intérêt
Européen que le protocol a été signé et cet intérêt prévaut
encore aujourd'hui et nous est commun," rief der Kanzler.
[He was interrupted by an usher who brought a telegram from
Kiel with news of a fight near Missunde.] Der Vice Kanzler war

über dieses Telegramm tief erschüttert und brach mehrmals in die bereit angeführten Worte aus: "C'est la guerre générale. Vous aurez la France, l'Angleterre et la Suède contre Vous. La Russie jamais. Jamais elle ne marchera contre la Prusse."....

THUN TO RECHBERG, TELEGRAM, ST. PETERSBURG, JAN. 18, 1864; 11:35 A. M.-2:40 P. M.

No. 2. Le Cabinet britannique se montrant inquiet des démarches des Cours de l'Autriche et de la Prusse vis-à-vis du Danemarc, Prince Gorchacov croit urgent de le tranquilliser sur nos véritables intentions, pour prévenir scission entre les *"quatre Cours conservatrices."*

THUN TO RECHBERG, ST. PETERSBURG, 26/14 JAN., 1864.

No. 1 B. Les relations entre les Cabinets de St. Petersbourg et de Londres deviennent de jour en jour plus intimes. ....
Le P^{ce} Gortchacow qui, il n'y a pas longtemps, semblait vouloir laisser au Danemarc seul la responsabilité de sa mauvaise foi dans ses rapports avec l'Allemagne, en est maintenant, grâce à l'influence de Lord Napier, à considérer l'intégrité de la Monarchie danoise comme une nécessité européenne de laquelle il fallait tenir compte n'importe que ce pays remplisse ou non ses engagements internationaux.

Je crois devoir mentionner ici quelques mots addressés par le Vice-Chancelier à Lord Napier en ma présence. "Nous pourrions parler," lui a-t-il dit, "plus énergiquement à Copenhague mais comme l'Empereur est décidé à ne faire marcher un homme ou à dépenser un sou ni pour, ni contre le Danemarc, je dois me borner à des conseils."

J'ai pris acte de cette déclaration, mais comme il ne coûte rien au P^{ce} Gortchacow de revenir sur sa parole il me parait qu'il ne faudrait cependant pas y attacher une trop grande valeur.

THUN TO RECHBERG, ST. PETERSBURG, 4 FEB./23 JAN. 1864.

No. 2 A.-B. .... Le Vice-Chancelier revient dans chaque entretien sur son idée favorite de l'alliance intime des quatres grandes Puissances en disant qu'il fallait sacrifier des intérêts, graves sans aucune doute, mais minimes en comparaison du grand but qu'on se propose, c'est à dire le maintien et la consolidation de la paix européenne.

Le Prince m'a encore répété, qu'en reconnaissant formellement l'intégrité de la monarchie Danoise nous ferions un grand pas dans cette voie. Aussi a-t-il été fort satisfait lorsque je lui ai communiqué le télégramme de Votre Excellence concernant les notes identiques remises à Londres. Il considère cette démarche comme étant de nature à calmer les appréhensions du cabinet anglais. ....

THUN TO RECHBERG, TELEGRAM, ST. PETERSBURG, FEB. 22, 1864; 3:6-9:20 P. M.

No. 3. .... Prince Gortchacow considère l'entrée dans le Jutlande très grave; il m'a dit: Mr. de Bismarck se fait illusions sur l'attitude de la France et l'Autriche en sera la victime innocente.

KNORRING TO RECHBERG, *Particulière*, VIENNA FEB. 22, 1864.

Les nouvelles reçues à St. Petersbourg de Londres et de Paris signalent une irritation fort vive produite par l'annonce de l'entrée des troupes austro-prussiennes en Jutlande. M. le Prince Gortchacow m'exprime l'appréhension que les avantages que cette mesure pourra avoir momentanément sous la rapport militaire ne soient contrebalancés par de sérieux inconvéniens politiques. Il croit d'ailleurs devoir abandonner à la sagesse des deux Cabinets alliés de peser les conséquences de la résolution qu'ils viennent de prendre. ....

KNORRING TO RECHBERG, *Particulière*, VIENNA, FEB. 28, 1864.

D'après des informations transmises par notre Ambassadeur à Londres, on croyait y savoir qu'une explosion insurrectionnelle était imminente en Galicie.

Les nouvelles que je reçois de diverses parts viennent à l'appui de cette donnèe. ....

KNORRING TO RECHBERG, *Particulière*, MAY 28, 1864; *Matin.*

Je crois ne pas devoir perdre un seul moment à informer Votre Excellence que, d'après un télégramme du Vice-Chancelier qui vient de parvenir, notre Plénipotentiaire à Londres maintiendra les principes du droit public. Selon M. le Pce. Gortchacow il est urgent que la succession ne soit pas préjugée, mais réservée à celui qui prouvera juridiquement les droits historiques, conformément à la doctrine qui a été soutenue jusqu'ici par les grandes puissances allemandes. Il en résulterait une combinaison, dans tous les cas, moins dangereuse pour la cause de l'ordre que ne le serait le choix de Duc d'Augustenbourg. Le Prince Gortchacow espère que Votre Excellence voudra bien faire munir Mr. le Comte d'Apponyi d'instructions d'urgence a cet effet. ....

KNORRING TO RECHBERG, VIENNA, JUNE 14, 1864.

Un mot du P^{ce} Gortchacow de Berlin m'informe que d'après les nouvelles données par le Bn. de Brunnow, il avait été décidé dans le dernier conseil de faire des ouvertures à la France pour s'entendre avec elle sur les mesures à opposer aux nouvelles exigences des puissances allemandes. L'Angleterre se verrait ainsi poussée à rendre l'Empereur Napoléon l'arbitre de la situation. Il dépendra de lui de rétablir l'alliance entre la France et l'Angleterre sur la base qui lui convient le mieux.

Dans cette situation un prompt retour de la part des puissances allemandes dans la voie de la modération parait le seul moyen d'éviter à l'Europe l'humiliation de voir l'Empereur Napoléon appelé à décider de son sort.

Le Prince Gortchacow aime à compter à cette effet sur l'esprit de conciliation du Cabinet de Vienne qui moins que tout autre saurait méconnaître le danger de la combinaison que l'attitude actuelle des puissances allemandes rend imminente.

Ne pouvant plus espérer de voir Votre Excellence avant Son départ, vue l'heure avancée de la matinée, j'ai cru remplir un devoir de conscience, en Lui exprimant par écrit, sans retard, les graves réflexions que M. le Vice-Chancelier m'avait chargé de signaler à Son attention.

NAPIER TO RUSSELL, SECRET AND CONFIDENTIAL, ST. PETERS-BURG, MAY 24, 1864.

No. 267. My despatch to your Lordship No. 265 of the 23rd inst. contains the formal report of my confidential question to Prince Gortchakoff and of His Excellency's reply in regard to the contemplated adjustment between Denmark and Germany on the basis of the separation of Holstein and of a portion of Schleswig from the Danish monarchy. The conversation did not however pass off so simply. When I asked Prince Gortchakoff whether he would give his energetic support to Her Majesty's Government in securing a defensible frontier for Denmark, irrespective of the mere question of local nationality, I hinted that it might be necessary to take a firm stand and make the Germans feel that there was a point at which they would meet an armed resistance to their extravagant pretensions.

The Vice Chancellor smiled rather significantly and said that in forming his views on this subject, he ''did not take even into contemplation the contingency of armed intervention from any quarter whatever.''

I said to the Prince that his expressions were important, I had certainly never led Her Majesty's Government to hope that Russia would give armed assistance to Denmark against Germany, but neither had I ever said that in no case whatever would Russia go to war for Denmark. From his present expressions I understood that not only he had resolved in no case to go to war in this quarrel, but that he believed no other Government would ever go to war.

The Vice Chancellor then qualified his first expressions and said that he did not mean to affirm that under no circumstances whatever would Russia take up arms for Denmark, no Government could bind itself by such absolute declarations, he meant that the contingency of armed intervention seemed so improbable and remote, that he did not allow that consideration to affect his resolutions.

I made no doubt however, that the first expressions used by the Vice Chancellor conveyed his real opinion. He is under the impression that Her Majesty's Government will accede to any terms which the German Powers may impose on Denmark and that under no circumstances will England have recourse to arms. This belief is shared by Baron Brunnow and by the German Representatives in the Conference and the attitude of the Russian Cabinet is no doubt in some degree influenced by this consideration. I am bound, however, to state that in the instructions addressed to Vienna, Prince Gortchakoff has gone rather beyond his own real impressions by constantly conveying to Count Rechberg the opinion that there is a point beyond which it would be dangerous to count upon the inaction of England.

Prince Gortchakoff, in my humble judgment, believes that Her Majesty's Government will swerve from the principle of a military frontier in Schleswig, just as they are ready to swerve from the Treaty of 1851 [sic] and the integrity of the Danish Monarchy. The political necessities which have conducted England to the first concession will conduct her to the second. With such impressions it seems natural that the Russian Minister should make no great efforts and incur no great risks with his German allies in contending for the interests of Denmark. The intervention of Prince Gortchakoff on behalf of Denmark will be proportioned to the estimate which he makes of the eventual attitude of England. If he believes that England will yield, he will interfere faintly and formally for Denmark. If he believes that England will fight, he will interfere earnestly and zealously and push his mediation almost to the verge of an alienation from

Prussia. The Vice Chancellor must be aware that a war between England and the German Powers would probably involve the explosion of the revolutionary forces in Italy, Hungary and Poland. Such an explosion would be extremely hazardous to Russia and would be pregnant with incalculable contingencies to all the Continental Governments. To avoid such a catastrophe, the Russian Sovereign would no doubt make considerable exertions, but while the catastrophe is regarded as impossible, he will make no real exertions at all.

In my humble opinion therefore, Her Majesty's Government will do well if they desire to have an effectual support from Russia, to make up their minds to stand at all hazards on certain terms and having done so they will do well to make their resolution known and felt here and the impression will soon be conveyed to Vienna and Berlin.

In offering this respectful expression of my opinion, I need not say that I disclaim all pretension to reflect on the past policy of Her Majesty's Government or to advise on their future course. The sentiments which I submit are conditional and hypothetical. It is consistent with my local knowledge and duty to state to Her Majesty's Government that if they look for support at St. Petersburg, they ought in my mind to do this or that, but it belongs to Her Majesty's Government who possess a view of our foreign relations on every side to put the alternative of peace or war in the Danish question under any circumstances. I think on the whole it might be done with safety on the question of a defensible military frontier in Schleswig, for I think that Russia and Austria would make Prussia yield, but there would probably be a dangerous crisis and Her Majesty's Government who have cognizance of the intentions of France can alone determine whether the hazard is one which ought to be confronted. (Rec'd May 30.)

NAPIER TO RUSSELL, MOST CONFIDENTAL, ST. PETERSBURG, MAY 25, 1864.

No. 271. I learn from Prince Gortchakoff this morning that the Russian Cabinet is disposed to support the proposal for a separation of Holstein and of a portion of Schleswig from Denmark, leaving the Danish kingdom in the possession of a military frontier on the South. This plan will, however, not be advocated without the assent of the King of Denmark, for the Emperor would not have the appearance of exerting an ungenerous pressure on the resolution of the Danish Sovereign.

Instructions were despatched in this sense to Baron Brunnow yesterday by telegraph and this morning by messenger.

In making this communication to me the Vice Chancellor having made use of expressions which implied a justifiable regret that the basis of the Treaty of 1852 was probably to be abandoned, under the pressure of irresistible political necessities, I asked the Prince whether he was disposed to make a last effort for the preservation of that Treaty, for if such was the case I would immediately communicate his view to Her Majesty's Government.

The Vice Chancellor replied that he was not disposed to do so, he would not be "more Catholic than the Pope," the Danish Government itself seemed to prefer the principle of separation to that of a personal union with onerous obligations.

Should the principle of a division of Schleswig be adopted, no doubt a formidable dispute will arise on the nature and locality of the frontier. If Her Majesty's Government be determined to secure the benefit of a defensible military boundary for Denmark, irrespective of the ethnological features of the population behind it, and if they look to the zealous cooperation of Russia for this purpose, I take the liberty of recording my opinion that such cooperation can only be secured by making the Russian Government feel that England will support that settlement at all hazards, if necessary by arms. (Rec'd May 30.)

APPENDIX IX

Bismarck and Sweden

There appear occasionally in the sources for the year 1863, statements that Bismarck had approached the Swedish government with suggestions for an eventual division of the Danish Monarchy between Prussia and Sweden. It is difficult to check the accuracy of such reports but there may be some foundation for them. It is clear that Bismarck kept in mind the possibility of tempting Sweden to support, or at least, not to oppose his designs on the duchies of Schleswig and Holstein. The sober reports of the Prussian minister at Stockholm and the information that leaked out about the negotiations for an alliance of Sweden with Denmark made the prospects of Swedish co-operation in an anti-Danish policy seem very slight and Sweden played no part in Bismarck's calculations comparable to those of the Great Powers. Swedish aid to Denmark would, however, have made the operations in Schleswig more difficult. Early in December 1863, therefore, a Prussian officer, *Oberst-Leutnant* Voight-Rhetz, was sent to Sweden to observe and report on the military preparations of that state.[1]

The following report of the Prussian minister at Stockholm is of especial interest. It was written at a time when pressure was being put on King Charles in the hope of ensuring his support for Denmark and when the Swedish minister at Copenhagen seems to have raised the hopes of the Danish Minister President.[2]

Rosenberg to Bismarck, Stockholm, December 15, 1863. (Berlin Archives).

Eure Excellenz haben bereits vor einem Jahre meine Aufmerksamkeit auf dem Werth einer Verständigung mit Schweden

---

[1] Roon to Bismarck, December 2, 1863, (Berlin Archives).
[2] Cf. pp. 147 ff., 153 f.

über die dänische Frage namentlich in Hinblick auf den Plan eines skandinavischen Reiches gelenkt. Bis jetzt ist zu dieser so wünschenswerthen Eventualität, wie meine Berichterstattung und der Gang der schwedischen Politik Eurer Excellenz bewiesen haben wird, keine Aussicht vorhanden gewesen. Der Skandinavismus hatte, während ich hier bin, eine so deutschfeindliche Richtung, und die erlauchten Personen, aus deren wahren Interesse man mit Recht den Wünsch einer Verständigung mit Deutschland über Dänemarks Zukunft folgert, hatten in der polnischen, wie letzthin in der Allianzfrage sich als die besondern Träger dieses falschverstandenen Skandinavismus hingestellt so dass die Möglichkeit einer Verständigung nicht hervortrat, es vielmehr im preussischen Interesse nur zu liegen schien, die, auf eine Stärkung des dänischen Widerstands und Einverleibung Schleswigs hingerichteten Bestrebungen des schwedischen Skandinavismus entschieden zu bekämpfen. Ungeachtet meines begrenzten Wirkungskreises und der beschränkten Hilfsmittel welche mir zu Gebote stehen, glaube ich in dieser Hinsicht nicht ganz ohne Erfolg thätig gewesen zu sein.

Seit dem Tode Königs Friedrichs VII hat sich die Lage verändert. Die persönlichen Engagements der beiden nordischen Könige hat der Tod des einen gebrochen. Der neue König hat seine skandinavische Probe noch nicht abgelegt und bei seiner unsichern Stellung, und den sich an einen etwaigen Regierungswechsel knüpfenden Hoffnungen wünscht man, wie mir versichert wird, an gewisser Stelle nur eine solche Politik Dänemark gegenüber einzuschlagen, die der, für die Pläne der Bernadottes unerlässlichen Popularität in Kopenhagen, nicht aber dem König Christian zu Statten kommt.

Aus diesem Gesichtspunkt entsprang das Bedauern welches Prinz Oskar geäussert haben soll, als das Ableben des Königs von Dänemark den Aufschub der Allianzunterzeichnung nach sich zog. "Hätten wir jetzt," so soll der Prinz ausgerufen haben, "die Allianz geschlossen, und stünden wir mit 20,000 Mann in Schonen, so würden sich die Dinge in Kopenhagen etwas anders gestaltet haben."

Diese dynastische Wünsche dürften indess, wie in dem ganzen

Verlauf der letzten Jahre, durch die Stellung der Kgl. Familie im Lande ihre natürliche Grenze finden, in dem sie zwar populär aber nicht von entscheidenden Gewicht ist. Das Land versteht sich wohl zu skandinavischen Demonstrationen, nicht aber zu wirklichen Opfern für die Dynastie. Es ist in der Theorie allenfalls skandinavisch; die praktischen Konsequenzen würde es nur dann übernehmen, wenn es vollkommen ungefährlich geschehen könnte.

Ein weiteres Hinderniss eines entschiedenen Vorgehens liegt in der Persönlichkeit des Königs. Die Schwierigkeit, diesen Monarchen zu einem grossen Entschluss zu bringen, im Verein mit Seiner Leichtigkeit Sich bei den ersten Hindernissen zu entmuthigen, dürften diesen, sonst zu einer militärischen Rolle so geeigneten Fürsten, für eine kühne und rücksichtslose Politik nicht besonders befähigen.

Im Allgemeinen darf man nicht vergessen, dass Schwedens Auftreten durch die Stellung der Grossmächte zu Dänemark bemessen wird, und dass namentlich die Haltung welche Preussen zu den verschiedenen Gestaltungen einnimmt, denen die Dänische Frage entgegengeht, von einem gewissen Gewicht fur die hiesigen Entschlüsse sein wird. . . . .

APPENDIX X

DID BISMARCK ENCOURAGE DANISH RESISTANCE, DECEMBER 1863, JANUARY 1864?

In a well known passage in his memoirs, Beust discusses Bismarck's policy in the Schleswig-Holstein question and describes one of the latter statesman's qualities as one "for which only the English language has an adequate expression—unscrupulous."[1] As an illustration of this he tells how, in the course of a conversation with Bismarck at Gastein in 1865, he had said: "You forget one thing, and that is what would have happened if the Danes had avoided a combat." Bismarck replied: "That was all taken care of. I had let it be known in Copenhagen, that England, which was not really the case, had threatened us with effective intervention in the case of armed attack [on Schleswig]."[2]

In somewhat different form, the statement appears in the diary of Dalwigk, the Hessian minister president and in a letter of the latter to Gagern, his minister at Vienna. Dalwigk notes under date of September 9, 1865 that Beust showed him a report to his government, written on August 17 at Giessen, where he had had a conversation with Bismarck. The latter had said among other things, that "Prussia, before the entry of the troops into Schleswig, had intentionally posed conditions to the Danes which the latter could not have fulfilled. Then he, Bismarck, had secretly[3] stirred up the Danes to resistance and through his agents aroused in them the confident expectation of English aid, although he had

---

[1] Beust, *Aus drei Vierteljahrhunderten*, I, p. 350. "Uebersetzen lässt sich das Wort nicht. Rücksichtlos wäre zu wenig, gewissenlos zu viel. Man musste funf Worte für eines setzen: 'um die Mittel nicht verlegen,' "

[2] *Ibid.*

[3] "unter der Hand."

assured himself in advance that England could not and would not give this help. .... "[4]

It is possible that in speaking of ''secret agents,'' Bismarck was exaggerating. There seems to be no other evidence of their action and it is not easy to conjecture how they would have operated under the given circumstances. It is possible that what Bismarck had in mind was a statement which appeared in the *Norddeutsche Allgemeine Zeitung* on January 1, 1864, as semi-official[5] and was reprinted in the *Berlingske Tidende* and other Copenhagen newspapers on the morning of January 2. This stated that the British Government had already protested against the Austro-Prussian proposal to the Diet at Frankfurt for the occupation of Schleswig, and had informed the German Governments that "in case German troops crossed the Eider, England would give Denmark the aid desired.''

Count Bernstorff, the Prussian ambassador in London, in a report of January 4, 1864 called Bismarck's attention to this article and expressed his surprise that, if the information were well-founded, Earl Russell had not given him or the Austrian ambassador any indication of it.[6] In his reply Bismarck explained that such a declaration of the British government had not indeed, been contained in the dispatches to the British ambassador which had recently been read to him but that information from Vienna and the utterances of the British ambassador up to the last few days, had offered some justification for the statements published.[7]

Bismarck did not, however, explain to Bernstorff that he himself, in various conversations with the British ambassador, had urged that the British Government use stronger language in its notes to Germany. ''The only suggestion which he had to make on the nature of Your Lordship's proposed communi-

---

[4] W. Schüssler, *Die Tagebücher des Freiherrn Reinhard v. Dalwigk zu Lichtenfels*, p. 185. Cf. Dalwigk to Gagern, September 20, 1865, in Vogt, *Die Hessische Politik*, pp. 212 f.

[5] ''Unter halbamtlichen Anstrich.''

[6] Berlin Archives.

[7] Bismarck, *Die gesammelten Werke*, IV, p. 274.

cation [to the Diet]," Sir Andrew Buchanan reported on December 26,

> was that the language which Her Majesty's Government proposed to use is not sufficiently decided, as an impression prevailed throughout Germany, which is daily increased by the Liberal press, that Great Britain will not seriously oppose an attempt of the Confederation to separate Holstein and Schleswig from the Danish Monarchy. It was desirable therefore in a communication which was in reality addressed to the people and the Governments of Germany, that Her Majesty's Government should use the strongest language compatible with diplomatic forms, to convince them and more particularly the people of the Northern Sea-board that they are following a course which may expose their coasts to a blockade by a British Fleet.
>
> If Her Majesty's Government therefore, are in earnest, he said, they should let the people of Germany know the risk they are incurring, and he had no doubt the more sensible among them would then think how far it would be wise to allow the passions of the day to carry them.[8]

A few days later, on December 31, Sir Andrew reported that "in regard to your Lordship's last communication to the Diet at Frankfurt, [Bismarck] said he feared it was expressed in too mild language for the occasion—as the people and the Governments of Germany believe that they may carry out their views on the Danish Duchies with impunity. ...."[9]

Bismarck may have desired to impress on the people and governments of Germany a sense of the danger they were incurring and so to make them more amenable to Prussian and Austrian influence, but strong notes from Great Britain and even more, the article in the *Norddeutsche Allgemeine Zeitung*, were as likely to rouse the expectations and the spirit of resistance of the Danes.

[8] Buchanan to Russell, No. 642, December 26, 1863 (Record Office, London). The passage cited has been marked with a pencil line on the margin of the original.
[9] No. 644 (Record Office, London).

APPENDIX XI.

GENEALOGY OF THE HOUSE OF OLDENBURG, TO ILLUSTRATE THE SUCCESSION TO THE DANISH MONARCHY. (BRANCHES WHICH HAVE NO IMPORTANCE IN THE NINETEENTH CENTURY ARE OMITTED).

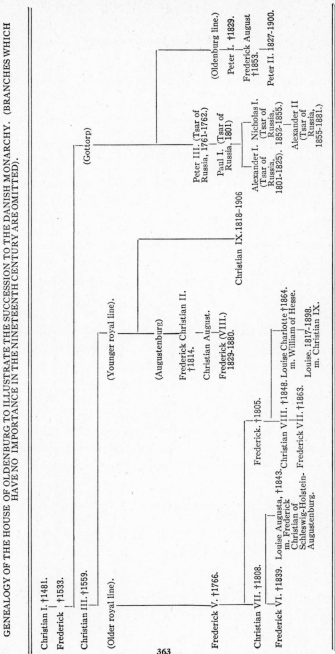

Christian I. †1481.
Frederick †1533.

Christian III. †1559.

(Older royal line).

(Younger royal line).

(Gottorp)

(Augustenburg)

Frederick Christian II. †1814.

Christian August.

Frederick (VIII.) 1829-1880.

Christian IX. 1818-1906

(Oldenburg line.)

Peter I. †1829.

Frederick August †1853.

Peter II. 1827-1900.

Peter III. (Tsar of Russia, 1761-1762.)

Paul I. (Tsar of Russia, 1801)

Alexander I. (Tsar of Russia, 1801-1825.)

Nicholas I. (Tsar of Russia, 1852-1855.)

Alexander II (Tsar of Russia, 1855-1881.)

Frederick V. †1766.

Frederick. †1805.

Christian VII. †1808.

Frederick VI. †1839. Louise Augusta, †1843. m. Frederick Christian of Schleswig-Holstein-Augustenburg. Christian VIII. †1848. Louise Charlotte †1864. m. William of Hesse. Frederick VII. †1863. Louise. 1817-1898. m. Christian IX.

363

BIBLIOGRAPHY

BIBLIOGRAPHY

MANUSCRIPT SOURCES

AUSTRIA. In the Vienna Archives (former *K. u. K. Haus-, Hof-, u. Staatsarchiv*), I have used the correspondence with the Austrian representatives at Copenhagen for 1851 and January 1864; at Berlin, London, Paris, and St. Petersburg from January 1, 1863 to August 1, 1864; Stockholm, 1863-64; the protocols of the Council of Ministers and the *Vorträge* of the minister for foreign affairs for 1863 and the first half of 1864; and the papers in the *Nachlässe* of Rechberg and Gablenz.

DENMARK. In the Copenhagen Archives (*Rigsarkiv*), I have used the correspondence of the Danish minister to Russia for 1850-51 and the correspondence with the Danish representatives at London, Paris, and St. Petersburg for 1863-64. Most of this material had been used by Thorsøe and Neergaard but it was worth while to read the dispatches in the original (most of them are in French) and *in extenso* to get an impression of the personalities of the writers and of the character of the information on which the government was basing its decisions.

FRANCE. In the archives of the Ministry of Foreign Affairs at Paris, I used the political correspondence with the French representatives at Berlin, Copenhagen, Frankfurt, London, St. Petersburg, Stockholm, and Vienna from the beginning of 1863 to the date in December after which the principal documents are published in *Les Origines diplomatiques de la guerre de 1870-1871.*

GREAT BRITAIN. In the British Archives (Public Record Office, London), I used the correspondence of the British representatives at the capitals of the Great Powers for the years 1848 to 1850 inclusive; the collected correspondence on the Schleswig-Holstein question from 1851 to 1860 (F. O. Supplement, Denmark, Schleswig-Holstein Question, 120-153); the correspondence with Berlin from 1861 to 1864 inclusive; and the correspondence with the British representatives at Copenhagen, Frankfurt, Paris, St. Petersburg, Stockholm, Vienna, and the capitals of the lesser German states for 1863 and 1864. I have also made some use of the Russell papers (on deposit in the Public Record Office) and of the Layard papers (in the British Museum).

HANOVER. In the Hanover Archives, I used the packet "1863. Betr. die Verfassungsangelegenheit der Herzogthümer Holstein und Lauenburg."

PRUSSIA. In the Berlin Archives (*Preussisches geheimes Staatsarchiv*, now at Berlin-Dahlem), I used the materials on the Schleswig-Holstein question from the beginning of 1863 to the end of July 1864 and those on Napoleon III's proposal for a European Congress. I was also allowed to use the protocols of the Prussian Crown Councils from November 1863 to June 1864 in the Archives of the Prussian Ministry of State (*Staatsministerium*).

NOTE ON REFERENCES TO DOCUMENTARY MATERIALS. As I was requested by the officials of one of the Archives in which I studied not to give exact archival references

(i. e., to volume and folio), and as the documents in at least one of the Archives have been rearranged since I studied them for this monograph, I have merely indicated the general source for the documents cited (e. g., Berlin Archives; Record Office, London, etc.). They can be located easily from the index in each of the Archives mentioned.

PRINTED SOURCES

The following list contains the books and articles which were of especial value for the preparation of this study. Because so many of the works contain both secondary and primary source material, it has not seemed desirable to classify the items. It is hoped that the alphabetical arrangement will facilitate reference and will not make it too difficult to determine the extent of the bibliography and the character of the materials used.

No attempt has been made to draw up a complete bibliography of the Schleswig-Holstein question. Supplementary references can be found in the well known German and Danish bibliographies, Dahlmann-Waitz, *Quellenkunde der deutschen Geschichte*, 8th edition, (Leipzig 1912) and B. V. A. Erichsen and A. Krarup, *Dansk historisk Bibliografi, systematisk Fortegnelse over Bidrag til Danmarks Historie til Udgangen af 1912* (3 volumes, Copenhagen, 1917-1927), continued most conveniently for this subject in the lists of literature given annually in the *Historisk Tidsskrift*, (Copenhagen), and the *Zeitschrift der Gesellschaft für die Geschichte der Herzogthümer Schleswig, Holstein und Lauenburg*.

Note: In the general collections of documents, there is much duplication. E. g., most of the material found in the British *Parliamentary Papers* is reprinted in the *Archives Diplomatiques* and the *Staatsarchiv*.

ALLEN, G. G. C. "Die Volkssprache in dem Herzogthum Schleswig zeit 1864," in *Z. f. s-h. G.*, XXI (1891), pp. 3-136. Includes a study of the nationality statistics before 1864.

Allgemeine Deutsche Biographie. 56 Volumes. Leipzig, 1875-1912.

ANDRÆ, POUL. *Andræ og Fællesforfatningen af 2. Oktober 1855*. Copenhagen 1903. Based on the papers of C. C. G. Andræ. Covers the period 1854 to 1864.

ANDRÆ, POUL. "En Brevvexling mellem Andræ og Krieger under Londonerkonferencen. 1864," in *Historisk Tidsskrift* (Copenhagen) 6R. V, (1894) pp. 121-182. Correspondence between the most influential Danish plenipotentiary and a prominent politician of differing political views.

"Aktstykker vedkommende den dansk-tydske Strid. I. Aktstykker der belyse den svensk-norske Regjerings Stilling til Sagen. (1858-1864)." In *Historisk Tidsskrift*, (Copenhagen) 3 R., III, (1864), pp. 677-792. Reprint of documents published officially in 1864. Some are in extract, and must be supplemented by those published by H. Koht.

Archives diplomatiques; recueil de diplomatie et d'histoire. Paris, 1861—Includes documents published by the Danish Government, which are not contained in the other collections listed. For other material, this is less satisfactory than the *Staatsarchiv*, as all the documents are translated into French.

ARUP, ERIK. "David og Hall. Krisen i Danmarks historie 1863," in *Scandia*, I, pp. 119-179. Arup attempts a critical study of the fragmentary memoirs of C. N. David (cf. Aage Friis, "C. N. Davids Optegnelser om Aarene 1863-1865" in *Historisk Tidsskrift*, 8 R., V, pp. 45-99) His most important conclusion is that from the accession of King Christian until the end of December 1863, Hall aimed to produce a crisis in the affairs of Denmark in the hope that out of it would come the Scandinavian union. The reasoning does not seem convincing to me and I have left my account of Hall's policy unchanged. The first part of Arup's article, dealing with the problem of David's and Sir Augustus Paget's roles at the time when King Christian was making up his mind whether or not to sign the November Constitution, has been attacked, and on the whole successfully, by Aage Friis, *Historisk Tidsskrift*, 9 R., VI, pp. 133-248.

ARUP, ERIK. "Danmarks krise 1863" in *Scandia*, III, pp. 1-51. Arup's reply to the criticisms of Friis.

ARUP, ERIK. *Rids af Danmarks Historie til Brug ved Universitets-undervisning.* Copenhagen, 1921.

ASHLEY, [ANTHONY] EVELYN [MELBOURNE]. *The Life of Henry John Temple, Viscount Palmerston. 1846-1865.* 2 Volumes. 2nd. edition. London, 1876.

BERNHARDI, THEODOR VON. *Aus dem Leben Theodor von Bernhardis. Tagebuchblätter.* 9 Volumes Leipzig, 1893-1906. Volume V. *Der Streit um die Elbherzogthümer. 1863-1864.* Volume VI. *Aus dem letzten Tagen des deutschen Bundes. 1864-1866.* Bernhardi was a well-known writer on Russian and military history. He was a friend of Roon and of other prominent Prussians and had good sources of information. In December 1863, he went to London, where he acted as an agent for the Prince of Augustenburg. He remained there until after the London Conference. He was in touch with all the elements in London favorable to the Augustenburg cause, notably with Bernstorff, the Prussian ambassador, and the Princess of Hohenlohe-Langenburg, half-sister of Queen Victoria.

BERNSTORFF. See Ringhoffer.

BEUST, FRIEDRICH FERDINAND, GRAF VON. *Aus drei Viertel-Jahrhunderten. Erinnerungen und Aufzeichnungen.* 2 Volumes. Stuttgart, 1887. Beust was Saxon Minister President and represented the German Confederation at the London Conference. He was a man of considerable ability but his vanity exaggerated his own importance. His memoirs must be used with caution. He reprints his most important reports from the Conference.

BISMARCK, OTTO, FÜRST VON. *Gedanken und Erinnerungen.* 2 Volumes. Stuttgart, 1898. As this work was written in the 1890's, and as Bismarck made it his political testament, it must be used with great caution and checked wherever possible with contemporary material.

BISMARCK, OTTO, FÜRST VON. *Anhang zu den Gedanken und Erinnerungen von Otto, Fürst von Bismarck.* 2 Volumes. Stuttgart and Berlin, 1901. Volume I. "Kaiser Wilhelm I. und Bismarck." Volume II. "Aus Bismarcks Briefwechsel." An important collection of letters.

BISMARCK, OTTO, FÜRST VON. *Die gesammelten Werke.* Berlin, 1924. "Blixen Finecke og Bismark. En Brevvexling," in *Danske Magazin*, 7 R., II (1916), pp. 364-387. Bismarck's correspondence with a prominent Danish politician. Edited with an introduction by Professor Aage Friis of Copenhagen. Of especial importance in relation to the so-called "Blixen episode" in October 1863.

BLOOMFIELD, GEORGIANA [LIDDELL] BLOOMFIELD, BARONESS. *Reminiscences of Court and Diplomatic Life.* 2 Volumes. London, 1883. By the wife of the British ambassador to Austria. Important only as she was in London during the critical days at the end of January 1864 and mirrors the prevailing sentiments there.

BRANDENBURG, ERICH. *Die Reichsgründung.* 2 Volumes. Leipzig, 1916. (2nd, revised edition [1922.]). *Untersuchungen und Aktenstücke zur Geschichte der Reichgründung.* Leipzig, 1916. The latest general work in German. The account of the Schleswig-Holstein Question in 1863-1864 is short but fairly good. More important is the section in the "Untersuchungen" on *Bismarck and Napoleon III, 1863-1866.* Brandenburg has had, in addition to the published materials, copies of a few important, previously unpublished, documents from the Prussian archives. He is able to correct Sybel at a number of points.

BRANDES, GEORGE MORRIS COHEN. *Levned.* 3 Volumes. Copenhagen, 1905-1908.

BRANDT, OTTO. *Geistesleben und Politik in Schleswig-Holstein um die Wende des 18. Jahrhunderts.* 2nd edition. Stuttgart, 1927.

BRANDT, OTTO. "Zur Vorgeschichte der schleswig-holsteinischen Erhebung," in *Archiv für Politik und Geschichte,* 1926, pp. 470-521.

BRICKA, CARL FREDERIK. *Dansk Biografisk Lexikon.* 19 Volumes. Copenhagen, 1887-1905.

British and Foreign State Papers. Compiled by the Librarian and Keeper of the Papers. Foreign Office. London 1841-.

BROCK, JOHANNES. *Die Vorgeschichte der schleswig-holsteinischen Erhebung von 1848.* Göttingen, 1916. The best work on the development of the Duchies from 1815 to 1848. Deals with social and economic as well as with national and constitutional development. Contains a good bibliography.

BUSCH, MORITZ. *Bismarck; Some Secret Pages of his History.* 3 Volumes. London, 1898.

Cambridge History of British Foreign Policy. 1783-1919. Edited by Sir A. W. Ward and G. P. Gooch. 3 volumes. Cambridge 1922-1923.

CARLQUIST, GUNNAR. *Ur Henning Hamiltons Brefsamling.* 2 Volumes. 2nd edition. Stockholm, 1914. Letters to the Swedish Minister at Copenhagen. Of especial importance are those from C. C. Hall and P. Vedel, both during Hamilton's term of service and after his retirement.

CHARLES-ROUX, FRANÇOIS. *Alexandre II., Gortchakoff et Napoléon III.* 2nd edition, Paris, 1913.

CIERPINSKI, F. "Die Politik Englands in der schleswig-holsteinischen Frage von 1861 bis Anfang Januar 1864," in *Z. f. s-h. G.* XLIV (1914), pp. 220-297; "Die Politik Englands in der schleswig-holsteinischen Frage im Anfange des Jahres 1864," in *Z. f. s.-h. G.* XLV (1915), pp. 86-115. A convenient summary of published material. The second part is the better.

CLASON, SAMUEL. "Skodsborgmötet och Ulriksdalskonferencen," in *Historisk Tidsskrift (Stockholm),* XXIV 1914. pp. 61-107. Based on the Swedish archives and a confidential memorandum of Count Hamilton written in 1864, this article supersedes all other accounts of the relations between Sweden and Denmark from July to September 1863.

CLAUSEN, JULIUS. *Af Orla Lehmanns Papirer.* Copenhagen, 1903. Lehmann was a leading Danish politician and Minister of the Interior in the Hall Cabinet.

CLAUSEN, JULIUS. *Skandinavismen.* Copenhagen, 1900. An old and somewhat superficial account.

DAHL and LINVALD. See *Sønderjylland.*

DASENT, ARTHUR IRWIN. *John Thadeus Delane.* 2 Volumes. New York, 1908. The standard biography of the famous editor of the London *Times.*

DAVID, CHRISTIAN GEORG NATHAN. "Optegnelser om Aarene 1863-1865," in *Historisk Tidsskrift,* 8 R., V, pp. 45-99. Edited by Professor Aage Friis of Copenhagen. David was a close friend of Christian IX and a member of the cabinet which took office after Monrad's fall in July 1864. His notes are in two sets, one written soon after the events described, the other some twenty years later. There are some irreconcilable differences in his accounts of the events from November 15 to 18, 1863.

DE GEER, LOUIS GERHARD FRIHERRE. *Minnen.* 2nd edition. Stockholm [1906].

[DE GEER, LOUIS GERHARD FRIHERRE]. *Ur Louis de Geers Brevsamling.* Stockholm [1929.] Contains some letters from Manderström and others from the period of the Schleswig-Holstein crisis.

[DENMARK, General Staff.] *Den dansk-tydske Krig 1864.* Udgivet af Generalstaben. 3 Volumes. Copenhagen, 1890-92.

[DENMARK, RIGSDAGEN.] *Rigsdagstidende.* Copenhagen 1850 ff.

[DENMARK, RIGSRAADET.] *Rigsraadstidende.* Copenhagen 1856 ff.

Denmark and Germany (No. 1). Correspondence respecting the Maintenance of the Integrity of the Danish Monarchy. (1864) c. 3257, 1864. The Austro-Prussian identic notes of January 31, 1864.

Denmark and Germany (Nos. 2, 3, 4, 5, 6, 7). Correspondence respecting the Affairs of the Duchies of Holstein, Lauenburg and Schleswig. c. 3267, c. 3272, c. 3276, c. 3300, c. 3371, c. 3382, 1864. See also [Great Britain, Papers presented to Parliament].

Deutscher Liberalismus im Zeitalter Bismarcks. Eine politische Briefsammlung. I. Band: Die Sturmjahre der preussisch-deutschen Einigung 1859-1870. Berlin, 1925. See Heyderhoff, Julius and Wentzcke, Paul.

Dictionary of National Biography. 22 Volumes. London, 1908-1909.

DÖHLER, KARL. *Napoleon III, und die deutsch dänische Frage, unter besondere Berücksichtigung der Französischen Politik während des Konfliktes von 1863-64.* Leipzig Dissertation. Halle a-S., 1913. The best of the German studies called forth by the publication of the *Origines diplomatiques de la guerre de 1870-1871.*

DRIAULT, J. EDOUARD. "La Diplomatie française pendant la guerre du Danemark," in *Revue Historique,* CVII (1911), pp. 79-94. A sketch based on *Les Origines diplomatiques de la guerre de 1870-1871.*

DROYSEN, GUSTAV. *Johann Gustav Droysen.* Leipzig and Berlin 1910.

[DROYSEN, JOHANN GUSTAV], *Johann Gustav Droysen Briefwechsel.* Herausgegeben von Rudolf Hübner, 2 vols., Berlin and Leipzig 1929. *Deutsche Geschichtsquellen des 19. Jahrhundert,* XXV, XXVI.

DUNCKER, MAX. *Politischer Briefwechsel aus seinem Nachlass.* Herausgegeben von Dr. Johannes Schultze. Stuttgart and Berlin, 1923.

ENGEL-JANOSI, FRIEDRICH. *Graf Rechberg. Vier Kapitel zu seiner und Oesterreichs Geschichte.* Munich and Berlin, 1927. Based on Rechberg's papers.

ERNST II., DUKE OF SAXE-COBURG-GOTHA. *Aus meinem Leben und aus meiner Zeit.* 3 Volumes. Berlin, 1887-89. As brother-in-law of Queen Victoria, he was in

close touch with affairs in London. He took an active part in favor of the Prince
of Augustenburg, but his real influence was less than he believed. That his Memoirs
must be used with caution, has been shown by various German writers.

ERNST, OTTO. *Franz Joseph I. in seinen Briefen.* Vienna, 1924. Letter to Prince
Albert of Saxony, February 16, 1864. pp. 159 ff.

ERSLEV, KRISTIAN SOFUS AUGUST. *Augustenborgernes Arvekrav.* Copenhagen,
1915. *Fortegnelse over Akter om den Sönderburgske Hertuglinie.* Copenhagen, 1915.
A calm and scholarly study of the question of the Augustenburg claims to the
succession to Schleswig. Professor Erslev re-examined the published materials
and found new sources which led him to the conclusion that the Augustenburg
claim to the Duchy after the extinction of the direct royal line was justified up to
the renunciation by Christian August in 1852. These views are now almost unanimously accepted by the Danish scholars. All attempts to refute Erslev's
conclusions have failed.

ERSLEV, KRISTIAN SOFUS AUGUST. *Frederik IV og Slesvig, en historisk Fortolkning
af Arvehyldingsakterne af 1721.* Copenhagen, 1901. The first of the publications
in which Erslev reëxamined the traditional Danish view of the legal situation of
Schleswig.

FABRICIUS, KNUD. *Danskhedens Udvikling i Sønderjylland i det 19. Aarhundrede.*
Copenhagen, 1919. A short sketch.

FALCK, NIELS NIKOLAUS. *Sammlung der wichtigsten Urkunden, welche auf das
Staatsrecht der Herzogthümer Schleswig und Holstein Bezug haben.* Kiel, 1847.
Falck was professor of jurisprudence at the University of Kiel and took a leading
part in the controversies in the first half of the nineteenth century. This is the
standard edition of documents bearing on the legal aspects of the Schleswig-
Holstein controversy.

FITZMAURICE, EDMOND GEORGE PETTY, 1ST BARON. *The Life of Granville George
Leveson Gower, Second Earl Granville, 1815-1891.* 2 Volumes. 3rd edition. London
1905. Granville acted as the Queen's mouthpiece in the discussions as to the
British intervention during 1863 and 1864.

FLEURY, EMILE FELIX, COMTE. *Souvenirs du Général Cte. Fleury.* 2 Volumes.
3rd edition. Paris, 1897-98.

FRAHM, FRIEDRICH. "Die Bismarcksche Lösung der schleswig-holsteinischen
Frage" in *Zeitschrift der Gesellschaft für schleswig-holsteinische Geschichte,* LIX
(1930), pp. 335-431. Frahm's interesting article on the Bismarckian solution of the
Schleswig-Holstein Question is marred by his attempt to prove that a group of
forged documents on the relations of Austria, Prussia, and Russia, which appeared
in the London *Morning Post* at the beginning of July 1864, are genuine. He argues
that these documents, most of which became known to various European cabinets
in April and May 1864, were put in circulation by Bismarck with the object of discouraging Swedish intervention which might have brought on a general European
war. I cannot prove the negative—that Bismarck did not give out these papers—
but Frahm's thesis seems to me to be untenable. I am convinced, however, both
from internal evidence and from examination of unquestionably genuine dispatches
of the same period and, in some cases, of the same dates, that the *Morning Post*
documents are palpable forgeries. Frahm asserts that the reason why these documents have not appeared in collections published from the Prussian Archives (he
seems to have studied only printed materials) is due to the fact that Bismarck gave

out *the genuine originals*. Assuming that this could be done without leaving any traces, Frahm's argument falls unless he can explain why the Austrian Archives contain no evidence of the documents that purport to be of Austrian origin. I expect to deal with this problem more completely in another place.

FRAHM, FRIEDRICH. *Bismarcks Stellung zu Frankreich bis zum 4. Juli 1866.* Kiel dissertation. Kiel, 1911. Goes only to 1859.

FRAHM, FRIEDRICH.'' Die Politische Lage beim Ausbruch des Deutsch-Danischen Krieges,'' in *Historische Vierteljahrschrift,* XVI (1913), pp. 520-536. Based on the *Origines Diplomatiques de la Guerre de 1870-1871.* Frahm overestimates Napoleon III's desire for German territory.

[FRANCE, Ministère des Affaires Etrangères.] *Les Origines diplomatiques de la guerre de 1870-1871. Recueil de documents.* Paris, 1910 ff. The political dispatches of the French Foreign Office archives. The series begins with December 25, 1863. Volumes I to IV (to November 5, 1864) cover the period of this monograph. Well edited and of very great value, especially for the conversations of foreign statesmen with the French diplomats. Somewhat less valuable for French policy because of Napoleon III's secret dealings with the foreign diplomats and with secret agents. Many important dispatches and letters are missing, but that is the fault of the archives, not of the editors.

FRIEDJUNG, HEINRICH.''Graf Bernhard von Rechberg,'' in *Historische Aufsätze.* Stuttgart and Berlin, 1919. First published in 1899.

FRIEDJUNG, HEINRICH. *Der Kampf um die Vorherrschaft in Deutschland 1859 bis 1866.* 2 Volumes. 6th. edition. Stuttgart and Berlin, 1904. Friedjung's chief contribution is his notes on his interviews with Bismarck and Rechberg. In general, his brief account of the Schleswig-Holsein Question is based on von Sybel.

FRIEDJUNG, HEINRICH. *Oesterreich von 1848 bis 1860.* Volume I. 2nd edition. Stuttgart and Berlin, 1908. Volume II. Part I. Stuttgart and Berlin, 1912.

FRIIS, AAGE. "C. N. David, Christian IX og Sir Augustus Paget i November 1863" in *Historisk Tidsskrift* (Copenhagen) 9 R., VI, pp. 133-248. A criticism of the first part of Erik Arup's article, "David og Hall. Krisen in Danmarks historie 1863," with an appendix of documents from the British Archives.

FRIIS, AAGE. *Den danske Regering og Nordslesvigs Genforening med Danmark* Copenhagen, 1921.

FRIIS, AAGE. "Holstens Indlemmelse i Danmark i Aaret 1806. En historisk Undersøgelse." In *Historisk Tidsskrift,* 7 R., VII, pp. 1-107. A study of the circumstances under which Holstein was incorporated with the Kingdom of Denmark after the dissolution of the Holy Roman Empire in 1806.

FRIIS, AAGE. " 'Under Junigrundloven' og dens Forfatter," in *Historisk Tidsskrift,* 9 R., I, pp. 89-128. A valuable essay on Neergaard's great work.

FRIIS, AAGE. Review of "Holger Hjelholt, Den danske Sprogordning og det danske Sprogstyre i Slesvig 1850-1864," in *Historisk Tidsskrift,* 9 R., III., (1925), pp. 407-418.

FRÖBEL, JULIUS. *Ein Lebenslauf. Aufzeichnungen, Erinnerungen und Bekenntnisse.* 2 Volumes. Stuttgart, 1890-91. After a varied career, during which he narrowly escaped execution during the revolution of 1848, Fröbel entered the Austrian service at the beginning of 1862 and was employed in the press bureau.

GEBAUER, JOHANNES HEINRICH. *Christian August, Herzog von Schleswig-Holstein.* Stuttgart and Leipzig, 1910.

GEBAUER, JOHANNES HEINRICH. *Herzog Friedrich VIII. von Schleswig-Holstein.* Stuttgart and Berlin, 1912. These two biographies are based on the Augustenburg archives at Primkenau and contain much valuable material. They represent the Augustenburg point of view but less violently than Jansen and Samwer.

GOOCH, GEORGE PEABODY. *The Later Correspondence of Lord John Russell, 1840-1878.* 2 Volumes London, 1925.

GOSCH, [CHRISTIAN] CARL AUGUST. *Denmark and Germany since 1815.* London, 1862. Danish point of view. Gosch was a Dane and was subsidized by and sometimes attached to the Danish Legation in London. Although the book is, in a sense propaganda, it is a keen criticism of the German claims.

[GREAT BRITAIN. *Papers Presented to Parliament.*] *Correspondence respecting the affairs of Denmark. 1850-53.* c. 3301, 1864.

[GREAT BRITAIN. *Papers Presented to Parliament.*] *Correspondence between Austria, Prussia and Denmark. 1851-52.*

[GREAT BRITAIN. *Papers Presented to Parliament.*] *Accessions to the Treaty of London of May 8, 1852, relative to the Succession to the Danish Crown.* c. 3270, 1864.

[GREAT BRITAIN. *Papers Presented to Parliament.*] *Correspondence respecting the Affairs of the Duchies of Holstein, Lauenburg and Schleswig. 1858.* c. 3383, 1864.

[GREAT BRITAIN. *Papers Presented to Parliament.*] *Correspondence respecting the Affairs of the Duchies of Schleswig and Holstein. 1860-61.* c. 2830, 1861. February 16, 1860, to March 11, 1861.

[GREAT BRITAIN. *Papers Presented to Parliament*]. *Correspondence respecting the Affairs of the Duchies of Holstein, Lauenburg and Schleswig.* c. 3038. March 18, 1861, to January 21, 1863. See also *Denmark and Germany.*

GUEDALLA, PHILIP. *Gladstone and Palmerston, being the Correspondence of Lord Palmerston with Mr. Gladstone 1851-1865.* New York and London, 1928.

GUICHEN, EUGÈNE, VICOMTE DE. *Les Grandes Questions Européennes et la Diplomatie des Puissances sous la Seconde République Française.* 2 Volumes. Paris 1925, 1929. Based on extensive archival studies.

HÄHNSEN, FRITZ. *Ursprung und Geschichte des Artikels V des Prager Friedens; die deutschen Akten zur Frage der teilung Schleswig (1863-1879).* 2 Volumes. Breslau, 1929. [Veröffentlichungen der schleswig-holsteinischen Universitäts-gesellschaft, Nr. 21.]

HAGENAH, HERMANN. *Revolution und Legimität in der Geschichte der Erhebung Schleswig-Holsteins. Untersuchungen zur Enstehungsgeschichte und zur Politik der provisorischen Regierung.* Leipzig 1916.

HAGENAH, HERMANN. "1863. Die nationale Bewegung in Schleswig-Holstein," in *Zeitschrift der Gesellschaft für die Geschichte der Herzogthümer Schleswig, Holstein und Lauenburg,* LVI, pp. 271-396.

HANSARD, THOMAS CARSON. *Parliamentary Debates.* London, 1812.—

HANSEN, JENS JULIUS. *Les Coulisses de la Diplomatie. Quinze Ans à l'Etranger. (1864-1879).* Paris, 1880. A Dane who went to Paris early in 1864. Wrote for the Paris press on Danish questions. Established relations with Drouyn de Lhuys. Has some information of doubtful value obtained from French diplomats in regard to the Anglo-French rapprochement in February 1864.

HASSEL, PAUL. *Aus dem Leben des Königs Albert von Sachsen.* 2 Volumes. Berlin, 1898-1900. Some material from the Saxon archives.

HASSELL, WILLIAM VON. *Geschichte des Königreichs Hannover.* 2 Volumes, in 3 parts. Bremen, 1898-1901. Anti-Prussian point of view. Much material from the Hanoverian archives, sometimes inaccurately used.

[HAYM, RUDOLF]. *Ausgewählter Briefwechsel Rudolf Hayms.* Herausgegeben von Hans Rosenberg. Berlin and Leipzig 1930. *Deutsche Geschichtsquellen des 19. Jahrhundert,* XXVII.

HAYM, RUDOLPH. *Das Leben Max Dunckers.* Berlin, 1891.

HEDEMANN-HEESPEN, PAUL VON. *Die Herzogthümer Schleswig-Holstein und die Neuzeit.* Kiel, 1926.

HEIBERG, JOHANNE LUISE, and KRIEGER, A. F. *En Samling Breve 1860-1889.* Udgivet af Aage Friis og P. Munch. 2 Volumes. Copenhagen, 1914-15. Volume I covers the period 1860-1864. Most of the letters are from Frau Heiberg. They throw much light on conditions in Copenhagen and, through her acquaintance with many prominent politicians, give some political information.

HENGELMÜLLER, LADISLAS FREIHERR VON. "Graf Alois Karolyi," in *Deutsche Revue,* October 1913, pp. 35-40; July 1914, pp. 33-47; August 1914, pp. 217-227; June 1915, pp. 294-301; July 1915, pp. 76-85. An account of the activity of the Austrian Minister at Berlin. Extends to the beginning of the war of 1864. Based on the Austrian archives.

HEYDERHOFF, JULIUS and WENTZCKE, PAUL. *Deutscher Liberalismus in Zeitalter Bismarcks. Eine politische Briefsammlung.* 2 Volumes. Berlin, 1925.

Historisk Tidsskrift udgivet af den Danske Historiske Forening. Copenhagen, 1840 ff.

Historisk Tidsskrift utgitt av den Norske Historiske Forening. Christiania, 1870 ff.

Historisk Tidsskrift utgifven af Svenska Historiska Föreningen. Stockholm, 1881 ff.

HJELHOLT, HOLGER. *Den danske Sprogordning og det danske Sprogstyre i Slesvig mellem Krigene (1850-1864).* Copenhagen, 1923.

HJELHOLT, HOLGER. "Den slesvigske Stænderforsamling i 1860. Et Bidrag til Belysning af slesvigske Politik under de danske Styre mellem Krigene," in *Historisk Tidsskrift* (Copenhagen) 9 R., III, (1925), pp. 209-344.

HOETZSCH, OTTO. *Peter von Meyendorff, ein russischer Diplomat an den Höfen von Berlin und Wien; politischer und privater Briefwechsel, 1826-1863.* 3 Volumes. Berlin and Leipzig, 1923.

JANSEN, KARL. *Schleswig-Holsteins Befreiung.* Herausgegeben und ergänzt von K. Samwer. Wiesbaden, 1897. The first important history from the Augustenburg standpoint. Hostile to Bismarck. Contains much of value both in the text and in the appendix of documents.

JANSEN, KARL. *Uwe Jens Lornsen, Ein Beitrag zur Geschichte der Wiedergeburt des deutschen Volkes.* Kiel, 1872.

JANSEN-SAMWER. See Jansen, Karl. *Schleswig-Holsteins Befreiung.*

JESSEN, FRANZ DE. *Manuel historique de la question du Slesvig; documents, cartes, pièces justificatives et renseignements statistiques.* Copenhagen, 1906. Propaganda, but contains several useful historical and statistical sections.

KAISER FRIEDRICH III. *Tagebücher von 1848-1866.* Mit einer Einleitung und Ergänzungen herausgegeben von Heinrich Otto Meisner. Leipzig 1929.

KAISER WILHELM I. *Briefe an seine Schwester Alexandrine und deren Sohn Grossherzog Friedrich Franz II.* Bearbeitet von Johannes Schultze. Berlin und Leipzig, 1927.

KAISER WILHELM I. *Weimarer Briefe.* Bearbeitet von Johannes Schultze. 2 Volumes. Berlin and Leipzig, 1924.

KEUDELL, ROBERT VON. *Fürst und Fürstin Bismarck. Erinnerungen aus den Jahren 1846 bis 1872.* Stuttgart and Berlin, 1902. Of especial importance for Bismarck's statements at the end of December 1863 and beginning of January 1864.

KOHL, HORST. *Bismarck-Jahrbuch.* 6 Volumes. Berlin, 1894-99. Contains many letters to and from Bismarck. The following are of special importance for the Schleswig-Holstein Question: *Zweiunddreissig Briefe des Grafen Robert v. d. Goltz an Bismarck, 1850-1864.* Volume V, pages 193-253. *Aus den Briefwechsel zwischen Graf Bernstorff und Bismarck,* Volume V, pages 105-193.

KOHL, HORST. *Dreissig Jahre preussisch-deutscher Geschichte 1858 bis 1888 in amtlichen Kundgebungen.* Giessen, 1888.

KOHL, HORST. *Die Politischen Reden des Fürsten Bismarck.* 14 Volumes. Stuttgart, 1892-1905. Volume II contains: *Die Reden des Ministerpräsident von Bismarck-Schönhausen im Preussischen Landtage 1862-65.*

KOHT, HALVDAN. *Die Stellung Norwegens und Schwedens im deutsch-dänischen Konflikt, zumal während der Jahre 1863 und 1864.* Christiania, 1908. Originally published in: *Videnskabs-Selskabets Skrifter,* II, Hist.-Filosof. Klasse, 1907, No. 7. By one of Norway's foremost historians. The fullest and best account of the policy of Sweden-Norway from 1848 to 1864 in the Schleswig-Holstein Question. In addition to the previously published material, Koht has used the protocols of the meetings of the Norwegian Cabinet and the documents annexed thereto. The important ones are published as appendices. Except for the negotiations of July, August and September 1863, where it has been superseded by Clason, Koht's work remains the standard.

KRIEGER, ANDREAS FREDERIK. *Dagbøger, 1848-1880.* Copenhagen, 1920 ff. Edited by Elise Koppel, Aage Friis, P. Munch. The third volume ends with July 31, 1866. A source of great importance for Danish policy. Krieger was a leading National Liberal politician, was in close touch with what went on in political circles in Copenhagen, and was one of the plenipotentiaries to the London Conference.

KUPKE, GEORG. *Vor fünfzig Jahren. Briefwechsel zwischen Dr. Karl Lorentzen und den Führen der Augustenburgischen Partei. 1863-1866.* Volume II in Quellen und Forschungen zur Geschichte Schleswig-Holsteins. Leipzig, 1914.

LAGORCE, PIERRE FRANÇOIS GUSTAVE, DE. *Histoire du Second Empire.* 7 Volumes. Paris, 1894-1905. Volume IV includes the Schleswig-Holstein Question.

LANG, ANDREW. *Life, Letters and Diaries of Sir Stafford Northcote, First Earl of Iddesleigh.* 2 Volumes. 2nd. edition. Edinburgh and London, 1890. Biography of a Tory statesman.

LAUGHTON, SIR JOHN KNOX. *Memoirs of the Life and Correspondence of Henry Reeve.* 2 Volumes. London, 1898. Reeve had been leader writer of the London *Times.* In 1863 and 1864 he was editor of the *Edinburgh Review.* Had influential friends both in London and Paris and was sometimes used for informal negotiations. His relations with the Earl of Clarendon were especially close.

LAURIDSEN, PETER. "Sønderjydske Førere i 1850 erne," in *Historisk Tidsskrift* (Copenhagen), 9 R., II, (1921-23), pp. 233-280.

LAURIDSEN, PETER. *Da Sønderjylland vaagnede. Skildringer og Breve.* 6 Volumes. Copenhagen, 1909-1919. Volume I in second edition, 1911. Studies of the leaders in the development of the Danish national movement in Schleswig. Publishes many contemporary letters. The best work on this development, but deals almost exclusively with the leaders, neglecting too much the progress of their ideas among the mass of the people. A popular edition, omitting the documents, was published in 1920.

LEE, SIR SIDNEY. *Queen Victoria, a Biography.* New and revised edition, London, 1904.

LENZ, MAX. *Geschichte Bismarcks.* 4th edition. Munich and Leipzig, 1913. The best short account of Bismarck up to 1871. Lenz's account of Bismarck and the Schleswig-Holstein Question is brief but excellent.

Letters of Queen Victoria. A Selection from Her Majesty's Correspondence between the Years 1837-1861. Edited by A. C. Benson and Viscount Esher. 3 Volumes. Reissue. London, 1911.

Letters of Queen Victoria. Second Series. A Selection from Her Majesty's Correspondence and Journal between the Years 1862-1878. Edited by G. E. Buckle. 2 Volumes. London, 1926.

LINVALD, AXEL. "Stemninger og Tilstande i Sønderjylland ved Krigens Udbrud, 1864," in *Danske Magazin,* 7 R., III, pp. 101-174. Reports of Danish officials in Schleswig to the Ministry for the Duchy of Schleswig in Copenhagen at the end of January and beginning of February 1864.

LORD, ROBERT HOWARD. "Bismarck and Russia in 1863, "in *American Historical Review,* XXIX, No. 1, October 1923, pp. 24-48.

LYALL, SIR ALFRED COMYN. *Life of the Marquis of Dufferin and Ava.* 2 Volumes. London, 1905. Lord Dufferin was Napoleon's guest at Compiègne early in December 1863 and gives an excellent account of the Emperor's attitude on the Congress question.

MACKEPRANG, MOURITZ. *Nordslesvig, 1864-1909.* Copenhagen, 1910.

MADVIG, JOHAN NIKOLAI. *Livserindringer.* Copenhagen, 1887. Madvig was a National Liberal politician, but of calmer temperament than most of the leaders. He was President of the Rigsraad in 1863.

MADVIG, JOHAN NIKOLAI. *Den nationale Politik og det danske Monarchie.* Copenhagen, 1864.

MAGER, F. *Herzog Ernst II und die Schleswig-Holsteinische Frage 1863-1866.* Greifswald, 1910. A critical study of Ernst II, *Aus meinem Leben und aus meiner Zeit.* Has used the Gotha archives. Mager's criticism of Ernst's account of his visit to Paris in March 1864 is in places too severe.

MALET, SIR ALEXANDER. *The Overthrow of the Germanic Confederation by Prussia in 1866.* London, 1870. The author was British Minister at Frankfurt.

MALMESBURY, 3d EARL OF. *Memoirs of an Ex-Minister.* 2 Volumes. 2nd edition. London, 1884.

MANTHEY, AUGUST CHRISTIAN. *Dagbøger for Aarene 1856-1874.* Christiania, 1909. Manthey was a member of the Norwegian Ministry.

MARCKS, ERICH. *Kaiser Wilhelm I.* 6th and 7th edition. Leipzig, 1910. Especially good on the relations between King William and Bismarck.

MARCKS, ERICH. *Otto von Bismarck. Ein Lebensbild.* Stuttgart and Berlin, 1915.

MARMORA, A. LA. *Un po' più di luce sugli eventi politici e militari dell' anno 1866.* Florence, 1873.

MARTIN, SIR THEODORE. *The Life of His Royal Highness the Prince Consort.* 5 Volumes. London, 1875-80.

MAURICE, SIR JOHN FREDERICK. *The Balance of Military Power in Europe.* Edinburgh and London, 1888. The writer believes that Great Britain could have intervened effectively in the war of 1864.

MAXWELL, SIR HERBERT EUSTACHE. *The Life and Letters of George William Frederick, fourth Earl of Clarendon.* 2 Volumes. London, 1913.

MEYER, ARNOLD OSKAR. *Bismarcks Kampf mit Oesterreich am Bundestag zu Frankfurt, (1851 bis 1859).* Berlin and Leipzig, 1927.

MEYER, ARNOLD OSKAR. "Die Zielsetzung in Bismarcks schleswig-holsteinischer Politik von 1855 bis 1864," in *Zeitschrift der Gesellschaft für die Geschichte der Herzogthümer Schleswig, Holstein und Lauenburg,* LIII, pp. 103-134.

MØLLER, ERIK. "London-Konferencens Hovedproblem" in *Festskrift til Kristian Erslev fra Danske Historikere* (Copenhagen 1927), pp. 515-536. A keen and valuable study of the problem of the division of Schleswig, with special reference to Danish policy at the London Conference. Møller emphasizes the difficulties in the way of a division that would have satisfied Danish state and national interests. It may be suggested that perhaps he underestimates the possibility that acceptance by Denmark of one of the compromises suggested (e. g. neutral mediation to determine the line) might have made it difficult for Bismarck to escape from the necessity of also accepting it. Such a compromise might have resulted in splitting the difference between the Schlei-Dannevirke and Apenrade-Hoyer lines and so, as suggested on page 242 above, have given Denmark approximately her present frontier. Whether or not that would have been a satisfactory solution in 1864 is, of course, another question.

MONRAD, DITLEV GOTHARD. *Deltagelse i Begivenhederne, 1864. En Efterladt Redegørelse.* Udgivet af Aage Friis. Copenhagen, 1914. Monrad's account of events in 1863-64, written in letter form some twenty years later, brings no new information but his views and comments are interesting.

MONYPENNY, WILLIAM FLAVELLE, and BUCKLE, GEORGE EARLE. *The Life of Benjamin Disraeli, Earl of Beaconsfield.* 6 Volumes. New York, 1910-1920.

MORLEY, JOHN. *The Life of Richard Cobden.* 2 Volumes. London, 1881.

MORLEY, JOHN. *The Life of William Ewart Gladstone.* 3 Volumes. London, 1903.

MURET, P. "La Politique française dans l'Affaire des Duchés et les premiers essais d'intervention européenne jusqu'à l'invasion du Slesvig. (25 Décembre 1863-16 Janvier 1864)," in *Revue d'Histoire Moderne et Contemporaine,* XVI (1911), pp. 137-169, 300-333. A brilliant study by one of the editors of *Les Origines diplomatiques de la guerre de 1870-1871.*

NEERGAARD, NIELS. *Under Junigrundloven. En Fremstilling af det danske Folks politiske Historie fra 1848 til 1866.* 2 Volumes. Copenhagen, 1890, 1916. In nearly three thousand pages, Neergaard has written the history of Denmark from 1848 to 1866. Neergaard began his studies of this period in the 1880's and the first volume, (to 1853) appeared in 1892. The work was then interrupted by the writer's political activities, but eventually began to appear in sections, the completed work coming out in 1916. As the work progressed, Neergaard gained access to more and more sources. The available printed material has been quite thoroughly used and supplemented by many unprinted sources, both private letters and diaries and the archives of the Foreign Office. In addition, Neergaard had the advantage of the advice and information given him by P. Vedel, who became Under Secretary in the Ministry for Foreign Affairs in 1858. For a detailed account of this work, see Friis, ''Under Junigrundloven og dens Forfatter.''

NIRRNHEIM, OTTO. *Das erste Jahr des Ministeriums Bismarck und die öffentliche Meinung.* Heidelberg, 1908. Deals with the Schleswig-Holstein Question from the fall of 1862 to the death of Frederick VII.

Nouveau Récueil Général de Traités Conventions et autres Transactions remarquables, servant à la connaissance des relations étrangères des Puissances et États dans leur rapports mutuels. Continuation du grand recueil de G. Fr. Martens par Charles Samwer.

OLLIVIER, ÉMILE. *L'Empire Libéral, études, récits, souvenirs.* 17 Volumes. Paris, 1895-1915. Volume VII. *Le démembrement du Danemark, etc.*

ONCKEN, HERMANN. ''Grossherzog Peter von Oldenburg (1827-1900), ''in *Historisch-politische Aufsätze und Reden.* 2 Vols. Munich and Berlin, 1914. II, pp. 35-92. First published in 1900.

ONCKEN, HERMANN. *Die Rheinpolitik Kaiser Napoleons III. von 1863 bis 1870 und der Ursprung des Krieges von 1870-71; nach den Staatsakten von Oesterreich, Preussen und den suddeutschen Mittelstaaten.* 3 Volumes. Stuttgart, 1926.

ONCKEN, HERMANN. *Rudolf von Bennigsen: ein deutscher liberaler Politiker. Nach seinen Briefen und hinterlassenen Papieren.* 2 Volumes. Stuttgart and Leipzig, 1910.

Les Origines diplomatiques de la guerre de 1870-1871. See [France, Ministère des Affaires Etrangères.]

OSTENFELD, J. S. M. *Studier over Stemninger og Tilstande i Holsten (1815-30).* Copenhagen, 1909. In parts superficial.

OTTOSEN, JOHAN. *Peter Hiort Lorenzen's historiske Gœrning.* Copenhagen, 1896.

PAGET, WALPURGA EHRENGARDE HELENA (LADY VON HOHENTHAL). *Scenes and Memories.* New York, 1912. By the wife of the British Minister to Denmark. Of slight value.

PAHNCKE, ROBERT. *Die Parallel-Erzählungen Bismarcks zu seinen Gedanken und Erinnerungen.* Halle a-S., 1914.

PASOLINI, PIETRO DESIDERIO. *Giuseppe Pasolini. Memorie raccolte da suo figlio.* Imola, 1880. In November and December 1863, Pasolini was in Paris and London trying to influence Napoleon III and Palmerston to do something for Italy. He tried to bring about a rapprochement between France and Great Britain in spite of the rejection of the Congress.

PHILLIPSON, MARTIN. *Das leben Kaiser Friedrichs III.* Wiesbaden, 1900.

PLOUG, PARMO CARL. *Digte.* 2 Volumes. Copenhagen, 1901.

POSCHINGER, HEINRICH, RITTER VON. *Aktenstücke zur Wirthschaftspolitik des Fürsten Bismarck.* Volume I. Berlin, 1890.

POSCHINGER, HEINRICH RITTER VON. *Bismarck-Portfeuille.* 5 Volumes. Stuttgart and Leipzig 1898-1899.

POSCHINGER, HEINRICH, RITTER VON. *Preussen im Bundestag 1851 bis 1859. Documente der k. preuss. Bundestags-Gesandtschaft.* 4 Volumes. Leipzig, 1882-84. Bismarck's dispatches from Frankfurt.

POSCHINGER, HEINRICH, RITTER VON. *Preussens Auswärtige Politik, 1850 bis*

1858. Unveröffentlichte Dokumente aus dem Nachlasse des Ministerpräsidenten Otto Frhn. v. Manteuffel. 3 Volumes. Berlin, 1902.

PRECHT, HANS. *Englands Stellung zur deutschen Einheit, 1848-1850.* Munich and Berlin, 1925. (Beiheft 3 der Historischen Zeitschrift).

Protocols of Conference held in London relative to the Affairs of Denmark. c. 3336 1864. The official protocols of the London Conference. To be found also in various other documentary collections.

[PRUSSIA. General Staff.] *Der Deutsch-Dänische Krieg 1864.* Herausgegeben vom Grossen Generalstabe, Abtheilung für Kriegsgeschichte. 2 Volumes. Berlin, 1866-1887.

RAMSAY, ANNA AUGUSTA WHITTAL. *Idealism and Foreign Policy.* A study of the relations of Great Britain with Germany and France, 1860-1878. London, 1925. Based on the British Archives but superficial and inaccurate.

RASCHDAU, LUDWIG. *Die politische Berichte des Fürsten Bismarck aus Petersburg und Paris, 1859-1862.* 2 Volumes. Berlin, 1920.

REDESDALE, ALGERNON BERTRAM FREEMAN-MITFORD, BARON. *Memories.* 2 Volumes. 5th edition. London, 1915.

REDESDALE, ALGERNON BERTRAM FREEMAN-MITFORD, BARON. *Further Memories.* London, 1917.

REDLICH, JOSEF. *Das Oesterreichische Staats-und Reichsproblem.* 2 Volumes. Leipzig, 1920-1926.

[REICH, C. E.] "Chr. E. Reich's Dagbog fra 1864," in *Danske Magazin,* 7 R., II, pp. 152-180. Edited with an introduction by Professor Aage Friis of Copenhagen. For a time in 1864, Reich was Minister for War. His notes are of especial value for the council meetings in May and June.

REVERTERA, FRIEDRICH GRAF. "Rechberg und Bismarck 1863 bis 1864," in *Deutsche Revue,* 1903, October to December, pp. 1-14, 129-141, 264-276. Revertera was Austrian civil commissioner in Schleswig.

RINGHOFFER, KARL, editor. *Im Kampfe für Preussens Ehre. Aus dem Nachlass des Grafen Albrecht v. Bernstorff, und seiner Gemahlin Anna geb. Freiin v. Koenneritz.* Berlin, 1906. Of greatest value for Bernstorff's term as Prussian Minister for Foreign Affairs and for the London Conference.

RIGSDAGSTIDENDE. Cf. [Denmark. Rigsdagen.]

RIGSDAGSTIDENDE. Cf. [Denmark. Rigsraadet.]

ROBERTSON, CHARLES GRANT. *Bismarck.* London, 1918. Robertson's account of the Schleswig-Holstein Question is stimulating if not always accurate in detail.

ROON, ALBRECHT THEODOR EMIL GRAF VON. *Denkwürdigkeiten.* See Roon, Waldemar von.

ROON, WALDEMAR GRAF VON (Editor). *Denkwürdigkeiten aus dem Leben des General-Feldmarschalls-Kriegministers Grafen von Roon.* 3 Volumes. 5th Edition. Breslau, 1905.

RUBIN, MARCUS. *Frederik VI's Tid. fra Kielerfreden til Kongens Død.* (1814-1839). *Økonomiske og historiske Studier.* Copenhagen, 1895. By a leading authority on Danish economic history. Includes studies of the economic relations of Denmark and the Duchies, and of the beginnings of the Schleswig-Holstein movement.

RUBIN, MARCUS. *Mænd og Bøger.* Copenhagen, 1920. Collected essays. The most important are those on *A. D. Jørgensen, P. Vedel, 15 November 1863*, and *Under Junigrundloven*.

SALOMON, FRITZ. "Eine neue französische Aktenpublikation über den Ursprung des Krieges von 1870-71," in *Historisches Vierteljahrschrift*, XIV (1911), pp. 396-413. A critique of the first four volumes of *Les Origines Diplomatiques de la Guerre de 1870-1871*.

SALMONSENS *Konversationslexikon*. 2nd edition. 25 Volumes. Copenhagen, 1915-1928.

SCHIEMANN, THEODOR. *Geschichte Russlands unter Kaiser Nikolaus I*. 4 Volumes Berlin and Leipzig, 1904-1919.

SCHLITTER, H. "Die Frage der Wiederherstellung Polens im oesterreichischen Ministerrat 1863," in *Oesterreichische Rundschau*, LVIII (1919), pp. 63-69. Based on the Protocol of the Ministerial Council of November 1, 1863. Shows the position of the Austrian Government on the eve of the crisis.

SCHLÖZER, KURD VON. *Petersburger Briefe 1857-1862 nebst einem Anhang Briefe aus Berlin-Kopenhagen, 1862-1864*. Berlin, 1923.

SCHLÖZER, KURD VON. *Römische Briefe, 1864-1869*. 15th and 16th edition. Berlin, 1926.

SCHULTZE, JOHANNES. *Die Briefe Kaiser Wilhelms I*. See *Kaiser Wilhelm I*. etc.

SCHULZE-DELITZSCH, HERMANN. *Schriften und Reden*. Volume III. Berlin, 1910.

SCHÜSSLER, WILHELM, editor. *Die Tagebücher des Freiherrn Reinhard von Dalwigk zu Lichtenfels aus den Jahren 1860-71*. Stuttgart and Berlin, 1920.

SCHWEINITZ, HANS LOTHAR VON. *Denkwürdigkeiten des Botschafters General von Schweinitz*. 2 Volumes. Berlin, [1927].

SEIGNOBOS, CHARLES. *Le déclin de l'Empire et l'établissement de la 3e République, 1859-75*. Paris, 1921. Being Volume VII of Lavisse, E., *Histoire de la France contemporaine*.

SIMPSON, FREDERICK ARTHUR. *Louis Napoleon and the Recovery of France, 1848-1856*. London, 1923.

Sønderjylland, Redigeret af Svend Dahl og Axel Linvald. 2 Volumes. Copenhagen, 1919.

Sønderjydske Aarboger. 1889-1914. Published by the Danes of North Schleswig in the interests of their nationality. Contains some important articles on the history of the Danish movement in Schleswig.

SPRINGER, ANTON HEINRICH. *Friedrich Christoph Dahlmann*. 2 Volumes. Leipzig, 1870-72.

Staatsarchiv, das. Sammlung der officiellen Aktenstücke zur Geschichte der Gegenwart. Hamburg, 1861 ff. Reprints most of the diplomatic dispatches, speeches from the throne, etc. Especially useful for German diplomatic dispatches and the protocols of the sessions of the Diet of the German Confederation. Material is printed in the original language.

STEENSTRUP, JOHANNES C. H. R. and others. *Danmarks Riges Historie*. 6 Volumes. Copenhagen, 1897-1907. Volume VI, 1814 to 1864, by A. D. Jorgensen and N. Neergaard. The standard general history of Denmark.

STERN, ALFRED. *Geschichte Europas seit den Verträgen von 1815 bis zum Frankfurter Frieden von 1871*. 10 Volumes, Stuttgart and Berlin, 1894-1924.

STERN, ALFRED. "L'Insurrection polonaise de 1863 et l'impératrice Eugénie," in *Revue Historique*, CXXXVII, (1921), pp. 66-73. Metternich's reports of the Empress's views on the remaking of the map of Europe.

STERNFELD, RICHARD. "Der Preussische Kronrat von ⅔ Januar 1864," in *Historische Zeitschrift*, CXXXI, pp. 72-80.

Sveriges Historia til vara dagar. Utg. av Emil Hildebrand, Stockholm, 1919. Volume XII. *Oskar I och Karl XV.* By Carl Hallendorff. Stockholm, 1923.

SYBEL, HEINRICH VON. *Die Begründung des Deutschen Reiches durch Wilhelm I.* 7 Volumes. 4th Revised edition. Munich and Leipzig, 1892-1895. Volume III deals with the Schleswig-Holstein Question. Now that the Prussian archives have been opened to students, Sybel's work loses its significance as a unique source for the documents contained there.

SYBEL, HEINRICH VON. *Kleine historische Schriften.* 3 volumes. Stuttgart 1880.

TATISHCHEV, SERGIEI SPIRIDONOVICH. *Imperator Alexandr II*, [In Russian.] 2 Volumes. St. Petersburg, 1903. The account of Russian policy in the Schleswig-Holstein Question is based on published materials, principally von Sybel, *Die Begründung des Deutschen Reiches.*

THORSØE, ALEXANDER. *Kong Frederik den syvendes Regering.* 2 Volumes. Copenhagen, 1884-1889. A standard Danish history. Has made use of much unpublished material from the Danish archives. Although the first one and one-half volumes of Neergaard's *Under Junigrundloven* cover the same period with much more material on Danish politics, Thorsoe's work is still important for foreign relations. In some respects it is more useful than Neergaard as it gives the dispatches in less summary fashion.

TIEDEMAN, CHRISTOPH VON. *Aus Sieben Jahrzehnten. Erinnerungen.* 2 Volumes. Leipzig, 1905, 1909. Volume I. *Schleswig-Holsteinische Erinnerungen.*

Urkundenbuch zur deutsch-dänischen Angelegenheit. Vom 29 October 1857 bis 26, December 1861. Hamburg, 1862.

Urkundenbuch zur Geschichte der Holstein-Lauenburgischen Angelegenheit am Deutschen Bunde in den Jahren 1851 bis 1858. Frankfurt a. M., 1858. These two collections contain the principal negotiations between Denmark and Germany from 1851 to 1861 and the action of the Diet in respect to them. The first contains the German text of the important correspondence of December 1851 and January 1852.

VIEL-CASTLE, COMTE HORACE DE. *Memoires sur le Régne de Napoleon III., 1851-1864.* 6 Volumes. Paris, 1883-1884.

VITZTHUM VON ECKSTAEDT, COUNT CARL FREDERICK. *St. Petersburgh and London in the years 1852-1864.* 2 Volumes. London, 1887. With preface by Henry Reeve. Vitzthum von Eckstaedt was Saxon Minister in London. His book contains for each year a summary written later and a series of his contemporary letters to Dresden. He gives much information on British politics. He seems to have been in close touch with Derby and Disraeli.

VOELKLE, C. *Die Haltung Englands in der deutsch-dänischen Frage, Herbst 1863-Juli 1864.* Heidelberg dissertation. 1913.

VOGT, ERNST. *Die Hessische Politik in der Zeit der Reichsgründung, 1863-71.* Munich and Berlin, 1914. A small but useful work. The writer has been able to use the papers of Heinrich von Gagern, Hessian Minister in Vienna. They throw some interesting light on Austrian policy.

WAHL, ADALBERT. "Die Unterredung Bismarcks mit dem Herzog Friedrich von Augustenburg am 1, Juni 1864," in *Historische Zeitschrift*, XCV (1905), pp. 58-70. The writer has too much confidence in Bismarck's good faith, and too little conception of the versatility of his policy.

WALPOLE, SIR SPENCER. *The History of Twenty-Five Years.* Volume I. 1856-65. London, 1904.

WALPOLE, SIR SPENCER. *The Life of Lord John Russell.* 2 Volumes. 2nd. edition. London, 1889.

WARD, SIR ADOLPHUS WILLIAM. *Germany, 1815-1890.* 3 Volumes. Cambridge (England), 1916-1918. The author was a son of J. Ward, who was British representative to the Hanse towns in the 1860's. He was personally acquainted with many of the participants in the events of 1863-64. The point of view is liberal German, and, while in general very fair, the book suffers from lack of knowledge of more recent Danish works. The account of the campaign of 1864 in Volume II as written by Spenser Wilkinson.

WARD, SIR ADOLPHUS WILLIAM. "The Schleswig-Holstein Question 1852-1866," in *Cambridge History of British Foreign Policy*, II. Cambridge, 1922.

WARD, JOHN. *Experiences of a Diplomatist, being recollections of Germany, founded on diaries kept during the years 1840-1870.* London 1872. Ward was British envoy to the Hanse towns. He sympathized strongly with the Augustenburg party and was a personal friend of many of the leaders.

WELLESLEY, FREDERICK ARTHUR. *The Paris Embassy during the Second Empire. Selections from the Papers of Henry Richard Charles Wellesley, 1st Earl Cowley, Ambassador at Paris 1852-1867.* London, 1928.

WEMYSS, MRS. ROSSLYN. *Memoirs and Letters of Sir Robert Morier, G. C. B., from 1826-1876.* 2 Volumes. London, 1911. Morier was attached to the British Embassy in Berlin. He was in close touch with liberal circles in Prussia, including the Crown Prince and Princess. He sympathized with the German view of the Schleswig-Holstein Question.

Zeitschrift der Gesellschaft für die Geschichte der Herzogthümer Schleswig, Holstein und Lauenburg. Kiel, 1870 ff. Cited: *Z. f. s.-h. G.*

ZWIEDINECK-SÜDENHORST, HANS VON. *Deutsche Geschichte von der Auflösung des alten bis zur Errichtung des neuen Kaiserreiches, 1806-1871.* 3 Volumes. 1897-1905.

NEWSPAPERS: *Allgemeine Zeitung* (Augsburg); *Berlingske Tidende* (Copenhagen); *Dagbladet* (Copenhagen); *Faedrelandet* (Copenhagen); *Times* (London); *Morning Post*, (London).

INDEX

INDEX

Adelheid, princess of Augustenburg, 79.

Agreements of 1851-52 (of Denmark with Austria and Prussia), negotiation of, 9-13; terms of, 13, 267-273; effect on Holstein and Schleswig of, 14; and March Patent, 56; and November Constitution, 72; and Treaty of London, 99; basis for occupation of Schleswig, 102, 182, 190; abandoned by Austria and Prussia, 217.

Ahlefeldt-Olpenitz, emissary of the Prince of Augustenburg, and Bismarck, 224.

Alexander II, tsar of Russia (1855-81), opinion of, on November Constitution, 130 f.; support of, for Bismarck and Rechberg, 200 f.; opposition of, to Augustenburg claims, 234; cession of claims of, to Grand Duke of Oldenburg, 241, note.

Alexandra, princess of Denmark, betrothal of, to Prince of Wales, 46.

Algeria, revolt in, 206, note.

Alsen (Als), island of, 169 f., 189, 249; capture of, 250.

Angeln, district of Schleswig, Germanization of, 4, 242.

Anglo-Austrian-French *entente* of 1863, breakup of, 114.

Apenrade (Aabenraa), 241.

Apponyi, Rudolph, Count, Austrian envoy at London (1856-60), ambassador (1860-71), on Palmerston's attitude towards Austria, 175; as plenipotentiary at London Conference, 226, 234 f.; and Palmerston, 244.

Arup, Erik, Danish historian, on Hall's policy in November and December 1863, 146, note.

Armistice, agreed on by London Conference, 227; expiration of, 249.

"Article V," of Treaty of Prague, and North Schleswig, 261 f.

Augustenburg, branch of House of Oldenburg, and succession to the Duchies of Schleswig and Holstein, 7. *See* Chris-

tian August and Frederick, Prince of Augustenburg.

Austria, and agreements of 1851-52, 9-13; diplomatic action of, against Denmark in 1856, 19; in 1857, 21; supported by Russia, 26; rejection by, of British proposal for a Conference in 1861, 39; negotiations of, with Denmark in 1861, 41 ff.; claim by, of right to negotiate on Schleswig, 42; and March Patent, 57; international situation of, November 1863, 96; support of, for Federal Execution, 100; and Treaty of London, 101 f.; acceptance by, of suggestion for Conference, December 1863, 162; identic note of, to England, January 31, 1864, 167 f.; opposition of, to consultation of population of Duchies, 207 f., 241, note; and question of disposition of Duchies, 231 f.; Augustenburg claim supported by, 232; program of, for disposition of Duchies, 233, 332-348; views of, on military operations, 249; comments on policy of, 255 f.; and German question, 257-261; and Schleswig-Holstein question after the war with Denmark, 257-261; and France, 96; and Prussia, 1863, 60, *see* German Great Powers; Bismarck on policy of, 84; rumors of Prussian guarantee for non-German possessions of, 184 f.; proclamation of state of siege in Galicia, 208. *See* Apponyi, Austrian fleet, Austro-Prussian convention, Biegeleben, Francis Joseph, Rechberg, Schmerling.

Austria-Hungary, modification of Article V of Treaty of Prague by, 262.

Austrian fleet, reported bound for Copenhagen, 177 f.; in the Channel, 244; in battle off Helgoland, 204 f.

Austro-Prussian Convention, of January 16, 1864, negotiation of, 102 f.; dating of, 103, note; article V of, published by Bismarck, June 1866, 261; of March 6, 1864, 202, 207.